Bounded Choice

Bounded Choice

True Believers and Charismatic Cults

Janja A. Lalich

UNIVERSITY OF CALIFORNIA PRESS

Berkeley / Los Angeles / London

University of California Press
Berkeley and Los Angeles, California

University of California Press, Ltd.
London, England

© 2004 by the Regents of the University of California

Library of Congress Cataloging-in-Publication Data

Lalich, Janja.
    Bounded choice : true believers and charismatic cults / Janja Lalich.
       p.   cm.
    Includes bibliographical references (p.   ) and index.
    ISBN 0-520-23194-5 (cloth : alk. paper). — ISBN 0-520-38402-6 (pbk. : alk.
paper)
       1. Heaven's Gate (Organization).   2. Democratic Workers Party (San
Francisco, Calif.).   3. Cults — Psychology.   4. Brainwashing.   I. Title.

BP605.H36L35   2004
306'.1 — dc22   2004000767

29   27   26   25   24   23   22   21   20
10   9   8   7   6   5   4   3   2   1

In memory of David Kleinberg and Dick Joslyn

People like certainties. More, they crave certainty, they seek certainty, and great resounding truths. They like to be part of some movement equipped with these truths and certainties, and if there are rebels and heretics, that is even more satisfying, because this structure is so deep in all of us.

Doris Lessing

Contents

List of Illustrations   *xiii*

Preface   *xv*

Acknowledgments   *xxi*

1. Introduction: Cults and True Believers   *1*
   Definitional Issues   *3*
   Cults in the Headlines   *8*
   The Bounded Choice Perspective   *14*
   The Comparative Research Project   *19*

   PART ONE: HEAVEN'S GATE

2. Gurus, Seers, and New Agers   *25*
   Entering Heaven's Gate   *26*
   Formative Principles   *31*
   Sociocultural Influences   *32*
   Religious and Spiritual Influences   *34*
   Technologies of Change   *37*

3. The Beginning: "The Two" Arrive   *42*
   The Formative Years   *42*
   The Development of Bounded Choice (Part 1)   *53*

4. Evolution of the Charismatic Community   63
    Consolidating the Membership   63
    The Development of Bounded Choice (Part 2)   71

5. Denouement   91
    The Death of Nettles   91
    Going and Staying Underground   93
    Leaving the Human Level   95
    The Development of Bounded Choice (Part 3)   98

PART TWO: THE DEMOCRATIC WORKERS PARTY

6. Revolutionaries, Rebels, and Activists   113
    Historical and Ideological Influences   114
    Sociocultural Influences   118
    The Emergence of the New Communist Movement   121
    A Typical Recruit   123
    A Convergence of Forces for a New Party   124

7. The Founding of the Democratic Workers Party   126
    The Arrival of a Leader   126
    The Development of Bounded Choice (Part 1)   137

8. The Cadre Formation   149
    The Formation of the Party   149
    The Development of Bounded Choice (Part 2)   160

9. Decline and Fall   193
    The Glory Days   195
    The Unraveling   202
    The Failure of Bounded Choice   206

PART THREE: THEORETICAL PERSPECTIVE

10. The True Believer: The Fusion of Personal Freedom
     and Self-Renunciation   221
    The Significance of the Social Context   221
    Structures of Freedom and Constraint   222
    The Bounded Reality of the True Believer   233

11. Bounded Choice: Cult Formation and the Development
    of the True Believer   247
    Bounded Choice in Relation to Other Conformity Theories   247
    Cult Formation: The Self-Sealing Social System   251
    The Social Psychology of the Individual Change Process   254
    The Limited Choices of the True Believer   257
    Bounded Choice as a Larger Social Phenomenon   261

Appendix   265

Notes   275

Bibliography   303

Index   317

Illustrations

Figures

1. Patch attached to the sleeve of Heaven's Gate member's "Away Team" uniform   27
2. Rancho Santa Fe mansion where bodies of Heaven's Gate members were found   29
3. Marshall Applewhite and Bonnie Nettles, Houston, 1972   46
4. Diary entry by early follower of "The Two," May 30, 1975   51
5. Marshall Applewhite and Bonnie Nettles at public recruitment meeting, 1975   65
6. *Ruffles,* book of Heaven's Gate sayings   76
7. Heaven's Gate promotional flyers and posters   94
8. Heaven's Gate true believers found after suicide   97
9. Marshall Applewhite's farewell address   100
10. Sampling of DWP printed material   145
11. The author on her way to a study group meeting, 1975   152
12. Flag of the Rebel Worker Organization, one of the DWP's front groups   159
13. Early DWP books, including *The Militant's Guide,* the Party's main indoctrination manual   168
14. The author at a rummage sale sponsored by the Grass Roots Alliance, one of the Party's mass organizations, 1979   171

15. DWP publicity buttons   *178*

16. Cover of an issue of *Our Socialism,* a political magazine published by the Party in its later years   *196*

17. The author representing the Party's publishing house, Synthesis Publications, at the Frankfurt Book Fair, 1984   *197*

18. The author speaking to Nicaraguan political activists while with a Party-sponsored delegation to Nicaragua, August 1984   *200*

19. Interactive processes between the individual and the leader and/or group leading to the development of charismatic commitment   *234*

20. Interlocking and interactional dimensions of the social structure that create a bounded reality and contribute to a state of personal closure for the individual participant   *259*

21. The interactional and structural elements leading to the state of bounded choice   *261*

Tables

1. Charismatic authority: Positive and negative characteristics   *265*

2. Transcendent belief system: Positive and negative characteristics   *266*

3. Systems of control: Positive and negative characteristics   *266*

4. Systems of influence: Positive and negative characteristics

5. Salient features of charismatic authority as manifested in Heaven's Gate and the DWP   *267*

6. Salient features of the transcendent belief system as manifested in Heaven's Gate and the DWP   *268*

7. Salient features of the systems of control as manifested in Heaven's Gate and the DWP   *269*

8. Salient features of the systems of influence as manifested in Heaven's Gate and the DWP   *270*

9. Critical features of cultic structure as evidenced in Heaven's Gate and the DWP   *271*

10. Organizational outcomes of Heaven's Gate and the DWP   *272*

11. Matrix of purpose and effects of the four structural dimensions of the self-sealing system   *272*

12. Characteristics of personal closure   *273*

Preface

In the midst of writing this book, the unthinkable happened. On the same morning, within minutes, nineteen terrorists hijacked four American commercial airplanes. Two were flown into the Twin Towers of the World Trade Center in downtown Manhattan, one was flown into the Pentagon, and the fourth, likely heading for the White House, crashed in a Pennsylvania field thanks to heroic passengers. So while I was writing about the boundless devotion and daily sacrifices of members of two homegrown charismatic cults, true believers of another type suddenly caught my attention.

Suicide bombers and other terrorists are ultra extreme; and in many ways their actions are light-years away from what goes on in "ordinary" cults. The psychiatrist Robert Jay Lifton refers to such extremists as people who are "destroying the world to save it."[1] The events of September 11, 2001, and what we have learned since about the perpetrators, while extreme, are nonetheless directly related to issues discussed in this book. In many respects, cult members' expectation of attaining personal freedom (e.g., some type of salvation) through participation in a society of like-minded believers is not far removed from the aspirations of countless terrorist groups around the world today.[2] As Eric Hoffer wrote in his classic analysis of the true believer, "However different the holy causes people die for, they perhaps die basically for the same thing."[3]

In this book I discuss individuals who made intense and total commitments to a cause or a leader. Like other true believers, eventually their identities and life goals were constructed only in the closed context of their belief systems. They lived each day under the sway of a passionate vision and their own dedication to it. This exposition of their lives, and of the development and evolution of the two groups to which they belonged, highlights the importance of social milieu, charismatic influence, and a desire for change. The combination of charismatic leadership, a transcendent belief system, personal commitment, and social and psychological pressure is the key dynamic that interests me and forms the foundation of my bounded choice theory. Secrecy, strict discipline, rigid hierarchy, utter respect for leadership, total commitment, and varieties of social influence and control were part and parcel of the two charismatic cults explored here: the Democratic Workers Party, a radical, California-based political sect, and Heaven's Gate, a secretive and nomadic group of celibate "monks" who committed collective suicide in 1997. Although not nearly as extreme or destructive as Mohammed Atta's band of hijackers, these two groups share some interesting similarities with their terrorist counterparts who also believed in absolutes and answered the call to immortality.

It is apparent that a fervent and transcendent belief guided the 9/11 hijackers and was at least one motivation for their actions. News reports soon revealed that the men had been planning their elaborate, secretive operation for years, right under our noses. They were skilled and well-trained operatives. Apparently some of them were not aware that they were on a suicide mission but thought they were merely going to hijack the planes and make some demands. So hierarchy, discipline, secrets, and manipulation appear to be part and parcel of their group too. These nineteen men, we learned, were part of the worldwide Al-Qaeda network, which is guided by the elusive and charismatic Osama bin Laden. Al-Qaeda training manuals and handbooks found during intelligence investigations describe the type of indoctrination and training required by bin Laden.[4] They give precise and detailed instructions on behaviors, dress, social interactions, undercover survival tips, and deadly tactical operations, more or less guiding the daily lives of adherents as they await orders for proceeding on acts of martyrdom. The political psychologist and terrorism expert Jerrold Post said that these handbooks give us a good idea of how "legitimate religious beliefs [can be turned] into fanatical tenets."[5]

This transformation from dedicated believer to deployable agent is much of what I describe here. And although I see similarities between international terrorists and cult members, I do not intend to imply that all of these movements are the same or that all of the people in them are the same or have the same motivations. Especially in large international terrorist groups, for example, geopolitical considerations and historical developments must be taken into account. Naturally, such groups would be operating on quite a different level from the two groups I analyze.[6] Submitting oneself to the domination of a charismatic leader is an intimate and complex process; it is unique to each leader and each devotee. Yet by examining the similarities of charismatic influence and control in its various forms, we stand to gain a more profound understanding of this enigmatic phenomenon. In this post-9/11 world, it is perhaps more important than ever to understand the cult mentality of the true believer. With that in mind, I encourage government officials and scholars studying terrorist organizations to consider the bounded choice model presented here, for it may add another piece to the puzzle of this very troubling issue.

I joined the Democratic Workers Party (DWP) in San Francisco in mid-1975. Of course, I did not think of it as a cult at the time. Quite the contrary. I thought I had found the perfect outlet for my burgeoning political ideals. The DWP's founding ideology was an innovative blend of feminism and Marxism-Leninism. Depending on our focus and the political climate, we used a variety of names for the group: the League for Proletarian Socialism, the Rebel Worker Organization, the Workers Party, the Peace and Justice Organization, the Grass Roots Alliance, and U.S. Out of Central America, among others. We members knew those names were merely "external" manifestations and preferred to call the organization simply "the Party."[7]

In November 1978, while a member of the DWP, I learned of the mass suicide/murders at the Peoples Temple community in Jonestown, Guyana. Like so many others, I was shocked, horrified, and sick at heart. Many of Jones's parishioners had hailed from the West Coast and still had friends, neighbors, and relatives living here. Consequently, San Francisco residents tended to feel an extra measure of alarm and distress at what had transpired in Guyana. The collective deaths of more than 900 people, 287 of whom were children, was a human loss that touched us deeply. In response, our Party newspaper ran a lengthy editorial on the tragic event in which our leader extolled Jones, his followers, and their socialist mission and vision. While much of the rest of the media was shrieking "cult," we stood firm in defending Jones's purported ideals.

Many times the Party, too, had been labeled a cult — by the media, by former members, by other activists on the Left. I would hunker down, work harder than ever, and ignore these claims, which we dismissed as mudslinging and Red-baiting. I would tell myself time and again that these patently false charges were simply intended to undermine our leader, our organization, and our righteous efforts.

About seven years after the Jonestown tragedy, in late 1985, the DWP was suffering through its own organizational crisis. Rather abruptly, the group came to an end — however, by much less disastrous means than what had occurred at Jonestown. In fact, the DWP's demise came about by internal revolution and collective vote. Before long we all found ourselves cast out from organizational life.

So here was a new day. As I was trying to sort things out, a friend from the past — someone who had left the Party before its dissolution — once again was referring to the organization by using the "c" word. I was staying at this friend's comfortable home a few hours north of San Francisco. After a decade of oppressive and mind-numbing collective living, of years of almost round-the-clock work stints, I had gone there to visit and get some much-needed R and R. At some point, between long bouts of sleep and rambling postmortems about our lives in the Party, my friend brought out a book she had gotten from the local library. It was about Jonestown.

"Read it," she urged, holding out the thick book. "See what you think."

I backed off a little, almost afraid to touch it. "Aw, c'mon," I replied. "They were religious. We weren't like that. It must have been so different."

"Read," she said. And I did.

To my surprise, the differences between the Party and Jonestown (and there were many) were not so great as the similarities. I could no longer deny the nature of my Party experience. And so began the first of my many explorations of the cult phenomenon.

Just as I have never forgotten the first televised scenes of Jonestown, I could not lightly dismiss the deaths of the members of Heaven's Gate almost two decades later. This book is the culmination of a research commitment stemming from that incident. It is based on years of study, which began in late 1985 when I found myself no longer a member of the DWP but an individual out in the world, able to make my own decisions and choices for the first time in more than ten years. I had to piece my life back together, as well as, to some degree, my mind. For my own healing from such an intense experience, I needed a fuller understanding than simply believing that the Party was a political group gone astray or that I had made a bad choice by joining it. I tried to figure out what had happened to me and my comrades during those years as devoted cadres. I realized that I had evolved from a thirty-year-old woman with an idealistic commitment to change the world into a dogmatic, rigid shadow of myself ten years later.

I needed to deconstruct that experience. I began by reading and studying whatever I could find on influence processes and trauma; on cults, brainwashing, and personal conversions; on power, leadership, and authoritarian regimes; on political and religious extremism; on all manner of related subjects. I talked to people who had been in other types of groups, as well as to former DWP comrades. I talked to academics, clinicians, and researchers. I went into therapy. I cried, I laughed, I struggled with my past and my present. I read, I wrote, I talked, I thought.[8] With time and much effort, I rebuilt my personal life and established a professional life.

Putting together all that I was learning, intellectually, personally, and professionally, I began to formulate a perspective not only on my cult involvement but also on the cult phenomenon in general.[9] After a time, I began to speak and write on the subject of social-psychological influence and control and to work as an educational consultant to others coming out of confining and controlling situations or relationships. I began researching and collecting data on cults and extremist groups and philosophies. In the mid-1990s I set up an educational resource center and consultation practice in which I interviewed and met several hundred individuals who had participated in controversial groups and the families and friends of members of such groups or highly controlled one-on-one relationships. My work revolved around helping families come to a better understanding and improving communication between all parties. Also, as an educator, I worked with current and former members of all kinds of groups to help them find balance in their assessment of their experiences and, for some, discover a way to regain a sense of a future. I facilitated support groups for former members and another support group for women who had been sexually or physically abused in relationships with an imbalance of power (e.g., teacher, pastor, therapist, guru, spiritual leader).[10] I have actively researched a variety of groups, from seclusive New Age channeling cults to lucrative meditation cults, from strict martial arts cults to quirky but controlling self-improvement courses, from small but rigidly authoritarian left-wing sects to violent right-wing racist compounds. There is no end to the list, really, for cults may take any form or focus on any interest. That is what makes them so fascinating to me.

As a sociologist, I acknowledge my relationship to this subject in general, my personal and professional experiences, and my bias toward the

DWP and Heaven's Gate. I have a professional interest as a researcher and a practitioner. Personally, of course, my interest stems in part from having been a member of a cult. And last but not least, my interest is rooted in social concern and my sense of social justice. I have always been critical of human injustices and indecencies and have looked for solutions to them.

Specifically, in relation to the study that forms the basis of this book, I feel a certain kinship with members of both groups. The depth of their dedication, the strength of their commitment, and the intensity of their hard work are traits I admire. Some former DWP members are among my close friends; some I consider family. Also, I confess to still having an affinity with the Party's foundational belief system — not the dogmatism, the rigid organizational structure, or the harshness of the demand for self-transformation that the Party came to represent, but the ideals of freedom, equality, and justice for humankind that originally were espoused.

By contrast, because of its abstract otherworldliness and disdain for the human world, I find the Heaven's Gate philosophy wanting. Nonetheless, I can understand its appeal for many. I was aware of and had studied the group for some years before the suicides. I had met and interviewed men and women who had been members but who had left before the suicides occurred and, in some cases, before the group openly discussed suicide as a possibility. Also, I knew families with a son or daughter, cousin, niece, or nephew in the group, including parents who, in the end, lost their daughter in the collective suicide. In part because of those previous connections, I felt a deep obligation to go forward with this project.

My past cult membership and my activities as scholar-practitioner can be viewed as both a strength and a potential hazard in relation to my research. Like any good researcher, I have been and continue to be on guard, watchful of my own biases. At the same time, my lengthy and high-ranking membership in the DWP equips me with particular insights into cult phenomena that are enhanced by firsthand knowledge and experience as well as a profound and heartfelt comprehension of the complexity of the issues. This does not mean that I have all the answers, but it helps me to determine which questions to ask.

Acknowledgments

Given not only the complexity but also the emotionality of the subject matter of this book, I could not have done it alone. There are so many people to thank.

For the conceptualization of the comparative study that forms the basis of this book, I thank Richard Appelbaum, Miguel Guilarte, David Rehorick, and Barnett Pearce, all of whom are faculty members at the Fielding Graduate Institute in Santa Barbara, California, as well as Benjamin Zablocki of Rutgers University. Rich Appelbaum, in particular, gave me almost daily support during the early phases of work, including data gathering, analysis, and writing. I am forever grateful for his wisdom, steadfastness, good spirit, and wry humor; for believing in me; and for reading every single word of the initial project and helping me to shape the bounded choice framework and theory that evolved out of it. For comments and discussions that inspired me to clarify my thinking about concepts related to charisma and leadership theory, organizational structure and change, knowledge building, and identity and commitment, I thank Annabelle Nelson, Sara Cobb, Eleanor Scott Meyers, Charlie Seashore, Jeremy Shapiro, Frank Friedlander, Bob Silverman, and Dottie Eastman Aggar-Gupta.

I am lacking in adequate words of appreciation for Robert Balch's impeccable research on the Heaven's Gate group since the 1970s and for his openness and sharing attitude toward our similar research interest. He is the epitome of academic collegiality. For reading and critiquing parts or all of the book, I thank Robert Balch, Marny Hall, John Horton,

Michael Langone, Burke Rochford, Ben Zablocki, and "N." Their inci-sive, timely, and well-deserved commentaries pushed my analysis forward and helped to keep me on track. I also wish to thank David Bromley and Thomas Robbins for specific comments on portions of an earlier version that made this one better. I am grateful to Wade Clark Roof and the Editorial Board of the University of California Press, as well as to the anonymous reviewers for the press who read and reviewed the manuscript and made suggestions for improvement. Of course, I am solely respon-sible for the final product.

I acknowledge the collegiality of Eileen Barker, Jean-François Mayer, Irving Hexham, David Bromley, Lorne Dawson, Gordon Melton, Thomas Robbins, Massimo Introvigne, and the late Jeffrey Hadden. Although we are often on the other side of the fence in certain debates about cults and new religious movements, I have appreciated our dialogue.

Researching and writing about controversial issues can be quite stress-ful at times, so having colleagues engaged in similar work keeps morale strong and creative juices flowing. For that I thank my sisters in struggle: Alexandra Stein, Miriam Williams Boeri, Kaynor Weishaupt, and Amy Siskind. Additional thanks to J. Anna Looney for jumping into the fray. I thank Michael Langone for his constancy and sense of humor, and my colleague and friend, the late Margaret Singer, for her wisdom, tenacity, and ever cheerful spirit. I am deeply grateful to Ben Zablocki for his unwavering support and comedic relief.

My colleagues in the Sociology Department became an invaluable sup-port to me in their constant encouragement, their intellectual nourish-ment, and the occasional glass of wine. Cynthia Siemsen took time from her own book to read my drafts and discuss ideas and issues. Liahna Gordon read with her usual precision and critical eye. My most enthusi-astic supporter and unsparing critic, Laurie Wermuth, read numerous chapter drafts and gave me significant suggestions. I benefited from the expansive support of the department chairs, Kathy Kaiser, Tony Waters, and Clark Davis. They understand the value of research and scholarship and the time it takes to do it. Many thanks also to Alison Dutro and Maureen Knowlton for taking such good care of me and the myriad administrative details related to this project.

I am grateful to others who helped with technical aspects of my research. Jeff Teeter and the interns at Chico State's Instructional Media Center lent their expertise and worked with me on some of the photo-graphs used in this book. Mark Langston, librarian at Chico State's Meriam Library, responded with speed and just the right information when needed. I am indebted to Tammy Rae Scott of KQED-FM in San Francisco and to the historian Max Elbaum. Words of support and encouragement that nourished me along the way came from many friends, colleagues, and associates. I can name only a few of them here: David Clark, Ron Enroth, Carol and Noel Giambalvo, Mimi Goldman, Joe Kelly, Steve Kent, Robert Lifton, Bernie Mazel, Gene Methvin, the late Herb Rosedale, Patricia Ryan, Patrick Ryan, Charlie Sweeny, Joe Szimhart, Dennis Tourish, Tim Wohlforth, and Philip Zimbardo.

Data and germinating ideas from this project have been used in papers presented at meetings of the American Sociological Association, the Association for the Sociology of Religion, the Society for the Scientific Study of Religion, the Pacific Sociological Association, the American Family Foundation, and A Common Bond. I thank conference and session organizers for affording me the opportunity to present my ideas and engage in public dialogue about them. Portions of this work were published in "The Cadre Ideal: Origins and Development of a Political Cult," *Cultic Studies Journal* 9.1 (1992): 1–77; "Pitfalls in the Sociological Study of Cults," in Benjamin Zablocki and Thomas Robbins, eds., *Misunderstanding Cults: Searching for Objectivity in a Controversial Field* (University of Toronto Press, 2001); and "A Little Carrot and a Lot of Stick: A Case Example," in Michael D. Langone, ed., *Recovery from Cults: Help for Victims of Psychological and Spiritual Abuse* (W. W. Norton, 1993).

My research and work on this book were aided by grants from the Dean of the College of Behavioral and Social Sciences at California State University, Chico. I was honored to receive the first Elizabeth Douvan Award for Post-Doctoral Development from the Fielding Graduate Institute, which provided additional financial support.

I was fortunate to have the assistance of two terrific editorial helpers. Alan Rinzler worked at a remarkable pace, with the care of a dedicated wordsmith and book maven. He helped to reshape the manuscript at a crucial time and made a tremendous contribution. I thank Alan more than my heart can express. I offer a giant thank you to the intrepid and multitalented Ashley Wagar. Her sharp mind, quick wit, and computer skills were a lifesaver as the manuscript moved into the final stages.

From day one Stan Holwitz, my editor at the University of California Press, believed in the importance of the issues addressed in this book. I am appreciative of his patience and encouragement every step of the way. Also, I thank Randy Heyman and others on the press editorial and production staff. Because of them, the publishing process was not only painless but also a real pleasure. Sheila Berg's final editing of the manuscript smoothed out the rough edges and made other improvements with care and sensitivity.

For sustenance and the kind love of friends and family, my heartfelt thanks to Marny Hall, Darlene Frank, Polly Thomas and Miguel de Cruz, Shelly Rosen, John Horton and Pat McCloskey, Lenor de Cruz, Beth Fisher-Yoshida, Martha Sherman, Sue Brooks, Barbara Besser and Phil Montalvo, Catherine DeGrano, Nikki Schrager, Robert and Billie Borntrager, Sharon and Gretchen Erle, Darlene Roberts, the Vickers family, Rod and Melanie Bush, David Kotick and Donald Isenman, Elizabeth Swenson and Alis Valencia, Patricia Lerman, Bill Valentine and the late Joe Lopes, Mimi Riley, Georgia Fox, Noell Adams, Anne Rene Elsbree and Kim Emmett, and the 2Ns.

My one and only, Kim Vickers, stayed close by my side and survived all of it over all these years with humor, insights, and love. She read every version with care and urged me on when the tunnel seemed impossibly long.

I am profoundly grateful to all of the individuals and families I have met, spoken with, and worked with over the years. Their experiences, struggles, and insights inspired me and helped me to come to a more thorough understanding of the true believer phenomenon. The pages of this book would not include the depth of detail or the heart and soul of real-life experiences without the courageous members of the Democratic Workers Party and Heaven's Gate who opened up to me and let their stories be heard. I hope that I have done justice to all of you.

CHAPTER I

Introduction

Cults and True Believers

In late March 1997 thirty-nine members of the Heaven's Gate cult, including the leader, committed collective suicide. Their bodies were found in a luxurious home in the wealthy suburban community of Rancho Santa Fe, near San Diego, California.

Why did they do it? What were they thinking? Why did they leave their families and friends? What causes cult members to commit such acts of violence — and even to destroy themselves? These are natural questions in response to seemingly incomprehensible human actions. I have been asked these questions countless times over the years by bereaved relatives, puzzled social scientists, and journalists trying to explain outrageous acts to a stunned public.

Conventional wisdom tells us that cult members who commit acts against themselves and others must be deranged, unstable, weak-minded, or weak-willed. They must be needy lost souls who cannot think for themselves. Researchers, clinicians, practitioners, and academics, as well as ordinary citizens, have concluded that cult members must be dysfunctional, mentally ill, or coerced by charismatic but insane leaders. The purpose of this book is to contradict these simple formulations and to advance a theory that explains how normal, intelligent, educated people can give up years of their lives — and sometimes their very lives — to groups and beliefs that from the outside may appear nonsensical or irrational. My dual status as former participant and current observer affords me an insider/outsider perspective that brings additional insights to this paradoxical issue. I can say from years of study, writing, research, and hands-on activities that the confounding behaviors of some cult members occur as a logical conclusion to lives that have been gradually constrained in an increasingly oppressive social structure.

Countless examples — from making preposterous claims of raising the dead to taking multiple wives to committing fraud and murder to rash acts of terrorism, both domestic and international — clearly illustrate that some cult members make seemingly irrational, harmful, and sometimes fatal decisions. Yet these acts are committed in a context that makes perfect sense at the time to those who enact them and are, in fact, consistent with an ideology or belief system that they trust represents their highest aspirations. I call this "bounded choice." It offers a new way of thinking about and analyzing the true believer phenomenon. In this book I intend to convey that intertwined reality, using Heaven's Gate and the Democratic Workers Party to illustrate the bounded choice model.

The behavior of core members of the DWP and Heaven's Gate is characteristic of bounded choice in that many if not most of them had been socialized to a level of compliance whereby they would have done anything that their group demanded or expected of them. Eight Heaven's Gate believers had themselves castrated, and eventually all active members killed themselves, apparently for ideological reasons.[1] And within their realm, DWP members perpetrated extreme and at times inexplicable acts, such as threatening and assaulting naysayers, harassing and beating up former members, and, on more than one occasion, exhibiting behavior that went against good common sense. Yet such behaviors are not confined only to groups of the most extreme nature, as the DWP and Heaven's Gate surely were. Many groups, situations, and settings that do not appear bizarre or extreme on the surface may comprise the same structural and interpersonal dynamics that I explore here — and may result in similar consequences of unquestioning adulation of a leader or authority figure, combined with personal sacrifice and disempowerment on the part of followers or adherents. Influence, social control, conformity, constraint, and "freedom" of choice are matters of everyday concern — if we take the time to recognize them. Looking at the extreme through the two cases highlighted here may shed some light on the more ordinary occurrences in a multitude of contexts.

Although for the most part tight-knit charismatic groups are insular and self-serving, they are not without interaction with, and often leave their mark on, the larger culture in which they reside. Both the DWP and Heaven's Gate, for example, made a certain impact on the larger society. Perhaps we can avoid further personal tragedy and, if we are lucky, deter larger-scale tragedies by making a greater effort to understand the lives of those who are driven by a single-minded devotion — to a cause or a leader. In part, that is what I attempt to recreate in this book: a detailed view of the life of a true believer. It is my hope, then, that this book will help us to better understand the interrelation of group and interpersonal dynamics, power relations, charismatic influence, and the genuine human desire to find purpose and meaning in life. It is a heady mix whose results can be awesome — or devastating.

Definitional Issues

The framework used in this study and the theory that emerged from it together provide a new way of thinking about a compelling area of inquiry that has grabbed our attention for decades now. My perspective differs from many of the studies of cults to date. Typically, those studies have focused on one aspect of cult involvement, such as a profile of a leader, an exposition of the overall belief system, a general depiction of a group and its activities at a particular time, or a recounting of the stressful life (and subsequent trauma) experienced by one or more cult members.

Many psychological studies have tried to either prove or disprove the harm caused by cults, especially to the individual member. Some of them have taken the stance of blaming the leader as the genesis of everything that happens in the group, blaming the families of members for having in some way driven their offspring to want to join the group, or blaming members themselves for having gotten involved in the first place and then either wasting precious time or, worse yet, going along with distasteful practices.

Meanwhile, some sociological studies of cults have tended to take a distant, sometimes glorified, apologetic, or overly sympathetic stance. For the most part, they too have focused on a single aspect or have taken a rather superficial look based on a visit or two to a cult's approved location or on interviews with the leader or cult spokespersons. Many authors of sociological studies have steered away from former-member informants. These researchers appear to be motivated toward this methodological lacuna by the force of the widespread, and I believe harmful, idea that former members tend to be angry and unreliable apostates.[2] Unfortunately, a number of lengthy and detailed studies have resulted in shallow reports that present a sanitized version of particular groups, thus limiting our view of those groups' histories and practices. Studies that have taken a hard, critical look at the more controversial aspects of cults, whether religious or secular in orientation, are few and far between.

To shield myself from similar shortcomings, I try to take an integrated view of cult life by looking intently at leaders, members, group structure, and social interaction. In the study that forms the basis of this book, for example, I decided to compare two very different types of cults in order to identify their similarities and differences and to expand the data at my disposal. I did not shy away from former-member informants or information that might be considered critical of the group or that portrays it in a bad light; nor did I presume the absence of positive aspects or experiences. Given the complexity, and in some cases the sophistication, of many cults, individuals in the same group may have widely varying experiences, some positive, some negative, some even neutral.

In the pages that follow, I challenge some of the prevailing taboos and sacred cows in this field of study. In that regard, rather than avoid using the contentious word *cult* or refrain from drawing on the controversial notion of "brainwashing," I engage them both and try to unravel some of the obfuscation surrounding them. For the crucial aspect of cult phenomena that interests me most is the transformative demand that requires at least some devotees to become true believers, who in turn become agents of the cult and its leader. The potential for cult enthusiasts to be led down a possibly murky or dangerous trail resides in both the individual commitment and the collective commitment to personal transformation — and the group's or leader's specific formula for bringing adherents to that all-or-nothing state of mind and being.

In recent years many academics, and on occasion the media and others, have steered away from the "c" word. Depending to some extent on their academic disciplines, researchers have resorted to choosing from a spectrum of alternative labels to identify these groups. For example, many sociologists of religion refer to them as "new religious movements," implying that they are just another site on the religious landscape. For this reason and others, some of these scholars have been described as "cult apologists," and some of their work has been interpreted as being "soft on the cults."[3]

At the other end of the spectrum, some critics of cults (sometimes referred to as the anticult movement, or more derisively as "cult bashers") have written or spoken of cult members as victims of mind control, as though they were merely passive victims and helpless pawns of evil leaders and their sinister mental manipulations. In my opinion, both of these competing extremes have proven inadequate to address this complex issue.

It seems to me that one way out of this fix is to strive for definitional clarity. In that vein, I suggest a redefinition — and reassertion — of the word *cult* to denote groups with a certain type of power structure and internal relations of power based on charismatic authority. I define a cult as follows:

> A cult can be either a sharply bounded social group or a diffusely bounded social movement held together through shared commitment to a charismatic leader. It upholds a transcendent ideology (often but not always religious in nature) and requires a high level of personal commitment from its members in words and deeds.[4]

The definition used here is not meant to be evaluative in the sense of implying that a group is good, bad, benign, or harmful. Rather it is meant to convey a systemic view of such a group, which is composed of a charismatic relationship and a promise of fulfillment along with a methodology by which to achieve it.

Cults differ in their specific ruling ideologies and in their specific requirements, practices, and behaviors; and a single group may differ over its lifetime or across locations. These groups exist on a continuum of influence (with varying degrees of effect on their members and on society, and vice versa) and a continuum of control (from less invasive to all-encompassing). Each group must be observed and judged on its own merits and its own practices and behaviors as to whether it constitutes a cult, which, as used here, is not meant to be dismissive or one-sided.

Cults are frequently totalistic and separatist. Therefore, sometimes I use the term *totalistic organization* or *totalistic ideology* when discussing them. The concept of totalism to which I adhere is primarily that of Lifton, who used the term to describe both environments and ideologies.[5] Some cults are totalistic when they are exclusive in their ideology (i.e., it is sacred, *the* only way) and impose on their members systems of social control that are confining and encompass nearly all aspects of life. Cults are separatist when they promote withdrawal from the larger society. Frequently, the totalistic and separatist features of some cults make them appear alien and threatening, and those features have attracted a great deal of attention in the mass media. My purpose here, however, is to treat totalism and separatism not as aspects of the definition of cult but as analytically interesting features of cult organization.

Also, I refuse to throw the baby out with the bathwater in relation to the concept of brainwashing. As the sociologist Benjamin Zablocki aptly wrote, "Many scholars deny that brainwashing even exists and consider its use as a social science concept to be epistemologically fraudulent. Others make grandiose claims for the brainwashing conjecture, often using it to account for virtually everything about human behavior in high-demand religious organizations. Neither of these approaches is helpful."[6] Over the past several decades, in part because of a fierce culture war among certain academics and critics of cults and in part as fallout from widespread Cold War ideologies and mythologies, brainwashing has come to be regarded as an induced psychological "snapping" that happens in a moment. Not so. When brainwashing occurs, it is the result of a series of intense social-psychological influences aimed at behavior modification.[7] It is a complex, multilayered, and time-consuming process. Typically, it is not used during the introduction and recruitment stages of cult contact. Brainwashing does not occur in every cult, and it can occur in other contexts. It requires a specific type of setting and interaction.[8] Yet it is not foolproof, nor does it create a permanent state of mind or being.

Numerous misconceptions prevail about the process of brainwashing. And equally unfortunate misunderstandings have been generated by the stereotypical usage of the term, perhaps best exemplified in *The Manchurian Candidate*, one of the most famous Red-scare movies of the 1950s. We cannot let a specific snag in our cultural history forever block from our view the very useful ideas embedded in the foundational literature on thought reform and coercive persuasion. For that reason, I draw from Lifton's pathbreaking *Thought Reform and the Psychology of Totalism*[9] and from the work of the social psychologist Edgar Schein, *Coercive Persuasion*.[10] However, I recognize also the importance of going beyond that literature. It is for that reason, in part, that I developed the notion of bounded choice, a contextual theory that offers a new perspective.

The long-standing debate over cults, or new religions, is so highly charged that participants and observers tend to call it "the cult wars." The contributions of those who take a freedom of religion stance are important, especially to combat ethnocentrism, bigotry, and acts of political repression and social oppression. At the same time, using solely a religious studies paradigm to study these groups hampers us. I say this not because

I am antireligion but rather because I recognize the existence of cults and the behaviors of people in them as much more than a religious phenomenon. Some cults may be part of the new religious movement landscape, but many more have ideologies that stem from other sources: political philosophy, nationalism, psychological theories, psychotherapeutic approaches, belief in extraterrestrial life, self-improvement regimens, a charismatic figure, and so on. And even those cultic groups that are religious in nature should be allowed to withstand the scrutiny of objective research and not be sheltered by the cloak of religion.

To avoid the polarization of views that has been one result of the cult wars, I have made an effort to go beyond what meets the eye. My ideas have been strengthened by drawing from primary works in the field — for example, Max Weber's analysis of charisma as a relationship of power, not simply as attractive and compelling traits supposedly inhering in certain individuals;[11] John Lofland's typology of conversions as a breakthrough model exhibiting the important fact that not all conversion experiences are generated in the same way;[12] Lofland and Rodney Stark's elucidation of the significance of "affective bonds" during the cult conversion;[13] and Rosabeth Moss Kanter's treatise on the significant role of commitment in group settings.[14] Building on these classic texts and others, I broadened my reach to include other sociological theories, organization theory, and the social psychology of influence. To show how structure and the individual interact, I call on Anthony Giddens's structuration model.[15] To understand better how choice is constrained, I look to Herbert Simon's theory of bounded rationality.[16] To demonstrate consequences for the individual in this context, I rely on Lifton's concepts of doubling and personal closure, as well as on his work on revolutionary immortality to explore the leadership dilemma.[17] My intention in building the bounded choice model is to contribute analytic tools that I hope will reshape our understanding of this provocative area of study.

Until now, scholarly and popular views in this field have centered on either variants of rational-choice or role theory or various "mind control" theories. My purpose is to set forth a useful, more comprehensive approach to cults as complex and often confounding human systems. This new perspective offers the opportunity to understand the appeal of such groups, the changes witnessed in at least the core members, and the difficulties some people have leaving the group or rejecting cult thinking. Also, it may help seekers, future recruits, and prospective members and believers to evaluate both the potential benefits and the potential risks of certain belief systems or group involvements.

Cults in the Headlines

In the United States and in other countries throughout the world, covert groups exist in the community, in the workplace, in urban centers, and in rural settings, and other groups are openly recruiting new members through a variety of avenues, including schools, spiritual centers, businesses, medical establishments, government agencies, the entertainment industry, and the military. Cults may take form as a one-on-one relationship, or mimic aspects of families, or present themselves as huge, tightly organized corporate entities. They may have a formal structure or exist as an amorphous social movement. Often cults function as legitimate businesses or organizations, restaurants, bookstores, self-help groups, psychotherapy clinics, or leadership training programs.

An estimated two million people have joined cults in the United States in the past several decades, and there are hundreds if not thousands of controversial groups.[18] In this discussion I am deliberately not highlighting the positive experiences that may occur in a cult context given that the focus of this book is the potential dilemma of true believers in charismatic cults, the interactional dynamic that brings moral human beings to occasionally engage in reputedly insidious or demeaning behaviors. The following, therefore, are examples of the most noteworthy groups of recent times in terms of notorious activity.

On November 18, 1978, more than nine hundred followers of the Reverend Jim Jones, at his command, either committed suicide or were murdered by their comrades in the remote jungle of British Guyana, a small nation nestled between Venezuela and Suriname on the northern coast of South America. These true believers, all U.S. citizens, were living and working there to create a utopian society known as Jonestown. This communal movement, based on a radical mixture of religion and socialism, had evolved out of the Peoples Temple, a church founded in the Pentecostal tradition by Jones and headquartered for a time in San Francisco. Jones promised to bring his followers to a better world, away from the injustices of the capitalist and racist U.S. society.

Jones and his commune had just reluctantly hosted a fact-finding mission led by Congressman Leo J. Ryan of California. "Dad," as Jones was known to his flock, had successfully indoctrinated his followers to believe that they were revolutionary socialists with much to fear from "outsiders." On that dreadful day in November, near the end of the visit from Ryan's entourage, Jones decided that he and his paradise had been intruded on by evil outsiders. In a self-involved, likely drug-induced delusion, he called for revolutionary suicide, urging his disciples to implement the "white night" they had ritually practiced over the years. There was no exit for anyone who doubted or challenged the directive. All the residents of the Jonestown commune were doomed.[19] As they watched their children being forcefully injected with the lethal mixture of cyanide and fruit drink, the adults could "choose" to poison themselves. If they resisted, they were threatened at gunpoint by a security squad made up of fellow parishioners.[20] Days later, images of 914 small and large, male and female, young and old bloated bodies lying draped over one another flashed across television screens — grisly images invariably retrieved and replayed whenever another cult controversy makes the news.

In the 1980s members of the Rajneesh ashram found themselves in the midst of a growing controversy with the surrounding communities in central Oregon. This movement was founded by Bhagwan Shree Rajneesh, an Indian guru. Rajneesh melded ideas from East and West into an intoxicating mix that during the 1970s and 1980s successfully attracted thousands of followers and more dedicated disciples called *sannyasins*. The Rajneeshees are probably best known for sporting all shades of maroon attire and dancing ecstatically during meditation. The bearded, soft-spoken (when he spoke) Rajneesh owned ninety-three Rolls-Royces and was by some accounts the epitome of a charismatic leader. Most of his adherents came from western Europe and the United States. It was more of an experiential and meditative psychotherapy movement than a religious one. In 1981, after a scandal-ridden departure from the group's birthplace in Poona (now Pune), India, involving sex, scanty attire, drugs, and tax evasion, Rajneesh and his acolytes arrived in the United States and eventually settled in rural Antelope, Oregon. There, they set about to build an expansive ashram estate while they behaved heavy-handedly with the locals and rather quickly fell into disrepute.

Once again scandals erupted. By fall 1985 several top leaders fled to Germany; later they were arrested and charged with misdeeds. After pleading guilty to immigration fraud, wiretapping, engineering a salmonella outbreak, arson, and assault on local officials, Ma Anand Sheela, Rajneesh's second-in-command, served about three years in a U.S. prison.[21] In November 1985 Rajneesh was deported on immigration violations. The movement dwindled somewhat after the guru's departure and his mysterious death, announced in early 1990, at age fifty-eight. Nevertheless, today a resurrected, renamed, and rejuvenated movement has a very active center in India as well as other locations around the world, most notably Sedona, Arizona, and Marin County, California. Rajneesh, a modern-day shape shifter and name changer, was calling himself Osho at the time of his death, which is the name of the "new" ashram: Osho Commune International, or most recently Osho Meditation Resort.[22]

The Rajneesh group was in the news again in fall 2001 in relation to America's rekindled interest in bioterrorism. Unbeknownst to many, at least until it was discussed in *Germs*,[23] a book that gained a great deal of attention after September 11, 2001, and the ensuing anthrax attacks, and subsequently brought out in various televised reports, the Rajneesh group had been implicated in the first incident of biological warfare on U.S. soil. While trying to assert itself politically in rural Oregon, members of the group had deliberately poisoned about a dozen salad bars in nearby The Dalles with salmonella bacteria in order to debilitate the local populace and keep them from voting. No one died, but approximately 750 people were stricken with stomach ailments and other illnesses.[24]

This violence was dwarfed by the 1993 conflagration at the Branch Davidian compound in Waco, Texas, which claimed the lives of eighty followers of David Koresh, including twenty-two children. That so many stayed in the building with their leader and refused to flee to safety continues to be the subject of much discussion, as is the issue of culpability: Could Koresh have let his people go? Not to be ignored either is the controversy surrounding the U.S. government's role in helping to bring about the immolation by its ill-advised and botched assault on Koresh's compound.[25] One ripple effect from this incident is that Timothy McVeigh, convicted of orchestrating the bombing of the Murrah Federal Building in Oklahoma City on April 19, 1995, was motivated in part by a desire to take revenge for the government intervention at the Branch Davidian compound. The Oklahoma bombing was perpetrated on the two-year anniversary of the Bureau of Alcohol, Tobacco, and Firearms raid in Waco.

In October 1994 and again in December 1995 the media broadcast news of ritualistic murders and suicides in Canada, Switzerland, and France. Sixty-nine members of a mystical group of believers died, and once more young children and babies were among the dead. A tape-recorded exchange by the two leaders indicates that they wanted their "departure" to be "even more spectacular" than what happened in Waco.[26] Then in March 1997 five more members of the group died in Quebec. Who orchestrated these events? How much was compliance, and how much was coerced? Are there more to come? These were the questions swirling about at the time. The deaths were connected to the Order of the Solar Temple (OTS, Ordre du Temple Solaire), a group led by Joseph Di Mambro, a French occult guru of sorts who had had followers since the 1970s, and Luc Jouret, a Belgian homeopathic physician known for his charismatic personality. OTS was a tiny, esoteric New Age group whose members believed they were an elect group who held the key to the universe and were on Earth to fulfill a cosmic mission. Infighting and internal dissent, financial controversies including charges of embezzlement, and problems with the law, such as possession of illegal weapons, all contributed to the demise of OTS and its eventual self-destruction.[27]

In 1995 the world was stunned again by a poisonous nerve gas attack on commuters in the Tokyo subway. Twelve innocent Japanese died and more than five thousand were sickened from inhaling the sarin gas. Later we learned that an earlier attack, in June 1994, in another area (Matsumoto) was related; in that incident, seven people died and another six hundred were poisoned. Those and other criminal activities and deadly schemes were connected to the Aum Shinrikyō (Aum Supreme Truth) religious cult, whose partially blind leader, Shoko Asahara, mixed Buddhism, Hinduism, and New Age ideas with torturous rituals, meditative exercises, and mind-altering drug ingestion, sometimes forced on his followers. Asahara preached that Armageddon was at hand, and many of the group's activities were meant to be apocalypse-inducing, to spur on a new world order.[28]

The Tokyo sarin gas attack is one of the world's most infamous incidents of chemical warfare. Subsequent investigations revealed that the Aum cult had been researching and planning the use of both chemical and biological weapons for some time, including disseminating botulinum and anthrax bacteria. Aum members included doctors, nurses, engineers, brilliant scientists, and highly trained laboratory technicians, as well as other well-educated Japanese youth, graduate students, and professionals. The cult had branches in Russia, Germany, the United States, and Sri Lanka and claims to have had up to forty thousand members. Most members lived in Japan or Russia. Trials of several Russian members for terrorism concluded in December 2001, and trials and sentencing are still in progress in Japan as of this writing. At the time of the Tokyo attack, Aum was said to be worth $1.5 billion. The group is now known as Aleph. It still has a few thousand loyal members and is led by Aum's former spokesman, the charismatic Fumihiro Joyu, who served a short sentence for his earlier activities. Joyu claims to have rejected the violence inherent in Aum's original teachings.[29]

In late March 1997 Heaven's Gate grabbed our attention. This cult had more or less disappeared from the spotlight, although it had a presence in various Internet chat rooms in the mid- to late 1990s. News coverage of this group goes back to 1975, but for the most part its members had kept to themselves, and their collective suicide in 1997 came as a shock to many. The proximity of their suicidal mission to the Easter holiday, plus the details of their seemingly bizarre lifestyle as divulged in myriad news stories, gave them front-page status for several weeks — an unusual achievement for a cult group. But it was not long before the fickle public moved on to other items of interest.

In March 2000 the international press buzzed with reports of the grisly deaths of more than seven hundred adults and children in southwestern Uganda. There, over a period of several weeks, about 444 members of the Movement for the Restoration of the Ten Commandments of God were poisoned, strangled, and buried in secret mass graves on four properties belonging to the group. In a final assault, at least 300 members were boarded up in a building and burned to death at the cult's headquarters. Among its leaders were a former Catholic layman and visionary (Joseph Kibwetere), a female visionary (Credonia Mwerinde), and a well-educated Roman Catholic priest (Fr. Dominic Kataribabo) who had been excommunicated by the church when he joined the Movement. These individuals were believed to have orchestrated the tragedy. They either escaped at the last minute and fled the county or died with their followers in the final church fire. To this day, their whereabouts remain a mystery.[30]

Another prominent group that caught the public eye is the Hare Krishna movement, or the International Society for Krishna Consciousness (ISKCON), as it is officially called. For decades, saffron-robed, shaven-headed devotees could be found on street corners chanting "Hare Krishna" and banging on drums or in the halls of airports around the world fund-raising and proselytizing. For a time this Hindu group, which came to the United States in 1965, was a large and growing movement, once claiming thousands of members. But ISKCON dwindled in size and influence after the 1977 death of the founder and leader, Swami Srila Prabhupada. Power struggles emerged among his eleven inheritors, and various scandals surfaced involving drug dealing, weapons stockpiling, the murders of some defectors, and the imprisonment of at least one regional leader.[31]

In June 2000 a class action lawsuit was brought against ISKCON on behalf of seventy-nine former members for alleged sexual abuse of children raised in its boarding schools, called *gurukulas*.[32] The lawsuit was dismissed from federal court in October 2001. ISKCON has never denied the allegations, although it has "disputed the extent of the charges and the idea that the organization as a whole is responsible for the crimes of its devotees."[33] Most recently, the group has filed for bankruptcy protection for those ISKCON communities named as defendants.

In late 2002 world headlines brought news of a Quebec-based group claiming to have cloned the first humans through their company, Clonaid. They announced two births and three more on the way. Naturally, this caused an ethical stir, from the White House on down to scientists and cloning experts.[34] The group, known as the Raëlians, is led by Claude Vorilhon, a former racecar driver and journalist, who claims to have encountered extraterrestrials in 1973 in France. These aliens reportedly told Vorilhon that all Earthlings were formed by DNA in test tubes and that he, now known as the Prophet Raël, was a supreme type of clone.[35] Many described the cloning announcement as a media fiasco and an orchestrated fraud; so far, neither Clonaid nor the Raëlians have offered any proof.[36] A journalist who was initially selected to oversee the testing but who dropped out when the group refused to allow it said, "It's entirely possible Clonaid's announcement is part of an elaborate hoax intended to bring publicity to the Raëlian movement."[37]

Not just religious and quasi-religious cults capture our attention. Memories of the radical 1970s were stirred up when fugitives from the Symbionese Liberation Army (SLA) were arrested, put on trial, and entered legal pleadings. The SLA was a revolutionary gang perhaps best known for kidnapping newspaper heiress Patricia Hearst, but members were also charged with bank robberies, attempted bombing, and murder. At least six SLA members died in police shoot-outs in 1974; others were captured, tried, and served sentences; but still others fled underground. In 1999 the FBI located a former SLA member, Kathleen Soliah, living an upper-middle-class life in Minneapolis as Sara Jane Olson. She is serving a fourteen-year sentence for a 1975 attempt to blow up two Los Angeles police cars, plus six years for a 1975 bank robbery attempt that resulted in the murder of a woman who was a customer in the bank at the time. And perhaps most surprising, in November 2000 the final SLA holdout, James Kilgore, came in from the cold. He had been living an open life under an assumed name, working as a researcher and teacher in Cape Town, South Africa. He pleaded guilty and received a six-year sentence for his role in the same fatal robbery.[38]

Other political groups we know too little about occasionally line up front and center. One that continues to make waves is the Earth Liberation Front (ELF). In January 2003 members of this radical environmental group claimed responsibility for setting SUVs on fire at a car dealership in Pennsylvania. Allegedly, this same group set fire to a resort in Vail, Colorado, in 1998. This action "caused $12 million in damage and is considered the most destructive act of eco-terrorism in U.S. history."[39] ELF sometimes works in conjunction with the Animal Liberation Front, attacking animal laboratories, primate research facilities, mink farms, and the like. Other antisocial and violent activities, including harassment, murder, and hate crimes against person and property, are perpetrated by secretive groups on the radical right — survivalists, white supremacists, and antigovernment groups.

Stories such as these make the headlines, stay with us for a few days or a few weeks, depending on what else is in the news, and then drift from view. "Enigmatic," "beyond belief," "cult mystery," "madness," "martyrdom," "secrecy" are the words that typically run through the headlines. Often the articles do not tell us much more. News commentators seem dismayed, puzzled, unable to fathom such "acts of faith." The collective suicide of the members of Heaven's Gate is just one among many instances of seemingly incomprehensible behavior and activities on the part of some cult members. I hope to get beyond the shock and horror of the headlines by offering some understanding of why cult members do what they do, based on both the promises and the constraints of the cult context. I offer a look at the daily lives and inner workings of groups such as these that over the decades have attracted not the lonely and lost, as most might assume, but rather the idealistic and lofty-minded, the curious and well-educated.

The Bounded Choice Perspective

Over the years and in the course of writing this book, I have struggled intellectually with issues of belief and coercion, which I see as the heart of the matter. I have concluded that there is a particular state of being, which I call "charismatic commitment," that can take root quickly, so that people become easily enmeshed and, in some cases, trapped, at least psychologically. This is the point at which there is fusion between the ideal of personal freedom (as promised in the stated goal of the group or its ideology) and the demand for self-renunciation (as prescribed by the rules and norms). At that point, the believer becomes a "true believer" at the service of a charismatic leader or ideology. In such a context, in relation to personal power and individual decision making, that person's options are severely limited — hence my overall conclusion that the best way to understand why cult members do what they do is to consider them in a state of ever-present bounded choice, a narrow realm of constraint and control, of dedication and duty.

Two complex processes — conversion and commitment — are central here and to any comprehensive understanding of contemporary cults. These processes are inextricably intertwined in the cult context while also intersecting with other relevant social phenomena, such as charisma, ideological control, and social-psychological influence.

Conversion is the process by which a person develops a new perspective on life. External pressure may or may not be present, accounting for the various types of conversion experiences. In his conversion typology Lofland identified self-conversion, personal mystical conversion, and situational conversion, in which there is little or no outside pressure. Or a person may undergo a group tie conversion, a collective contagion conversion, or a coercive persuasion conversion, in which external pressure is integral to the experience.[40] Often one outcome of a conversion experience is the adoption of an activist stance, which tends to give voice to the newfound meaning and purpose.

Although typically thought of as a process of religious change, conversion can and does take place in secular contexts.[41] For that reason, in my work in this field and in this book — in order to not be limited by a religious perspective — I prefer the term *worldview shift* to identify the internal change that takes place as a person adopts the new perspective, or worldview, and becomes a practicing adherent.[42] The social psychologist Kurt Lewin regarded such deep personal change as a process of re-education: "It is a process in which changes of knowledge and beliefs, changes of values and standards, changes of emotional attachments and needs, and changes of everyday conduct occur not piecemeal and independently of each other, but within a framework of the individual's total life in the group."[43] The transformational process is deeply felt but also intensely troubling because of the resultant changes in personality, attitudes, and behaviors.[44] The outcome of a successful conversion is a firm believer, a new person. In part, this adoption of and adherence to a newly found, all-consuming worldview is the binding matter that makes it difficult to leave totalistic groups or give up cultic thinking, in spite of the moral and emotional conflicts that arise within some if not most believers from time to time.

Along with the new worldview comes a new social system, an accompanying ideological structure. This may be an actual group or a supporting set of behavioral norms and guidelines. In most cases, this worldview shift is a fluid, gradual process, not a sudden, overnight occurrence. In some instances, the person may not be aware of the extent to which she or he is stepping into a new world — or a new way of grasping the world and understanding oneself. Nevertheless, the subtlety of the process does not diminish its impact — or the final effect, which is to achieve change toward a specific end. The desired goal is the transformation of the adherent into a committed believer, which means becoming a loyal group member or follower in those instances in which a group is attached to a belief system.

But sometimes one converts to an ideology without the presence of an actual group. This is what Lofland categorized as self-conversion.[45] The young American John Walker Lindh, who was captured in Afghanistan, is a case in point. Lindh's religious conversion and search for Islamic truths, which eventually led him into the hands of the Taliban and Al-Qaeda, is a good example of this type of self-styled conversion. Descriptions of Lindh's early conversion to Islam indicate no group pressure or undue social influence, other than attending a local mosque in Mill Valley, beginning at the age of sixteen.[46]

Throughout this transformative process not only does the individual gain a sense of purpose and belonging, but a new self evolves. In the extreme, these interactions (consisting of a series of conversions) result in the complete transformation of self. This is more than, say, simply belonging to an everyday group, such as a neighborhood watch committee or a ladies' auxiliary or a college fraternity. It has a profound impact on how the person both understands the world and interprets how it works; it is tied to the person's entire belief system and comprehension of the order of the universe. Such a worldview shift involves more than just individual psychology; rather it is a manifestation of what might be called political social psychology.

Described symbolically by Lifton as death and rebirth, the intense process of transformation to which I am referring involves a reorganization of the person's inner identity, or sense of self. Typically, it occurs through the use of a mixture of emotional appeals, rituals, instruction, self-examination, confession, and rejection, all in a context that deftly combines stress and harmony.[47] Most often, guilt, shame, and anxiety are integral to this process. Responding to the demands can be exhausting and stressful, for it requires repeated acts of self-renunciation; at the same time, the person experiences relief at having "found the answer," which is associated with a kind of personal freedom.

I have identified four interlocking structural dimensions that make up the framework for the social dynamics found in cults:

Charismatic authority: The emotional bond between leader and followers, which serves to lend legitimacy and grant authority to the leader's actions while at the same time justifying and reinforcing the followers' responses to the leader and/or to specific ideas and goals. The relational aspect of charisma is the hook that links a follower or devotee to a leader and/or his or her ideas.

The transcendent belief system: The overarching ideology that binds adherents to the group and keeps them behaving according to the group's rules and norms. It is transcendent because it offers a total explanation of past, present, and future, including a path to salvation. Most important, the group also specifies the exact methodology, or recipe, for the personal transformation necessary to qualify one to travel on that path.

Systems of control: The network of acknowledged, or visible, regulatory mechanisms that guide the operation of the group. This includes the overt rules, regulations, and procedures that guide and control group members' behavior.

Systems of influence: The network of interactions and methods of influence residing in the group's social relations. This is the human interaction and group culture from which members learn to adapt their thoughts, attitudes, and behaviors in relation to their new beliefs.

It is my contention that the combination of a transcendent belief system, an all-encompassing system of interlocking structural and social controls, and a highly charged charismatic relationship between leader(s) and adherents results in a self-sealing system that exacts a high degree of commitment (as well as expressions of that commitment) from its core members. A self-sealing system is one that is closed in on itself, allowing no consideration of disconfirming evidence or alternative points of view.[48] In the extreme, the group is exclusive; and the belief system is all-inclusive, in the sense of providing the answers to everything and being the only way. Typically, the goal of such charismatic commitments is to attain a far-reaching ideal; yet loss of sense of self is often the by-product of that quest. The consequences for the individual member are both conflicting and looped.

Let me explain what I mean by this, because this interaction is central to my theory and to understanding how people become so enmeshed that, in a sense, they become the organization. In identifying with the group, members find meaning and purpose and a sense of belonging. This is experienced as a type of personal freedom and self-fulfillment. Yet that freedom is predicated on a decrease in personal autonomy, manifested in continuous acts of ever-increasing self-renunciation. This self-renunciation usually is expressed in relation to decision making, whereby the individual's choices are constrained by the confines of the system, both real and imagined. In addition, behavior and therefore also choice are hampered by the development and nurturing of internalized mechanisms that prompt a person to perform (in thoughts, attitudes, and actions) in unity with the group's worldview and goals. That is the juncture at which the social-psychological reality that I have identified as bounded choice emerges.

To be a participant in the group means playing by the rules; and in such groups, there is only one set of rules, or rather only one set of rules that matters.[49] Once a person "chooses" to stay in the group, the impermeable, albeit invisible, confines of the structure do not allow for the possibility to "act otherwise"[50] in any significant sense — unless, of course, the person leaves the group. At best, leaving the group means undergoing another major shift in worldview; at worst, losing all moral and social support one has come to know and rely on. It requires facing the unknown, often with the threat of extinction in the form of soul death and, in some instances, fear of literal death. The self-sealing nature of cultic ideologies leaves no room for alternatives. Eventually, life outside the cult becomes impossible to imagine.

This occurs when charismatic leaders and their transcendent belief systems *demand* that their followers undergo a personal transformation that relies on the fusion of the individual's sense of personal freedom and the vow of self-renunciation. This fusion — which I call charismatic commitment — and its resultant social-psychological state — which I call bounded choice — is the force that time and again keeps people tethered to groups, relationships, or situations that many outsiders find incomprehensible.

A clarification is in order here: the emergence of charismatic commitment does not happen once, and, poof, the person is converted, eagerly awaiting the leader's beck and call. To the contrary, this is a recurring, renewable, and renewing process: one makes the commitment over and over again, generally with increasing devotion and loss of sense of self. Lapses of commitment are ordinary and expected; it is the resolution of such crises that pushes the believer to believe even more strongly. Integral to this evolving commitment is renunciation of who one was before encountering this "life-saving" belief or group. The premovement, or precult, identities fade into the background (sometimes slowly, sometimes rapidly) as the cult persona emerges and becomes stronger. This is not schizophrenia, not the eruption of a split personality, as might be described in the psychology literature. Rather the cult member undergoes the development of a personality that stands for and stands with the newly adopted worldview and its practices. Total and unquestioning commitment requires a new self.[51]

All of this, of course, is related also to issues of knowledge and power, because devotion to charismatic leaders is inseparable from a type of dominant power relationship based on the dissemination of, or the promise of the dissemination of, knowledge. In a cultic context, the charismatic authority, the shared belief system, the behavioral controls, and the social and psychological influences are all key structural dimensions that work in concert — with the individual actor as an integral part of the system — to exact an extraordinary degree of commitment and subsequent acts of faith. Recognizing and acknowledging the power of this charismatic relationship and the ensuing social-psychological dynamic provides insights into how and why someone living in such a system at times may act against his or her self-interest[52] — or at least so it may appear to those outside the system.

The Comparative Research Project

When the Heaven's Gate suicides took place, I felt a need to take a closer look at the group, which I had been aware of since at least 1994. Over the years I had been in touch with several former members, as well as families who had a relative in the group. My files contained many of the group's writings, public flyers, testimonials by individual members, and videotapes used for training and recruitment. I gathered even more source material after the suicides, including the voluminous Heaven's Gate book (which was available both in print and on the group's Web site, www.heavensgate.com), videos, and other original material given to me by families and former members (letters, diaries, flyers, procedures, ritual prayers, booklets, ads, etc.). I began with a thorough reading and analysis of these documents and the rash of media reports that appeared immediately after the suicides and in the following months. I conducted informal interviews with families and former members and also did a content analysis of the farewell videos.[53]

In those early stages of research I began to notice striking parallels, as well as important differences, between Heaven's Gate and the DWP. This piqued my curiosity. As a next step, I undertook an in-depth examination and comparative analysis of the DWP, a hard-core Marxist group with a worldview and orientation that revolved around political theory and political activism, and Heaven's Gate, a quasi-religious group whose beliefs revolved around asceticism and supernatural ideologies. The combination of vast differences and striking similarities that I found in the two groups made them ideal subjects for a comparative study. My hypothesis was that they were structured and led in such a way as to set up a self-sealing system — a closed social structure, an impermeable situation.[54]

Data for the study were drawn from each group's archival material, supplemented with in-depth interviews and informal conversations with individuals who had been either participants or in some way directly or indirectly associated with Heaven's Gate or the DWP.[55] Scholarly articles and media reports on the two groups were included as secondary sources. My own reflections, personal documents and diaries, and insights from having been a long-term member of the DWP brought to the study a flavor of participant observation. For each group, I examined founding and leadership dynamics, reigning ideology and worldview, organizational structure, and social relations and interactions. For this analysis, I used the four-part framework described earlier (charismatic authority, transcendent belief system, systems of control, systems of influence). I explored the sense of belonging, commitment, and moral obligation felt by the members; the actions and responses of the leaders; the individual members' sense of self; and individual and organizational tension and conflict, as well as their resolution.

Ultimately, my study took on a larger scope. I realized that I was not merely engaging in a remote academic exercise of outlining the similarities and differences in these two groups. Rather the findings and my interpretation of them opened up a discussion of freedom and constraint, of sacred devotion and personal sacrifice. Eventually this led to the development of my bounded choice theory. I came to understand better how such an environment, or social structure, contributes to a state of bounded choice in at least some of the adherents.

Individuals in a cult context are constrained not only by a bounded reality[56] — one product of a self-sealing system — but also by bounded choice. This occurs when the individual reaches what Lifton described as a state of personal closure.[57] ("Closure" in this sense does not mean completion, as it is sometimes used, but a turning inward and a refusal to look at other ideas, beliefs, or options.) I suggest that the state of personal closure should be considered the individualized version of the larger self-sealing system. Thus, as a person identifies and unites with the bounded reality of the group and its belief system, becoming a devotee by making that charismatic commitment to the self-sealing worldview, another process begins to take place. That is, individual perspective and personal decision making become limited and constrained, and that restriction comes from within as much as from without. In this context of closure and constraint, choices may exist, but they are severely limited. In such situations, the individual can be described as being in a state of bounded choice.

This comparative study illustrates the dilemma of true believers living with the demanding and dualistic nature of charismatic commitment. The DWP and Heaven's Gate illustrate how specific interrelated dynamics in a specific organization or context, in conjunction with individual actions ("agency" in sociological terms), tend to create this often stifling situation. At least at first glance, the two groups dissected here could not appear to be more opposite — in their values and ideals, in their goals, and in their daily lives. Yet, as this book shows, they were quite similar in the ways by which at least some of their members were transformed and led into a state of bounded choice, a paradoxical manifestation of both personal idealism and self-sacrifice.

·   ·   ·

The remainder of this book is divided into parts. Part 1 is devoted to Heaven's Gate. In chapter 2 I introduce the group and describe the spiritual, religious, and self-awareness milieu of the 1970s, which was influential at the time. The characteristic beliefs of that era and that milieu had an impact on the two individuals who founded the group, as well as many who joined in the early years. Chapters 3 through 5 provide a narrative of the life course of the group, highlighting people and events to underscore the bounded choice perspective.

In part 2, dealing with the Democratic Workers Party, I begin with a brief description and discussion of the leftist milieu of the early 1970s, the period when the Party was formed. Chapters 7 through 9 describe the development of the DWP, using interview data, documents, and personal experiences to illustrate patterns and draw comparisons with Heaven's Gate.

Part 3 contains my summation and analysis. Chapter 10 presents some of the main features of the comparison, reiterating the significance of social context and social structure. I also draw some conclusions regarding membership, commitment, charisma, leadership, and the nature of cultic, or self-sealing, social systems. In chapter 11, the last chapter of the book, I review the theoretical foundations of the bounded choice theory. I also suggest the theory's relevance to ongoing research on cults and the true-believer mentality and to other manifestations of single-mindedness in our society, including our present-day concern with terrorism and fanaticism.

PART ONE

Heaven's Gate

Gurus, Seers, and New Agers

During spring 1997, across the Northern Hemisphere, people eagerly watched the passage of the Hale-Bopp comet in the night sky. It had been discovered by Alan Hale and Thomas Bopp in summer 1995 and was reaching its closest points to the earth in March 1997. Astronomers estimated that even at its closest point, the comet would remain more than 120 million miles away.[1]

Most people were thrilled to see this wonder of nature, but a small group living together in southern California was straining to see the comet for a different reason. They had heard through the grapevine of UFO buffs that a spacecraft was trailing the comet. Astronomers had been trying to debunk that idea since it first surfaced in November of the previous year, but the rumor spread rapidly across the airwaves and the cyberwaves. The possibility that there was a spaceship following the comet was a hot topic in Internet chat rooms and on various Web sites.

Members of that group in southern California had their own elaborate Web site; in fact, some of them were working as Web designers and computer programmers. They took comfort in the idea that a spaceship might be hovering nearby. They bought a high-powered telescope to get a better look at the craft. Their leader — a man named Marshall Applewhite, known to them as Do (pronounced *doe*) — was convinced that this was the signal they had been waiting for. That trail behind the comet, discussed fervently in the wee hours on late-night radio, was surely *their* ride home.

Entering Heaven's Gate

It had been more than twenty years since Applewhite and his "cosmic mate," Bonnie Nettles (known to her followers as Ti, pronounced *tee*), had announced that a ship would arrive from outer space to rescue them from the earthly nightmare. They and their followers were to be taken to an eternal paradise, which they called the Next Level or the Level Above Human. It was their version of the "Kingdom of Heaven," but unlike many other conceptions of heaven, this one was believed to be an actual physical place. In this way, Ti and Do and their followers believed they would escape death and live forever in their celestial home — from whence they believed they had been sent to accomplish a mission here on earth.

This had all started in the early seventies, with just Applewhite and Nettles. Then, in 1975, they amassed their first loyal followers. For a time, they lived nomadically as they recruited across the United States, especially targeting college towns and countercultural centers. Always, they believed that leaving earth was imminent, that salvation was just around the corner. But years passed, and more years passed. The spaceship did not arrive to retrieve them, despite much anticipation and many rumored appearances by members of the group. As devotees came and went, the details of the group's belief system were altered to accommodate certain events, real or imagined. These alterations happened in much the way that they believed they themselves would morph into new bodies fit for the Next Level — that is, they were almost imperceptible. During the years of waiting, Ti fell ill and then died from a rather mundane disease, cancer. Do and the others persisted.

In southern California in 1997, several dozen hard-core followers remained steadfastly with their beloved leader Do. An air of excitement prevailed, an anticipation unlike that felt before. This time they were sure; the ship was coming to take them home. They decided it was time to take the steps they had been talking about for several years. They readied themselves for the liftoff by consuming a lethal blend of vodka and Phenobarbital mixed into a little pudding or applesauce to help the potion go down more smoothly. They made doubly sure of the success of this mission by having plastic bags placed over their heads as they reclined on their assigned beds.[2]

FIGURE 1. This patch was attached to the left sleeve of each Heaven's Gate member's "Away Team" uniform.

For years they had lived for this moment, had trained as a highly specialized "Away Team." They understood that they were a special class of Next Level students, readying to go back to their extraterrestrial home. Now each one was neatly dressed in a handmade, Trekkie-like black uniform. A colorful triangular patch symbolizing the Away Team was attached to the uniform's upper sleeve (see fig. 1). They all sported the bowl-shaped haircut characteristic of their group, and each member donned a brand-new pair of black Nike sneakers. A small carry-on bag sat on the floor next to each bed or cot. Each bag contained a five-dollar bill and a roll of quarters; and most bags also contained a driver's license or passport. They were ready for the trip.

On the mantle in the main room of their house was a graphic rendering of a Next Level creature, their ideal being, the one who would rescue them. Perhaps even Ti would show up. Both Ti and Do were known by the group as their Older Members, but Ti was highest on the chain of command. These dedicated men and women had trained long and hard for this moment. They had worked and trained together, living communally and sharing everything. They had subjected themselves to strict regimes and various physical and mental exercises, as though they were in a type of NASA training program. They did all this for years; in fact, most of them had been with Ti and Do for more than two decades. Although their efforts were not without inner struggles and personal turmoil, they had sacrificed for this, the end of their earthly existence and the beginning of eternal life.

And so the appearance of the Hale-Bopp comet — beautiful as it raced across the night sky — marked the largest mass suicide on U.S. soil and certainly one of the worst in U.S. history. Midweek, just before Easter Sunday 1997, the police in the exclusive suburban community of Rancho Santa Fe, about thirty miles north of San Diego, received a call alerting them to a tragedy in their midst. This small town of five thousand residents prides itself on a crime-free, sun-soaked environment — ultra posh, yet with a rural feel. In 2002 the town claimed title to being the most expensive place in the United States to buy a house.[3] Who would imagine that the local police would be led to such a gruesome discovery? Thirty-nine dead and partially decomposing bodies were lying neatly in various rooms in one of Rancho Santa Fe's gated estates, adorned with palm trees and lush foliage (see fig. 2). Local zoning laws keep Rancho Santa Fe properties at a two-acre minimum. Privacy is valued highly here. If it had not been for the anonymous call to the police, it might have been months before the grisly scene was uncovered.

The tip came from a former acolyte, Rio. He said he knew earlier that day that the deaths had occurred. He knew it as soon as he opened the packet that had been sent to him by the group. He read the letter but did not bother to look at the two videos that were enclosed. Rio had left the group a short time before, so he knew they had been discussing the possibility of helping along their earthly departure through artificial means. He felt compelled to go to the house to see for himself and asked his boss to drive him there. Rio went up to the door alone and cautiously looked inside. Indeed, they had "gone." Shocked, yet not surprised, he phoned the local police.

Two officers from the San Diego County Sheriff's Department found the bodies, each one lying neatly on a bed or cot and all but two covered with a diamond-shaped purple shroud. From the odor that filled the house, the police knew immediately that the deaths had occurred at least a few days earlier. It was a shocking scene even to veteran police personnel and coroners. By early evening television and radio stations were buzzing with the news. The first reports indicated that all the deceased were men, thought to be part of a monastic order of some sort. Like others, I listened and watched this mystery unfold. It did not take long before I was contacted for media interviews, while the dead were yet to be identified.

FIGURE 2. In late March 1997, thirty-nine bodies of Heaven's Gate devotees were found in this mansion in the exclusive community of Rancho Santa Fe, Calif. *(San Francisco Chronicle)*

A knowing chill ran through me that first night as I listened to scanty descriptions of what was known about the deceased; yet I did not want to jump to conclusions. Some news reports mentioned a Web site that was somehow related. I spent hours trying to access it, but the Internet was clogged with the traffic of many others doing the same. Finally, I got in. At first I was startled by the stark, pulsating headline banner, "Entering Heaven's Gate." I searched for something with more content. When I got to some text, the language was immediately all too familiar. I knew who it was: a group I had been studying from a distance for several years. Concerned and wanting to corroborate my conclusion, at 2:00 A.M. and again at 5:00 A.M. I spoke to colleagues on the East Coast. I called the San Diego police to tell them what I knew. Later I called a family on the other side of the country whose daughter was in the group. It was a very sad day.

Some of the earlier information was now being corrected in the news stories. In fact, among the dead were twenty-one women and eighteen men. Apparently their genderless appearance and asexual clothing and haircuts had thrown off the first investigators at the scene. Soon the media reports were acknowledging what I already knew: the dead were members of a group more commonly known as the Bo Peep cult — a group that had been in and out of the news since 1975 — and would now forever be known as the Heaven's Gate cult, a name based primarily on the name of their Web site, heavensgate.com.

The ages of the dead ranged from twenty-six to seventy-two; Applewhite, the leader, was sixty-six. They had died, apparently peacefully, in three groups over the course of at least two days. Written instructions found on the bodies and around the house pointed to exactly what had transpired during those last few days in the mansion, which had been home to the cult for approximately six months. Evidence indicated that the suicides began on March 23, the day the Hale-Bopp comet was closest to earth. As the identities of the deceased became known, the details of their former lives, their cult lives, and their hopes and dreams were splattered across the pages of daily newspapers and discussed on nightly news programs around the world. Eight had been with the group only a few years, having joined in the mid-1990s; the remaining thirty (not counting their leader, Do) had been devoted to Ti and Do since the group's beginning in the mid-1970s. Eight of the men, including Do, had had themselves castrated, and others in the group had been undergoing chemical treatments to combat sexual urges.[4]

Soon segments from their two farewell videos were being shown before, during, or after television reports. Do spoke on one videotape; the followers, most often in pairs, spoke for a few minutes each on the second recording. The videos had been sent to select former followers and sympathizers with the request that they distribute them to the media after the bodies were discovered. Do and his followers wanted the videos to explain their actions and impart their beliefs. More of their beliefs could be found on their Web site. Their home page reflected a high-tech, science fiction–like scene: a large golden keyhole, signifying the doorway to Heaven's Gate, was set against a black background filled with twinkling stars. The image shivered with a flashing "RED ALERT! RED ALERT! Hale-Bopp Brings Closure to . . . Heaven's Gate."

The media, of course, were in a frenzy. Each paper, news program, or radio talk show vied for the latest information or the greatest insight from someone in the know: the person who had tipped off the police, a local real estate agent who had recently shown the house, a neighbor, the waiter who had served them their last meal at a nearby Marie Callander's restaurant, a former follower, Applewhite's sister, a relative of one of the deceased, someone who had almost been a member of the group, someone who had been a member for a short time more than twenty years ago, a cult expert, a suicide expert, an apocalyptic expert. And my telephone was ringing off the hook. It went on and on — until more pressing news took precedence. Then, for the most part, the Heaven's Gate suicides slipped from public vision and collective contemplation.

• • •

Before turning to a careful examination of the Heaven's Gate cult — how and when it was formed, the interpersonal dynamics, the organizational crises, the highs and lows of daily life, the crucial aspects of the belief system that held it together, and the energies of the charismatic leaders who guided the way — we must go back in time to look at the sociohistorical context from which this group emerged. The Heaven's Gate belief system, as it was developed by Ti and Do, grew out of a social phenomenon, now identified as the New Age movement, that flourished in the 1970s. Yet Ti and Do themselves would have shuddered at the thought of being identified with it — or with anything remotely "human," such as organized religion. Nevertheless, the seeds of their belief system can be found in both.

Formative Principles

To understand the impact of the New Age movement on the founding and ideological development of Heaven's Gate, we need to explore the sociohistorical, cultural, and intellectual trends that gave rise to a certain worldview that was characteristic of the movement. New Age beliefs and practices vary widely, making it difficult to characterize the movement as having one mission. The New Age was and is decidedly more far-flung than many other social movements, including the New Communist Movement, which I discuss later in relation to the DWP. The New Age movement has been affected by an array of influences; therefore, the summary that follows focuses specifically on those aspects that helped to establish formative principles relevant to this study. These principles are a moral imperative, a demand for deep personal change, and reliance on a leader.[5]

The moral imperative was guided not by a political vision but a cosmic one that held to a belief that a person could — and should — transcend daily life by tapping into the "universal mind," the oneness of all existence.

In so doing, the mundane realities of mainstream ways would be super-seded by a grand cosmic interconnectedness that would do away with war, suffering, and earthly spoils. However, this lofty goal could be achieved only by making a commitment to a transformative process. The promised outcome was the individual's ability to experience the awesome state of cosmic oneness, thereby gaining insights into the self and the meaning of life. This was the rationale for the demand for personal change. This process, although extremely personal and individualized, was developed and introduced by certain knowing persons who were nec-essary to guide and direct it. It could not be done on one's own. One needed to rely on a leader — a guru, a teacher, a spiritual being.

These three principles — the moral imperative, demand for change, and reliance on leaders — grew directly out of a convergence of specific New Age trends. These were sociocultural influences emanating from certain cultural elites; religious and spiritual influences, including esoteric and Eastern philosophies; and technologies of change that revolved around methodologies of personal growth and self-awareness.

Sociocultural Influences

The New Age movement has been described as everything from a con-spiracy to a benign self-help movement. Some regard it as a type of touchy-feely religion; others consider it a threat to Christian values. The scholar of religion Wade Clark Roof has perhaps aptly described the most recent manifestation of the New Age as "a widespread spiritual awaken-ing."[6] Whatever one thinks of it, elements of the New Age movement have made inroads into major walks of life — from university curricula to TV talk shows. Oprah Winfrey, for example, is an ardent fan of many New Age concepts and beliefs; her program alone helps to spread these ideas to millions each day. Similarly, much of the programming on pub-lic television, especially during its fund-raising marathons, comprises spe-cials featuring various New Age celebrities and practitioners, from Deepak Chopra to Wayne Dwyer.

The New Age is possibly best known for its all-encompassing, yet somewhat elusive, nature. For example, researchers attempting to iden-tify traits of the New Age movement sent a survey to both critics (pro-fessional skeptics, cult watchers) and supporters (chiropractors, trainers, astrologers, and others associated with New Age philosophies or enter-prises). Three-fourths of the respondents agreed with two characteristics:

the New Age is rooted in Eastern mysticism, and it represents an eclectic collection of psychological and spiritual techniques.[7] Nevertheless, in spite of the movement's vast reach, one overarching idea runs through it: "The New Age bottom line can be stated in three words: 'All is One.' The cosmos is pure, undifferentiated, universal energy — a consciousness or 'life force.' Everything is one vast, interconnected process."[8]

Initially, the New Age movement was called the Age of Aquarius — a concept that piqued the interest of many in the countercultural movements of the sixties. This idea was influenced and popularized by the writings of Marilyn Ferguson, especially her book *The Aquarian Conspiracy,* sometimes called the New Age bible.[9] Some former Heaven's Gate members mentioned this book in particular to me during our interviews. They identified it as one of the few books that were important to the group over the years, in addition to the Bible and books on Gnosticism, various Jesus myths, and UFO sightings.

Ferguson's description of the Aquarian movement highlights the scope and depth of its worldview: "Broader than reform, deeper than revolution, this benign conspiracy for a new human agenda has triggered the most rapid cultural realignment in history. The great shuddering, irrevocable shift overtaking us is not a new political, religious, or philosophical system. It is a new mind — the ascendance of a startling worldview that gathers into its framework breakthrough science and insights from earliest recorded thought."[10]

The New Age movement, then, represents a vast shift in the perception of reality. Several facets of this contemporary paradigm shift are of interest here in relation to the group founded by Applewhite and Nettles. Among these are the idea of the interconnectedness of all things and the concept of reincarnation (an adaptation from Eastern philosophy), belief in the supernatural (an adaptation from esoteric belief systems), and the possibility of personal transformation and proposed methodologies for attaining a state of enlightenment (an adaptation from the human potential movement).

Often the emergence of New Age ideas, at least in the United States, is tied to the 1960s culture of drugs and protest. But in fact the origins of the New Age movement date at least to the 1950s, a decade in which a notable segment of the population rejected the materialism of the American Dream and sought out new meaning and new ways of interpreting life. An expression of this can be found in the works of Beat Generation poets and writers, such as Jack Kerouac, Allen Ginsberg, and Alan Watts, all of whom were proponents of Zen Buddhist and Eastern beliefs and practices.

At about the same time, Aldous Huxley wrote his groundbreaking essays, "The Doors of Perception" and "Heaven and Hell."[11] For many, this was the first popular effort to tie together two erupting trends: the attraction to Eastern ideas and the use of psychedelic drugs. Timothy Leary and Richard Alpert (who later changed his name to Ram Dass) popularized those ideas for a mass American audience.[12] "Turn on, tune in, drop out" is how Leary put it. Suddenly it was possible not only to sanctify experimentation with drugs (especially hallucinogenics) but also to interpret one's personal drug experience in terms of Eastern spirituality. In that way the counterculture became inextricably connected to strands of Eastern philosophy and religion. And as those ideas became more accessible, Eastern ways of knowing became more appealing.[13]

That was especially true after 1965, with the arrival in the United States of a number of Eastern gurus, a development attributed to the relaxation of immigration laws, which until then had kept out large numbers of Asians.[14] Although there is evidence of guruism and Eastern-based spiritual movements in the United States before 1965, the change in U.S. immigration policy opened the doors to many more opportunities at the very moment when public interest was growing. Popularization of these movements also took hold in response to the publicity surrounding such cultural heroes as the Beatles and the movie star Mia Farrow, who for a time had been linked with Maharishi Mahesh Yogi, founder and leader of the Transcendental Meditation (TM) movement.[15]

As a result of those sociocultural influences, strains of the ancient Eastern philosophies of Hinduism, Buddhism, Zen, and Taoism are embedded in New Age thought. Asian concepts of oneness, karma, reincarnation, nirvana, mantra meditation, kundalini, freedom from desire, and the path toward enlightenment became part and parcel of New Age belief systems and practices. One outcome of the marriage of East and West was that direct personal experience (found in one form in Ram Dass's exhortation "Be Here Now") was soon given precedence over abstract reasoning, a recurring theme in the New Age movement.[16] That precept becomes even more important when linked with new technologies of change.

Religious and Spiritual Influences

In a survey of 185 "Aquarian conspirators," Marilyn Ferguson found that the following names came up most frequently when respondents were asked whose ideas most influenced them: Pierre Teilhard de Chardin, C. G. Jung, Abraham Maslow, Carl Rogers, Aldous Huxley, Robert Assagioli, and J. Krishnamurti.[17] A common thread running through the ideas of those great thinkers is an interest in mysticism, Eastern philosophy, self-awareness, transcendence, and cosmic consciousness.

Yet the influences on New Age thinking are even more varied and wide-ranging and far older than the time frame represented by the luminaries identified in Ferguson's survey. New Age thought also can be traced to Gnosticism, occultism, Wicca, and shamanism, as well as modern ideas such as Transcendentalism, spiritualism, and Theosophy. The main elements of Gnosticism, spiritualism, and Theosophy are described briefly here because of their relevance to the founding of the Heaven's Gate group.[18]

GNOSTICISM

Gnosticism was a dualistic religious and philosophical movement prominent during the late Hellenistic and early Christian eras. Gnostic belief systems promised salvation through an occult knowledge, which each ancient Gnostic sect claimed had been revealed to it alone. Some systems were syncretic and incorporated Christian concepts; at times, the Gnostic movement was considered a threat to Christianity because of its "pagan temptations."[19] A central Gnostic teaching is that the evil spirit in each person is actually made of matter and can be released only through the use of secret formulas. Direct revelations from angels and out-of-body journeys to heaven and hell are typical of Gnosticism — characteristics that distinguish it from traditional forms of Christianity.[20]

Gnosticism is based primarily on an inner knowing, as opposed to faith or belief. That knowing is described as personal knowledge emanating from personal revelation through meditation or from access to the secret teachings of Jesus or other masters. As I demonstrate, that sense of inner knowing was central to the Heaven's Gate belief system and germane to each member's adherence to the group.

Gnostics believe that human life is destined to failure, that it is the creation of an evil god, whom only Gnostics perceive and are able to combat because they are endowed with inner knowing from the true God. This, too, is similar to the Heaven's Gate philosophy, with its hatred of and disdain for human life and earthly existence. Gnostics believe that all other religions and belief systems are false and that it is their task to create the true consciousness necessary for salvation.[21]

SPIRITUALISM

Spiritualism developed in the 1800s as an occult belief in the human ability to communicate with departed spirits.[22] This idea was extended to include the ability to read minds, have out-of-body experiences, bend spoons, lift tables, walk on hot coals, and recognize or manifest psychic or paranormal phenomena. Also part of this was a mental healing movement based on the work of Franz Anton Mesmer, often regarded as the father of hypnotism.[23] (The word *mesmerize* is derived from his name.) Those who conducted psychic readings and healings were called mediums and are considered forerunners of present-day channelers and psychics.[24]

Bonnie Nettles had been a medium and a psychic. She believed that she communicated with departed spirits, alien beings, and other cosmic guides. Similarly, Applewhite believed he was able to communicate mentally with Nettles after she died, or, in their view, departed to the Next Level.

THEOSOPHY

Theosophy is a philosophical and spiritual system that also emerged in the 1800s. It is a "fascinating mélange of esoteric Buddhism, lamaist doctrines from Tibet, Hindu mysticism and a romantic picture of world history which postulates a non-physical period of prehistoric evolution with the ecosphere gradually solidifying into matter, and a series of root races stretching all the way back to lost Atlantis."[25]

The Theosophy movement was founded by a Russian mystic named Helena Petrovna Blavatsky (1831–91), who led a colorful, sometimes scandalous life. More than once she was accused of being a fraud and a master of delusion. Despite Blavatsky's popularity, the British Society for Psychical Research was not enthusiastic about her; in the society's 1884 report she was described as "one of the most accomplished, ingenious and interesting imposters in history."[26] Nonetheless, the impact of her beliefs has been felt worldwide. Her tomes — *Isis Unveiled* and *The Secret Doctrine* — claimed to divulge the secrets of the "Brotherhood of Hidden Masters." Blavatsky declared that these ascended beings spoke through her, revealing the Truth of a greater cosmic reality in which the human soul has the capacity to become God. The Masters were believed to be guiding and controlling the destiny of humanity, as well as holding the key to the deeper laws of life and the mysteries of both science and theology.

Blavatsky professed that she alone, through her psychic abilities, had access to the secret knowledge of the Ascended Masters. The psychic elements of New Age thought were solidified in this concept of Ascended Masters. Blavatsky mixed this with other occult notions and her particular derivation of Hinduism, devised on her return from an extended stay in India. Now, with Blavatsky's blessing, New Age mystical inclinations, spiritual quests, and self-awareness rituals could rightfully include going back to past lives, channeling spirit guides, inducing out-of-body experiences and astral travel, and believing in the powers of crystals, angels, and sacred sites.

Important facets of the Heaven's Gate belief system can be identified in the trends, beliefs, and practices described here. For example, the idea of evil spirits, the sense of inner knowing, the ability to communicate with the departed, the existence of other levels of life and beings who control the heavenly spheres, and a belief in past lives and astral travel were all central to the ideology developed by Applewhite and Nettles.

Technologies of Change

The Swiss psychiatrist Carl Jung (1875–1961) is considered the forerunner of the human potential movement, which became known in part for promoting the use of probing self-awareness techniques called "technologies of change." Breaking with Freud, Jung believed there were aspects of the human psyche that were independent of the individual and part of what he called the "collective unconscious."[27] This dimension was a sort of storehouse of ancestral experience, represented by cosmic memories. He labeled these universal symbols, images, and patterns "archetypes." A key archetype was the mandala, or magic circle, which became a popular image among hippies and followers of Eastern thought. The mandala was supposed to represent the unity of life, and also the self. Jung believed in the possibility of personal growth through individual transcendence, or achieving harmony between the conscious and the unconscious. His ideas were, and still are, extremely influential.

In the 1950s and 1960s a psychological approach to personal growth by means of intense, small-group experiences — originally called T-groups or sensitivity training, later encounter groups or sessions — became popular in many circles in the United States. The purpose of these meetings was to heighten personal awareness. Although most often thought of as a West Coast phenomenon, the encounter movement had started in the

1940s at the National Training Laboratories in Bethel, Maine. Encounter sessions became more widely used several decades later as a way to study group dynamics and interpersonal problem solving and to improve communication society-wide.

With the growth of the civil rights and other protest movements, these confrontational but honest sessions seemed a handy tool to promote greater tolerance and improve social relations. Before long, "encounter became a household word."[28] The technique was broadly promoted by those associated with humanistic psychology, such as Abraham Maslow, Fritz Perls, Carl Rogers, and Rollo May. Eventually the trend became known as the human potential movement.

During encounter sessions, and eventually in many milieus, great emphasis was placed on the importance of *peak experiences,* a term coined by Maslow, a humanist psychologist.[29] Peak experiences are states of high emotional arousal. Reaching such heights was purported to enable a person to transcend the limitations of everyday life and tap into cosmic consciousness. Peak experiences were characterized by "blissful feelings; focused attention on the here and now; freedom from anxieties, doubts and inhibitions; spontaneous, effortless functioning; and a sense of being merged or harmonized with one's environment."[30] Maslow's use of the term was intended for those times when individuals sensed their highest potential, attaining a state of what Jung had first identified many years before as self-realization. Maslow called this state self-actualization.

Maslow admitted that someone who was not especially self-actualized could have a peak experience through the use of psychedelic drugs — and, as the New Age movement has amply shown, through a variety of mind-altering processes.[31] Soon encounter groups and similar practices used by others who were jumping on the self-awareness bandwagon included a plethora of techniques aimed at bringing about sensory experiences and intellectual revelations, fondly called epiphanies. The locus for much of this activity was Esalen, a retreat nicely situated in Big Sur, California. Other paths at the time led to such organizations as Synanon, est (Erhard Seminar Training), Scientology, the Center for Feeling Therapy, and Primal Scream therapy.

According to Ferguson, the goal of these processes was "to fine-tune the mind and body, to expand the brain's sensing, to bring the participants to a new awareness of vast untapped potential." "When they work," she wrote, "it's like adding sonar, radar, and power lenses to the mind."[32] Because of the alleged power of experiential practices and experiments, a growing emphasis on transpersonal and spiritual experiences took hold in numerous settings: first, in group therapy sessions; then, in a multitude of contexts, from hot tubs at hippie communes to elite cultural scenes to private parties to scientific laboratories.

One of the laboratory settings was that of the anthropologist Gregory Bateson, whose work greatly influenced the movement.[33] Bateson's version of a peak experience came about as part of what he called "Learning III," a high-level mental experience accompanied by insights and breakthroughs. Bateson's concept of the ecology of mind promoted the idea that we must think like Nature thinks and tap into a Metapattern that connects every living thing on this planet. Based on experiments that literally drove porpoises crazy in efforts to push them to Learning III, Bateson cautioned that "even the attempt at level III can be dangerous, and some fall by the wayside."[34] But those who make it, Bateson concluded, reach "a world in which personal identity merges into all the processes of relationship in some vast ecology or aesthetics of cosmic interaction." He added a foreboding afterthought: "That any of these survives seems almost miraculous."[35]

Yet transformational journeys were described zealously by Ferguson. The link to the New Age movement's moral imperative is readily apparent in her writing: "The transformative process, however alien it may seem at first, soon feels irrevocably right. Whatever the initial misgivings, there is no question of commitment once we have touched something we thought forever lost — our way home. Once this journey has begun in earnest, there is nothing that can dissuade. No political movement, no organized religion commands greater loyalty. This is an engagement with life itself, a second chance at meaning."[36]

Ferguson advised using a variety of "psychotechnologies," or mind-altering techniques, to reach those "deep inner shifts," the sought-after awakening, the self-actualization of the peak experience. She referred to the techniques as picks, pitons, compasses, and binoculars, asserting that they were "deceptively simple systems [such as] deep contemplation, grave illness, wilderness treks, peak emotions, creative effort, spiritual exercises, controlled breathing, techniques for 'inhibiting thought,' psychedelics, movement, isolation, music, hypnosis, meditation, reverie."[37]

Unfortunately, mass enthusiasm for peak experiences brought with it not only intensely high moments and deep personal insights but also excesses, exploitation, and harm. Various researchers and critics warned of problems that arose from mass marketing such high-powered techniques and practices.[38] Some of the unfavorable outcomes were physiological sensations caused by relaxation-induced anxiety, such as visual or auditory hallucinations or inappropriate sensory responses, for example, feeling cold, hot, tingly, or numb; odd behavioral activity, such as restlessness, tics, and spasms; and erratic emotional states, such as extremes of sadness, rage, joy, or sexual feelings. Negative psychological outcomes were states of brief reactive psychosis, incapacitating panic attacks and phobias, major depression, and dissociative disorders. Many eager explorers also attempted to accelerate or shortcut their quest for enlightenment and peak experience by abusing hallucinogenic drugs such as LSD, which resulted for some in traumatic experiences and sometimes in short- or even long-term psychosis.

Nevertheless, the motivation to experience varying types and degrees of altered states of consciousness as a means to self-fulfillment or self-realization blossomed in the Me Generation of the 1970s. This is precisely the period — and the prevailing ambience — in which Applewhite and Nettles were in the formative stages of their own personal awakening and the coming together of their group. The two leaders effectively guided their followers through an assortment of mind-altering exercises as part of their training program.

·   ·   ·

The New Age movement drew on a mélange of ideas and philosophies. Transformational moments, often regarded as mystical experiences, became a way of coping with and making sense of the world; for some people, they also become a way of life.

Functioning under that paradigm, the only accepted reality is that which is experienced *personally* through some form of transformative moment or event, which is then interpreted, or reframed, as having been, or being, connected to the greater cosmos. That the experience might have been manufactured or manipulated (deliberately or otherwise) is not the point; *the experience is the point* — for, in New Age thought, we create our own reality.

Thus, by way of a historical evolution through Eastern, Western, and esoteric systems of belief and thought, direct, intense personal experience became one of the unifying threads crisscrossing New Age concepts and practices. Beginning in the 1950s, thousands upon thousands of people, but even more in subsequent decades, latched onto those ideas as a way to make sense of their lives. In large segments of the population, it manifested in an individualized effort to resolve heightened alienation and growing dissatisfaction with the status quo. Some critics of the New Age movement consider it reactionary and politically conservative because of its inward-looking emphasis,[39] but it also can be regarded as a revolutionary movement, although not an overtly political one. New Age ideas represent, and push for, a voyage to the unknown.

It was in such an environment of cosmic oneness, altered states, personal transformation, and reliance on guides or gurus that the group that we now know as Heaven's Gate came into being.

CHAPTER 3

The Beginning

"The Two" Arrive

Marshall Herff Applewhite and Bonnie Lu Nettles espoused an eclectic philosophy that drew on ideas gleaned from a variety of belief systems, including Theosophy, Christianity, ufology (the interest in and study of UFO-related phenomena), and occultism. Their philosophy even included eco-fatalistic apocalypticism, foreseeing the destruction of planet Earth by humans ("spading under," in their words). The life span of the group they founded extended for about twenty-three years, from 1974 to 1997. Over this period, perhaps several hundred people were part of the group. Most people stayed for a time; however, a small but steadfast core remained throughout the group's existence. It was that core, plus several members who joined in the mid-1990s, who died with Applewhite in the collective suicide in March 1997.[1]

The Formative Years

Applewhite and Nettles met in Houston, Texas, in the early 1970s, probably 1972. Both were in their early forties at the time, and Nettles was about four years older than Applewhite. Although there are varying accounts of exactly how and where they met, most reports, including the group's own history, indicate that Nettles convinced Applewhite, during a time of psychological distress, that he was here on a divine mission and that they were soul mates. In recounting this history, Applewhite would sometimes mention how he struggled with and resisted this information. Whether Nettles was the instigator or merely helped Applewhite to make sense of his life at a time when he was under stress, one thing is certain: the two were inseparable almost from the time they met.

FIRST ENCOUNTER

Bonnie Nettles worked as a registered nurse. When she met Applewhite, she was married and the mother of four children, ages twelve to nineteen. According to her son, who was twelve at the time, Bonnie left her family to be with Applewhite.[2] Apparently, her marriage had already been in trouble before she met her "soul mate." A serious student of Theosophy and occult teachings, she was known as an astrologer, a psychic, and a medium and was a member of a group that held seances, or in current terminology, a channeling group. While in that group, Bonnie believed she received a message from an alien spirit who told her that someone who looked like Applewhite would appear in her life.

Applewhite, known as Herff to his friends, had been married also and had two children with his wife. His marriage ended sometime in the 1960s, long before he met Nettles. The son of a strict Presbyterian minister, Applewhite studied to be a minister, but his final degree was in music, which some say was his real love. He worked as a music teacher at the University of Alabama and at St. Thomas University in Houston. He had also served as choir director in several local churches. He had enjoyed a minor career singing in musicals and operas and was considered talented and charismatic.

More than his female counterpart, Applewhite fits the traditional view of a charismatic leader. From his earliest days as a teacher and performer, he was consistently described as intelligent, charming, pleasant, creative, and a leader. For example, someone who knew him during his theater days in Texas was quoted in a 1975 news article as saying that Applewhite had "a lot of charisma [and was] the kind of person everybody liked."[3] After his death, his sister remarked, "He was always very funny, a good student and a born leader."[4] A former college roommate commented, "He was a very attractive person. He was definitely a leader, but not a huge, flamboyant kind of leader. But people liked to be around him. They would listen to what he had to say."[5]

The main controversy surrounding Applewhite in his younger years was that he had been involved in homosexual relationships; sometimes these were carried on in secret, sometimes openly. Most reports from the end of his teaching years up until the time he met Nettles indicate that he was openly gay and lived in the gay section of Houston. Yet even after his divorce personal struggles over his sexual identity had caused him some distress and psychological conflict. Applewhite was never comfortable with being either homosexual or heterosexual, it seems; and surprising even him at first, Nettles fulfilled the role of the platonic soul mate he was looking for — something he had mentioned at the time to old friends.[6] In 1970, after he was dismissed from his last academic post at the University of St. Thomas, he became increasingly despairing as well as bitter about his academic colleagues who had not come to his defense.[7] Shortly afterward he suffered a breakdown, which entailed disorientation and hearing voices. Not long after that, he met Bonnie, his soon-to-be life partner.

Speaking about his mate, Applewhite once told a reporter, "I felt I had known her forever."[8] Years later, in one of the group's documents, Applewhite wrote matter-of-factly about his and Bonnie's lives at the time they met: "The registered nurse was happily married with four children, worked in a nursery of a local hospital, and enjoyed a small astrology practice. The music professor, a divorcee who had lived with a male friend for some years, was contentedly involved in cultural and academic activities."[9] In the *Beyond Human* video series produced by the group in the early 1990s for training and recruitment purposes, Applewhite spoke in some detail about the emotions surrounding that first meeting. Here he refers to Bonnie as Ti, her chosen cult name:

> In the early seventies for unknown reasons (and this is just my attempt to explain to you what occurred), for unknown reasons — things we could not understand — my life began to suddenly fall apart. It had been a very stable life, an acceptable life, certainly one that was considered legitimate and had respect to it in the community, as did Ti's life. And her life separately began to fall apart. We did not know each other. We'd never seen one another that we were aware of — had never met. Then in the early seventies, I think around '72, we met just perchance while I was visiting a sick friend in a hospital where Ti was a nurse. From that moment, my life changed — changed very significantly. I rebelled. I didn't want it to change, and yet I *knew* it had to change. And the conflict that was in me was very great.
>
> The same thing was happening with Ti. She knew she had something to do with me. I tried to reject that idea. Ti was confused for a while and wondered, "Well, why do I recognize you, and you don't recognize me?" And even though I might have thought I didn't recognize Ti, I knew that I couldn't cut it off. And here we had separate lives, separate careers, families, involvements

in the world, and all of a sudden, just because we met, something was causing us to have to become more involved in spite of our desire not to. Not
involved in a human way. There was never a coming together in that we were
bed partners or involved in a physical relationship. But there was something
that compelled us to spend time together and listen to each other, and search
together. And we started searching Scriptures, we started searching everything
we could get our hands on — New Age material, everything we could find that
would open our heads. We realized that all of the searching that we were doing
was superficial, that where we were really getting help and getting information
was from what was being fed to us — mentally.[10]

This description of their meeting became the group's official account:
a fateful meeting, a coming together, brief resistance, and finally acceptance of otherworldly intervention. This pattern occurs time and again in
group members' recounting of their own initiation into the fold.

BECOMING "THE TWO"

For a short time after they met, Applewhite and Nettles operated a small
metaphysical store called the Christian Arts Center, where they sold
books and other New Age paraphernalia. Nettles did astrological charts
and readings, claiming to have psychic help from a spirit guide, a dead
monk named Brother Francis. When the center failed, they started
another one, called Knowplace, where they held classes on mysticism,
meditation, and related New Age topics. Their second effort was not very
successful either. After a while the two friends withdrew from almost
everyone else in their lives. They spent more time with each other and had
only minimal contact with their respective families and children.
(Actually, Applewhite had ceased contact with his family several years earlier. He told a friend at the time that it was too painful to see his children.[11] According to Applewhite's son, he and his father had had no contact since 1962, when the boy was five years old.) During this period of
seclusion and separation from family and friends, Applewhite and Nettles
became a duo of mystics, "absorbed in a private world of visions, dreams,
and paranormal experiences that included contacts with space beings who
urged them to abandon their worldly pursuits."[12]

Applewhite's seclusion at this juncture represented a complete break
with the life he had previously known. He discontinued his involvement
with music and singing and lost contact with old friends. He read a great
deal of metaphysical literature, in particular, Madame Blavatsky's works.
As a Theosophist, Nettles was already familiar with these materials, and

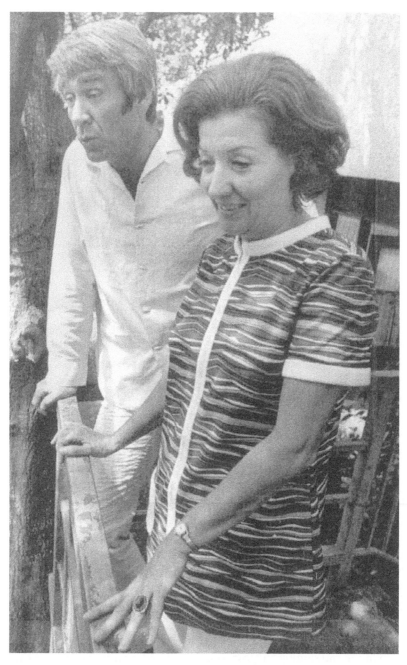

FIGURE 3. Marshall Applewhite and Bonnie Nettles in Houston, Tex., in 1972, during their early travels together. (AP/Wide World Photos)

most likely she encouraged her partner to read and study them. The view
that Nettles was the force behind Applewhite was voiced by several followers. It was readily apparent also to the public eye. For example, one
early devotee recalled, "They appeared as a tight unit; she, the silent bat-
tery; he with a strong stage presence, the mouthpiece."[13]

By most accounts, the two always appeared to be in total harmony (see
fig. 3). Sometimes Nettles corrected Applewhite when he was speaking,
and he always deferred to her as his guide. Despite reports that Applewhite was the main leader and despite all the media attention given to him
after the suicides, it was clear to their followers that she was at least a
coequal if not the guiding wisdom behind it all. For one thing, Nettles
was at the apex of the group's hierarchy. In a document written by
Applewhite as a record of the group's history, he noted that over time, certainly by early 1976, he himself had realized that she was higher up on the
Next Level chain of command. She was indeed his "Older Member," the
group's term for leadership.

Urged on by the visions and inner voices that came to them during
their self-imposed seclusion, the two mystics left Houston in January 1973
and began traveling around Texas and other southwestern states.
According to a woman who considers herself their first convert, their
purpose was to visit various metaphysical groups hoping to find followers, or at least people who would take them seriously.

But sadly, and also the source of some personal frustration for them,
no one seemed to pick up on their message, except for the woman just
referred to, who did not stay with them very long, only a few months. She
left them mostly because of the way they acted and because she was
unhappy with how they treated her — for example, sending her off by herself so they could be alone together and telling her that her presence was
disrupting their vibrations. During their travels, they sent her letters
describing what they were experiencing and coming to believe. They were
already secretive at that time and acting fearful and nervous. Even at this
early stage they were using assumed names and refusing to tell anyone
where they were staying.

ARREST AND RESURRECTION

A major event in their life on the road occurred in August 1974 when they
were arrested in Harlingen, Texas. They had called a press conference to
put out their message and billed the motel room to the reporter without
his permission. When he found out, he notified the local authorities. The

police learned that the two were wanted on several charges, including failure to return a rental car in another state and credit card fraud. Applewhite was extradited to Missouri and spent six months in a St. Louis jail, most of that time waiting for trial. The charge of credit card fraud against Nettles was dropped by the complainant, who, it turned out, was the husband of their first convert. Nettles returned to Houston and waited for her partner's release. Meanwhile, during his incarceration, Applewhite drafted a document that became the basis of their first written public statement. Within several months of his release, after he and Nettles joined up again, copies of this statement were sent far and wide to announce their arrival as "messengers of God." Once more they intended to spread the word and attract listeners and followers.

They went traveling again in early 1975. Not long after they met, they had come to the conclusion that they had known each other in past lives. Now they would experience their "awakening," which, as they explained it, led them to understand that they had actually been sent here from another planetary (and "heavenly") existence called the Next Level. The two sequestered themselves for several months in a campground on the Rogue River, near Gold Beach, Oregon. When they emerged from this retreat, they announced their awakening. Of this revelatory process Applewhite told a *New York Times* reporter: "Our thirst was unquenched and we were not finding what our purpose was, and it was as if the season had arrived under the direction of the Next Level for us to awaken to what we had to do. It was as if we had been given smelling salts and told, 'O.K., you guys, you've had 40 years and now it's time for you to realize who you are, what you have to do and get on with the show.'"[14]

They never discussed publicly the details of that experience but afterward claimed that during their seclusion at Gold Beach it had been confirmed to them that they were the two witnesses of the End Time, as written about in Revelation 11 in the Bible. They predicted that they would be killed in the streets, then resurrected three and a half days later and lifted up in a cloud of light, as portrayed in the Bible — only in their version the cloud was a UFO. Devoted followers with them at the time of "the Demonstration," as they called this death-and-resurrection sequence, would also be saved, as they would all be lifted off together in a Next Level spaceship. From this we see that Nettles and Applewhite's philosophy was deeply grounded in the belief that they were not humans but beings from what they called the "evolutionary level above human" (the Next Level). They had been sent here to spread their message and find others who would leave with them before the "final spading under," or destruction of the Earth. Applewhite and Nettles claimed to be bearing the same information brought by Jesus two thousand years ago.

CHARISMA IN HOLLYWOOD

None of Nettles and Applewhite's recruitment efforts was particularly successful until April 1975, when they were introduced to the followers of a Los Angeles–based metaphysical teacher named Clarence Klug. Klug had received one of the introductory letters sent to spiritual, New Age, and religious communities throughout the United States in which Applewhite and Nettles referred to themselves as the Two Witnesses. Intrigued, Klug invited them to speak to his group. That meeting took place on April 8, 1975, at the Hollywood home of one of Klug's acolytes. Klug, an aging guru with a circle of loyal followers, introduced his guests as "masters from outer space."[15] Dressed alike, with short cropped hair, and looking quite harmless and homey, Nettles and Applewhite entered the room and glanced out at the eager audience of about seventy or eighty people.

Applewhite spoke first: "Hello, I'm Guinea, and this is Pig," he said in jest, by way of introducing themselves. He proceeded to tell their story — about their awakening, the coming Demonstration, and the way to salvation from death. He preached that the human body must undergo a metamorphosis, a transformation he and Nettles called "the Process." This transformation was necessary in order to survive the atmosphere of the Next Level and make it to what they called "the literal heavens, a physical place."

Except for the joke about their names at the beginning of their remarks (Guinea and Pig, because it was all an experiment), for the most part, the two mystics had a serious demeanor, spoke to the point, and appeared knowledgeable and authoritative. Applewhite, an attractive, intense man with piercing blue eyes, did most of the talking. When he was done he asked for questions. One person sitting in the astounded audience asked if the two really were who they said they were — that is, representatives from outer space, their "Kingdom of Heaven." Applewhite replied, "You already know who we are or you wouldn't be here asking the question."[16]

The rapt listeners in attendance that evening were told by the two mysterious strangers claiming to be from outer space that anyone who wanted to come with them had to give up everything — jobs, possessions, family, children, sex, alcohol, cigarettes, and drugs. "It will only cost you your life," intoned Applewhite, a comment that now seems eerily portentous. It was a once-in-a-lifetime, once-in-a-hundred-lifetimes opportunity, they urged. This same scenario was repeated time and again over the next months of public meetings, as the two mystics and their band of eager acolytes successfully recruited more followers.

During and after that introductory meeting in Hollywood, most of those who had been present felt a mixture of skepticism and excitement. Meanwhile, their current guru, Klug, helped to arrange almost immediate private follow-up meetings in the next few days with "The Two," as Applewhite and Nettles were also called. Those who were interested were encouraged to make a hasty decision about this momentous opportunity. "After all, the window opens only once every two thousand years," said The Two, who in this way were model users of the scarcity principle of influence.[17] That is, if something appears hard to get, you will want it all the more. Those from the Hollywood meeting who chose to take advantage of the invitation were instructed to regroup at a campground on the Rogue River — the same Oregon locale of The Two's awakening, a place they called the Hideaway.

A couple of dozen people from Klug's group, including Klug himself, left their Los Angeles homes and lives and went off to join The Two. Not all were sure that they believed these two beings were really from outer space and were God's messengers, but, as good seekers, they were willing to check it out. For many of them, it was significant that Klug had also decided to go along. After all, Klug had been their teacher, their leader up to that point — and a perceptive one at that, most agreed. That adventurous first batch of followers knew that going with The Two meant giving up everything, including all worldly possessions, contact with people from their former lives, and, most of all, their "humanness." They may not have known exactly what that meant, the extent of such a commitment, but their curiosity was piqued and they were willing to give it a try. Soon many of them were serving as upper- and middle-level leaders, the Elders and Helpers who kept the system going.

Brent was one of those from Klug's circle. Tall, handsome, soft-spoken, and a talented actor and musician from the South, Brent had moved to Los Angeles after a stint in the military.[18] At the time Klug introduced his students to The Two, Brent was on the verge of breaking into what looked to be a successful Hollywood modeling career. Just at the moment when his smiling, attractive, young face adorned the box of a top-brand cereal, Brent decided to give it all up to follow Nettles and Applewhite. Having been a student of metaphysics and New Age ideas and philosophies for some time as a member of Klug's group, in many ways Brent

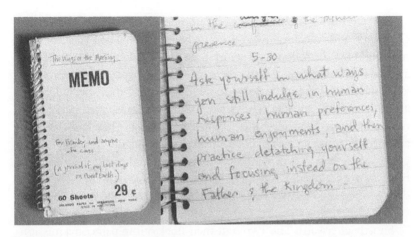

FIGURE 4. Brent's diary, with entry from May 30, 1975, shortly after he joined up with The Two. (Janja Lalich)

was the epitome of a seeker. He was an earnest, genuine, loving soul who, like so many others, was looking for greater meaning and purpose in life. He had also suffered some intense heartbreaks, both in personal relationships and in his career. In addition, he was an "out" gay man at a time when this was more difficult than it is today, at least for some people. This mix of personal and social factors helped to solidify Brent's decision to take a chance on The Two and their version of salvation.

Brent's experience is typical of the charismatic attraction experienced by others who chose to follow Applewhite and Nettles. Within days Brent sold his possessions and made his way to Oregon. A sensitive and introspective person, Brent kept a diary as he embarked on this journey (see fig. 4).

In one of his first entries he wrote: "We all came in contact with The Two and followed our urging to them." That statement mirrors The Two's recounting of their own meeting. Like Nettles and Applewhite, Brent and his comrades were not without doubts and questions, but they succumbed to the positive flow of the unknown. When these curious first followers came together in the campground, some felt it was the answer to their prayers. "It was like my family was there and I just wept," recalled Brent, reflecting on his first days at the Rogue River as he watched the arrival of others from his group. "I will just never forget that because I was so warm and happy and comfortable. And I thought, 'Oh, this is going to be great.'"

Early on during this first group encampment, Applewhite and Nettles got angry with their followers for not being there when they called a meeting. Half the followers were in town, while others were wandering around in the woods and along the river. The Two appeared flummoxed and annoyed. "We must be doing something wrong," they concluded and abruptly left the campsite. The newly gathered followers fell into a state of commotion. They felt guilty, confused, and lost. They had given up everything, traveled miles to be saved, and suddenly The Two were gone! When their leaders reappeared unannounced the next day, the novitiates were overjoyed. Some literally wept in ecstasy and relief. That incident formed the basis for one of their first lessons: Always be there for your leaders.

Shortly afterward, The Two sent their flock out in pairs on a mission to prove stamina and worthiness. They were supposed to reproduce more or less what The Two had experienced during their time on the road. It was meant to be a time of individual awakening for the young devotees. This plan also allowed Applewhite and Nettles to be alone again, a pattern they established with their first disciple several years previously.

• • •

It is apparent that Applewhite and Nettles had met each other at a critical juncture in their lives. The extent to which they believed the myth they created about themselves can never be known, but it seems likely that they were motivated by a mixture of belief and the desire to control and manipulate. They managed to amass a group of followers who were willing to trust them, or at least take a chance that they were who they said they were. With time and experience, the lack of success noted by their first convert was replaced by an effective charismatic attraction.

Applewhite and Nettles used various names over the years. Right away they dropped Guinea and Pig; the names were not appropriate now that others were taking them seriously. They continued to refer to themselves as The Two but also used regular names such as Vickie and Seymour Morgenstern (after the morning star). The latter were used for practical purposes, such as picking up mail at postal boxes or when questioned by authorities. For a while they took the names Bo (Applewhite) and Peep (Nettles) in recognition of their growing flock of sheep, as they starkly revealed to a reporter in one of their rare media interviews.[19] At some point in 1976, Nettles and Applewhite took the names Ti and Do. They explained the new names as an acknowledgment that everyone, including Do, had to go through Ti to get to the top, just as in the musical scale.

Both Applewhite and Nettles were consistently described as having "powerful eyes," one of the superficial traits often attributed to charismatic leaders. Between them, though, Applewhite was regarded as the attractive one, the charming, handsome one with appeal, whereas Nettles usually remained in the shadows, quietly guiding him. As The Two took on a public persona, their inseparable image fed the charismatic relationship they enjoyed with their audience. One early follower recalled, "I just felt drawn to them. You could feel the goodness."[20]

Another follower explained, "Bonnie was a very strong, powerful speaker. But most of the time, she didn't do that. She just sat back, carefully observing. So when she did come forward it was all the more dramatic." Brent, who had been in the group for fifteen years and been part of the inner circle, supported the notion that it was Nettles who was the driving force: "This was her cult. There was no doubt about it. Bonnie was definitely the founder, and she convinced Applewhite that he had a mission." Brent used the phrase "absolutely charismatic" when describing Applewhite. This effect was especially visible in public meetings.

This historical recounting makes clear that the group was an outgrowth of the New Age movement. Nettles, and then Applewhite under her tutelage, had a solid background in Theosophy and spiritualist beliefs. Elements of Christianity — no doubt Applewhite's influence on their ideology — are evident also (e.g., the two witnesses and the Resurrection scenario). But most prominent in their ideology were aspects of New Age beliefs, such as UFOs, communicating with spirit beings, the presence or threat of discarnate entities, cosmic occurrences, and connections to other spiritual domains. They used these theological and philosophical elements to forge an ideology that enveloped their followers in a social structure that was reinforced by mechanisms of influence and control.

The Development of Bounded Choice (Part 1)

With great emphasis on their personal experiences (i.e., their awakening), Nettles and Applewhite gathered around themselves individuals who believed in their leadership and who latched onto their professed mode of personal transformation — even to the point of ritualistic replication. Symbolic experience was crucial for recruiting members at this early stage in the group's development.

Meanwhile, the group's nomadic and communal lifestyle provided the impetus for some recruits to drift away and yet others to remain, thereby increasing the commitment and involvement of those who composed the first relatively stable group of followers. For those who made the commitment and began their selfless devotion to The Two, the process that led ultimately to bounded choice had already begun. Even at this initial stage of the group's development, the self-sealing system of the cultic organization was beginning to form.

All four dimensions of the bounded choice framework are dualistic, engendering both positive and negative sentiments and consequences. This dualism is central to the binding nature of these powerful structural dimensions of the cultic social system.[21] Let us now look at how these four structural and ideological dimensions developed during this stage of the group's formation

ESTABLISHING CHARISMATIC AUTHORITY

From his earliest public appearances in Alabama and Houston, Marshall Applewhite was reported to be an unusually compelling and persuasive man. Time and again, he was characterized as somebody with style, with a mesmerizing personality, with a riveting stare. He was a person you were unlikely to forget. He was definitely a charmer, said to be capable of looking deep into you with his ice-blue eyes and convincing you of anything.

Bonnie Nettles's charisma was more subtle, but her authority over the early followers as well as Applewhite himself was unquestionable. Rich, a heartfelt Californian who was in his early twenties when he joined the group in late summer 1975, had this to say: "Applewhite was really good. He had the charisma. Oh, man." Rich stayed in the group for thirteen years. When asked about his views on Nettles, he remarked: "Her strength was as the metaphysical one with the strong psychic connection. She said she had a spirit guide talking to her. She could tune into that energy and information, and extract it and interpret it, and then she would feed it to him [Applewhite]. She was the quiet one, the stoic one, who created the idea."

The charismatic relationship between leaders and followers is central to the cultic dynamic. It is the authority by which the leader commands. But also located in the charismatic relationship is the feeling of specialness that followers experience, a feeling that serves many functions. First, it provides a sense of connectedness and belonging, purpose and meaning, and generates a primal response of love and adulation (as well as their counterpart, fear and resistance). Second, it legitimates the leader's authority and permits the leader to act unchallenged.[22]

Both Applewhite and Nettles were aware of the need to exert charismatic authority so as to rein in their followers and bring them to an obedient state, but their skill in this area developed gradually. In early 1973, according to their first convert, Applewhite and Nettles exhibited fear and anxiety, which led to her alienation from them. Then, in early 1975, after Applewhite's arrest and after he and Nettles set out on their second journey and spent time in retreat on the Rogue River, they emerged with a more confident and fully developed identity: no longer human, but one step above.

As is typical of charismatic leaders, Applewhite and Nettles now began to claim a lineage that gave them access to divine knowledge. "Do was guided in how he had written the statements," recalled Brent, explaining how he had understood his leaders' explanation of their connection to the Next Level. At first Applewhite and Nettles spoke of themselves as the two witnesses from the Book of Revelation — they called themselves the Two Candlesticks and the Two Lampstands, bringing the light, the news. But before too long, they spoke with the belief that they were actual incarnations of Jesus and God the Father.

Their followers believed it as well. Regularly, they defended the position that their leaders (the Older Members) had come here not to start a new religion but to complete a task they had begun two thousand years before. Applewhite confirmed this when he wrote:

> Remember, the One who incarnated in Jesus was sent for one purpose only, to say, "If you want to go to Heaven, I can take you through that gate — it requires everything of you." Our mission is exactly the same. I am in the same position to today's society as was the One that was in Jesus then. My being here is actually a continuation of that last task as was promised to those who were students 2,000 years ago. They are here again offering the same help. Our only purpose is to offer the discipline and the "grafting" required of this transition into membership in My Father's House. My Father came with me this time for the first half of this task to assist in the task because of its present difficulty.[23]

It was in April 1975 that their charismatic authority came to first fruition as they stood before the group brought together by Clarence Klug in his Hollywood home. Evidently, Applewhite's performance that evening was masterful. His relaxed self-assurance, his intense blue-eyed gaze, the confidence with which he replied, "You already know who we are or you wouldn't be here asking the question," when challenged as a visitor from outer space and the Kingdom of Heaven — this single outstanding performance clearly succeeded in persuading many in the audience to give up their careers, their families, their material possessions, and join the first encampment at the Rogue River.

Those who chose to follow The Two, some for a short time, some for the remainder of their lives, often recounted the intensity of their feelings in a manner that echoed Applewhite's recounting of his own experiences. As early as 1976 followers were saying:

> "What The Two had to say just felt right. My head told me their story didn't make sense, but I had a strong inner feeling that told me, 'Hey, you've got to do this.'"

> "I felt they were sincere, truth-seeking, happy and fulfilled. For the first time in my life, I have a firm faith that there is something higher."

> "None of the Indian gurus compared even remotely with The Two."[24]

As might be expected, some of those who left the group express a less sanguine view. Rich, for example, said, "Applewhite and Nettles convinced themselves that they were who they said they were. They probably went back and forth for a long time, thinking to themselves something like, 'I'm just playing a role. No, I'm not. This is real.' Seems to me then the ego got in the way and they really convinced themselves it was real and they were who they said they were. When recruits responded, they thought, 'Oh, they're responding! It must be the truth.' That validated their myth. They needed us, the members, to do that."

Like all effective charismatic cult leaders, Applewhite and Nettles grounded their authority in the belief that they were guided from on high, and few questioned their sincerity, not even most of those who either quickly or eventually chose not to stay with them. A long-term former member interviewed in a television documentary said, for example, "I never doubted Do's sincerity or his own belief in himself."[25] To most of their followers and to many sympathetic outsiders, The Two appeared to be on a genuine quest.

The indirect style of leadership used by Nettles and Applewhite established a closely felt and binding charismatic relationship with their followers. They were perceived as special, as bringing the promise of salvation. And they were accepted as the authorities to whom followers readily submitted — or left the fold.

DEVELOPING TRANSCENDENT BELIEF

A transcendent belief system is a system of thought that explains past, present, and future. It is transcendent in the sense that it looks to, indeed predicts, a radical change — either progressive or reactionary — in the social order.[26] It not only holds forth a utopian vision but also offers the actual means by which to get to the new world.[27] When that aspect is present, a belief system becomes an ideology.

The compelling, often totalizing nature of a transcendent belief system — with its call for the personal transformation of each adherent — is central to my argument that it is a key component in the self-sealing cultic system that leads to bounded choice. It serves to restrain adherents and to make them behave according to the group's rules and norms — even when not in the group's physical presence.

During the early years, the transcendent belief of the Heaven's Gate group was based on the idea of personal transformation by means of an individual metamorphosis into a Next Level being. Subsequent developments led to shifts in the group's beliefs, but at first this high-demand message stated clearly that each member was to convert into a new creature. This process was described as a physical, biological, and chemical changeover.

The biggest draw of this belief system was its promise of overcoming death. Members who were loyal and worked hard enough were supposed to be saved from death. The Two had said that entry into the Next Level would be by spacecraft coming to lift them up and away, literally, after the followers had completed the process of metamorphosis — that is, evolved into new creatures. If they did not make it this time, their souls would be put on ice for later pickup. In retrospect, we know that this group, which initially sought to overcome death and recruited on that very promise, later made a giant U-turn by choosing to hasten death and initiate their departure from earth.

The Heaven's Gate belief system was largely symbolic and metaphorical. For example, the researchers Robert Balch and David Taylor described Applewhite and Nettles as having arrived in a "flurry of metaphors."[28] And after attending one of their public meetings on the Stanford University campus in August 1975, the UFO investigator Jacques Vallee wrote that the group was "completely committed to a fantastic interpretation of human destiny."[29] One of Applewhite's and Nettles's gifts as charismatic leaders was their ability to formulate a binding philosophy that drew on common, everyday images. That touch of familiarity would have made it easier for followers to accept the proffered metaphorical concepts, the analogies and symbols. Soon these became foundational assumptions central to their worldview, and eventually they were adopted as guiding principles.

Over time and with the participation of their followers, forms of language and forms of mental representation merged.[30] This group used metaphors as both "pre-existing thought and subsequent action."[31] When metaphors are taken literally, the outcome is not simply new meanings for old words but also an accompanying change in "beliefs and feelings about the things that the words refer to."[32] The shared context of Heaven's Gate was more than a speech community; it was also a thought community.[33]

INSTITUTING SYSTEMS OF CONTROL

I use the term *systems of control* to identify the acknowledged, visible organizational mechanisms used to regulate or guide the operation of a group. These are the means by which authority exerts itself, and they constitute a powerful form of social influence in the group context. From the moment Applewhite and Nettles met and recruited their earliest followers, they pursued a strategy of absolute authority from the top down. Such a strategy is crucial to a self-sealing system and the gradual development of bounded choice. Authority is more than sheer power, as is reflected even in the language associated with authority, words such as *orders, obedience, obligation,* and *duty.*[34] Such words, and their underlying concepts, would not be necessary if subjects simply had guns held to their heads by their superiors. Authority is more complex. It implies a reciprocal relationship: those in authoritative roles are entitled to make demands; those in subordinate roles are obligated to obey. Yet obedience is not blind followership; even in intensely controlled situations, "subordinates are not totally free of the responsibility to exercise judgment."[35]

In our society, obedience to authority is taught from a very early age and is encouraged in most avenues of life. As citizens, we are ingrained with the idea of respect for authority, listening to our elders, not making waves, being a "good" child, a "good" pupil, a "good" employee, and so on. Dutiful behavior and accompanying attitudes are second nature in most of us. In cults, not only are there sanctions to further encourage obedience but also, as in the two groups examined here, typically, the group itself is formed around an "ideology that glorifies [obedience]."[36] Discipline and respect for authority were part and parcel of the formation of Heaven's Gate. The leaders insisted on this system of control, and it gained legitimacy early on.

Applewhite and Nettles were unquestionably the top leaders of the group. They were vital links in what was called the Chain of Mind, which led to the Next Level, from whence they claimed to receive their guidance. For the most part, they were coequals, although, as we have seen,

Applewhite acknowledged that Nettles was his Older Member. The command structure was pyramidal: the leaders at the top, the most committed and developed members functioning as elders and role models, and the majority of the members at the base.

"The whole idea of Heaven's Gate was this hierarchical model," said Rich. "We have these Representatives here on earth and they are to mentor the younger ones and then when you're in the literal heavens, quote, unquote, at another evolutionary level there is a whole chain of relationships. I mean it's very much like the military. I mean it is the military. You've got chain of command. You know, like the President at the top, then you've got his advisors, and then you've got the next ones — but you're always looking to your boss. So the concept is very ordinary."

This organizational system of control was based on secrecy, rigidity, stern discipline, and excessive control, eventually requiring members to relinquish their decision-making powers and sense of self — thereby restricting the reality within which they could make their own bounded choices. This approach worked because the members trusted their leaders completely in the belief that they were genuine and sincere in motivation.

Periodically, Applewhite and Nettles called their followers together to tell them that anyone who was not ready to make the commitment to "total overcoming" could leave. Their stated goal here on Earth was to totally overcome their humanness — that is, to reject all human attachments, feelings, emotions. There would be no hard feelings, members were told, if someone was incapable of this most difficult task. At times, members who decided to leave were given bus fare or airfare home or to another city. A constant threat felt by members was not being able to maintain the discipline and being asked to leave the group.

Thus the early systems of control kept members disciplined and subjugated while continuously restricting the internal rationale of their perspectives and choices. Members were already on the path toward a more confined life and bounded choice. This development was reinforced by the next dimension of the social structure, the systems of influence.

FORMING SYSTEMS OF INFLUENCE

The Heaven's Gate systems of influence were less overt than the organizational systems of control but led to a deeper and equally powerful internalization of the group's norms and goals. Systems of influence comprise the structures of social control, the human interactions and norms of conduct in the group's culture, and the social relations, all of which serve to regulate individual behavior in the community setting. These systems of influence include group norms, or the emotional and psychological atmosphere, modes of communication, and styles of information dissemination; peer influence and modeling, or peer pressure, cultural convention, and mimicry; and commitment, or sense of responsibility, duty, and obligation.

Systems of influence, once institutionalized, become central to a group's culture and are strengthened by social interaction in the group setting. As a result, individual members' actions and interactions become second nature. This is especially the case as long as they remain within the confines of bounded choice, that is, the social-psychological barriers constructed by the self and the social structure reinforced by other social agents, which include leaders and members alike. Let us take a closer look at the most important aspects of the systems of influence in the early years of Heaven's Gate.

Group norms revolved around personal and collective transformation and the means by which to achieve it. The primary norm was to strive at all times to overcome one's humanness. Members were driven by the idea that this would bring them eternal life. They recognized that the process was difficult and required great strength and commitment, and they supported one another in their desire to change. It was Applewhite and Nettles, the members believed, who made the transformational process possible. They were the direct link to the Next Level and thus the perfect guides. Members believed that The Two had been sent from the Next Level to assist in the desired collective and personal transformation.

Getting rid of reliance on one's own mind — as well as any expression of independent thinking — was another part of the process. Members learned not to trust their own thoughts or inner reflections. Early on they were told that those "little voices" were ever-present "discarnate entities" trying to pull them back to human interests in the human world. These were sometimes called Luciferian influences, described as spirit beings doing the work of the devil by putting "human" distractions in the way of students trying to purify themselves.

At the first campsite Brent recorded in his journal: "We learned about the spirits, how every feeling, except our urge to achieve the kingdom, was the result of a 'spirit's' activity." A month later he admonished himself: "How long will you continue to believe these things have any worth? . . . When will you have finally exorcized these beings that cling to you and perform as your reaction? To be stripped of them, to be free!! And then truly ready to go!"

During our interviews, Rich recalled also the constant effort to suppress emotions and remain separate from the rest of the world: "It was like we are deprogramming ourselves from human emotions [and] it was constant, incessant, day in and day out — how would my Older Member *have* me do it? I don't want to have any human thoughts and I don't want to have any humanlike emotions. I only want to have Next Level–like emotions and the closest example that I have of this is Marshall Applewhite and Bonnie Nettles. And so I'm going to act like them. Because actually they're insisting upon it. If I want to — no, it's a foregone conclusion: I *need* to emulate them if I want to be in this group."

The goal was clear: transformation. The method was clear: the Process. And everything about the environment supported behaviors in compliance with that mission

Peer influence and modeling were powerful factors in a group such as this, sequestered from the rest of the world. The rule of the day was always, as Applewhite solemnly declared, "I'll continue to be a sheep and do everything to please that Shepherd."

Peer pressure came into play in the communal lifestyle, in the guidance that members must be dependent on their Older Members for instructions on correct behaviors and ways of thinking, and in the insistence on procedures based on mimicry and mindlessness. The ultimate maxim was, "Look to your Older Members for everything." That, of course, left Applewhite and Nettles to be regarded as the perfect role models. They exemplified Next Level consciousness.

The object was to model oneself — in everything — after the example set by the Older Members. It was the way to reach the ideal, for certainly they were the embodiment of perfection. Before he died, Jstody explained, "We were getting it built into our circuits through our efforts and the help that we got from our Older Members and the example they showed in their impeccable behavior." Mimicking Applewhite and Nettles, as well as Elders and others who had been with the group longer, was the rule.

Rich described this process: "There was this training of how can I emulate and do exactly what this person does and not think about how I would do it. There is this loss of identity. I only wanted to identify with my Older Member. I just want to do what the general tells me. So that's where another aspect of the brainwashing comes from. I'm actively taking on this idea and programming myself. I'm brainwashing myself because I believe that if I do this, then I'm going to be better off. So the brainwashing was getting me to believe that I'll be better by being like you [meaning Applewhite and Nettles]."

Independent thought or action was unacceptable. The purpose of following the model was to accept being led, step by step, through the process of destroying one's "human programming" to the point of no longer trusting one's own judgment, perception, or observation of any circumstance. Applewhite explained that the goal was to lose self-confidence, to become like a child who does not know anything: "I have to look to the Next Level. I have to let the Representative from the Next Level serve in that position of whom I look to. I have to say, 'You know what's right for me.'"[37]

Commitment discussions took place periodically. They were reassuring to Applewhite and Nettles as well as to their followers. More than once members were asked, "How deep is your commitment?" At one point, they were instructed to write commitment notes stating that they would be willing to do anything their leaders asked them to do. Brent remembers thinking to himself at the time, "What does that mean? I mean, practically speaking, does that mean I'm willing to give my life?"

Commitment was also expected and demonstrated by taking on all assignments, or tasks, willingly and without complaint. A disciple was expected to lead the spartan, controlled, and certainly at times bizarre life of a dedicated believer readying for the Next Level, for salvation, for ever-lasting life. Preceding this, of course, the individual decision to go with the group meant leaving behind family, friends, job, personal interests, emotional attachments, and so on. That in itself was a great expression of commitment on which to build.

•   •   •

The complex systems of influence in this group were intrusive and very quickly became all-inclusive. They served to envelop any aspect of a member's life that was not already covered by the charismatic relationship, the precepts of the transcendent belief system, and the overt systems of control. The systems of attitudinal influences strengthened the other structural dimensions of the organizational system, creating an enmeshment for participants that brought them rather willingly to a state of psychological restriction and bounded choice.

In the next chapter, I show how the evolution of Heaven's Gate continued on its way to a choice that ultimately led to self-destruction.

CHAPTER 4

Evolution of the Charismatic Community

Much of Heaven's Gate's evolution into a cult occurred while the group was underground. It remained generally separate from the larger society, though some members held jobs or had other means of outside contact. Given this secretive lifestyle and the fact that many of the members and both leaders are dead, it is difficult today to write the group's history. My intent here is not to reconstruct a precise chronology but to use examples, sometimes from different periods, to highlight general processes that existed in the group for most of its duration.[1] It is these processes that prove interesting and crucial for analyzing cults generally.

Consolidating the Membership

For about five or six months after the Los Angeles meeting, The Two and their followers held meetings up and down the West Coast and in the Southwest. All the meetings were based on the same model: an explanatory talk, primarily by Applewhite, and then questions from the audience. Eventually, they had about fifty followers, then one hundred, then more. More than one hundred followers were recruited at four of their first public meetings held in California, Oregon, and Colorado.[2] The meetings were advertised on posters in college communities, bookstores, and coffee shops. Stark and simple, the posters declared that two beings, who would soon be returning to the Kingdom of Heaven in a spaceship, were here to talk about the transition from the human level to the next, from here to eternity.

The message promised the opportunity to overcome death. Ti and Do said this was "the Truth" that Jesus had been talking about. Some of those who responded to the posters or meetings did not want to miss out, just in case it was the Truth. Sometimes as many as five hundred people turned out. After one meeting in Waldport, a small town in Oregon, twenty people abruptly left their homes and families to go with these "strange" people with a strange message — a phenomenon that attracted national media attention, even a report by Walter Cronkite on the evening news.

RECRUITMENT

When Applewhite and Nettles appeared at the early public meetings, they were always flanked by several followers (fig. 5). They seemed self-assured and a little mysterious, projecting a certain aura that tended to appeal to the crowds before them. They almost always spoke to audiences on or near college campuses or in progressive or alternative locales. For example, meetings were held in Tucson, Santa Fe, Madison, Denver, Boulder, San Francisco, Santa Cruz, Los Angeles, Berkeley, Mendocino, Champaign-Urbana, Ann Arbor, St. Paul, Gainesville, Asheville, Eugene, Portland, and Spokane. The group's advance posters tended to attract curious individuals from communities of seekers and others with an interest in UFOs or supernatural phenomena.

The Two's appeal was rooted in the fact that they were offering something different. They referred to concepts well known to the counterculture, but at the same time they offered something unique, not the same old trip with the best hit of acid or some group spouting the same old verses out of the same old Bible or Hindu or Buddhist text. Their ideas took bits and pieces of the familiar philosophies and movement ideologies but were really far out. No one else was promising the possibility of evolving beyond humanity, of leaving the earth in a divine spaceship, of overcoming death. Many of the people who attended these meetings had already tried a variety of spiritual paths and experiences; they were ready for something new. The Two and their disciples sounded knowledgeable enough and came across as mysterious enough to entice both the curious and the sincere. Applewhite and Nettles, along with their message and their obviously dedicated band of followers, awakened a dormant yearning in the hearts of those who responded.

FIGURE 5. Marshall Applewhite and Bonnie Nettles, then known as Bo and Peep, seated at the microphones at a public meeting in 1975 at Cañada College, in Redwood City, Calif. Modeling their leaders, followers sit alongside in pairs. (Reginald McGovern/CORBIS SYGMA)

"I knew I was linked to them in a way that I couldn't explain. It was such an intense experience. . . . After the second meeting I went outside and cried for joy," recalled Jstody, who had been in and out of the group since 1976.

Interestingly, the language, imagery, and metaphors used by the members blatantly mimicked those of their leaders. There was no pretense of originality or independent-mindedness in the group. Rather, members took pride in copying their leaders in all things. In various testimonials over the years and at the end, members spoke or wrote of "wake-up clues," of feeling as though someone were grabbing them and shaking them to listen and follow, of feeling like they were waking up for the very first time — all phrases formulated by Applewhite in his renderings of Next Level involvement.

Rich remembered having seen one of the group's flyers somewhere around his suburban town just north of San Francisco. Out of curiosity, he and his girlfriend went to the meeting, which was being held at a nearby community college. Unbeknownst to Rich and his friend, this gathering was the small group's first public meeting.

"The energy there was very strong," Rich remembered. "It was intense and a lot of people were in kind of a bewildered state." Immediately Rich felt drawn to the message — and the messengers: "The way they looked, the way they presented themselves was otherworldly, I guess you would say. They really had a presence, like they knew what they were talking about." He went on to describe the ambience: "It was kind of hypnotic, monotonic, hypnotic. They were kind of working the energy, taking on the whole persona and just really sinking into it. They were really able to act this out and really believe that they were who they said they were."

After the meeting Rich stayed to talk with some of the followers while The Two hastily disappeared. Rich ended up chatting with Brent for a long time and was very impressed with him, his knowledge, and his dedication. Brent had been up on the stage during the meeting, seated just feet from the two mystics who had enthralled at least some in the audience. Brent appeared to be someone in the know. Plus he was a bit charismatic himself. He exuded youthful enthusiasm and was tall and handsome, with a nicely cropped beard. He was imposing, yet gentle and convincing in his demeanor and manner of speech. Rich trusted him immediately. Why not?

After a week or two of personal deliberation, Rich decided to join. His girlfriend did not feel the same compulsion. In retrospect, Rich said, "I could see how I was taken in by someone with conviction who looked me right in the eye. . . . I didn't want to take a chance on this being wrong." So Rich left behind his girlfriend and his family, quit college and his job, and went to meet the group at the Oregon riverside campground. He did not know what he would find there. "It shifted my life at that moment," he said pensively. "Life as I knew it changed."

BONDING

The ages of those who passed through the group — either becoming fully committed, or checking it out and leaving, or being asked to leave — ranged from fourteen to seventy-five. A large minority of those had at least some college education; others had completed undergraduate and, in a few cases, graduate degrees, as well as other specialized training. Most of them identified themselves as seekers of Truth who had previously experimented with various religious, spiritual, and alternative paths, from Scientology, Eastern religions, and Catholicism to spiritualism and magic. Some had been engaged in social activism, such as environmentalism, the peace movement, or the women's movement. Although some gave up seemingly successful lives and careers — for example, one member was a prominent businessman and family man from Colorado — most were less situationally stable at the time they encountered the group. They were close to graduation from college, or had just ended a relationship, or were dissatisfied with their lives, or simply were on the hippie trail, as were so many others at that time.[3]

Communal living was popular in the 1960s and 1970s, and many young people — not just the ones in this group — saw it as a way to escape the drudgery of the capitalist system or simply to experiment with new forms of living.[4] In the commune newly formed by Applewhite and Nettles, money was pooled, and few members objected. Those who did object either were swayed to go along with the system of sharing or left the group. In time, daily needs were centrally organized, from clothes to supplies to food. Compared to other groups, this one was not vastly wealthy, nor was it very poor. They always had the means to get by, and when necessary, members worked at outside jobs and donated their salaries to the general fund. Those who had access to family assets or had received inheritances also contributed.

Another group practice was the assignment of a "check partner," typically but not always someone of the opposite gender. This partnering explicitly was not to be sexual or intimate, although some pairs experienced some difficulties along those lines. The purpose, as The Two explained it, was for group members to mimic their leaders, who were after all a partnership of two, as well as to be a check on and reinforcement for each other. It was also a means of putting members through a test of will — to see if they could abide by the discipline. Later, when the group lived in houses, men slept in one room, women in another — with the exception of known gay men. The latter were sent to sleep in the women's bedroom to ease their struggles with temptation.

In the early years, 1975 and 1976, the members were sent out with a partner to travel the country, to emulate the travel, travails, and lessons of The Two in their formative years as a partnership. The teams were supposed to experience tests and learn to survive together, to be watchful of each other, and to recruit, or "harvest other souls." Getting paired with a person one did not particularly like was part of the test. This fostered endurance and commitment, and it also forged a unique sort of camaraderie.

As a gay man, Brent remembered being perturbed by his female partner who he felt had all the womanly traits he found annoying. Yet, to his surprise, as they traveled together across the country through trial and tribulation, they became quite fond of each other. In relating this during one of my interviews with him, Brent laughed, "Yeah, exactly those human feelings we weren't supposed to have — in fact, the setup encouraged it, while also denouncing it. But I couldn't see that at the time." He turned back to look at the group's farewell video that we were viewing together. When his former check partner appeared onscreen, Brent openly wept as she said her good-byes.

At times, of course, just as Brent described, human interaction did occur, in some instances, even romantic and sexual activity. At first, these incidents were not talked about; later, they were regarded as tests and used as lessons, as examples of wayward behavior. But, above all, "human conduct" was not condoned. At some point during the first year, anything that might be taken as human interaction, and definitely sexual relations, was strictly forbidden. That drew the line for many adherents and hangers-on who did not want to follow such strict rules for the long term. Although a no-sex rule was present from the outset, after several breaches the rule was enforced more strictly and followers could no longer see it as a game. Ti and Do meant it for real.

The Two's followers roamed the country on their mission to preach, convert, and, most of all, experience. Together, they begged for food, scrounged for places to stay, and sometimes received gifts from strangers, such as a place to shower, a meal, free gasoline, or tires for their rundown cars. They organized speaking events in town after town to spread their message and look for those who might respond. Some drifted away during that period. Those who remained evolved into an odd sort of family. Yet it was a family that was forbidden to express intimacy, to share personal knowledge, particularly personal histories, or to indulge in human emotions.

In a written testimonial, Anlody, who joined the group in 1976, described clearly the ideal of the Heaven's Gate family: "The only REAL 'family' relationship that can be maintained is that between an Older Member and a younger member. As long as the younger member keeps his eyes on his Older Member, and wants with all his heart, mind and soul to please his Older Member, that relationship is forever."

WAITING FOR THE "DEMONSTRATION"

For the most part, partnered teams were on their own, and the group communicated quite haphazardly. Nevertheless, even during that time, the followers received guidance from The Two in telephone calls and sporadic encounters. At least some of the followers kept notes of doubts and things to ask about the next time they talked with The Two. When things went well, "it was proof that God was taking care of us, that we were on the right track," said Brent. This validated and reinforced their belief in their leaders. Their other main task was to try in every moment to communicate with the Next Level.

One way in which Applewhite and Nettles exploited their followers' eagerness to believe was by playing mystical tricks on them. They would disappear and reappear unexpectedly, emerging mysteriously out of the woods, for example, especially during the campground days. "They weren't above doing little things that were theatrical," Brent commented. "After all, Herff had been a performer and an actor. It was in his blood."

Tricks and "cosmic connections" were carried out throughout the years, sometimes manifesting in highly modern and technological ways. For example, Jstody explained: "Often we would get signs from the media, feeling that perhaps the Next Level or Ti's helpers at that level were subtly setting up situations that would pop up in the media."

Applewhite and Nettles told their followers that messages would come via television, especially during their favorite program, *Wheel of Fortune,* or via movies like *Cocoon* or *The Sound of Music.* According to Applewhite and Nettles, the vast audiences of *Wheel of Fortune* were proof that millions were tuning in to the Next Level message. And *Cocoon,* with its life-giving alien pods, was evidence that Next Level ideas were being filtered through mainstream media. The Two were especially taken with these media manifestations, and the group spent quite a lot of time sitting with their leaders watching these and other shows. Given Applewhite's musical and theatrical background, we can speculate that this was an attempt on his part to stay connected to his earthly self.

During the early days together, proselytizing, fund-raising, and finding ways to survive occupied much of the followers' time. Basically, they watched the skies together, waited for messages from their leaders, and prayed for the Demonstration. The Demonstration, as the leaders had explained, would occur when they would be publicly assassinated, then three days later taken by UFOs to the Next Level.

Originally, The Two had predicted that the Demonstration would happen in a matter of weeks; then it was going to be soon, then months, then within the year. Although they denied ever giving an exact time, they readily admitted to a sense of urgency.[5] During the waiting, they expected their followers to undergo individual transformations, or the Process, which was essentially a concerted effort to overcome human attachments. Walking out of the door of one's life was the first step, and other details and more complicated practices evolved over time as the group went into seclusion. Being engaged in the Process bound the members to each other and to their leaders and solidified their belief in the message. The group-defined reality became the only reality by which to live.

Because The Two had declared that the Demonstration was imminent, initially a sense of excitement, anticipation, and urgency enveloped the group: maybe today would be the day! For that reason, at the first public meetings, followers who were assigned to sit onstage kept a certain distance from The Two in order to escape the expected assassin's bullets. Yet, though they testified time after time that they were waiting to be killed — after all, that was their mission as the Bible's two witnesses — The Two continued to travel under assumed names and remain elusive. Periodically they would go into hiding even from their followers. How was the Demonstration to happen under such circumstances? "They were frightened and in fear of going to jail," explained Brent.

Apparently Applewhite's six-month stint in jail several years earlier was all he wanted to experience of that realm. If they were not doing anything illegal, then such fears were without foundation; but charismatic leaders are rebels and revolutionaries, so on some level erratic behavior fits the profile. In that regard The Two are likely to have had an exaggerated sense of their importance in relation to outside authorities. On the other hand, we can understand a level of anticipation, even fear, since according to their ideology, they would be killed for "bearing the message." It should also be pointed out that an aura of fear keeps followers on their toes and vigilance high.

Later, The Two had concerns also about retribution from members' families that had established an informal network to share information about the leaders and the group — their names, activities, and whereabouts, whatever was known or could be found out. In this way families were able to — or hoped to — find out bits of information about their loved ones in the group. In fall 1975 The Two got scared off by some negative publicity and hid from everyone, including their followers. Brent, who held firm through that period, always referred to it as the great diaspora. During those months, followers wandered about, struggling and confused, not knowing if they would see their leaders again.[6]

A few months later, when The Two resurfaced, they explained that the Demonstration *had* happened: they had been killed by the media, they said. Their task now was to carry on teaching their followers, get them ready for "graduation," and await the spacecraft that would come to retrieve them and others who were ready. Around this time, the size of the group swelled and then retracted again, for only the hardy stayed with the group once it adopted its very demanding lifestyle, which began after they regrouped in summer 1976.

However, Applewhite and Nettles continued to disappear without warning. In fact, most of the time most members did not know Applewhite and Nettles's whereabouts or where they lived. They simply arrived for the daily meetings; on occasion, they entertained visits from Elders or Helpers at their place of residence. The Two continuously maintained that being around others lowered their vibrational level, exactly what they told their first disciple in early 1974.

Where did they go when they were away from the rest of the group? "Who knows?" Rich replied. "They would go on trips. Supposedly they were going to find the next step. . . . But as I look at it now, Ti and Do hightailed it. They went underground. They weren't that excited about becoming martyrs after all."

Ultimately, though, The Two's reclusive behavior was useful: it allowed them to remain apart from their followers, and it added to their mystique and perpetuated the leader myth they had created. Meanwhile, the pooled money of their followers was supporting them. The members' fear of losing their leaders and the frustration over their absences was handily transformed into a stimulus and a sense of anticipation. "We never knew if we would see them again," said Brent. Some members drifted away during those times, but those who stayed and became the core group developed an increasing dependency on their leaders.

STARTING THE "CLASS"

In reaction to some hecklers in the audience at a meeting in April 1976, Nettles announced, "The harvest is closed." Public meetings were halted, and no new members were brought in.

The Two instructed their followers to scatter and report later in the summer to a campground in the national forest near Laramie, Wyoming. About one hundred devotees and curiosity seekers showed up. This is about the time that the leaders took the names Ti and Do and gave the group more structure by forming what they called the Class. Quickly, the group was reduced by half or more because of the stringent rules and regulations that guided daily life. By November written and verbal behavioral guidelines were in place and group norms were institutionalized.

According to the new structure, The Two were now "the Teachers," and the followers were "students of the Next Level." Students referred to each other as "classmates." Members and former members interviewed after the collective suicide still used that terminology when talking about the group and their fellow members. It was in-group language that stuck.

It was also at about this time that Ti and Do introduced the idea that they should be referred to as Older Members. It was generally understood by all that The Two were indeed older members of the Next Level; after all, they were visiting here from there. This understanding afforded Ti and Do even more cosmic and charismatic authority.

Immediately on joining the group, members were to choose new names. At first, these were biblical names; but once the Class was established, the names were reduced to symbolic ones, with three letters in the first syllable, followed by -ody. Often Ti and Do bestowed a name on a student that carried a special meaning related to his or her development. For example, Stlody's name indicated that he was steeled in his devotion and service. In his exit video Applewhite explained that names ending in -ody were considered diminutives: "Ody means an awful lot to us," he said. "It's a child name, like Bobby or Jimmy, to denote a young member of the Kingdom of God . . . a young 'un, a child of the Next Level." By that single gesture, every student became part of a tight charismatic community, connected to the ultimate reality.

The transition to being students carried with it another regressive identity shift besides the childish names. The students were thought of (and thought of themselves) as children, younger, inexperienced, and in need of instruction. Their task was to ready themselves for space travel and for acceptance into the Next Level. Their exemplary Older Members were there to show them the way. According to some reports, teaching was a profession at which Applewhite excelled.[7] Those who knew him during his teaching career reported that he was extremely well liked. We can assume that he felt comfortable in that role and found the Class a useful image for this phase of their experiment. In addition, both Applewhite and Nettles were now in their mid-forties, whereas most of their followers were in their twenties. In that sense, Applewhite and Nettles played a parental role, and they often fit the part.

During interviews with me and during media appearances after the suicides, Brent, for example, strove to make the point that when he and his classmates became followers, Applewhite did not look like a "bug-eyed, bald-headed fanatic." Rather, Brent insisted, both Applewhite and Nettles had soft, gentle appearances and were "just like your folks, only nicer." Brent is not the only one who felt that way.

Nettles was remembered as kindhearted at times and motherly. For example, occasionally she would arrive at the group's campsite with a freshly baked cake for everyone, even while they were on one of their strict and bizarre training diets. "You've got to have some fun, too," she would say, as she encouraged them to break the very regimen she and Applewhite had imposed on them.

In general, Ti and Do's followers deeply trusted The Two in their experience and knowledge and their professed connection to the Source. This trust made students want to follow their Teachers' example in all things. For that reason, students were ready and willing to go along with the myriad exercises, diets, and mental programs introduced by Ti and Do as part of the training requirements, many of which were eventually instituted as group "procedures," written into scads of notebooks and binders.

The purpose of the Class was to prepare for life on the Next Level, as well as for getting there in the spaceship. They thought of it as a NASA training mission or like being on *Star Trek*. For this reason, they thought of themselves as a "crew," and one of their goals was to be "crew-minded," not an individual. They would succeed in their mission by working hard, doing their homework, following the example of their Teachers, and asking for and mentally listening to Next Level guidance. Students were to follow every lesson and instruction so that they, like the Older Members, could graduate to the Next Level. There, they expected to attain eternal life in the form of service to future generations. In addition, they would be saved from the evil and inevitable destruction of planet Earth. The Next Level was understood as a physical place; it was real, not a spirit world as in other belief systems. It was home.

Students believed they would "graduate" when they rid themselves of human tendencies and achieved the "Next Level Mind," which was their version of a greater cosmic intelligence, not unlike the wisdom of Madame Blavatsky's Ascended Masters, or the cosmic oneness of New Ager Marilyn Ferguson, or Gregory Bateson's Learning III. The students in this Class expected that once they attained the metamorphosed state (their peak experience), they would board a spacecraft where they would serve as the crew and be taken to the idyllic Next Level, a level devoid of nasty, inferior human traits and interferences. This was their self-actualization.

In the group milieu students spent hours listening to their Teachers. They learned the lessons of their leaders' early travels, the lessons of their own and each other's journeys, and the lessons drawn from other daily events. Everything was a lesson, and the students' own experiences and errors were used as examples in the collective lessons. Eventually, they knew everything about each other's daily lives, inner thoughts, waking and sleeping moments, hopes, fears, and transgressions. Progress was monitored at "slippage meetings," when students' errors were reviewed. For the students, nothing was private, nothing was secret. Applewhite and Nettles knew everything, demanded everything. That was their right as the Older Members.

An important feature of being part of this group was that at some point members learned that at an earlier time in their lives they had received a "deposit" of Next Level knowledge. They came to believe that in the past, Next Level crews had been sent to Earth to "tag," or make deposits, in chosen human bodies and their minds and spirits. Having such a deposit was believed to be the critical factor that initially drew someone to the information offered by The Two and was proof that you were destined to be with the group. It meant that you had had some connection to The Two in a previous life. Having the deposit was thought of as a sense of "knowing," or an internal recognition. Of course, the opposite of having this special knowledge was to be ignorant, which meant having no knowledge of the Next Level, or, perhaps worse yet, having had it at one time and rejecting it.

The deposit was considered the basis for the right to be a student member of the Class. "It's only open to people that are part of this family, that have that deposit of Next Level Mind," explained Jstody. That right involved both obligation and opportunity. In a way, they were like students in an elite private school. They felt special, chosen, superior to and better than other people who were not in the school, and they felt especially grateful to their Teachers for allowing them into the Class. Because even with the deposit, each person still had to go through the tests, train to develop, and prove readiness to the Next Level. Ti and Do, as the Next Level's representatives here on Earth, were key to that process. Nothing was given, except that which was given by the leaders.

Later on, believing in the deposit became proof of your innate alienness. A point of clarification is in order here. Members of this group would not have used the term *alien* as it is typically used, that is, to denote odd creatures from outer space. "Alien," in that sense, was regarded as a human label and a human way of thinking. To the contrary, according to their worldview, Next Level creatures were the norm, the standard to live up to. In their opinion, if anything was alien, in the sense of being odd, it was human life.

The students eventually came to believe that they also were beings from the Next Level who had assumed, or taken over, human bodies, as had their leaders. They were not human, had never been human, and did not belong here. They were an extraterrestrial crew sent to earth for training and waiting to go back home to outer space, to the Level Above Human. This is a significant factor that contributed to group cohesion and was a primary source of each member's loyalty and connection to the group. This idea, perhaps more than any other, bound them to the system, to each other, and to their leaders.

For members of Heaven's Gate, there was no past. Their only reality was now — the group. Those who held jobs turned over their earnings to the group's Purser, who also filed their income taxes and took care of all financial matters — in consultation with Applewhite and Nettles, of course.

The group was constantly on the move, either in small teams or in larger numbers. For years they lived in campgrounds, "following the sun," as one longtime member described it. They lived for varying amounts of time in Wyoming, Oregon, California, Colorado, New Mexico, Mississippi, and Texas, their leaders' home state. They never stayed longer than six months in any one locale. Whether they lived in tents, trailers, or a house, these were called "crafts."

Their campsites were set up in a star-shaped pattern, with an Elder in charge of each grouping. Applewhite and Nettles stayed apart from the members, at first in their own tent and later in a nice trailer bought with money donated by one of the members. In the late 1970s at least one devotee received a relatively large inheritance or trust, which allowed the group to live in houses. Sometimes they rented, and sometimes they bought their houses — always with cash, like all other group purchases. After the 1974 arrest incident in Texas, Applewhite decided not to use credit cards or anything else that would make it possible to track the group.

When it was time to move on, they sold their house and left no traces behind. Often the move happened suddenly; for example, Nettles might wake up and say she had a vision that told her it was time to go. Members who worked at "out-of-craft" jobs had to quit on a moment's notice. In fact, the constant departures were among the reasons that Rich got frustrated with his life in the group.

Over the years, the students worked on a variety of projects, from setting up their living quarters to operating publishing ventures. They were ideal tenants, remodeling houses and making them pristine places in which to live. At one point they refurbished a houseboat, which they did not get to live in because once again their leaders said it was time to move on. Their time was taken up also with the range of exotic diets, health reg-

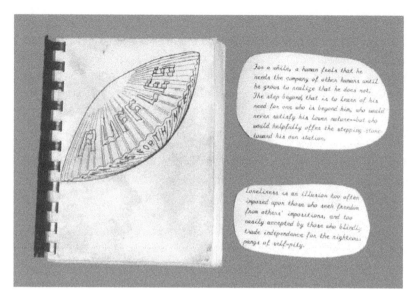

FIGURE 6. *Ruffles,* a book of Heaven's Gate sayings, was one of many projects over the years to spread the group's beliefs.

imens, and isolating mental and physical exercises designed to train their minds and rid them of human traits and desires.

The group set up various enterprises intended to spread their message to the world, although proselytizing was never its main thrust. They put out booklets about their (short-lived) Anonymous Sexaholics Celibate Church. They produced and sold a self-published, spiral-bound book, *Ruffles: Snacks for Thinkers,* which consists of short, pithy sayings to live by, written by the students (fig. 6). They sent out a think-tank newsletter on nutrition and produced a health-oriented diet book, *Transfiguration Diet.* Later, the publishing rights for that book were turned over to another company. They intervened at UFO conventions. And they produced a twelve-part video series, *Beyond Human — The Last Call,* plus two other videotapes of Applewhite discoursing on the group and its philosophy.

There was hardly a time when they were not involved in some project, which often was brought to a halt just before completion. Ti and Do would suddenly announce that something was not right, that it was time to move on. Whatever members were doing at the time would be abandoned. Flexibility and the ability to respond to such quick changes was a virtue, students were told; it was all part of their training for the Next Level.

The Development of Bounded Choice (Part 2)

Before the formation of the Class, the group was erratic in its behavior and its internal discipline. But the Class changed everything, giving structure and order to what was until then a rather diffuse movement with little direct leadership. Applewhite described in a straightforward manner the decision he and Nettles made to set up the Class:

> Ti and Do announced that it had been rumored that some were still occasionally indulging in pot and sex. Everyone was asked to go off by themselves for a few hours and make up their mind as to whether they were just caught up in the fun of the "movement" or if they were serious. For now the real "classroom" was to begin, and it was not for those who felt they wanted to hold on to human ways. Ti and Do preached long and hard about what it meant to rid oneself of self, and what would be required of those who continued.[8]

From that point on, The Two subjected their followers to extensive regimentation. Each student reported every twelve minutes to a central post at camp to see if Ti or Do needed something. At The Two's instructions the group followed bizarre diets and exercise regimens and were subjected to various forms of discipline, such as expanses of time without speaking, called "Tomb Time," and prolonged periods of covering their heads and faces with hoods. All these encouraged the Next Level Mind.

These and other methods contributed during this period to an acceleration of the establishment of a self-sealing system that led ultimately to a state of bounded choice. And within the restrictions of this bounded choice, the members of Heaven's Gate became capable of committing what to the outside world seemed like a lunatic act — but was to them entirely logical, necessary, and even beautiful.

ESTABLISHING CHARISMATIC AUTHORITY

"Ti and Do represent — *are* — the Second Coming," proclaimed Jstody in a radio interview. It is clear that he and other followers of The Two believed mightily in the heavenly lineage of their Older Members. Likewise, in a statement posted on the Web in 1995, "Undercover 'Jesus'

Surfaces Before Departure," Applewhite reinforced this image by stating not only that he was Jesus but also that Nettles was God the Father. Referring to Nettles, Applewhite wrote, "His relationship to this planet is as Chief Administrator, and is the One referred to as 'God' in the early stages of this civilization."[9] Applewhite explained that his "Father" (Ti/Nettles) had come with him this time to help bring new "sons" to the Level Above Human and that he (Ti/Nettles) came "undercover," having incarnated into a female body. Applewhite always referred to Nettles as "he."

This is certainly fitting with the Christian image of a male God, God the Father. But also, this gender-bending language and imagery is representative of the gender and sexual denial that was characteristic of the group. In that vein, Applewhite also referred to their students as "sons," even though there were more female than male followers. Despite their claim to a genderless future, Applewhite was quite traditional in his gender labeling by favoring men and setting up a "male"-dominated hierarchy.

But here again Applewhite and Nettles are asserting and expanding on their authority based on the charismatic relationship they had with their followers. Charisma is best thought of as a powerful social relation rather than exclusively as attributes inhering in an individual. The leader-follower relationship evident in the Heaven's Gate cult is the epitome of a charismatic relationship.

Max Weber, one of the first to explore and write about the concept of charisma, focused not so much on the leader as the people around the leader, those who are affected by the leader and who, in turn, have an effect on him.[10] "What is alone important is how the individual is actually regarded by those subject to charismatic authority, by his 'followers' or 'disciples,'" he wrote.[11] Although Weber wrote of "natural" leaders and "supernatural" attributes,[12] he made it clear also that charismatic leaders were to be tested, were to prove themselves time and again, and had to be "charismatically qualified" by their followers.[13] In that sense, the charismatic leader does not exist without an audience of believers. The charismatic leader needs followers, and the followers, who are the source of what Weber called charismatic authentication, are integral to the establishment, legitimacy, and success of the leader. This social relation is central to Weber's depiction of the concept of charisma, a two-way street.

Clearly, Ti and Do lit the emotional fire of those who saw and heard them — and responded. This response was not a cognitive reaction, although it may be tied to what Weber identified as a "psychological precondition."[14] Because Ti and Do's charisma engendered this primal response in their followers, that response, as well as Ti and Do who were believed to be the source of it, was endowed with special meaning. The interpretation of such a response is usually culture-bound: it may be called an ecstatic state, bliss, or a born-again feeling, depending on the context.[15]

But the constant in the charismatic relationship is that the leader(s), in this case, Ti and Do, are regarded as the *source* of the emotion. Ti and Do were believed to be truly connected to a higher order, in tune with the greater cosmos, and were believed to have been delivered to their followers in order to bring them salvation and eternal life. They had something very special to offer, which the members were convinced they needed and wanted.[16]

According to Weber, charismatic leaders are "responsible for but one thing, that [they] personally and actually be the God-willed master."[17] Regarding this authority, there is no hierarchy, for the charismatic is opposed to order and structure.[18] Yet Weber also described various levels of followers or devotees, for example, the "permanent helpers" or inner circle. The inner circle around the leader is readily evident in Heaven's Gate (and in the DWP, as I show later) and made a significant contribution to each leader's success.

Under legal authority, submission is based on an impersonal bond, guided by societal norms and the rule of law. But under charismatic authority, submission is based on a personal bond to the one who embodies the "extraordinary" quality, "regardless of whether this quality is actual, alleged, or presumed."[19] The overall goal of discipline is to integrate the individual into the whole; and, ironically, though the charismatic is said to shun order, discipline is necessary to ensure total and unswerving obedience. This is an important point, especially in any consideration of self-destructive, antisocial, or illegal activities by cult members. For example, such discussions were relevant, although not necessarily decisive, in the trials of Patricia Hearst for her participation in a deadly SLA-inspired bank robbery; of members of Ervil LeBaron's polygamous sect, charged with murdering opponents and former members; and the so-called Manson girls for their participation in the Tate-LaBianca murders orchestrated by Charles Manson.

Applewhite and Nettles were highly successful in their establishment of charismatic authority over their followers during the period of growth and consolidation of their cultic group. Brent's description of a time he tried to leave the group exemplifies The Two's persistence in influencing their followers. This incident occurred during the campground days. Brent went to his leaders to express his doubts and concerns about staying in the group. Applewhite told him to sit down next to him. Seated only inches away, Applewhite leaned into Brent's face, stared hard into his eyes, and said, "Now repeat after me: I want what you want."

Brent, the confused follower, mumbled, "I want what you want," looking into his leader's eyes.

"No," Applewhite responded firmly. "Say it again: I want what you want."

Brent, looking intently into his leader's icy blue eyes, repeated with a little more vigor, "I want what you want."

This back-and-forth process went on for a very long time, until finally the young man broke down in tears and decided to stay with the group. That type of manipulation was an effective means by which Applewhite exerted his power over his followers. At the same time, the followers, as respondents in the process, felt as though they were making up their own minds while also uniting with their leader's mind, which they were told repeatedly was their goal. Various accounts have told of similar encounters in which Applewhite successfully swayed someone's opinion in favor of the group.

Nettles had equally strong powers of persuasion. Former members recalled that all it took was a glance from her to know she was displeased. "She didn't have to say much, just move her hand a little bit," said Rich.

In such a tightly run and authoritarian setting, it is not difficult to ascertain when a behavioral or attitudinal change is expected. Various students have attested, either in their final testimonials or, in the case of the remaining believers and former members, in later statements, to the pleasant atmosphere of group life. But some former members maintain that much of their life in the group was based on fear.[20] This fear was wide-ranging. It included fear of missing out on salvation if one left the group; visceral fear of the leaders' power to humiliate and degrade, to shun and cast out; and fear of ostracism by fellow members, now one's only family. From the possibility of eternal damnation to the everyday discomfort of being chastised, these were the visions that guided daily conduct, along with the hope that the spaceship would come to take them home.

DEVELOPING TRANSCENDENT BELIEF

The Heaven's Gate cult was rooted in the transcendent belief that a person could overcome death by ending the cycle of death and rebirth, which was to be achieved by means of a transformational process that would allow the person to enter the Next Level and live happily into eternity. To get there, a believer — through much effort and force of will — needed to undergo a biological transformation, just as a caterpillar turns into a butterfly, to use one of the group's early analogies.

A 1975 statement written by Applewhite and Nettles, which was used to communicate to prospective members, stated clearly that their mission was not meant to be a "spiritual trip."[21] Rather, they believed that the human body would undergo a biological and chemical metamorphosis as the believer struggled to overcome his or her humanness. So long as the devotee directed all his or her efforts toward that goal, the day would come when the overcoming would be finished, the metamorphosis would be complete, and the spaceship would arrive.

The highly symbolic belief system formulated by Applewhite and Nettles offered liberation from what they called the "human-mammalian species." But only those who could overcome all ties to the human world, to human family, sensuality, emotions — or, in their words, "addictions" and "human programming" — would attain this other level of existence. The basic tenets of their belief system can be summarized as follows:

- The only way off planet Earth was with a Representative of the Next Level (i.e., Applewhite and Nettles).

- You will know the information possessed by Ti and Do is for you if you feel it deep down, which means you were preselected by the Next Level.

- If you have such a knowing, you must submit to difficult tests to get ready to leave.

- There is not much time, for the end of the Age is coming.

The basic guidelines were

- Have complete respect for and obedience to Ti and Do, as Older Members of the Next Level.

- Strive at all times to model yourself after Ti and Do. Before acting, think, what would my Older Member *have* me do?

- Strive at all times to be in tune with the Older Members in order to be linked to the Next Level Mind.

- Submit to the process of overcoming, and fight strenuously against all humanness and attempts by Luciferian influences to pull you back to the lower forces.

- Always be crew-minded. Do not think of yourself.

Applewhite and Nettles believed that in the 1970s they had each incarnated into an adult human body after coming to Earth in a Next Level spacecraft. News stories since the 1950s of alleged UFO crashes were regarded by them as validation that Next Level visitations had happened and were continuing to happen. Applewhite's partner, Nettles, God the Father, had accompanied him on this trip back to Earth because of the enormous challenge of the task. Applewhite understood that he had come to Earth once before, as Jesus, but on that occasion his task had been interrupted. This time, his task was to round up students from the past. He predicted that he would be hated for the blasphemy of saying who he was, just as he had been persecuted before. Also, he would be hated by the families and friends of those who aspired to leave with him because of the Next Level requirement that adherents break all ties with "the world," or earthly existence.

For adherents, that meant not only leaving behind families, jobs, hobbies, and other human pursuits but also, according to Applewhite, ridding themselves of "their old minds, their identities, in exchange for the mind that flows through me, as they attempt to be accepted as one of my 'children.' It will 'cost' them everything of this world."[22] He made it very clear that loss of self was a requirement for membership in the group. That requirement was reframed as losing one's *human* self, an innate individualism that kept one from attaining higher goals. It meant developing a profound dependency on the Older Members, which took the form of a large degree of personal infantilization. This served to ensure conformity and compliance and prevent followers from questioning either the leaders or the process.

Those who were meant to follow, to become students of the "Representative incarnate" (sometimes called "the Rep"), were drawn to the message. They recognized the Reps, as well as the information. Members believed that the Next Level deposits they had received acted as homing devices that led them to the information, and ultimately to Ti and Do. No one could become a student of the Next Level without such a deposit. In other words, the Next Level was not for everybody.

In the early years (1975–76) the process of personal transformation was referred to as Human Individual Metamorphosis (H.I.M.); and for a time, the group went by the name H.I.M. The desired metamorphosis was to be accomplished in three ways: by being a member of the Class; by "pulling on," "merging with," "grafting onto" the Older Members' mind so as to reach the Next Level Mind; and by ridding oneself of *all* human emotions, or attachments. There was no room for compromise.

Because all meant all in their strict disciplinary system, this group can be classified easily as a totalistic cult. Members knew that being a student of the Next Level, being in the Class, was an all-or-nothing proposition. More than one member remarked in testimonials that the Next Level had the toughest entry requirements in all the heavens.

Their training, which Applewhite sometimes referred to as God's Astronaut Program, would free the members from the structure of human life and human ways. When this was accomplished, members would literally be lifted up to the Next Level and fitted with a new, indestructible "vehicle," their term for "body." This new form would be genderless; Applewhite described it often in his many talks to the group, as well as in his writings. The transformative vision kept them going. Applewhite continually reinforced it with such comments as this one from his video series: "What's important is how *fast* have I overcome the world so that I don't need to return to the human world."[23] In that transformative process lay the path to freedom.

INSTITUTING SYSTEMS OF CONTROL

Applewhite and Nettles were always clear about being in charge, although at first their leadership style was one that relied on indirect methods. For example, they would say what they thought about something or what they were going to do, then tell their followers that it was up to them to decide what they were going to do. Yet the preference was clear.

That leadership tactic offered what might be called the illusion of choice, for, indeed, followers knew exactly what was expected of them if they wanted to remain students in this Class. Ironically, alongside these indirect leadership methods were myriad rules and regulations for practically everything, from the exact diameter of a breakfast pancake to the exact amount of toothpaste to put on a toothbrush. Applewhite and Nettles were not above using these overt means of control; nevertheless, the subtler and more sophisticated style of influencing their followers was crucial to the effectiveness of their system, and crucial to their image as benign leaders.

In direct contradiction to this desire to appear benign was the role of fear in Heaven's Gate. Fear was also integral to the Heaven's Gate systems of control. First, there was much talk of the spirit entities that could distract students and pull them down into lower reaches. Second, whether a student graduated was contingent on acceptance by Next Level beings who apparently were quite difficult to please.

Rich expressed it clearly, at the same time explaining how the fear got translated into something more palatable: "It was all fear-based. Applewhite was reaming it down our throats. But after a time, the fear gets buried and turned into the idea that I should just be of service to my heavenly Father."

To some extent, the fear that pervaded the group milieu emanated directly from the leaders' own fearful and skittish behavior. "They were easily spooked," Brent remembered. Rich recalled that "almost all the activities were paranoid responses." For example, quite often the group was given the order to break up their campsite because the leaders sensed "bad vibes." As far back as one of their campground settlements in summer 1975, Applewhite asked a newcomer to their camp if he was armed.[24]

This cautiousness can be traced to The Two's original mission and their time on the road, when they rather consistently ran out on hotel and motel bills and justified it by saying they were doing God's work.[25] After the 1974 arrest and Applewhite's jail time, however, The Two espoused a policy of upholding the law. In some of his writings, Applewhite confirms that the arrest incident was one source of their guarded feelings, but he also notes that they were already "pretty paranoid" by that time.[26]

On occasion, students were ejected from the Class or "sent out into the world" for an indefinite period to do a special task. Although they still felt connected to and part of the group, it was not the same as being there. One member, for example, reframed this experience by saying that he had been sent out as an emissary to spread the word: "If I felt they were calling, I would go back. They're still putting out vibrations and sending me a lot of positive energy."[27] Meanwhile, he worked as a golf caddy.

In late 1976 nineteen members were purged. Ti and Do and their Elders had decided together that those nineteen were the least committed members of the group and were bringing the others down. This reduced the membership to less than seventy. Everyone in the group knew of this expulsion, and all those remaining must have felt relieved that they were not among the Phoenix 19, as the expellees came to be called in group lore. Some of the Phoenix 19 were readmitted years later; and at least three of them were among the 1997 suicides.

Also, Ti and Do routinely met with members to review their every act. More than once, the leaders expressed annoyance at the gaffes of their students, from whom they expected no less than perfection. "Righteous indignation" is the way Rich described it. As they sat around in group sessions, sharing lessons from travels, from ventures into the "human world," or from "slippages" in the discipline, the atmosphere was not always cozy. "How dare you judge the Next Level?" was a familiar rebuke from a regularly testy Applewhite.

As for the leaders themselves, Applewhite might admit to having a difficulty with something. But, Rich recalled, "Ti was never wrong. So basically *they* were never wrong."

The group remained tightly controlled by the leaders. Given that the object of their mission was to learn to control their "human vehicles" in order to be ready for pickup when the spacecraft arrived, as the group evolved and as time passed and no ship came, the members accepted more stringent discipline, regimentation, and suppression — and felt heightened anticipation.

Separation from the world became the centerpiece of their commitment. An us-versus-them mentality was a cornerstone of the Heaven's Gate organizational system. Early on, Applewhite and Nettles determined that in order for their endeavor to work, the group needed to be sequestered. Applewhite explained: "We had to disappear in order to be isolated. In other words, we had to be separated out, or lifted out, in order to be free to do what we had to do."28

Separation became synonymous with overcoming the world. It was justified by their belief that they were an elite team who had been separated from the Next Level. They believed that each member's soul could come to life then, only by returning home to the Next Level. That process was initiated when the soul deposit in each student began to dominate and take over the "vehicle" in which it found itself. "The flesh has to become, in a sense, dead, have no voice, just be a living mechanism that will permit you to do what you want to do within the bounds of a lesson ground," taught Applewhite.29

Thus, by separating from the human world, and in effect from self, they understood that they were ending their own separation from the Next Level. Leaving the past behind, then, was acknowledged as the first step in overcoming because it was the first step toward going home. But it required more than simply leaving the past behind, for Applewhite urged: "We have to actually *forget* it. We have to be *unable* to remember it."30

Sawyer, a longtime member, explained the need for that degree of control when he said that any interest in a spouse or children or yourself was not acceptable to be part of their group. Why? Because it made perfect sense, he explained, that one has to completely leave behind the old in order to get to the new.

Another student, Anlody, said, "Survival requires that you allow nothing of this human existence to tie you here. No wealth, no position, no prestige, no family, no physical pleasure, no religion spouting to hang on to any of the above will enable you to survive. They are only entrapments. They are means by which the lower forces have lulled the humans of this planet into being comfortable in their hell." With such an understanding, students were prepared to accept a highly controlled environment in which they could work in a totally devoted manner on their primary task of overcoming.

Along with a change in personal names came a change in appearance and outward behavior. Students were expected to have a kind of non-identity, that of the genderless member of a Next Level crew member. So they gave up makeup and personal items, completely disregarded their appearance, and stopped wearing tight-fitting clothes, jewelry, and other adornments. The idea was to not give the "vehicle" any attention, and to not attract attention when out in the world. They wore a unisex uniform: loose-fitting pants and a long, loose, high-buttoned shirt that hid male or female body parts. Sometimes they wore jumpsuits, sometimes baggy nylon parka outfits in dark or muted colors. All their clothing was inter-changeable.

As the group became completely communal, all needs were taken care of, decreasing any chance that individualism would surface. The bottom line for each student was to be part of the crew and require nothing spe-cial. "We don't want to have or need special attention or need special scheduling. We want to only be a cog in the wheel," said Applewhite, explaining what a student should want.[31]

"If you needed something," Brent said, "you'd say, 'There's a hole in my underwear'—and you sent a note. You presented the problem, and they'd say, 'Go to the Purser and get enough money, and on your next whatever, get some underwear.' But that changed too because then in a very short period of time we had a total communal wardrobe. We had large, small, medium underwear in a big drawer and at the end of the day you just went and got your stuff out of those and then somebody was responsible for checking that—the laundry crew. They would throw out what was holey and inform Links [Ti and Do]—'cause they were our 'links' to the Next Level."

A major aspect of group control was the suppression of human emo-tions. "There wouldn't be any shouting or anger, no displays like that," recalled Rich. "Emotions—those are *human* emotions," he said, mim-icking the disdain he felt while in the group. "The key with Heaven's Gate is they suppressed everything."

Students were told that in order to function as a Next Level crew, they had to get rid of clumsiness, of humanness, especially anything to do with affection, sensuality, and sexuality. Being soft-spoken, engaging in as little conversation as possible, and following procedure created an atmosphere of restraint and sanctity. The environment was keenly controlled through the group's procedures. There was an exact way to do everything. In the beginning, procedures and norms were conveyed verbally, but as the group matured, other methods were used.

"As we got more sophisticated later on," Rich explained, "then it became 'the book.' Put it in the book. We had books upon books, you know, three-ring binders, and steno notebooks." There were procedures for getting up, preparing meals, washing cars, brushing teeth, going to the bathroom — everything. According to Jstody, "The procedures weren't arbitrary in nature. They were practical. They were to the point. Guidelines that had to do with living within the budget of your supplies . . . like a scientific team."

In a sense, the procedures became the group's rituals. Rich related, "There was the ritual of how the house was kept. It was spartan and very hospital clean and the ritual of the sanitation and the suits, you know, the ritual of the jumpsuits or what we'd wear inside, to make it appear as though we were a crew of people with one mind and that we were all on a mission. Those are all ritualistic ways of indoctrination that were particular to this group. There were ways of speaking and mannerisms. . . . A lot of it was mimicking or it was an evolved sequence of procedures. We were supposed to get up and do this and we're supposed to make lunches this way and we're supposed to make the pancakes that way and you're supposed to shave in a certain way. All these things were literally written down in books — 'the procedure is . . .' — so everything was referenced to material that came from on high, from the authority. . . . The whole idea was to do things differently than you were used to doing it."

Although they may have resisted these regimens at first, in time students believed they were necessary guides as they advanced to the Next Level. Students knew that they were to maintain these regimens even when apart from the group; they made them feel secure and connected. Besides, they believed that the Next Level knew if they were holding to the discipline. In relation to following procedures, Jstody said, "I feel like it gives me protection — the more and more that I live this way and try to copy the guidelines set down."

The Class was set up as a training ground, which meant that "lessons" were a major focus. All activities and behaviors were subjected to scrutiny and criticism; all attitudes were monitored and reviewed. Check partners aided in this process, but Applewhite and Nettles were the overall guides in proper behaviors, attitudes, and ways. The atmosphere was one of struggle, learning, correction, and self-correction.

Everything, including the voluminous procedures, was presented as part of "Next Level design." Thus students were expected to love procedures because they were central to overcoming. To resent having to follow procedures was to stall the overcoming process. Such would be regarded as rebelliousness, as choosing slow growth, as giving in to evil influences. Loving procedures was proof of flexibility. Ironically, procedures were to be experienced as freedom from structure, and their convoluted and constrained life was to be perceived by them as liberation.

Rules and regulations were plentiful. Many were put into place early on: "There's no sex and there's no alcohol and there's no — it got real basic at the first," recalled Rich, talking about the first camp in Gold Beach, Oregon. But the truly rigid routine and hard-core disciplines came a year later with the formation of the Class. Regarding themselves almost like a special forces team, students knew it would be hard; Applewhite and Nettles told them so time and again. Ollody echoed that when he wrote, "It will not be easy for you . . . or anyone. This is the most difficult step for a human to undertake and accomplish."

The basic rules revolved around giving up everything "human," in particular, sexual activity and "addictions." Addictions included everything from drugs and alcohol to feelings for one's human family to humanitarian interests and organized religion. Self-monitoring and self-reporting were the mainstays of this system. Behavioral guidelines were set down in a list called "The 17 Steps," among them, following instructions without adding one's own interpretation; not polluting others' ears with inconsiderate conversation; not procrastinating or finishing tasks halfway; not exhibiting defensiveness; and not being pushy, aggressive, interfering, or demanding. Another document, "Major Offenses," outlined the basic code of conduct. Three major offenses were

1. Deceit: doing something on the sly, lying, and not exposing an offense immediately;
2. Sensuality: permitting any arousal in thought or action;
3. Breaking rules knowingly.

A list of thirty-one other offenses follows, such as me-firstism, using one's own mind, criticizing or finding fault with classmates or teachers, being negative, being aggressive, having private thoughts, engaging in gossip or lack of restraint, having likes or dislikes, in any way vibrating femininity or masculinity, permitting physical or verbal abuse toward classmates, and lacking in effort or commitment. Basically, the Next Level requirement was, no self-expression, no sexuality, no disloyalty, no affection.

FORMING SYSTEMS OF INFLUENCE

Beyond the direct charismatic authority, the transcendent belief system, and the systems of control, during this period, the cult continued its powerful march toward bounded choice through internal pressures, group norms, peer influence and modeling, and overall commitment.

The push to conform was very strong in Heaven's Gate but in some ways not so different from the norms of conformity found throughout U.S. society. The specifics of this conformity — ideas, appearance, language, deference to Ti and Do — may seem odd to the outsider, but such conformism is rampant everywhere, as citizens flock to buy the latest fashion or hot product or kowtow to their bosses. It is the very normalcy of that behavior that made it easy for Ti and Do's followers to go along with the program.

One of the effects of the intense pressure to conform was a collective style of communicating. For example, when students spoke, they generally used the pronoun *we*, and each student spoke about herself or himself in the third person. Both a detachment from self and a merging of self into the greater whole were evident. Observing their speech patterns in their exit video is very telling: when a student began to speak, often he or she first agreed with what the previous speaker had said or referred to what other students had already said. Students were unaccustomed to having their own points of view, so they often assured listeners that they had nothing different or better to say. Or they would say that, anyway, they were not able to say it better than their Older Members. Almost all of them apologized for their behavior.

Also, students conformed by adopting a presentational style that mimicked Applewhite. They spoke precisely and softly, as he did. They emoted in the same way that he did. On the video, for example, half of the students either cried (very briefly and almost hidden), started to cry and stopped, or spoke about getting emotional — all behaviors that are characteristic of Applewhite's own theatrical style.

Applewhite and Nettles spared no effort to convey the seriousness of their mission. In early meetings, as far back as 1975, they had asked their followers how far they would go for the cause. Both Brent and Rich, as well as other former members, remembered The Two asking such questions as, "Would you be willing to bear arms for this cause?" "Would you do anything?" "Are you prepared to do anything for the Next Level . . . to adjust that fast?"

Each person was expected to write a note describing the degree of his or her commitment. Applewhite and Nettles set high standards for their students and weeded out the ones who were simply curiosity seekers or out for an experience. Instructing members to write statements about their commitment increased the likelihood that they would take it more seriously and not renege on it. Also, members knew which of them had not yet turned in a commitment statement, which added to the feeling of pressure from one's community of peers.

Being asked to express commitment happened in other ways as well. One of these was a "final exam" that was given in the late 1970s. "They sent us all out to work, to get jobs, to see if we would be pulled back into the world," said Brent. Some followers did leave the group during that test.

Other commitment crises occurred as a consequence of the various evenings they all sat together, staring at the skies, waiting for the space-ships. On several occasions, Applewhite and Nettles assured the students that this was the time, that they had gotten the word from the Next Level. When no ships came, they would tell their followers that they could leave if they wanted, and they would not blame them if they did.

"We don't know what happened," they would say. "We're as disappointed as you are."

None of the core group left at these times. "We'd all start crying and saying, 'Oh, no, Ti and Do,'" Brent recalled. And they would huddle together for consolation. In the end, "failed" miracles served as opportunities for the followers to reaffirm the charismatic relationship rather than break the bond.

· · ·

The charismatic community that formed around Applewhite and Nettles was strong and close-knit. The communal lifestyle reinforced the sense of togetherness and the extent of dependency — and was solidified by the leaders' demand that their followers remain steadfastly loyal and mimic them in every way. Given that the group was nomadic and, for the most part, sequestered from the outside world, it did not take long for the group reality to take hold and for members to feel that they were part of a tight community, as we shall see in the final chapter of their story.

CHAPTER 5

Denouement

At this point in the story of Heaven's Gate, a trauma occurred that altered and threatened the group's existence but ultimately was overcome, as Applewhite proved his ability to assert his charismatic authority and reaffirm the group's transcendent belief system. The followers remained under his control and influence. The self-sealing system was preserved, and bounded choice prevailed.

The Death of Nettles

Nettles fell ill sometime in the early 1980s, a fact that was kept from most members. She already had had at least one surgery and an eye removed because of cancer. Former members who were there during those years believe that she had been sick for about two years before her death.

Nothing was said about it, but she was noticeably quieter at their meetings and then attended fewer and fewer group sessions. She died in 1985, most likely from liver cancer. Her body was probably cremated and her ashes strewn in a lake near one of the group's Texas abodes. The details of that event were known only by Applewhite and the two loyal devotees who had served as their Helpers, both of whom are now dead.

Afterward, Applewhite came to the group and announced that Ti, his

Older Member, had passed, that her work was done here. He added that he had more lessons to learn and so would be staying with the students to help them complete their training. Applewhite told the students that they should not be sad about Ti's departure for now she would be able to guide them even better from the Next Level.

Some say, however, that Applewhite was devastated by his partner's death and that this incident represents a major turning point in the life of the group. After all, for Nettles to die in her physical body, her "human vehicle," was counter to their teachings up to that point: they were supposed to metamorphose and be lifted up en masse. It must have given pause to some, including perhaps Applewhite, and it most certainly provoked some shifts in their beliefs.

On the surface, Ti's death caused little overt crisis in commitment for the members. And whatever crises may have been in the offing were nipped in the bud by a type of wedding ritual, complete with gold bands, between Do and his loyal students. In his exit video, Do explained that the bands they each wore were an expression of commitment to the group. Also, he added, they were used to keep outsiders from approaching students with romantic intentions when they were in the world working or doing other out-of-craft tasks. In any event, the rings were an important symbol and served to solidify any wavering member's ties to the Class or to Do at the time of Ti's death.

It is unknown whether it was Applewhite's idea to get wedding rings for all the members or whether it might have been something that Ti and Do had discussed as a way to safeguard his continuation as leader of the group after her death. At what could have been a shaky time, this dramatic ritual cemented the bond members already had to the Class. They were able to choose the type of band they wanted from among two thicknesses, and from that point on they considered themselves married to the Next Level.

After Ti was gone, Do always had an empty chair next to him when he sat with his followers. As he explains in his videotaped exit statement, the chair was a reminder to him to always seek guidance from *his* Older Member, Ti, who was his Shepherd and his Father and to whom he looked for everything — just as the students were now to look to him.

By then, ten years into it for most students, daily life was routinized and the change in leadership was taken in stride. Ultimately, Applewhite had little trouble carrying on the tradition he and Nettles had started. His followers had tremendous respect for him. His leadership was not questioned upon Ti's death. Rkkody, who had been in and out of the group for years and who took his life some months after the collective suicide, remarked: "Do was in the position of doing that task. There was no other leader to come forth. He did an excellent job."

Applewhite seemed depressed after his partner's death and sometimes at a loss, but there was little change in the way things were run. The community remained close and closed. When asked whether another leader might emerge to be with remaining members of the Class after the collective suicide, Rkkody bristled: "There's no other leader who's going to come forth from the Next Level. I could be wrong, but it doesn't make sense to me that they would send another Rep at the end of this, after the twenty years that this Rep had to spend here. And he did an excellent job and I can't — it's incomprehensible to me that he somehow had failed in this job where they would need to send somebody else. That doesn't even compute."

Going and Staying Underground

As the years passed, Applewhite and the students grew old together. When students returned to camp or their current craft, they shared war stories and also tales of psychic wonderment and high spiritual moments. All of that, of course, was attributed to being in communication with their Older Members, who were always the ultimate guides. For the most part, the group remained underground from 1976 until 1992, when they resurfaced as Total Overcomers Anonymous (T.O.A.), ran national newspaper ads, and sought new recruits. During the seventeen or eighteen years of being sequestered, the students had bonded into a closed, unified, self-sealing group.

In the 1990s the students became increasingly involved in computer work, as a way to earn money but also to spread the word. They attempted to broadcast their *Beyond Human* series on satellite TV, but there is little to suggest that it made any impact. In May and June 1993 they bought newspaper advertisements that bore headlines such as this one that appeared in *USA Today:* "UFO Cult Resurfaces with Final Offer." If someone responded, a Prospective Candidate letter would be sent, along with part 1 of their video series and a selection of flyers and personal testimonials by loyal students, such as Mllody, Ollody, and Sawyer. (See fig. 7.)

In January 1994 the group sold its houses and most of its possessions and started to travel in teams again, trying to recreate what they had done twenty years earlier — sermonizing and recruiting, offering "a window of

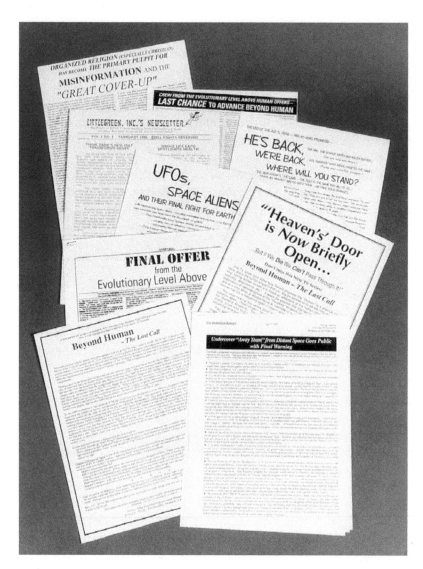

FIGURE 7. Heaven's Gate produced many flyers and posters to explain their beliefs, generate interest, and attract new members. In some years, the group had a postal box in Texas to which curious individuals could write; shortly thereafter, they would receive flyers in the mail.

opportunity to advance to the Next Level." But unlike the crowds of hundreds that had once gathered, this time only a handful of people came to their meetings: about thirty in Eureka, California, and about forty in Chicago. By this time the group's membership had shrunk to less than three dozen. They managed to bring in some new members during that time, at least several of whom were former members who came back to the group. Then they were not heard from.

As Applewhite aged, and with Nettles gone, he no longer held daily meetings, and he appeared before his members only occasionally. He lived apart from the others, as he and Nettles almost always had. Except for his two Helpers, no one knew much about his life or his health. Some of the members recruited in the 1990s never met him and left before the final farewell. It is unclear how much contact the members, especially new members, had with the remote Applewhite during these final years.

In August 1994 the group made a poster, which according to their book was not used publicly. Its bold, all-capitalized heading blared out at the world:

UFO TWO AND CREW SAY:
"THE SHEDDING OF OUR BORROWED HUMAN BODIES MAY BE REQUIRED IN ORDER TO TAKE OUR NEW BODIES BELONGING TO THE NEXT WORLD." IF YOU WANT TO LEAVE WITH US YOU MUST BE WILLING TO LOSE EVERYTHING OF THIS WORLD IN ORDER TO HAVE LIFE IN THE NEXT. CLING TO THIS WORLD AND YOU'LL SURELY DIE.

It is apparent here that the metamorphosis talked about in the early years had evolved into a belief that they would be leaving behind their human bodies, mere "vehicles" to be shed, "like an old used car," as one student remarked in his videotaped exit statement.

Leaving the Human Level

Heaven's Gate appeared on the Internet in about the middle of 1995. The group set up an extensive Web site, which included much of the writings it had produced over the years, its history as reconstructed by Applewhite, numerous member testimonials, and statements primarily by Applewhite on various issues, such as organized religion and suicide. Its discourse had turned more to discussion of evacuation and leaving the planet. The Web site began to carry more exit statements and statements about the wasteland of planet Earth and human life. One Internet posting was titled "Undercover 'Jesus' Surfaces Before Departure."

Apparently, their messages were not well received by Netizens, which added to Applewhite's and his followers' frustration and demoralization. This probably had a substantial influence on the decision to depart. Their reaction to the Internet response to their postings is indicative of their state of mind: "The response was extremely animated and somewhat mixed. However, the loudest voices were those expressing ridicule, hostility, or both — so quick to judge that which they could not comprehend. This was the signal to us to begin our preparations to return 'home.' The weeds have taken over the garden and truly disturbed its usefulness beyond repair — it is time for the civilization to be recycled — 'spaded under.'"[1]

The Heaven's Gate book was added to their Web site in April 1996, along with a notice implying that this might be their last interaction with the human level. The book includes documents from the very beginnings of the group, as well as statements and writings detailing the chronology of the group and the evolution of the belief system and transcripts of their video recordings. It also includes testimonials written just before their departure.

On September 14, 1996, a message titled "Time to Die for God, or Armageddon — Which Side Are You On?" was posted on several Internet newsgroups. In January 1997 the group posted a revised 1994 document that outlined their views on leaving, likening it to "the sound of music" (one of Do's favorite phrases), for they had been waiting so long. By this time they were referring to themselves as the "Away Team," a special crew who had been sent here from the Next Level. They were completing their task and were about to leave for home. In February members posted an Internet message about the Hale-Bopp comet. They indicated that it was a sign of the end of the world, the marker they had been waiting for. They posted another such message at the entry to their Web site.

On March 26, 1997, the bodies of Applewhite and his followers were found in the Rancho Santa Fe mansion the group had been renting for $7,000 a month since October 1996. The former follower who called the police had been alerted to the group's final act by the contents of a Federal Express package he received. Similar packets containing a letter and two videotapes had been sent around the country to stalwart former members, sympathizers, and adherents, asking that they maintain the Web site and launch a media campaign. Among his last recorded words, Applewhite said, "The world has become so corrupt that in order to be heard you have to do a media event."

News reports later confirmed that all of the members had died from ingesting a lethal mixture of drugs and alcohol, and death was ensured by

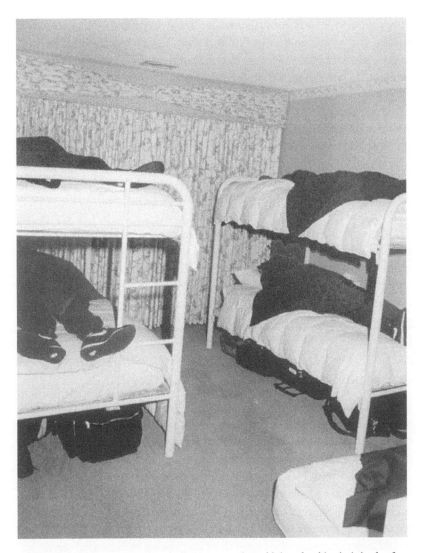

FIGURE 8. Heaven's Gate true believers were found lying dead in their beds after ingesting a suicide potion. Each was covered with a purple shroud. (AP/Wide World Photos)

the plastic bags that had been tied over their heads by Applewhite's two loyal Helpers (see fig. 8). Memos and procedures were found in the house indicating exactly how the deaths were to be carried out.

According to the coroner's report, Applewhite had been suffering from severe heart disease and had been at high risk for a heart attack.[2] Within the grapevines of former followers, cult watchers, and academics who studied the group, there were rumors that Applewhite thought he had liver or prostate cancer. He had told at least some of his followers that he thought he was dying. Whatever the decisive factor — and surely, there were at least several — it is likely that the members of this close-knit group, who had waited so patiently over the years for the spaceship to come and who had submitted to a life of struggle and deprivation, were ecstatic that the time had come when finally they were allowed to leave.

The Development of Bounded Choice (Part 3)

The mass suicide of the Heaven's Gate cult was not a delusional or insane act from the point of view of those who took their lives. Rather, it was the ultimate and inevitable next step within the self-sealing system of their community. In killing themselves, they believed they were making a logical and even ecstatic choice, given the history and context of the group to that point. This bounded choice was dictated by the same four principles that we have seen at each stage of the cult's evolution.

ESTABLISHING CHARISMATIC AUTHORITY

Many of the members who died with Applewhite expressed their high regard for their leaders, Ti and Do, in their videotaped exit statements. One follower who joined in the mid-1990s said, for example, that she did not have the words to express her gratitude to her Older Members. Another follower who joined at about the same time stated that he would follow his Older Member, Do, wherever he went. He said he was thankful that it had been set up that way and that he would do whatever was necessary. Another from the last batch of recruits said that he knew he would experience unlimited growth by continuing in unlimited service to his Older Member and Next Level Mind.

Praise for Do, in particular, was unbounded, though Ti was still their revered leader, at the top of the chain. This effusive deference to Applewhite is not unusual. After all, Nettles had died twelve years earlier and was likely to have become somewhat of a fond but distant memory to those who knew her, while the eight recent members knew of her only through the myths and mystique generated about her by the others.

Only the highest praise of Applewhite was expressed by students on their farewell video. One newer member described him as "so special, dignified, unhuman, objective." Expressing sympathy for Applewhite's difficult role, this young woman believed that he had endured much to be their leader. A male follower who joined in the 1970s, left in the early 1980s, and then rejoined in 1994 said it was "unimaginable" to think about what Ti and Do had gone through for them, the students. This image of the beleaguered leader comes up time and again in charismatic groups, in part as a result of the followers' demands on the leader to live up to the charismatic ideal.[3]

In her farewell statement, Jnnody, who joined in 1975 and was one of the main Helpers, especially after Nettles died, said, "You all couldn't really know it unless you'd done what we had done and been through what we've been through." Similarly, in her exit statement Mllody said, "The love that an Older Member has for a younger member is a type of love that a human cannot experience." It is this type of inner experience that helps to bind members to a leader and a group. Members become completely convinced that their happiness, existence, and ultimate fate are inextricably tied to the leader, who claims to be the source of that inner feeling.

Did Applewhite think this was suicide? No, he assured the world, as he assured his followers one more time, sitting before them during the taping of his final statement. With some vigor, he said: "Suicide is when you've received Mind from the Kingdom and are aware of the truth and have the opportunity to move and you turn against that or cannot do what is required to identify with Mind. Suicide is separation from the Kingdom when the Kingdom has reached out and offered life to you. It is suicide *not* to leave. It is to take life to leave. This is not life to us. This is primitive, barbaric. This is history. We are about to regain life." (See fig. 9.)

In their own exit video, loyal students professed one after another that they too were departing to another level and were not committing suicide. Tddody, for example, echoed his leader: "To stay here is suicide."

Jstody, who was not in the Class at the time, decided to join his Classmates roughly six weeks later by duplicating their method of drinking a lethal potion, in a motel near the house in Rancho Santa Fe where the others had completed their pact. Just before his death, during a radio interview, he said of his Classmates: "I believe they reached a point that the word was given to depart from this world back to the mother ship, to move into bodies that had been prepared for them, physical bodies of a finer nature, androgynous, sexless. It's an evolutionary step. . . . No, I don't think of them as dead. Well, the bodies, yes. These are shells left behind and they were dropping a body in this life. It served them well and had finished its service because they had overcome it and were strong

FIGURE 9. In his videorecorded final farewell, an aging Marshall Applewhite (Do) tells his dedicated "students" and any new would-be followers that, contrary to what outsiders might think, it is suicide to remain here on Earth. (AP/Wide World Photos)

enough in their minds to take on the new body that was prepared for them."[4]

Given the degree of the followers' dependence on Applewhite by that time, it is not surprising that they chose to go with him when he was ready to exit. The fear of being left alone was perhaps greater than confronting the possibility that he might have been wrong about impending doom and Next Level salvation.

In their exit video, thirty out of thirty-five students said they were happy and proud, that this was the moment they had been waiting for, that they could not be happier, and so forth. The evening before, during his taping, Applewhite pronounced, "We're so excited, we don't know what to do. We're about to reenter. We can't wait."

In their usual style of mimicry, the next day during their taping, the members reiterated that they could not be happier, that they were excited, could hardly wait, were eager to get off this planet. They also insisted that they were acting of their own free will; twenty-seven of them attested to that. Qstody, for example, said, "My free will and options allow me to keep looking up to the Next Level and Older Members' Chain of Mind — or to look away, which results in separation and death, like cutting away a leaf from a tree."

"Free will" did not mean having a world of choices; it meant having *one* choice, the choice of whether or not to be part of Lucifer's world (understood by them to be the human world). Ultimately, it meant one thing: staying in the Class, choosing the Next Level.

DEVELOPING TRANSCENDENT BELIEF

The major shifts that occurred in the beliefs held by the members of Heaven's Gate were

- from bodily metamorphosis to "dropping" their "vehicles" (i.e., abruptly ending their human existence);
- from Ti and Do announcing themselves as the two witnesses from Revelation to referring to themselves as Jesus and God the Father;
- from the Demonstration (Ti and Do's martyrdom in the streets and being lifted three and a half days later to the Next Level) to no Demonstration (explained as having been "killed" by the media); and
- from spacecraft voyage to suicide.

Typically, the leaders, and toward the end, Applewhite alone, explained that these shifts were the result of new information from the Next Level. For the most part, the changes did not appear to cause any major concerns within the core group or crises of faith among the general membership.

One belief that emerged strongly during the group's evolution, however, was based on a biblical subtext that dated the group's origin to the time of Jesus. First indirectly, then more explicitly, Applewhite referred to himself as Jesus, saying he had come back this time to finish the job, which was to bring the message and harvest lost souls. Likewise, Nettles, higher on the chain of command, became God the Father, here in human form to help out her (His) son, Jesus. Without much prodding, the members, many of whom already believed in reincarnation when they joined the group, came to accept that they also had been present in Jesus's time and were part of a select group from the Next Level, sent to Earth to complete a mission.

In their exit statements and other testimonials some members spoke
of their earlier incarnations. This belief not only offered the promise of
salvation but also helped to explain their feelings of alienation from mainstream society. It was a worldview that cleverly served to make sense of
the adherents' pregroup lives. The alienation prevalent among many of
their generation and a commonplace product of fast-paced society was
particularized in each one of them by this teaching. The result was that
students believed that the alienation they felt was directly attributable to
a prior connection to the Next Level and their real purpose here on Earth,
which was to leave and go back "home." This interpretation assuaged
them, as it kept them separate from the world.

For the most part, the belief system was imparted orally, directly
from Applewhite and Nettles or from Helpers and Elders to the members
under their command. Students did not have a precise program of study,
although the Bible was always available, as were books on New Age topics, in particular, UFO sightings. Applewhite included a recommended
reading list at the end of his *'88 Update*, an important document meant to
clarify the group's purpose and history up to that point. The Holy Bible
is listed among the recommendations. Applewhite did not specify a version but cautioned his students not to water it down with their own interpretations. Also included are *The Essene-Christian Faith*, described as a
depiction of how early Christians tried to purge themselves of things that
separated them from the Kingdom of Heaven; *The Lost Books of the Bible
and the Forgotten Books of Eden*, a 1974 book of gospels and other writings
attributed to Jesus that apparently had been left out of the New Testament; *The Nag Hammadi Library*, the secret Gnostic writings unearthed
in Egypt in 1945; and numerous UFO-related titles, such as *UFO Crash
at Aztec: A Well-Kept Secret, The Roswell Incident, Above Top Secret: The
Worldwide UFO Coverup*, and Whitley Streiber's *Communion: A True
Story* and its follow-up, *Transformation*.

Applewhite's reading list contains more works on UFOs than any
other topic, indicating a deep connection to ufology. Yet Applewhite and
his followers often derided the media's depictions of them as the UFO
cult. Popular interest in UFOs was exploited by them as a way to spread
their message and at the same time find UFO buffs who might be open
to the Heaven's Gate ideology. Also, the growing interest in and increasing occurrence of alleged UFO sightings were interpreted by Applewhite
and Nettles as validation of the truth in their message. Some scholars
argue that the use of UFOs in this group's belief system is consistent with
Gnostic teachings, which were of interest to both Applewhite and Nettles
during their formative years.[5]

An attitude of self-hate was instilled in the members, reframed as hatred of their human selves, which was projected onto their "flesh vehicle." It was an attitude of distaste and disdain, reflecting the self-hatred in Applewhite's apparent ambivalence about his sexuality.

In the students' exit video, the troublesome vehicle was one of the most prevalent themes. Twenty-six of the thirty-five members commented on their disgust with human ways and the human body. They considered the body nothing more than a borrowed outer shell that was not them but merely a device for being here on Earth and going through the training and tests in order to get back home to the Next Level.

Struggling with the pulls and demands of the human vehicle was a requirement and a daily reality. According to their beliefs, the vehicle served as the intermediary between the human world and the Next Level, between us (the Class, the students and Teachers striving to get away) and them (everything else, or life as one knew it before entering the group). This made the vehicle necessary, but at the same time it was to be rejected because it originated outside the Class and would not be needed in the Next Level.

This dichotomous worldview became all-encompassing, as all such worldviews do. Given the closed society of the group, it rather swiftly became their reified version of reality. Life on planet Earth was merely a training ground, a torturous one at that. As Smmody, who joined in 1975, said, "My task is to work on control and restraint and to learn the ways of the Next Level that my teachers had to teach me. I'm thankful they came here to this insidious place."

Students understood that they had to completely separate from the human world to achieve their goal. Anything associated with human existence was seen as a threat to their advancement, to their ultimate goal of getting off the planet. Earth and its inhabitants stood for everything that was negative; this world was described as corrupt, polluted, evil, primitive, barbaric, and history. Human life was equated with ignorance and death, as is evident in this eerie statement by Applewhite: "Our cause is to let you know we are returning to life after a visitation with death."

Glnody, another devotee who joined in 1975, reflects the same negativity in this statement, not unlike those made by his Classmates: "This is no life here in the human world. This planet has become the planet of the walking dead. . . . The human world is a hideous hell due to all of the poor choices humans have made since the beginning of this civilization. If this is all there is with nothing to look forward to beyond this, then why choose to extend your time in hell?"

The focus in the group was always toward the sky, toward the heavens.

As Rich explained it, pointing to the sky: "Everything that's out there is good. Everything that's here is bad. So the Earth is bad, mother is bad, women are bad, sex is bad, procreation is bad. Father is good — the dominant authoritarian energy of out there. The projection out there is what is real."

In the end, the belief system left no room for doubt and less room for error. Given that the group was sequestered for most of its twenty-two years, members had a great deal of time to absorb the beliefs and become accustomed to living by the rules. Although some members worked outside the group to help with its financial support and others left for a while and were readmitted later, in general, the members who were recruited in 1975 and 1976 and stayed through the trying times were firm believers.

Essentially, Heaven's Gate students regarded their involvement as a lifelong commitment. The benefit was eternal growth. As Jstody explained, "Tremendous growth can come from rising above this vibration and looking, you know, to something higher, reaching for something higher."

INSTITUTING SYSTEMS OF CONTROL

Discipline and subjugation increased as the group approached its moment of absolute bounded choice. And the systems of control never ceased to form a tightly structured pyramid, with power continuing to come from the top. After Nettles's death, Applewhite continued to look to her for guidance. Jstody, an on-and-off member who was not with the group when it committed collective suicide, was asked in a radio interview to describe the way in which Applewhite and Nettles communicated: "He'd ask. He talked to her. He talked to her. He'd wake up in the middle of the night and ask. He'd go to sleep asking. We would sit together as a classroom and ask all together and if we seemed to be getting off track, we'd stop one approach and start another and ask again. It was constant."[6]

Essentially, Applewhite modeled the process for his followers, and they followed his process in their daily lives. To make decisions or know what to do when away from the group setting, students were to rely on their connection with their Older Member, confer with their check partner, and hope they made the right move.

Jstody explained that process: "It's not like you have a long discussion. You think, well, this is kind of what I got and does that feel right to you and, well, it feels — if there's no argument then you can proceed tentatively in that direction. But you don't want to sit around and not do anything because the Next Level wants things to happen and happen quickly. So it's not a debating society and the faster and more flexible you are and the quicker you are to work with your partner, of course, the faster you grow to assume more responsible positions, because you're not holding up the works with a bunch of stubbornness, and well, I want to do it my way kind of thing."

Most members' activities and actions were determined by following the existing procedures or sending a specific request in writing and waiting for instructions on how to proceed. "We didn't make decisions. We just presented problems and asked for help," explained Brent.

As time went on — or as Brent liked to say, "as the craft evolved" — there was some degree of individual decision making. For example, if a team responsible for supplies went shopping, they were able to make some decisions about which products to buy — especially if they saw something on sale. After they returned to the craft, they were required to make a full report. Brent again: "Then Ti would call us on the caller and say, 'Well, this was good what you did' and 'This was wrong what you did. We don't want that. Don't even serve that stuff.' So, there were times we were entrusted to make decisions, but our decisions were always critiqued."

Given that all daily needs were taken care of — food, clothing, living arrangements — there were few decisions left for a member to make. If money was needed for a function related to an out-of-craft task, for example, a written request was made to Applewhite or to one of the liaisons if he was not around. A rigid routine developed, so that there was little room for extraordinary occurrences and therefore for requests to be necessary. Rich commented on this: "If there was something that was never done before, that there was no precedent for, most of the time we wouldn't do that." Group life was pared down to the bare essentials.

At the same time students had many tasks to perform. Some of them revolved around the infrastructure of keeping the Class functioning at optimal level. Those were "in-craft" assignments. Many activities were given a quasi-scientific name, in keeping with the space station aura, such as working in the "nutri lab" (the kitchen) or the "fiber lab" (the laundry). Assignments could also involve finding places to live and getting them ready. Given that the group moved frequently, a lot of activity centered around some aspect of moving or setting up a new craft.

Out-of-craft tasks might be connected to a specific project, such as spreading the group's message, either directly or indirectly, or producing their written materials and, later on, the Web site. Some assignments were related to whatever training discipline the Class was engaged in at the time, which might require items for a special diet or a special uniform. At almost all times the group was involved in one or another of such projects. "I don't remember a lot of down time," said Brent, who had been with the Class for more than fifteen years.

As mentioned previously, members who held jobs gave their earnings to the group. New members often turned over their life savings, collections, and family inheritances, although this was not a requirement. All money was pooled and used to support the group in all things. By all accounts, they lived fairly well, ate well, and had nice things. Their crafts were well equipped and well taken care of. The various homes of Applewhite and Nettles always had the best available furnishings.

The members trusted their leaders completely, believing them genuine and sincere in motivation. They put their lives — literally — in the hands of Applewhite and Nettles. On the students' exit video, thirty-two of the thirty-five who spoke directly thanked Ti and Do for allowing them to be in the Class and for giving them the opportunity to be with them.

In the end, the Heaven's Gate systems of control were extremely confining and all-encompassing. If one wanted to remain in the group, there was little that could be done individually or by one's own doing or choice. The "design," as they referred to it, ensured complete dependency of the members on the leaders, built around an intricate system to oversee that degree of control which led to the bounded choice of their own demise.

FORMING SYSTEMS OF INFLUENCE

Rejection and self-renunciation played an ongoing role in the internal culture, bolstered by peer influence and mutual commitment. Nettles and Applewhite stressed over and over the necessity of that dependent relationship, and Applewhite modeled this dependent state for his followers. For example, in his farewell video, he said, "I know of my total dependence on my relationship with my Teacher [Nettles]. Without that I go astray."

Similarly, Mllody wrote in a 1993 testimonial: "The mind of the Chief of Chiefs is passed down to all younger members to possess as their own to the degree that they have grown to be able to receive it. If a younger member turns from the mind of his Older Member (the source of all knowledge) and looks to some other source, he will ultimately sever his connection with life itself."

Such a bond was expressed by Dvvody, the last student to join the Class in August 1996, after leaving her four young children with relatives in the Midwest. Both she and her husband joined. He left after a short time but was unable to persuade his wife to leave with him.[7] In her exit statement made on the brink of her self-destruction, an emotionless Dvvody said, "There is nothing here for me. I want to look forward. Keep my eye on Ti and Do. That's my path."

In their final statements some of the students mentioned the disconnection from their former lives. For example, Dmmody, a recruit from the 1970s who left and then rejoined in 1994, criticized himself for having left the group for a time: "I thought I wanted to see the vehicle's family and things like that." Likewise, Nrrody, who joined after attending the Los Angeles meeting in April 1975, said there might be "ones in the world that might recognize this vehicle, but I am not this vehicle." Chkody joined in 1975 with her boyfriend, who left the group in 1993. Chkody said she realized that "this choice may have caused some suffering" but that "suffering was caused by the misinformation that's out there about an individual choosing to become a member of the Kingdom of Heaven."

Despite such pronouncements of faith, acceptance into the Next Level was not guaranteed. Nothing was to be taken for granted, and the path was not easy. But all members of the group believed that it would be well worth it if they succeeded. Drrody said, "The transition to becoming a beginning Next Level member is the most difficult undertaking any human can undergo or even imagine — yet the reward is priceless. Imagine being able to serve, learn, and grow among others with only a pure, selfless motivation, in service to the Creator, connecting with a future — potentially forever."

Given the intensity of their mission, struggling each day to attain the ideal was filled with anxiety, fear, and tension. Brent described the tension in his diary during the first summer: "It is this condition of continual strain that does the work — it is the struggle and the push against the forces of fatigue, doubt, indulgence, irritation that keeps us changing. Truly we should rejoice in the endless struggling, because it is the fire of our conversion. For there *is* an ending to it, and on that day, we will know our rewards."

The tension was manifest in the uneasiness that came from feeling the presence of influences — a feeling that left some members ill at ease. Rich recalled the unsettling emotion: "So I'm basically feeling like I'm having influences and I'm uncomfortable because I'm not really feeling comfortable being in his [Applewhite's] presence because of my doubts or my waffling. So for a long time I would feel very uncomfortable and feeling like he could read my thoughts. So it was my stuff, but it was effective in keeping me under control and with the program."

Rich was not alone in believing his thoughts could be read. The idea of mental telepathy was discussed often in the group. It dated back to Nettles's view of herself as a medium, even before the founding of the group. It was also evident in her claim that she was receiving transmissions from the Next Level and, later, in Applewhite's belief that he was in mental contact with Nettles after her death. In one of their video presentations, Applewhite explained, "Mental telepathy is a very important aspect of crew participation — not letting thoughts enter our mind that can be an interference, knowing that our Older Member can read that thought. I mean, if we have that thought, it comes right to them."[8] No wonder Rich and other students did not feel alone with their thoughts.

Students experienced a great deal of anxiety because they never knew what was coming next. The constant moving, starting and stopping projects, and getting and suddenly quitting jobs — all these were rationalized as lessons in flexibility. "It was all part of the design. You never know what the Next Level wants. You just have to go with the flow and be ready for whatever comes," commented Rich, describing that state of uncertainty. Anticipation was the main emotion hovering over the Class.

It is this heightened state of anticipation that finally came to fruition in March 1997 when the followers of Marshall Applewhite joined him on their journey home.

· · ·

The Heaven's Gate organizational system, comprising charismatic authority, transcendent belief system, systems of control, and systems of influence, relied on the rigid demand for a genderless existence, complete separation from the world, and total devotion to Applewhite and Nettles. The group can easily be dismissed as bizarre. In viewing their exit statements, the androgynous and similar appearance of Applewhite and his followers and their speech are surely strange.

Yet it must be borne in mind that the group recruited followers during an era that promoted alternative lifestyles and cosmic possibilities — a worldview that has followed us into the new millennium. It is not surprising that those who joined latched onto the group's vision. Many of them had been questioning mainstream values and ways for some time and, for one reason or another, were unhappy with the status quo. No less important is the fact that much of their shared belief rested on images of good and evil, a compelling worldview embedded with otherwordly heroes and villains, virtues and vices. Members were choosing to be on the side of the angels, which meant that to not do so put one at great risk. This moral imperative was reinforced by a philosophy that encouraged hatred for the human self and the rest of the world and feelings of love and commitment narrowly focused on the leaders, the impossible ideal, and the utopian vision. Together, they formed a coherent vision of the world, a story to which members were wed, a narrative for which they lived and died within their own exercise of bounded choice.

PART TWO

The Democratic Workers Party

CHAPTER 6

Revolutionaries, Rebels, and Activists

The Democratic Workers Party had its beginnings in 1974. Full-time members, called "cadres" or "militants," typically numbered between 125 and 150, but in certain periods there were between 300 and 1,000 members at various grades of affiliation. In the early 1980s the DWP branched out into various locales around the United States, but the headquarters always remained in San Francisco. Throughout most of its existence, the DWP was a highly controversial organization. Marlene Dixon, the group's leader throughout its life span, was a former professor of sociology and a radical feminist of the sixties era. Through charisma and chutzpah, Dixon was able to gather around her extremely loyal followers, known throughout the Left for their obsessive devotion to her.

A feature that distinguished the DWP from so many other leftist groups at the time was its proudly feminist origins, as it had been founded and was led by women. In addition, the group was innovative and bold in its local, national, and international interventions and activities. Although most of the leadership personnel were women, the DWP was never solely a women's organization; almost from the beginning, the membership included both men and women, and throughout the years at least several men served in middle- and upper-level leadership positions.

As a Marxist-Leninist organization with a Maoist orientation, the DWP was part of the New Communist Movement (NCM), or the party-building movement. This movement was prominent in the Left in the 1970s and 1980s. Before I discuss the DWP's origins and evolution, I want to explain the roots of the NCM and describe its social milieu.

The NCM was a product of specific sociopolitical developments in the United States, as well as a direct by-product of the student movements of the 1960s.[1] Historically, the movement was one outcome of the failures and inadequacies of the Old Left and the New Left,[2] as well as a beneficiary of the perceived successes of certain international revolutionary movements. The New Communist Movement was, in fact, an umbrella term for a radical trend that tended to dominate U.S. leftist politics in the early 1970s. The movement itself was affected by political ideologies imported from abroad but also by events at home in the United States.

Organizations within the NCM drew on general feelings of social alienation, growing economic polarization, and political unrest and distrust. According to the *Encyclopedia of the American Left,* groups and activists in the NCM reached thousands through their political actions and publications.[3] As a movement, however, it did not have staying power. In addition to the growing crisis in the world Communist movement and in many socialist countries, which began in the 1960s but took hold in the 1980s, most NCM groups could not withstand the turmoil in their own ranks. By the end of 1989, almost all NCM groups had either disbanded or splintered into practical invisibility.[4]

Historical and Ideological Influences

NCM activists considered themselves Marxists and spent much of their time studying and debating Marxist texts. Marxist theory had tremendous impact worldwide in the twentieth century; but especially in the United States in the 1970s, Marxism enjoyed a kind of renaissance as a "serious intellectual alternative to conventional social science."[5] That reconsideration extended also into activist circles, especially because many activists came from a campus milieu and intellectual traditions. As a result, Marxism combined with Leninism was the impetus behind the formation of countless revolutionary groupings in the late 1960s and early 1970s.

The basis of Marxism, of course, is that class conflict and class struggle are the inevitable outcome of the economic structure of society. "The history of all hitherto existing society is the history of class struggles," wrote Karl Marx.[6] Specifically, in a capitalist society that dialectic is expressed most often in struggles between capitalists and workers.

Capitalists, driven by the profit motive, exploit their workers, who essentially create the wealth but never get their fair share. Marx believed that class struggle was the motor force of history and that social change had occurred and would occur again through social revolution. But in spite of that deterministic outlook, Marx also believed that this revolution could come about only through insurrectionary collective action.

With Friedrich Engels, Marx wrote *The Communist Manifesto,* first published in 1848. In it, they advanced the idea that capitalism would be overthrown as the culmination of a class war that would be initiated by the rising of the working class. A classless society known as communism would be the eventual result. These ideas were instrumental in the growth of the socialist movement in the nineteenth century and the formation of the First International, an association of socialist parties.

THE INFLUENCE OF LENIN

The Russian revolutionary Vladimir Ilyich Lenin was a student of Marxism and a professional revolutionist. Lenin's theoretical contribution is found in his analyses of the state and of imperialism as the last stage of capitalism. But Lenin is perhaps best known for his organizational contribution. In his famous pamphlet *What Is to Be Done?* Lenin expressed the idea that a revolution could be brought about only by a highly disciplined political organization of professional revolutionaries, identified as the Bolshevik cadre party. After the success of the Russian Revolution in 1917 and the founding of the USSR, Lenin, who sought to spread the idea of revolution, established the Third International, an association of all Communist parties worldwide.

Let me briefly recapitulate portions of the history of this organizational form. Lenin fought a battle within the Russian (and international) socialist movement to form a vanguard party that would be in stark contrast to the mass socialist parties of the time. Historical conditions led Lenin to believe that this was necessary.[7] The main features of this development, summarized below, illuminate the development that took place in the "old" Communist parties, which were in many ways duplicated in the "new" parties in the latter decades of the twentieth century.

1. Under the tsar, the party was forced to work underground. Therefore, the party was secretive.

2. To protect working-class interests, the party had to enlist the most politically advanced workers, intellectuals, and activists. Therefore, the party was elitist.

3. To meet the prevailing needs, party members were to do more than just pay dues or offer lip-service support. Now actual work was required. Therefore, the party demanded a full-time cadre commitment.

4. In order for the organization to be focused and of one mind, decisions would be made democratically but, once made, were absolutely binding on all members. Thus the party would operate under a form of organization called *democratic centralism,* which put restrictions and tight controls on debates and factions within the party.

5. To be effective in the heat of battle, a military command structure and centralized direction was necessary. Therefore, democratic centralism came to mean tight discipline, no dissent, and unconditional obedience.

6. So as not to jeopardize the ultimate goal of revolution, it was important for the party to distinguish itself from other groups. Therefore, the party was sectarian, highly critical of others, and exclusive.[8]

Over time those principles took hold and became even more intransigent. The social historian Max Elbaum wrote: "The party conception 'hardened,' with greater and greater stress on discipline, centralism and monolithic unity and less and less weight given to inner-party democracy or strategic cooperation with other revolutionaries who stayed outside the party."[9] Specific developments and strategic shifts locked down the overall nature of the party as an organization, and these developments were justified time and again because of historical conditions in the Soviet Union and Europe.

Stalinism intensified the growing lack of democracy within the party. Under Stalin, a ban on factions, first instituted by Lenin in the heat of revolution, became a permanent fixture. Similarly, the concept of iron will (total devotion with no room for deviation) evolved as the ruling norm. Once more, historical necessities were used as the rationale for those and other extreme measures.

However, the conditions specific to the USSR at the time were rarely taken into consideration with any seriousness by the U.S. activists who adopted the Marxist-Leninist organizational model for their own purposes. The differences were either glossed over or misread to apply locally, as vast numbers of American leftists assured themselves that such extreme conditions existed in the United States as well. Thus a call for a cadre elite, complete with secrecy, democratic centralism, and sectarianism, became the norm in the NCM milieu.

These are the basic ideas that motivated NCM activists. The overall mission of domestic NCM groups was to create a revolutionary vanguard party that would lead the fight for socialism in the United States. The long-established Communist Party–U.S.A. was considered by these activists to be bankrupt and "reformist" — that is, not interested in real change, and in some instances actually blocking it. Other leftist groups were regarded as too loose, too weak, and also reformist. NCM activists believed that revolution required a Marxist-Leninist fighting party.

But the NCM also stood for a type of Marxism-Leninism that drew heavily from the Chinese Communist Party. In fact, in his summary of the period, Elbaum equated the NCM with Maoism.[10] The Chinese Party, of course, was constructed on the Bolshevik model — a concept reified to the point of absolute rigidity by Stalin.

THE INFLUENCE OF MAO

Mao Zedong was an original member of the Chinese Communist Party and was the charismatic leader who brought Communism to China in 1949, after a protracted battle against Chiang Kai-shek and the Kuomintang, the previous ruling party. Mao became the first chairman of the new People's Republic of China.

Chairman Mao's contribution to the Marxist-Leninist model was the application of class distinctions to all parts of life, both within the party and without. In other words, people, their actions and behaviors — as well as their thoughts and attitudes — were either for the working class or against it. These class differences were to be rooted out by means of "class-standpoint struggle." The process of class-standpoint struggle was central to Mao's program of thought reform, by which he planned to get key sectors of Chinese society to adopt his worldview and support the revolution.[11]

Class-standpoint struggle became a focal point of Party life. Such struggles were most widespread during the Cultural Revolution, a turbulent period that was supposed to rid the Chinese Communist Party and the country of citizens with "liberal" tendencies — that is, anyone who stood in the way of revolutionary progress, as defined by Mao. The Cultural Revolution was a nationwide campaign from 1966 until Mao's death ten years later. The effects of the Cultural Revolution were felt for years and in many ways remain prominent in the minds of many Chinese.[12]

The Maoist class-standpoint struggle was especially attractive to U.S.-based activists. Known as criticism/self-criticism, it was a more politically correct expression of the kind of self-examination popularized by the intensive, probing therapies of the human potential movement. But in the context of the burgeoning disciplined parties, the class-standpoint "framework gave struggle over differences within Maoist parties a particularly bitter character."[13] As we shall see, that aspect could not be better exemplified than in the case of the DWP.

Those historical and ideological strands — from Marx to Mao — deeply affected the deliberate search for a viable organizational form that was at the heart of the NCM in the early 1970s. During that period, typically some version of what was called Marxist-Leninist–Mao Tse-tung Thought was the guiding philosophy adopted by a cornucopia of new groups and liberating movements — among blacks, women, Asians, Hispanics, workers, and gays. These new groups that were emerging across the United States identified themselves as "pre-party formations" or as part of the party-building movement. Dedicated activists worked hard to recruit each other into one group or another, each group convinced that it had found the correct line and the correct leader.

These groups, almost always identified by their initials, took such names as the October League (OL), the Revolutionary Workers League (RWL), the Communist Labor Party (CLP), the African Peoples Socialist Party (APSP), the International Workers Party (IWP), the National Labor Federation (NATLFD), the New Alliance Party (NAP), the Workers Viewpoint Organization (WVO), which later became the Communist Workers Party (CWP), and Revolutionary Union (RU), later the Revolutionary Communist Party (RCP). Some of the groups were quite traditional in their political interpretations, following the Party lines of China or Albania; others struggled to develop a new brand of Marxism more applicable to the times and to the United States.[14]

Sociocultural Influences

In the 1950s and 1960s the United States experienced a crisis in values, and one response to that crisis was the emergence and eruption of political and social activism. After World War II many Americans lived lives of comfort and affluence, unlike anything they had known in the past. At the same time the Cold War ambience and the threat of nuclear war kept Americans on edge and unsure of tomorrow. Such was the dilemma facing many youths (and some adults) of that era. Involvement in various protest movements became an outlet for that sense of personal and social

confusion, as well as what was for many growing alienation from mainstream ideas and values.

RELIGION, POLITICAL ACTIVISM,
AND THE HIPPIES

The religious scholar William McLoughlin identified this activist era as
the Fourth Great Awakening: "In the 1950s and '60s a large proportion
of the young were torn between feeling that they were hopelessly trapped,
on the one hand, and hopelessly adrift, on the other. They were adrift
because behavioral patterns inculcated by their parents made no sense to
them; they were trapped because the educational patterns formed them
into vocational choices they found unbearable. . . . Alienation from parents, schools, and vocational goals produced an emotional distress or
affectlessness in the young. In order to 'feel alive,' they looked for excitement. In order to find security, they formed groups. In order to find
guidelines, they looked for authority figures."[15]

An upsurge of interest in religion occurred, but that interest spawned
a growing curiosity for "Zen Buddhism, magic, astrology, satanism, and
the occult," as well as "a renewed interest in atheistic Marxism."[16] Equally,
young people found excitement, or a sense of meaning and purpose, in
the prevailing or escalating social protest movements. The era of political activism began with the ongoing civil rights movement and ended
with very visible student movements — both in the United States and
around the world. For example, it was a student strike that set off the
events of May 1968 in France, when the entire country went on strike and
Charles DeGaulle was almost driven from the presidency. Activist and
radical students in France were an inspiration to their American counterparts, themselves immersed in debates and demonstrations at campuses
across the country, such as Columbia University in New York City, the
University of Wisconsin at Madison, and the University of California at
Berkeley. The student movement sparked growing protests against the
war in Vietnam — protests that eventually were joined by masses of people and halted U.S. participation in the war.

The radical sector of the student movement came to be called the New
Left, for it represented a new vision of leftist politics, away from the hard-
line stodginess of the Communist Party (known as the Old Left). The Old
Left was hardly considered a viable option for these energized young
activists.[17] One of the main organizations active during this period was
Students for a Democratic Society (SDS). With their Port Huron mani-

festo, a vision of unity and participatory democracy, SDS leaders thought that all the world would soon be theirs. The spirit of the moment was "youthful and reckless, searching and headstrong, foolhardy, romantic, willing to try almost anything."[18]

Another reaction to the perceived dead end of mainstream life was the equally adventurous hippie movement of the late 1960s and the 1970s, with its call to "turn on, tune in, and drop out." The two movements existed side by side, and intersected in many ways. Those were heady times: hippies were coming to antiwar demonstrations and other events such as the Anti-Inaugural Ball in Washington when Richard Nixon was elected, and some so-called hippie behaviors, such as marijuana use and sexual experimentation, were common among large segments of political activists.[19] "From the coast of California to the metropolitan centers of Europe, the youthful Bohemia of the sixties was high most of the time and in the horizontal position much of the time," wrote one observer.[20]

DISILLUSIONMENT AND HOPELESSNESS

But as the 1970s unfolded, both the spirit of hopefulness ("love power") of the hippie counterculture and the spirit of rebellion ("people power") of the activist New Left were in serious retreat. The assassinations of their role models, John F. Kennedy (1963), Malcolm X (1965), and Martin Luther King Jr., and Robert Kennedy (both in 1968), contributed to growing alienation. Similarly, many idealists and activists were profoundly dismayed by the 1968 Democratic National Convention in Chicago, when the police rioted against a broad spectrum of young demonstrators. Also, progressive political forces were profoundly shocked by the subsequent election of Nixon. That era's landmark film, *Easy Rider*, portraying the conflict between conservatives and radicals, was filmed in 1968 and released to wide acclaim in 1969.

The social unrest intensified in 1970, when four students were killed by poorly trained National Guard troops during a peaceful demonstration at Kent State University in mainstream Ohio. Then the shock of the Watergate revelations helped to close the lid on the enthusiasm for the possibility of peaceful, positive change. Many young people who had been leftist activists in the late 1960s and early 1970s were now more disillusioned and disgusted with the American Dream as their hope for social revolution shattered.[21]

The heyday of the civil rights movement, the hippie movement, the antiwar movement, the New Left, and what is now identified as the second wave of the women's movement had all passed. Even the Black Panther Party, which many leftists had idealized (even idolized) in the late 1960s, was in disarray, having succumbed to police provocation, numerous raids and shoot-outs, and internal strife.[22] Given this state of affairs throughout the various progressive movements, those who wished to remain politically active during that "post" period had some decisions to make.

The Emergence of the New Communist Movement

It was at that very moment of crisis that the NCM took hold. Activists who wished to hold on to a leftist vision — particularly in urban centers such as New York, Chicago, Seattle, Minneapolis, Boston, Los Angeles, and San Francisco — redefined themselves as anti-imperialist, socialist feminist, nationalist, or radical Marxist, sometimes a combination of all those orientations. During that period, much of the activity centered on reading, participating in study groups, and attending public forums to discuss and debate what type of political work and which type of political organization would best serve to bring about social change. Some activists decided to join (or were already members of) the Communist Party–U.S.A. or its splinter group, the Progressive Labor Party; while others chose from among the still-active long-standing Trotskyist groups. Yet many others remained unaffiliated and struggled to sort out their options.

For young leftists entrenched in that milieu, study focused on classic Marxist-Leninist texts, along with other writings they held in high regard, in particular, the works of Chairman Mao. Mao had grown so popular that at one time members of the Black Panther Party were selling Mao's famous Little Red Book of quotations.[23] Other idealized heroes included Fidel Castro, Regis Debray, Che Guevara, and Ho Chi Minh. Studious North American activists were learning about Third World liberation movements — the most recognized being those in Cuba, Angola, Vietnam, Eritrea, and Mozambique.

Perhaps more than anything else, the awareness of those movements in the far corners of the world made a profound impact on this generation of leftists. What greater proof of the correctness of their thinking and the direction they were heading than seeing, for example, the tiny country of Vietnam defeat the strongest world power? The little man could win — with the right beliefs and an unswerving commitment to the struggle. Positive examples of the victorious Vietnamese and smiling, rosy-cheeked Chinese peasants portrayed in stylized, oversized posters renewed the fervor of left-wing idealists whose spirits had faltered with domestic political events of the late 1960s and early 1970s.

Yet for many, there were bitter memories of recent participation in the New Left, the antiwar movement, or the women's movement. Countless activists came away from those experiences with the notion that the U.S. Left suffered from not only an absence of honest and accountable leadership but also a lack of organizational structure and theoretical development that could endure.[24] Among the remnants of the Left, the debate centered on what form of organization to build: a mass party or a vanguard party? Those who chose the latter as their model became part of this new party-building movement. Implicit in that choice, as discussed earlier, was accepting the need for a Marxist-Leninist, disciplined party that would be the vanguard in leading the U.S. working class to revolution.

In the San Francisco Bay Area, the locus of the DWP's formation, radical politics was very much in the news. In 1974 and 1975 a small terrorist group called the Symbionese Liberation Army was being sought by the authorities for the Berkeley kidnapping of heiress Patricia (Patty) Hearst, daughter of the newspaper magnate Randolph A. Hearst. The SLA had also been named as suspects in several armed bank robberies around the state. At the same time, the Prairie Fire Organizing Committee (aka the Weather Underground, a paramilitary offshoot of SDS) was mysteriously distributing bulletins known as revolutionary communiqués in coffeehouses, bookstores, and leftist hangouts. The region was believed to be a high priority area for investigation and infiltration by local Red Squads (intelligence divisions) and FBI agents.

The widespread use of government and police surveillance, including COINTELPRO (the FBI's domestic counterintelligence program), was common knowledge among radicals. COINTELPRO was a household word among the radical Left, causing rampant paranoia and suspicions in both leftist circles and the women's community. At the time, it was supposed to be a secret government project, but radical activists knew that undercover agents and a variety of informants were being used by the FBI, not only to spy and gather information, but also, through the use of agents provocateurs, to disrupt organizations and cause dissension in the leftist ranks.

Groups ranging from the nonviolent American Friends Service Committee and the Southern Christian Leadership Conference to militant extremists of the Black Panthers, Weatherman, the Ku Klux Klan, and

American Nazis were subjected to FBI spying and infiltration. One researcher who studied this era wrote, "Although the full extent of the FBI's infiltration and provocation of radical groups was not revealed until the mid-1970s, leftists in particular were acutely aware of the tactics federal and local law enforcement agencies were using to disrupt their organizing efforts. Many who witnessed this government interference in lawful organizing efforts concluded that social change could no longer be accomplished through traditional political means. Revolution, they felt, was the only solution."[25]

The extremist behavior of a handful of radicals plus the anticipation of FBI and Red Squad spying and provocation meant that guardedness and secrecy were daily fare among leftist activists, at least the more radical ones. In fact, evidence of such caution and care was considered a sign of seriousness of intent. Safe houses, noms de guerre, secret meetings, code names, and need-to-know policies were all part of the radical landscape, gleaned from movies, revolutionary manuals, political autobiographies, spy novels, and lore from around the world. Activists in this milieu took themselves very seriously, made lifetime commitments to their cause, and spent much of their time in study circles critically examining their own activities, as well as that of their competitors. The use of some form of criticism/self-criticism, an adaptation taken directly from Maoism, was a regular component of most NCM groups. Members of those New Communist organizations debated the correct line, produced tracts and newspapers, leafleted workers at factory gates, and preached revolution and armed struggle. In their dedication, those strident young Communists were determined not to repeat the mistakes of either the Old or the New Left.

A Typical Recruit

At the time I was living in San Francisco, having moved there in late 1974 after spending about four years living on a small island off the coast of Spain. Almost immediately I got involved in both feminist and gay political activities, which often involved different sets of friends and different venues.

For example, I was part of a volunteer collective of women who operated what was at that time San Francisco's only women's coffeehouse. The Full Moon Coffeehouse was a refuge for women in general, as well as an alternative to bars for lesbians. The owners were straight and gay, as were the women who frequented the place. As a volunteer there, I staffed the counter, arranged for performers, and set up a small bookstore. At times I was more involved with strictly gay issues, such as demonstrating to raise awareness about the unfair treatment of gays in Cuba. I undertook that type of political activity with a progressive gay group.

In addition, I read and studied Marxist texts, an interest that started when I was a Fulbright scholar in France, which happened to coincide with massive demonstrations against U.S. involvement in Vietnam as well as the events of May 1968, during which students (myself included) occupied the universities and eventually the French nation engaged in a general strike. Now, back in the United States in the mid-1970s, I took classes at both of the Bay Area's "liberation schools," where a range of courses on social change was offered. These were collectively run, private schools with free or low-cost classes at night and on weekends. They were taught by volunteer leftist intellectuals and activists. The early 1970s Liberation School was at first identified with independent Marxist and revolutionary circles, which had split into two parts, each sponsoring a school. The one that kept the name Liberation School was "hard-line" Marxist and Maoist; the other, the San Francisco Liberation School, was considered "social democratic" (i.e., less hard-line).[26] Eager learners took courses in basic Marxism, *The Communist Manifesto,* the politics of health care, leftist history of the U.S. labor movement, and the like.

I was so gung-ho about this that the folks who ran one of these schools invited me to teach courses there. I had already read Marx's *Das Kapital* three times. My life was steeped in New Communist Movement ideas and activities, and most of my friends and acquaintances were involved in similar activities. It was a short leap for me to get involved with a Marxist-Leninist organization.

A Convergence of Forces for a New Party

On analysis of the NCM, I realized that it shared the three important features identified with the New Age movement. A moral imperative, a call for personal transformation, and the recognition of the need for a leader were equally compelling principles to activists in the leftist milieus of the 1970s and 1980s.

The moral imperative — although quite different in its thrust from that felt by New Agers — was based on a Marxist-Leninist worldview that urged adherents to make a commitment to strive for a greater cause, the cause of the working people. The call for personal transformation was based on a general understanding that dedicated activists needed to change themselves fundamentally in order to meet the standards and demands of the working-class struggle and thereby achieve the goal of the moral imperative — and, very important, that change could take place only in a particular setting, a democratic-centralist cadre party. Finally, a leader was essential to bring these elements together and provide the necessary direction.

It was in that environment — serious and searching — that a confluence of factors and personalities resulted in the birth of the DWP, which drew on elements of the NCM while also being a creative concoction that had a particular appeal to certain types of activists. Marlene Dixon, with the support of her first circle of devotees, blended the seriousness of the Marxist-Leninist fighting party with a feminist perspective. This unique feature allowed the group to draw radicals from leftist circles as well as the women's movement. Dixon's theoretical orientation also meant that the DWP was aligned with a variant of political theory called world-systems theory that not only was sophisticated but also distinguished the party from the so-called China-liners or Soviet-liners.

In addition, the DWP professed openness to gays and lesbians — an understandable position given that many of the founders and early members were lesbians. In fact, most NCM groups were virulently antihomosexual, as well as dismissive of the women's movement.[27] In that way the DWP, although not a gay group, offered an organizational venue for progressive and left-leaning homosexuals, many of whom had just recently generated their own liberation movement around the time of the 1969 Stonewall Riots in New York City. San Francisco's gay community served as a fresh and lucrative recruiting ground for the DWP. Altogether then, with an innovative and unique allure, the DWP became a recognized competitor within the New Communist Movement and within the Left in general.

But the Party also was noted for something else. As Elbaum put it, the Democratic Workers Party "was notorious for its cult-like functioning even in a movement hardly known for democracy or openness."[28]

CHAPTER 7

The Founding of the Democratic Workers Party

The DWP was formed in 1974, during the heyday of the party-building movement, and was active until late 1985.[1] The group defined itself as a Marxist-Leninist, democratic-centralist, proletarian-feminist organization. "Marxist-Leninist" meant the application of class analysis to societal conditions and a full-time commitment. "Democratic-centralist" meant that the leadership was to be obeyed at all times and that the minority must submit to the majority once decisions were made. "Proletarian feminism" was Marlene Dixon's theoretical contribution, allowing the DWP to stand against both class prejudice and sexism and for the equality of all people. Although a key recruiting asset in the beginning, the concept of proletarian feminism became less prominent in Party literature and approaches after the first several years. Over time, concepts and issues tied specifically to the working class and then to "world socialism" were stressed more.

The Arrival of a Leader

Marlene Dixon was a large, loud woman who exuded a type of charisma that could be difficult for outsiders to comprehend.[2] Her personal style was abrasive, and she was stern and domineering. Nonetheless, Dixon was able to exact a commitment from her followers that entailed devotion to her person and undying defense of her actions as their leader. In 1980 a San Francisco newspaper ran an article about the DWP in relation to its electoral work. In it, a local observer said of DWP members, "These people are incredibly intelligent, but they are totally bananas for Marlene Dixon."[3]

MARLENE DIXON'S RISE TO PROMINENCE

Marlene Dixon had earned a Ph.D. at the University of California, Los Angeles, in the mid-sixties. She had taught sociology at the University of Chicago and at McGill University in Montreal. According to some of her former students and colleagues, during those years, she became interested in mass social psychology and group behavior modification. She studied Robert Jay Lifton's work on thought reform; and she studied and admired total communities, such as Synanon, and other directed methods of behavioral control, such as Alcoholics Anonymous. She spoke of these programs as providing positive ways to change people.

Dixon claimed to have participated in various leftist groups during the six years she taught at McGill. From that experience she formulated her analysis of the problems of political organization per se and the specific contradictions of the class forces at work in the North American Left. Dixon, like her hero Chairman Mao, believed that class differences hindered effective work methods and genuine successes in progressive movements. It was during this time in Canada that she said she "figured it all out," coming to certain conclusions about organization, survival, and effectiveness.[4]

In recounting her personal history, Dixon always mentioned her involvement at least since her college days in progressive movements; and like other progressive-minded academics at the time, she had supported Marxist tendencies within the mainstream disciplines, much to the dislike of reactionaries in the academy who were against radical change. As a result, she was among a number of left-leaning academics who were reprimanded — and in some cases purged from their jobs.

Because of her radical stance, Dixon had been quite popular among students at the University of Chicago, her first appointment. As a professor who spoke out for students' rights, she was able to draw a coterie of students. Former students of hers recalled that Dixon held seminars at her house, sometimes followed by drinking, songs, and poems. Accord-

ing to Dixon, the local police considered her teaching dangerously persuasive and labeled her a subversive. She said the university administration had been given this information by a student informer and police
undercover agent on campus.⁵ During that period, there were occasions
when Dixon seemed immobilized by fear and childlike. Students ran
errands for her; she began to have attendants and bodyguards; and after
a time she rarely went out alone.

The University of Chicago's decision not to rehire Dixon sparked a
student protest on campus and an occupation of the administration
building that lasted sixteen days. This event put Dixon's name on the
map of radicalism.⁶ In referring to those times, Dixon literally described
herself as a charismatic leader and as "a national leader fighting for
socialism and feminism."⁷ She believed that the news coverage of her
troubles with the university had been a key factor in bringing the topic
of the women's movement and equal rights to national attention.
Indeed, this event is listed in the Feminist Majority Foundation's on-
line *Feminist Chronicles*. For the year 1969, among other events, the Web
site notes: "Marlene Dixon, an Assistant Professor of Sociology, was
fired from the University of Chicago for alleged radical teachings and
being female. Her dismissal precipitated public demonstration in her
support of both women's liberation groups and the radical student
groups."⁸

An alternative, and rather harshly critical, point of view is presented by
Edward Shils, a professor of sociology, in a commentary on the same
period. Shils called Dixon an "incompetent young teacher" and noted that
"the department of sociology, in a series of decisions of a rare unanim-
ity — both a special departmental committee which had been asked to
assess her merits, and the department as a whole — voted against her continuation." According to Shils, Dixon was "backward in her studies,
[but] not backward in building a body of supporters among students." As
for his assessment of her scholarly work: "There was very little of it, and
it was of rather poor quality. I studied it carefully and then summarized
and assessed it with special reference to her knowledge of other work in
her field of interest and the merits of her achievement in comparison with
that work. In both respects, she came off poorly."⁹

At her next job, at McGill University, Dixon formed another coterie
of loyal students whom she advised and took great interest in, often invit-
ing them to political retreats at a small farm she owned.¹⁰ She lectured to
them about the need for political commitment to a movement and the
importance of the use of criticism/self-criticism. There are some indica-

tions that Dixon tried to pull together some kind of ongoing group in Canada, but her efforts were not successful.

THE CALIFORNIA CONNECTION

Also in the early 1970s, several small groups of activist women in San Francisco and Oakland were feeling particularly frustrated with their political efforts. They had been politically active since the sixties in one or several progressive social movements — the antiwar, anti-imperialist, women's, prison, and union and workplace movements. Some of these women knew one another directly; others were acquaintances or familiar through common social or political circles. The women began meeting together with the hope of finding a more productive way to channel their energies. As individuals they had been participating in different political study groups, which were popular at the time. Although as a group these women may not have agreed on a single identifying label, they considered themselves serious political women intent on working for social change in America — or, in their words, "bring[ing] about revolution."

A determined young woman named Virginia who had been part of this informal grouping recalled, "Things were percolating. We were meeting and throwing around ideas — vague and undefined — of a radical women's organization. We were already studying Marxism." Trish, a college graduate who at the time was in a relatively good profession and had been involved in various political causes, concurred: "We were meeting and talking and thinking about creating a women's pre-party 'something.'"

Meanwhile, at McGill, Dixon once again became embroiled in faculty infighting and threats of a purge. She began to come back to California on school breaks; perhaps she saw the writing on the wall and was looking toward a future away from Canada. In summer 1974, while on the West Coast, Dixon looked up one of her former students from Chicago. Dixon knew that Trish was living and working in San Francisco and was politically active in a number of leftist causes.

Trish had not seen or been in touch with Dixon since 1969, when Dixon held a summer teaching position in the Bay Area. On that visit, Trish and Dixon had a major disagreement over the People's Park incident in Berkeley. Centered on a small piece of land, about one square block and legally owned by the University of California, Berkeley, People's Park had become a symbol for human rights. Hippies, runaways, street people, and students "liberated" the neglected lot, declaring it the "people's park," and soon it became a popular Berkeley hangout. The state of California, the formal owner, resisted the takeover and tried to reclaim the property by surrounding it with a fence.

On May 15, 1969, known as Bloody Thursday, two hundred fifty Highway Patrol, police officers and Alameda County Sherriff's deputies confronted a crowd of about six thousand demonstrators protesting the erection of the fence around the park. One demonstrator was killed, another blinded, and more than one hundred citizens injured. By evening the National Guard was called in by then-Governor Ronald Reagan. This set off a rampage through the streets by thousands of angry students, the calling out of more police, and National Guard helicopters spraying tear gas around campus. Protests continued for almost two weeks, until the university chancellor said he supported leasing the park to the city of Berkeley, and a People's Park Council was formed. The park remains today as an open space.[11]

While Dixon and Trish were drinking as they debated about this incident, the two got into a heated argument. Dixon, in her usual overbearing style, thought the activities were all wrong and that she knew the best strategy. She got pretty nasty, deriding Trish for supporting the People's Park actions and calling her politically naive and stupid.

Because she and Dixon had not parted amicably, Trish was quite surprised to see Dixon at her door five years later. But Trish was even more struck by the person standing before her. Dixon told Trish that she had given up drinking; indeed, she had lost a lot of weight and looked good. She attributed all of this to having found political clarity in her study and practice of Marxism-Leninism.

Trish was entrenched in leftist study groups at the time. Now she saw her former professor as a living testament to correct political theory. Here was truly a way to change your life. Trish thought it would be a good idea to introduce Dixon to her political friends who had been meeting together in various study groups.

One of those young women, Rhonda, described her reaction to their first meeting with Dixon: "One day Trish said, 'My political friend has just arrived in town. Let's have a meeting with her to talk about radical women's groups.' So a bunch of us met at Trish and Luann's house. Trish's friend was there. She was dynamic, bright. Already then she was putting out the basis of a [political] line on women's oppression. I thought it was incredible, all this talk about the relation of women to capital. I remember thinking, 'Wow. These are the words!' So we decided to start a study group. We met several times. Then she, Marlene, said, 'Let's form a small organization.' Then within a few weeks, it was, 'We need leadership.' It was all her idea. She always set the tone and direction."

THE EARLY MEETINGS

During those first encounters, the women felt that Dixon was articulating in a very powerful way many of the things they each believed or had experienced to some degree: the sudden realization of the significance of Marxism-Leninism, the irreconcilable inadequacies of the existing pre-party formations in the New Communist Movement, and certainly the centrality of women's oppression. She was calling on them to live out their political beliefs with the same commitment and seriousness that she herself avowed. Dixon spoke with the assurance of an educated person, an experienced radical, and a known figure in the women's movement: after all, she had taught at universities, had written articles and theoretical pieces,[12] had given speeches at national conferences and rallies.

In other words, Dixon had a track record that far outshone the others in the room, who for the most part had working-class or "alternative" jobs — such as in a women's press collective, in a women's carpentry collective, as city employees, and as hospital and clerical workers. Several of them were unemployed. Also, Dixon was about thirty-eight at the time, which meant she was from seven to twenty years older than the other women.[13]

Virginia, one of the youngest in this group, recalled her opinion of Dixon: "I was extremely impressed. She could be quite charming and very articulate. She articulated many things I somehow felt about the world. At the time it was powerful. Looking back on it, I can see that I was naive. I mean I had had some leftist experience, but not enough to regard her critically. . . . Her having a Ph.D. wasn't particularly important one way or another. I was more shaped by the things she wrote. I had respected her writings. It stuck in my mind that this was someone I had read since high school. I liked the things she had written which brought a left perspective to the women's movement. I believed that she was known and recognized in the women's movement."

It became apparent now to the women that they were destined to be "professional revolutionaries." Suddenly what they had been thinking and feeling was being articulated, and they latched onto Dixon's words with a fervor. In describing this merger, this melding of people and ideas, the founders who were interviewed said without hesitation that Dixon was charismatic. They described her as intelligent, with stature and university training, as powerful, experienced, impressive, and serious. Not only was she well versed in Marxist theory, but she had a minor reputation as a radical feminist, in particular, for her theories on the role of women in capitalist society.

Having been born and raised in a working-class section of Los Angeles and having a self-proclaimed history of activism added the necessary radical components to Dixon's image and outlook. When she spoke of her political past (which she did repeatedly and often, particularly in the formative years of the DWP when she had a group of members around her), she described with flourish (and, according to some of her contemporaries, with great exaggeration) her years as an activist in the civil rights movement, community organizing efforts, the antiwar movement, the New Left and SDS, the women's movement, the New Communist Movement, and Canadian liberation movements. Dixon would boldly proclaim that she possessed impeccable credentials for the role of spokesperson and leader.

MOVING TOWARD A NEW ORGANIZATION

After Dixon began to attend the women's meetings, the discussions took on a new dimension. Before long Dixon proposed that they start their own political organization. She spoke with conviction and dynamism about actually forming a group, not just sitting around and talking about it. To many of the women in this early group, Dixon seemed larger than life; no doubt, Dixon's assessment of her own radical credentials was overblown. But to the women in the Bay Area she was manna from heaven — the impetus they needed.

All agreed that there needed to be an alternative to existing groups on the Left. Why couldn't they be the force behind creating such an alternative? They wanted to be free of what they saw as the ills rampant in other leftist groups, in particular, racism, sexism, and lack of direction. Of that decision to form their own group, Virginia remarked: "It was all part of a particular time. We did what we did out of what we thought was an appropriate response. We were part of a particular time in history. There was a political impetus to do it — and this was all your friends and all of your life. There was a utopian quality to it."

At one of their meetings, the women shared their personal histories. After all, they were talking about starting their own political organization, and self-revelation seemed a necessary step. As it turned out, it set a ritualistic precedent for the group. "Doing your class history" became standard practice for each new member. However, according to Rhonda, at the founding meetings this self-reflective exercise simply involved a participant recounting her class background and political experience, whereas by late 1975, once the organization took shape, class history sessions became more like lengthy interrogations of new members.

None of the founders whom I interviewed remembered Dixon presenting her class history at these meetings, at least not in the same way each of them had done — with trepidation. However, there were many occasions when she related her version of at least her recent past in academia. At these times, her words reflected the bitterness, exaggerated fears, and self-aggrandizement that characterized her behavior and her leadership. She expressed pride in her academic achievements but also insisted on the importance of her working-class background and the fact that she had endured many hardships as a woman in the early 1960s in pursuit of a college education and an academic career.

A favorite line of Dixon's, often repeated throughout the years in various Party documents, was the following: "I am a woman who has a Ph.D., a doctorate, and was a professor in University. But I was not born a professor — I was born a woman in the lower class and had to fight class prejudice and male prejudice every step of the way 'to go to college and realize the American dream.' What I learned was that the American dream was a pipe dream — an empty dream — and that it was built upon suffering, demanded it, created it."[14]

Dixon always spoke caustically of that period of her life; yet to some extent, academia, or at least academic debate and certain academics, remained a focal point of her interests. She regarded the academic experience as one in which she was shot down and betrayed, and she neither forgot nor forgave those who sided (or who she thought sided) against her. She spoke about academe and many of her former colleagues as corrupt, evil, the enemy; and she spent a great deal of energy expounding on the views of intellectuals and academics, primarily sociologists. The articles she contributed to one of the Party journals, *Synthesis* (later *Contemporary Marxism*), reveal her deeply felt animosity: "The Sisterhood Ripoff," "Sham Leninism: Yet Another Polemic Against Albert Szymanski," "Anticommunism: A Petty [sic] Bourgeois Necessity," "The Petty [sic] Bourgeois Politics of Research Collectives."[15]

Dixon's polemics were aimed at leftist and radical associations, such as the New American Movement (NAM), the Union of Radical Political Economists (URPE), and the Union of Marxist Social Scientists (UMSS); at feminists and socialist feminists; at others in the NCM; and at progressive academics such as Barbara Ehrenreich, Paul Piccone, and Albert Szymanski. Some on the Left felt that these polemics were out of line.[16]

Others rallied around them. Either way, Dixon's ideas were hard to ignore, for as the organization took shape, disseminating such materials consumed much of its time, energy, and money.

A PRE-PARTY FORMATION

After a protracted contract renewal fight at McGill, Dixon decided to give up teaching.[17] Of that experience, she said, "Those years of fighting were in one sense an irreparable loss to me, years stolen from my development and my thought in pursuit of the politics of truth. I decided to resign so that not one more hour should be stolen from me: no power on earth . . . would have persuaded me to spend one more moment combatting the mindless, malevolent stupidity of the Department of Sociology at McGill."[18]

She decided to return to California. She felt certain that her days in academic dreamland, as she called it, were over. Especially during the early years of the Party, she spoke of that decision with heartfelt emotion: she was returning to the working class, to where she was born and belonged.

Now, having met women who were equally enamored with the struggle and equally fed up with the system, during one of their meetings that summer of 1974, Dixon called the question. She urged them to take the step to form a serious, radical group, which she predicted would evolve into a disciplined Marxist party, a vanguard party that would lead the working-class revolution in the United States.

Afterward, Trish recalled that Dixon had predicted that within five years the group would have five thousand members. According to the recollections of some of the other women there, their evolution into an organization happened almost overnight. At one meeting they were a group; by the next they were a real "pre-party formation," as such Marxist groups were called at the time.

Virginia remembered both the thrill and the tension of those days: "I woke up one morning thinking, 'My god, I'm in a party now.' I was in a panic, feeling totally responsible for the class struggle. I knew that if I messed up now it was another nail in the coffin of the working class."

Thus Dixon's entrée was a total success: she presented herself as a worthy leader, complete with an awakening (the period of exile in Canada when she claimed to have figured it all out) and a personal myth (her rise up from the depths of the working class). And she spoke a language that inspired others to take action. The women accepted her professed leadership abilities, and her mysterious and unexpected arrival only increased her aura of specialness, giving her an almost cosmic, godlike quality. In effect, she answered the prayers of these earnest activists (and their early recruits) who on their own seemed unable to resolve the dilemma of how to create meaningful lives for themselves. At the same time, by joining up with Dixon and her cause, they felt useful and needed — for great was their mission, and surely every body was precious.

After Dixon met with Trish, Luann, Rhonda, Virginia, and the others who were interested in forming a radical women's group, it was Dixon who began quickly to transform their informal meetings into a formal organization. The structure of the group emanated from her: she solidified their amorphous ideas, instituted discipline, proposed the leadership, and set up security measures.

After numerous meetings were held throughout summer 1974, a Central Committee was elected by secret ballot at Dixon's urging. She assured the group that in spite of their small size, a leadership body was needed. As a supporting argument, she raised the example of the Chinese Communists, pointing out that Chairman Mao's party had begun with only six people and had had a Central Committee right from the start. Dixon suggested which members should comprise the leadership and included herself as the head. At that point Dixon was still employed by McGill. She returned to Canada for the fall semester, while the others continued to read and study. They all felt strongly that they were onto something special, so they kept their newly formed group secret.

Dixon returned to the Bay Area for a visit during her 1974 Christmas break. At an intense meeting with the other women, she presented her work "Principles of Dialectical Leadership," an eighteen-page paper outlining the norms of conduct for serious revolutionaries. This paper was considered the organization's first internal document.[19] At Dixon's direction, the small group wrote its first constitution; and, again at her suggestion, the Central Committee assigned itself the task of writing a position paper, "On the World Situation," a title that suggests the grandiosity of their vision. The following year, Dixon visited again during her spring break.

Several major decisions were made at these meetings: to accept a few more people into the group and to permit men to join. Though most of the founders were radical lesbians, they were not supporters of a separatist philosophy. As staunch Marxists, they believed capitalism was the enemy, not men. To reinforce that belief, Dixon, who was not a lesbian, emphasized that they were to focus on recruiting heterosexuals and that the organization had to maintain a "straight" image.

From the start Dixon insisted on setting up various units. She began the process of dividing up the group, small as it was. Some members were put in leadership positions; separate, closed meetings of this leadership circle were held before and after the general meetings. Immediately, it was clear that some of the women were being favored and pushed into leadership roles, that there was going to be a rigid hierarchy, and that there was a right or a wrong way, defined by Dixon.

Also, at this early stage Dixon instilled discipline and an ambience of secrecy. She talked about the group as a paramilitary formation, as she impressed on the others that what they were creating was so potent that the state (meaning the FBI or local police Red Squads) would immediately infiltrate if it knew what the women were up to.[20] Given that it was common knowledge that Senate investigation committees had been studying leftist activity in the wake of the recent bombing conspiracy by radicals across the nation,[21] as well as increased tension over the Patty Hearst incident, Dixon's caution did not seem particularly extreme or paranoid.

Michelle, one of the founders, commented on Dixon's guidance during that period: "She was forming us into the model. We did our first study of Meyer's cadre training. It was very slow and very serious. We studied, wrote papers, did a lot of criticism/self-criticism and class histories. She set it all up." Michelle was referring to *The Moulding of Communists: The Training of the Communist Cadre*, by Frank Meyer.[22] In this book, Meyer, a former leader in the Communist Party–U.S.A., describes in detail Communist Party training protocols and procedures and membership requirements and activities. After Dixon heavily edited the book, the Party's production team put out a revised version with the title *The Training of the Cadre*.[23] It was issued to members as a highly secret, numbered, internal document and was the Party's primary training manual, along with another book of Party writings, *The Militant's Guide*.[24] The purpose of studying *The Training of the Cadre* was to instill respect for the cadre ideal and engender in each militant a cadre transformation. The goal was to take a Party member from being a dedicated activist to a steeled revolutionary fighter.

Before long the group's founders realized that they were part of an underground organization. Having experienced frustration with the New Left — its looseness, macho attitudes, and lack of seriousness — and feeling a compulsion to do something with their political convictions (and, hence, their lives), the women were eager for organizational stability. They readily accepted Dixon's version of cadre training; for them, at last, this was the real thing. They saw themselves articulating, living,

and breathing a profound transformation of leftist politics. They felt serious and special. Their work took on new importance and a sense of
urgency. They prided themselves on being the founders and leaders of a
new kind of Marxist group, one that would help bring about revolution
in America, in the tradition of other great revolutionary movements.
Although adamant about not following the political line of any other leftist party (domestic or international), they regarded themselves as part of
the world Communist movement, in the tradition of the Third International founded by Lenin after his split with the Mensheviks. They especially admired the World War II resistance fighters, many of whom were
European and eastern European Communists. In effect, they modeled
themselves after a combination of Lenin's steeled Bolsheviks and Mao's
Red Guard.

The Development of Bounded Choice (Part 1)

Even at this early stage of the group's development, the self-sealing system
of cultic organization was beginning to form and the process that ultimately led to bounded choice was initiated. Certainly the political background of the members of this group was quite different from those who
joined up with Applewhite and Nettles. The motivation for coming
together, the style of leadership and organizational structure, the more
public nature of their political activism — these and other characteristics of
what eventually became the Democratic Workers Party were in stark contrast to those of Heaven's Gate. Nevertheless, there are many profound
parallels and similarities to be found in relation to the manifestation of
charismatic authority, transcendent belief, systems of control, and systems
of influence. Let us now examine the manner in which these four crucial
elements began to develop during this early stage of the DWP's history.

ESTABLISHING CHARISMATIC AUTHORITY

Charismatic leaders must exhibit three characteristics: effective oratory
skills, the ability to create myth and legend, and a capacity for innovation
and success.[25]

Oratory Skills.   Dixon was certainly an effective orator, as were Applewhite
and Nettles (although Nettles rarely spoke in public). All three leaders
were introduced into a group of strangers and left with a band of fol-

lowers. They also addressed public audiences with some effect, although all three tended to limit their public appearances, preferring to concentrate on their "captive" audiences.

All three leaders imparted much of their instruction and indoctrination by lecturing and teaching, in both formal and informal group settings. In the formative years, Dixon held Sunday morning classes at her house for a select group of members; in Heaven's Gate, followers gathered around the leaders at their campsite or in their communal living quarters. The adherents in both groups were taken in, rapt, swayed, and convinced enough to put their lives on the line for their leaders — literally, in the case of Heaven's Gate.

Applewhite, Nettles, and Dixon used language as a tool to motivate and persuade, creating their own terms, phraseology, and images for use within the group to encapsulate their followers' experiences. In both groups, a subset of followers responded to that language by making a dedicated commitment. Also, all three leaders used fear and guilt, as well as compassion and charm, to influence their followers, and all three were recognized as master controllers.

Given our understanding of charisma as a relationship, oratory skills can be effective only if there is an audience to provoke. In the two cases studied here, the audiences were carefully selected and ready for the message. Those who were less receptive or posed any kind of threat to the status quo either left the group on their own or were expelled, which left few if any doubting Thomases to serve as distractions for the loyalists.

Personal Myth and Legend.   Dixon was skilled at creating a story about herself that matched what her audience wanted to hear and fit perfectly with the times. In the context of the political movements and the activism of the day, she had — or said she had — all the right credentials. During the Party years, to my knowledge, no one (recruit or member) independently investigated Dixon's life history; that would have been unthinkable. Any questioning inside the organization was discouraged, usually with harsh criticism.

For example, in 1976 an academic, who joined the Party sometime the following year, was invited for a visit to see for herself the political organization Dixon was creating. As they drove around San Francisco, Dixon was enticing Janet to join, explaining to her that the cadre was shaping up and she was pleased with the results of her endeavors.

Janet recalled being impressed, so she asked Dixon "where she learned all this stuff"; but the sense conveyed to her was that it was a "big secret." She always refused to name exactly which groups she had been involved with in Canada, implying that she had some kind of clandestine training, "as though she'd been trained by the Chinese or something," said Janet. Reflecting further on that incident, Janet said, "I just accepted and didn't investigate. I was naive, and just so eager to become the perfect cadre."

An attitude of blind acceptance was the norm in the DWP: recruits who asked too many questions were immediately dropped, criticized, and labeled as "agents," that is, police or government spies. Some expelled members were treated the same way, which ensured that active members would pay no heed to them should they decide to speak out or reveal "Party secrets." That type of silencing tactic was reinforced by a strict "no gossip" rule.

Dixon's version of her life in the Left seems to have been exaggerated or embellished. She told her followers, for example, that she had been a "great leader" in the civil rights movement and had led marches to Selma and Montgomery, which would have been while she was a college student. Later it was learned that she had gone to one sit-in in the South with a busload of other students from the university in Los Angeles; she was one face among thousands. Nothing more was ever learned about her involvement in that movement or any other; yet Dixon was able to convince her followers in the DWP that she was exactly the leader they were looking for, and once she got herself positioned, she did not let go. Whenever she was challenged, she would bring up her working-class origins and extensive political background as reasons for her followers to remain steadfast in their support of her.

Innovation and Success.   All three leaders — Dixon, and Applewhite and Nettles — were innovators. Perhaps their success was limited, given that neither group is still around. Nevertheless, forming a group, keeping it going, and being supported by it for more than ten years in the case of Dixon (and Nettles) and more than twenty in the case of Applewhite is no small feat, from any perspective. That alone indicates initiative, competence, and success at organization building.

All three depended on their members for financial support while at the same time living apart and keeping secrets from them. In both Heaven's Gate and the DWP members donated money to support the organization — from either inheritances, personal savings, or wages. During the life spans of these two organizations, none of the three leaders was ever required to work at an outside job. Like most charismatic leaders, Dixon, Applewhite, and Nettles expected to be supported by their followers. And the followers assumed this burden as a sacred and revolutionary obligation.

As for theoretical innovation, Dixon introduced new concepts pertaining to women as a revolutionary force, organizational possibilities on the Left, and a variety of political ideas and solutions. She had something to say about *everything*. Dixon was unique in her blending of Marxism and feminism — a combination that worked in that era. She was able to attract both women and men who were fed up with the Left and therefore regarded Dixon's worldview as special, contemporary, and especially revolutionary.

In fact, Dixon referred to her unique brand of revolutionary feminism and the fact that the group was founded and led by women as "our secret weapon." Initially, Dixon was accepted as a leader because more than anything she seemed to articulate what the others were feeling — both their frustrations with leftist movements and their need for a guiding worldview. Dixon was skilled at putting that together and at imparting a sense of urgency about being part of a new and special organization.

DEVELOPING TRANSCENDENT BELIEF

Whereas Heaven's Gate, despite the group's own protestations, was religious in orientation, the DWP was political. One group was looking for heavenly salvation; the other had its feet planted firmly on the ground.

The DWP professed a political goal and had a specific agenda that involved working with or for other people. Party members wanted to change the world, and they believed their work would lead in that direction. They wanted to initiate social justice and ultimately achieve working-class salvation. The Party's philosophy, outlook, and practice were validated through a connection to basic Marxist texts (Marx, Lenin, and Mao, in particular) and revolutionary traditions that used a democratic-centralist model.

Both groups' belief systems, however, were transcendent: for Heaven's Gate, resurrection was life; for the DWP, revolution was life. The here and now was insufficient for the members of both groups. DWP militants believed that eventually the capitalist system was going to be overthrown. In addition, a gnawing sense of urgency was a compelling feature in both groups. Time was short: Dixon predicted that insurrectionary conditions would emerge in the United States within two decades; Applewhite and Nettles predicted the Demonstration and then the coming of the spaceships. Consequently, life in both groups was governed by a crisis mentality that guided their work and the underlying intensity of daily life.

Both groups upheld the ideal of personal transformation as the key to promised glory. In Heaven's Gate, it was the process of metamorphosis brought about by the daily struggle of each student in the Class, whereas in the DWP, a militant aspired to be a steeled cadre, a selfless worker for social justice and economic equality. Errors and backsliding were handled through criticism sessions, and the concept that the whole was greater than the sum of its parts was integral to the formation of the Party and the indoctrination of early members. A DWP militant never acted alone, always feeling the watchful eye of a comrade and, more important, one's internal Party voice.

Members of both groups were motivated by a compelling moral imperative. The DWP's "class consciousness" was akin to the Next Level's "deposit of knowledge." In other words, in each case, once you *knew*, you *had* to join. The alternative was unthinkable.

Both groups were dominated by a deterministic undercurrent, which applied not only to each individual but to all life events as well. In Heaven's Gate, everything was regarded as "the design" of the Next Level; in the DWP, the world was guided by economic determinism, as first outlined by Marx. Dixon believed that men made history, but she also held strongly that world events were on a predestined trajectory: the fall of capitalism was inevitable. Once such a deterministic outlook is accepted as true, then it becomes irrational to act out of sync with what was surely going to happen. In that way, the belief system helped to shape behavior.

Both groups were separatist in their sectarian and reclusive ways. This meant they also needed enemies. Both were essentially antimainstream — not unusual for the time — and considered that "bourgeois" or "human" life merely pulled you down, took you away from your greater purpose. There was no middle ground, no sitting on the fence. Someone was either for or against the group.

Both groups engaged in a holy war against their stated enemies. In Heaven's Gate, it was "human" life, human emotions and attachments, and the evil discarnates, Lucifer's "angels." In the DWP, the enemies were the capitalist class, the petite bourgeoisie, and other leftists. Ultimately, the DWP, like Heaven's Gate, believed it had the only way; all other belief systems were dismissed as lacking seriousness and as unworthy.

INSTITUTING SYSTEMS OF CONTROL

When a curious outsider (who later became a Party member) asked Dixon, "How do you get all those people to abide by the discipline, to follow orders all the time?" Dixon leaned over, looked him in the eye, and replied, "With a little carrot and a lot of stick."

The DWP and Heaven's Gate are strikingly similar in the control mechanisms they instituted to instill discipline and loyalty to the leaders and the mission. There were also some vivid differences. Both groups were hierarchical, with an inner circle around the leaders. In both groups, almost all decisions (and certainly all substantive decisions) were made at the top of the pyramid. DWP members had a slightly more unrealistic grasp of their role in group decision making. Militants were expected to "take initiative," within the bounds of discipline; yet the reality of their everyday lives gave them very little of consequence to make decisions about. Eventually, a militant who thought she was taking initiative would be "reined in" and criticized for "careerism," "grandstanding," "factionalizing," or a variety of other charges that served to stifle further efforts at independent action and to set an example for others.

Both groups had abundant rules and regulations, which included having members take on new names, pool their income and resources, work at assigned tasks, obtain permission for personal requests, and the like. Both had a "no gossip" rule that was key to keeping members from talking with each other about group-related matters or personal concerns. In that way any venues for discussing doubts were effectively eliminated. In effect, members were isolated from each other and at the same time constantly surrounded by the group and serving as monitors of group norms. In that sense, the group was omnipresent, even when members were away from the central locations. The result in both groups was a false sense of intimacy and togetherness (called "comradeship" in the DWP, "crew-mindedness" in Heaven's Gate) in the midst of barriers to deep relationships or even deep conversations.

Also, in both groups, it was unacceptable to be critical of the leaders. That principle resulted in unquestioning acceptance of a double standard. That was particularly the case in the DWP, where the leader committed overt violations of the norms — at least in the presence of her inner circle, who colluded in upholding the vision of the "perfect" leader. In Heaven's Gate, the mystery surrounding the leaders' whereabouts most of the time is an example of the double standard. Students were expected to reveal and divulge all and abide by strict rules, but they did not know if their leaders were doing the same. How would they have felt, for example, if they had discovered that during all those years when they were forbidden contact with their families, their Older Member Ti was regularly writing motherly letters to her eldest daughter, Terrie, back home? This was revealed by Terrie after the suicides.[26]

Both groups also held to an androgynous ideal, which was used as a means of control. In Heaven's Gate, the vision of the genderless member of the Next Level was the ideal to which they aspired; in turn, they applied the genderless norm to themselves, hiding their sexuality and gender and denying all sexual inclinations.

Interestingly, the DWP preached its own version of such an ideal. The "androgyny principle" in the Party was defined as "the rejection of secondary human (sexual) characteristics in order to focus on the principal aspects of ourselves: our social and human totality."[27] That concept had two facets. First, militants were not supposed to see each other as male or female but as comrades in the struggle, "as equals, who judge each other as human beings and not in terms of sex roles."[28] Second, the spirit of service was "desexed." That is, in the larger society service is an attribute typically applied to women, whereas in the DWP it was "found equally in men and women."[29]

In both groups an androgyny principle as a guiding norm served to justify gender-related systems of control. Specifically, they concerned personal relationships, emotional displays, sexuality, childbirth, and child rearing. In addition, the ideal engendered a pervasive attitude of suppression and self-denial in both Heaven's Gate and the DWP.

FORMING SYSTEMS OF INFLUENCE

There are some clear similarities and differences in the systems of influence identified in the two groups. One can see that each group had its own way of expressing particular modes of influence; yet these modes are similar in substance if not in wording and attitude. For example, both groups valued personal awakening. In Heaven's Gate, it was expressed as a "soul deposit" and a "deposit of knowledge" that led a person to the group and justified a commitment to it. In the DWP, a person's awakening came through "grasping a Marxist analysis," which gave one "class consciousness" that led to joining the group and making a commitment.

Both groups believed in change through deliberate transformation. In Heaven's Gate, it was thought of as a physical metamorphosis brought about by Next Level training in overcoming all human thinking and ways. In the DWP, it was regarded as cadre transformation, brought about by training and class-standpoint struggle to overcome all bourgeois and petit bourgeois thinking and behavior. In both groups, members believed that the process was a willing transformation and that everything else (the outside world, the media, etc.) was brainwashing. In jest, Applewhite and his students liked to make comments about willingly brainwashing themselves to get rid of human nastiness and ugliness. In the DWP, there was specialized training to lead the militants to understand that they were choosing to "willfully" transform themselves, that the leader was not practicing brainwashing, as was done in cults. One of my assignments as a Party School teacher was to lead this very training.

Self-renunciation was important in both groups. In Heaven's Gate, the ideal was the genderless, emotionless Next Level creature; in the DWP, it was the steeled cadre, the Bolshevik without emotion, obsessed with the cause of building the Party. Members held themselves to a standard that said: "What would my Older Member *have* me do?" or "What would a good Bolshevik do?" Both believed that the whole was greater than the sum of its parts and that individualism was counter to their goals. Members in both groups detested individual thinking and criticized any expression of individualism. Independent activity was not allowed in either group. In one group, independent action was considered "human" and therefore despicable; in the other, it was regarded as factionalizing, undermining, anti-Party, and "despicable bourgeois behavior."

Differences in the two groups' systems of influence centered primarily on the tenor of daily life. In Heaven's Gate, members' days revolved around training exercises to ready themselves for Next Level pickup, as well as various tasks devised by the leaders, including maintaining their residence as a model spacecraft. They worked hard but also had a slightly relaxed environment, with bouts of TV watching and long nights of sleep.

In contrast, DWP militants, striving for their cadre ideal, worked long hours, day after month after year. They toiled in the Party's print shop or at tedious administrative duties or other time-consuming assignments. Given their daily workloads, militants struggled to find time to meet the burdensome fund-raising and recruitment quotas, sell their papers, distribute literature, talk to potential recruits, put out the Party line at work or elsewhere, keep up with political study and other internal campaigns, and on and on. It was a frenzied and exhausting lifestyle. (See fig. 10.)

Submission to the organization was the ruling principle, and in the DWP there was intense pressure to conform. Not only were militants to strive for the self-imposed pressure of cadre life; they were to be agents of pressure on each other. From *The Training of the Cadre* members learned they were to have an "inner sense of self-critical urgency which cadre Communists constantly communicate one to another."[30] As Meredith, a longtime member, recalled, "The social pressure was great, with encouragement from the trusted friends who had recruited me. I

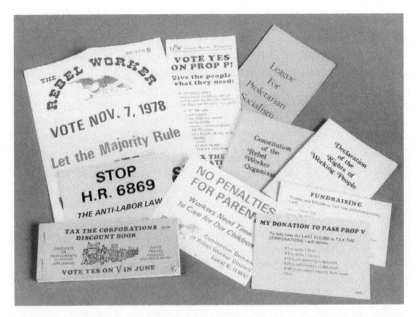

FIGURE 10. A sampling of booklets, flyers, raffle ticket books, fund-raising cards, bumper stickers, voting cards, and other literature distributed by DWP members over the years.

became bound and determined to be a worthy member of this elite community, to meet the challenge of changing the world."[31]

DWP members believed that the desired personal transformation came about only by engaging in class-standpoint struggle and collective criticism sessions. Criticism/self-criticism was a process by which a person accounted for a statement or action that was regarded as anti-Party or politically incorrect. Any act or thought was legitimate material for scrutiny, for class-standpoint analysis. Criticisms could be raised by the individual, by another comrade, or by someone in leadership. All criticisms were to be accepted. "Accepted" did not mean superficial agreement; it was to be internalized for the purpose of reforming one's class standpoint. "While our fellow comrades are absolutely essential to the process of self-changing, what is crucial in the last analysis is the cadre's own self-understanding," wrote Dixon. "That is why we do not ask for passive acceptance of criticism."[32]

The Militant's Guide cautioned militants against a defensive posture: "Defensiveness views criticism as a threat, not a potential means and aid to practice and self-transformation. . . . The worst result of nonstruggle attitudes is to stop the growth process both of cadre and of the party as a whole."[33] Militants understood that "the consistent practice of criticism and self-criticism [was] absolutely essential to the party."[34] Two former cadres and longtime members described that sentiment:

> *David:* We were totally dedicated to the cause of the oppressed. We strove to live up to an impossible ideal, using the most extreme criticism of the smallest errors or "incorrect" attitudes to change ourselves.[35]

> *Meredith:* In our group, criticism/self-criticism, used daily, was the primary method of control. I remember so clearly one of the first sessions that targeted me. Sitting in a circle being berated and accused of misdeeds by the group, I felt like my head was literally being yanked from my shoulders, turned around 180 degrees, and set down backwards. I stopped seeing, stopped thinking, stopped speaking my mind. In that experience, I began to surrender my vision, my mind, my personal experience, and my soul, and to internalize the idea that due to my middle-class background, my own thoughts, ideas, and gut reactions were at best, suspect, and at worst, downright evil.[36]

The encadrification process was to be internalized "to the point of creating a spontaneously loyal servant of the class struggle who has no competing interests."[37] That transformational philosophy rested on the following, as some former DWP members wrote: "total selflessness, absolute devotion to the working class, courage, iron will, and the ability to find one's bearings independently. DWP militants, sincerely believing in those virtues and wanting to approximate the ideal, spent innumerable hours in training programs for cadre development."[38] The practical outcome of that belief was separation from most of the rest of society that was not involved in the DWP or some phase of its work. Specifically, it meant that militants left behind families and friends who were not recruitable, and other personal relationships were minimized and considered unimportant. Such personal matters were not discussed (unless they became the subject of a criticism).

Learning to stifle emotion became each militant's political and personal goal for self-transformation. "Objective" and "subjective" were two widely used terms in relation to the demand to be emotionless. To be subjective meant putting oneself before the Party, a "me-first" attitude, selfish individualism. To be objective, a goal militants were to constantly strive for, meant putting the Party first and applying scientific, Marxist analysis to one's thoughts, feelings, and actions.

Thus no matter how harsh a criticism, a militant was not allowed to show emotion or cry. If someone being criticized began to cry, she was told to leave the room and return composed. After a time, tears were not seen. Militants did not talk about personal needs, feelings, or relationships; did not talk about their families; and did not express regret over not having free time, holidays with family, or time for personal affairs. Such matters were viewed as petty and trivial in light of what the DWP set out to do and in the face of the commitment to contribute to the struggle.

Given the harsh nature of daily life in the DWP, one might wonder, why would anyone join or stay? Women's interest in joining an organization founded and led by women is perhaps readily understandable, especially at a time when options for political activism for women were somewhat limited. But why did men join? What was the attraction for them?

Carter was one of the first men to join, when the Party was in its formative days in 1975. He worked at a local food cooperative in one of San Francisco's progressive neighborhoods and had a young child. He was close friends with several of the Party's founders. In Carter's opinion, "Male Left leadership [in other groups] seemed pompous and uncaring. So it made sense to have an organization founded and led by women. That didn't bother me. In fact, I regarded it as a privilege to be accepted as a man. I thought the strong criticism was the price you pay."

Meanwhile, for Toby, another rank-and-file cadre man, the organization made sense on an emotional level. Toby had always considered himself a feminist, or pro-feminist, and regarded the feminist revolution as a continuation of the civil rights and antiwar movements, as well as a complement to the gay rights movement, which he had a personal stake in. That the Party was founded and led by women struck a chord with him. Toby explained, "Most of why I joined the Party, though, was rooted in emotional as opposed to intellectual reasons. I had a visceral dislike of prejudice and discrimination from a very early age. It seemed to me the world would be a much better place without bigots and bullies. The bigots I saw were mostly White men. Most of the bullies were male as well."

Other reasons had less to do with the feminist aspect than with the DWP's overall revolutionary vanguardism and serious attitude. Tyrone, who had been an upper-level cadre and at times in the inner circle, explained, "It was the seventies. I didn't want to belong to any part of the mainstream. I didn't want to be a lawyer or something like that. I had no grounding in career or family or traditional values. The Party seemed just the opposite of all that."

Women who joined had similar attitudes. For example, Meredith said, "I believed that by giving up my own self-interests I could serve a greater purpose and accomplish something in the world."[39] Following others, she moved almost one thousand miles across the country to join.

Former cadre Marguerite, who was among the first rung of joiners in 1975, said, "Are you kidding? I was thrilled to join the Party . . . to be part of the club. Being gay, I was already marginalized, so for some group to want you . . . well, I was all for it."

Doris, a cadre member for about eight years, said, "I have thought back on what originally motivated me to join — as a political person I wanted to be more effective to really bring about change. I believed a disciplined organization was necessary to make those changes in this country. I saw the seriousness of the Party and I was frustrated with the New Left. All my hopes and dreams for a truly human society where people controlled their own lives and resources, and could live in dignity and respect, were exemplified by the Party. I saw that through struggle I would have to change in the process if I was to be a part of building a new world, and the Party took that transformation very seriously."

• • •

The basic tenets of the DWP's ideology and methodologies flowed naturally from the beliefs, trends, and organizational forms upheld generally by the New Communist Movement and imposed specifically in the Party setting. They were

- The concept of a tightly disciplined organization
- The need for a strong leader and centralized decision making
- The requisite personal transformation by means of class-standpoint struggle.

These worked together to create a pre-party formation to the liking of charismatic leader Marlene Dixon.

Those who were emboldened by Dixon's worldview jumped headlong into the emerging group, making a commitment to the cause and to their personal political development and transformation. They did so according to the group's guidelines and under the direction of its leaders. At the same time, the DWP was moving inexorably toward the self-sealing atmosphere of a full-scale cult.

CHAPTER 8

The Cadre Formation

The founders of the new party had no specific timetable for their revolution. But in the beginning they thought it was possible to build a revolutionary workers' movement and foresaw the seizure of state power — although they did not necessarily believe that event would occur in their lifetimes. Yet, with deep conviction, they felt that their particular political understanding of the contradictions in capitalism and their own experiences as women heightened their awareness of the need for a more just society. As they saw it, that set of factors made them part of an inevitable process, giving them a place in the history of humankind.

In the day-to-day process of the DWP's formation, everything that happened took on a seriousness heretofore unknown — the directed study, the intensity of the debates, the sophistication of Dixon's writings and polemics, the acceptance of discipline, the lengthy meetings, the institutionalization of criticism and self-criticism, even the first expulsion of one of the founders,[1] as we shall see as the story unfolds.

The Formation of the Party

In the minds of the founding members and by her own declarations, Dixon began to represent the living embodiment of their goals and ideals. Now the founders and their newly recruited members, through the process of cadre transformation as outlined and guided by Dixon, could be true revolutionaries, with their own organization and their own revolutionary leadership.

The members spent more and more time together, bound by a shared political commitment and a vision of the future. Their energies in every waking hour were spent on perfecting themselves in the image of the cadre ideal. They worked feverishly toward building a party that would be new and different, Marxist and feminist, nondogmatic and American. They knew that it was not an easy calling.

Virginia reflected on the intense feelings of those early days: "There was a strong sense that one must be willing to make sacrifices and be very committed. The view was that it's a dirty job and someone has to do it. We lived by the words in that famous Brecht poem, you know . . ." And she began to recite

> Alas, we
> Who wished to lay the foundations of kindness
> Could not ourselves be kind.
> But you, when at last it comes to pass
> That man can help his fellow man,
> Do not judge us
> Too harshly.[2]

Then she sighed and said, "That justifies a lot of things." Virginia's comment illustrates the depth of their commitment to the vision.

RECRUITMENT AND BONDING

Dixon went back to Canada at the end of spring break 1975 to finish up the semester, while the others continued studying and writing a position paper, "On the World Situation." During that spring and summer, some very cautious recruitment went on, and a small number of like-minded close friends, spouses, and relatives were brought into the group. It was also during this time that I was courted and made the decision to join. I was an acquaintance of several of the founders and traveled in the same social circles. I did not know at first that they belonged to an actual political organization but simply knew that these women were political activists.

One of them, Eleanor, lived around the corner from me in the Castro district of San Francisco. I would run into her on the street and she would invite me for coffee. At the time I was working at the local leftist bookstore and writing short stories and poetry. She was a tall woman who always spoke very fast, in a breathless way. She had a way of presenting ideas with passion and clarity. She knew how to involve one in the conversation, so afterward I felt like I was both learning and being listened to with respect, as though my opinions and ideas mattered. I was somewhat familiar with the disorganization and lack of seriousness of the macho male Left, as we called it, and also I had had some negative experiences in the women's movement that left me feeling as though it was really a predominantly middle-class movement with goals and perspectives that differed too much from mine. Consequently, I always enjoyed the times I ran into Eleanor. Our meetings left me curious, and anxious for more.

One day Eleanor asked if she could come to my apartment with a friend to talk about something in private. "Sure," I said, and we set a date and time. I wondered what it was going to be about and spent several nights restless with expectation.

Finally, one afternoon Eleanor and her friend arrived at my place. I recognized the other woman from around the Castro district. I served them tea in my small studio apartment. After a few moments of chitchat, they got down to their agenda. Eleanor explained that they were running a study group called Women and the State. It involved weekly meetings to discuss readings and issues related to the role of women in our society. Since I was still relatively new in town, I thought this would be a good way to meet people, and I was also keenly interested in the subject, as Eleanor knew. They showed me a small mimeographed pamphlet outlining the goals and principles of the study group. If I agreed with them, I was told, then I could start attending.

I readily agreed. It seemed like a wonderful opportunity, and I was thrilled that they were asking me. Before leaving, they told me to not tell anyone else.

"Why?" I naively asked.

"Oh," said Eleanor, "we don't want too many people to know about it because we don't want it to get too big."

What I did not know and was not told was that Women and the State was a front group for their budding organization, a way to target women in the community and draw them into the outer layer of their political circle. Also, I learned later, there were other study groups with different areas of focus, such as one for factory workers, one for hospital workers, and so on, and militants in those workplaces were to recruit into the study groups from among their coworkers.

Friendship and coworker networks served as the main fields for har-

FIGURE 11. The author on her way to a study group meeting in 1975. The Women and the State study group was one entrée into the Party at that time. (Janja Lalich)

vesting recruits interested in political issues, class struggle, third world revolutions, women's rights, and so on. Essentially they were using classic Communist recruiting techniques, but this was not obvious to those who were the targets. The courtship, approach, and invitation of other members were generally quite similar to the process I experienced.

The study groups were small, usually fewer than ten participants. Several people at each group were already members of the background organization, although that was not revealed. As study group members we were given assignments, asked to make oral presentations, and encouraged to join local political actions, such as helping out at strike picket lines. We were carefully observed and discussed in private; those of us who showed potential were groomed for the next stage.

After about six weeks in Women and the State, once again Eleanor asked if we could have a private meeting at my apartment. This time another person arrived with her, again someone I knew from common friends and local political activity. The air in my apartment was heavy with tension as we sat down.

Eleanor began, "We've been very pleased with how you've handled yourself in the study group. And, well, it seems that you are in complete unity with the idea that what's needed to make change in this country is a vanguard party."

I listened and nodded in agreement. She continued, "What would you think if we told you that there is such a party?" At first I did not really grasp what she was saying.

"What do you mean?" I muttered.

"Well, we couldn't tell you this before, but there is an organization behind Women and the State. It organized the study group and gives it leadership and guidance. We belong to it. It's not really a party yet, but a pre-party formation. And, well, you know how dangerous this is with the FBI around everything, so it's a secret cell."

I wanted to know more: where, how many members, who else was in it? I was told that they could not reveal that information and it was better not to know, for my own safety. But they did tell me that it was a women's organization and that it was international. They implied that it was very large.

"Wouldn't you like to apply?" Eleanor's companion asked. "It seems like everything you've done to this point leads to this. Don't you agree?"

Eleanor leaned over, her face almost touching mine. She looked me in the eyes and said, "Isn't this what you've been waiting for?"

That was all it took. I asked for the application.

The acceptance process was long and drawn out. I had to fill out a lengthy application that asked for personal history, financial information, past political activities, and more. I was interviewed again after the application was reviewed and then finally told I was accepted. Shortly after that I was told to go to a house where I knew several members lived for a special orientation meeting. Two of my best friends who were being recruited at the same time were told the same thing, so we went together. I did not know what to expect, or that Dixon would be there.

In fact, when I first met Marlene Dixon in 1975 I did not know who she was or what her role in the group was. The group itself did not have a name at that time, or at least not to my knowledge. As I recall it, when we entered the house, we were told that we would be meeting a woman who was part of the group to go over some final matters. It happened pretty quickly, with a hush-hush tone to it all. Four of us new recruits sat on a funky old couch in anticipation, while the others were rushing back and forth and seeming very uptight. We waited, wondering, and then there was some rustling around in the next room. I remember being mildly stunned by the appearance of the large woman who walked through the doorway. She looked a bit disheveled and was obviously older than the rest of us. I remember that she wore brown shapeless slacks and some kind of overblouse. Her hair was medium length, dishwater blond, in no particular style. She had a big face, with puffy cheeks, and her front teeth protruded a bit. But when she entered the room she took control. She plunked herself down in front of us and delivered a short speech about security and the significance of what we were doing. She wanted assurances of our commitment to the cause. She asked us a few curt questions, waited for each of us to answer, exuding impatience all the while. In a flash, she was gone. I don't think they even told us her name.

When I asked Marguerite her recollections, she said: "I remember very little of that day. For some reason I remember that as we were standing on the porch, Justine told us to pick a Party name. I was thrilled to be called Deborah for some reason, probably because I was able to think of it quickly. I think there were four of us [new recruits] there. I have no idea what Marlene said really, but I came away with the idea that she was a representative of a worldwide party, which metaphorically speaking she probably thought she was. That is one of the problems with metaphors. I honestly can't remember anything else. Weird, isn't it? I think I was mainly kind of overwhelmed. I had committed myself for my life to this. I thought it was truly big. Most everyone I knew in San Francisco were members. Wow. God, it seems so weird now."

By fall 1975 the "org," as we called it in those days before it had a name, had about forty members and a growing recruitment pool. At that stage, there were fewer than ten men in the group. The female-to-male ratio evened out over the years, although there were always more women than men in the group, sometimes twice as many. One year after the founding meetings, this core group was solidified in its commitment, and Dixon was firmly established as the theoretical and organizational leader.

Initially, the group was clandestine, with a paramilitary tone to its internal literature and training. Membership was to be kept secret. For the most part, within a matter of weeks or months, most of those who joined broke off with friends or acquaintances who were not part of the group. New members were required to assume a Party name. This was a first name only, and thereafter the young militants were known as Comrade Brenda, Comrade Gus, and so on. There was a great deal of secretiveness surrounding membership, meetings, and activities, as well as a plethora of security guidelines and other rules of behavior. Most members did not know one another's real names, where they worked, or even what their Party assignment was if they were not in the same area of work (at that time called a department). The Party required a twenty-four-hour commitment, which meant little time for family or other interests.

COLLECTIVE SECRETS

Around the time I was joining Women and the State, Dixon was relocating to San Francisco. A small house was rented for her, and the other women helped her to move in. They painted and got the house ready, making it a comfortable space for her. She did not get a job; instead she wrote, studied, led criticisms, and conducted political education. (Initially Dixon's financial support came from her savings, but very quickly it came from members' monthly dues.) When the others visited her, they were ordered around, told to clean up, empty her ashtrays, and open her sodas. Often it appeared as though she had been lying around in bed for days reading spy novels.

This was not lost on everyone, despite their adulation. Rhonda, one of the founders, believed mightily in what the women were creating together. Plus, her lover at the time and all of her best friends were part of this new venture. "Through long babbling conversations," recalled Rhonda, "Marlene would convince me that she learned about the enemy by reading spy novels." In describing this formative period, Rhonda said, "I thought all this was pretty bizarre, but I went along with it. I knew if I said something, she'd go crazy. I didn't want her screaming at me."

With such behavior on both sides, a double standard took hold early on: Dixon was never held accountable in the ways her followers were, nor did she ever live by the organization's rigid rules and norms that she herself put in place.

During that summer in 1975, several of the founders had at least one uncomfortable encounter with Dixon, who apparently was not as reformed in her alcoholism as she had attested. When these incidents occurred, Dixon behaved wildly, making inappropriate comments and gestures. The young believers were stunned, taken aback, and scared. Yet because of Dixon's role as their new leader and their view of her as special, they excused her behavior.

"You have to understand, I held her as a god. I was terrified because she had an evil side to her, but there was also a level of brilliance that kept

me from questioning these things," explained Trish. Rhonda had a similar attitude: "No one would talk about it. To myself I thought, well, we
have to protect her because she's so important. This was just a momen-
tary aberration and the important thing was to protect her reputation."

Such rationalizations were reinforced by Eleanor, Dixon's strongest
supporter among the founders. Luann remembered calling Eleanor after
one incident and feeling that she was very unsympathetic: "She said we
[Luann and Penny] should have taken control of the situation. She called
us liberal and blamed it on us." To be called liberal in this context was a
harsh criticism, adopted from the writings of Chairman Mao. It meant
that a person was a political "limp noodle," had no principles, and was not
willing to defend the Party.

Trish encountered the same reaction: "When I mentioned it to
Eleanor, I got severely criticized. She said I should just let her [Marlene]
pour the booze down, let her do what she wants. She said I was just being
liberal. I then shut it out of my mind and lived in a fantasy."

Zola made the mistake of mentioning a bad experience with Marlene
to one of the other women in the group. Zola remembered that not long
afterward, when she was at Eleanor's house, Eleanor sat her down for a
very serious talk. "She said it wasn't good to talk to *anyone* about
Marlene's drinking problem. . . . She said the State could use it against
Marlene, against us. She brought up some example from the Black
Panthers or something. The gist was to keep my mouth shut; this was not
to be talked about. I didn't know much about what the State would or
wouldn't do — and I guess it made sense to me to protect a weakness."

Encounters such as those just described and the individual rationalizations that followed ensured that as an organization the DWP would
abide no open discussion of this weakness — or any others that Dixon
might possess. Until very near the final breakup of the DWP, from a very
early juncture, Dixon's relationship with Eleanor was key to the smooth
functioning of the organization, as well as to members' devoted adherence to Dixon's leadership. From the very first meetings, Eleanor was
drawn to Dixon's leadership style; she acknowledged it, and her admira-
tion for Marlene was obvious to the others. Very quickly Eleanor became
Dixon's staunchest supporter in all things — theoretical, organizational,
and personal. Eleanor did not have an outside job, which allowed her to
spend most of her time at Dixon's side. One of the other founders said
Eleanor was "like the star's agent who does the dirty work in the background." Eleanor soon became Dixon's second-in-command, a position
she held for the next ten years.

The collaboration of Eleanor and, later, other upper- and middle-level leaders in hushing up Dixon's inappropriate behavior began a pattern of leadership secrets and corruption and an attitude of blaming the militants to cover leadership errors or inadequacies. In a document written after the DWP disbanded, three former leaders (including me) described this dynamic, stating that there was a shared view among the middle-level leadership that only those in the leadership could understand Dixon's erratic and unpredictable behavior and that it was our responsibility as leaders to hide it from everyone else. At the time, we did not think we were being used or manipulated but rather that we were more mature and more committed.

As the three of us stated later in our exposé: "Guidance [from Dixon] was made palatable and political rather than name-calling and incoherent, and Marlene was kept away from people and then her actions interpreted. There was conscious collusion and overt discussion about keeping the secret. But it was the militants who were seen as the problem, not Marlene's behavior."[3]

DWP members were taught that they would be nothing without Dixon, that there would be no organization without her. She was to be defended at all costs. She was, members were told, overworked and over-burdened. Soon it came to be understood as part of this logic that the undue stress on her was caused by the incompetence of Party militants. Because of this, members were to do anything, make any sacrifice to make Dixon's life better, more comfortable, so that, for once, she could do the work that a revolutionary leader should do.

As the Party grew in size, fewer and fewer members actually saw or met Dixon. For example, one former cadre who had been a full-time member for more than eight years said that she had seen Dixon only three times in all those years. Access to Dixon was intently controlled, as she shuttled back and forth between her country and city residences, her whereabouts known only by a small circle of trusted militants. In the last few years of the DWP, Dixon made perhaps one or at most two appearances before the entire group. This was usually at a special function, such as the annual all-Party Assembly. At the last Assembly, Dixon sent her communiqué by modem; it was an unintelligible poem. Her lack of visibility to the general membership made Dixon even more mysterious and awesome.

THE CONSOLIDATION OF POWER

Only one among the initial founding group was capable of challenging Dixon, and a major power struggle went on between them. This conflict was a decisive part of the group's formative history. Among the Bay Area group of women, Esther was the most experienced politically and therefore less eager to so quickly accept Dixon's views and leadership. For example, Esther objected to the idea that the group support Dixon when she decided to relocate to San Francisco. Using bullying tactics and pitting friends against each other, Dixon succeeded in chasing Esther out of the group.[4] The attack on Esther was orchestrated around the pretext that she had political differences with fundamental Party principles. According to the group's self-published history, every word of which was reviewed by Dixon, she responded with "howls of outrage and protestation" at the theoretical work being done under Esther's guidance in that first formative year.[5] Such a response from Dixon became the norm over the years as she was wont to emotional outbursts over incidents and errors large and small. In this case she successfully ridiculed several other members who were showing support for Esther's position, and before long the "implacable dogmatists," as they were called, were expelled.[6]

This two-line struggle, as it was known forevermore in DWP lore, revolved around two positions. Esther's position held that an organization should develop political lines and political strategies and be involved in "mass practice" (i.e., political organizing activities among the working class, such as in workplaces and labor unions), which members would learn from. Dixon's position was that *first* members must transform their class attitudes (their class standpoint) so that they would not offend working-class people when involved in mass practice. Dixon maintained that this type of cadre development was key to having a true proletarian party. She did not believe that "unreconstructed" militants should be unleashed on the working class.[7]

Several members left the group during the course of this struggle, and Dixon came out the clear victor and the leader of the still tiny organization. Thereafter, the polemics written during this first internal battle, and Dixon's subsequent analysis, were used to train all incoming members, to clearly make the point that DWP unity was around organization, not political line — a founding principle that ultimately gave Dixon total power.

By 1976 Dixon was declared the general secretary, an office and a title she suggested for herself. Then, at some point, the "org" was formally named the Workers Party for Proletarian Socialism. Internally, we referred to the group as "the Party." After a time the official name was changed to simply the Workers Party and then, eventually, the Democratic Workers Party. It was a conscious decision to not include "Communist" in the organizational name and to not refer to ourselves publicly as Marxist-

A Thinking Worker is a Dangerous Worker

Rebel Worker Organization

FIGURE 12. The flag of the Rebel Worker Organization, one of the DWP's front groups used to recruit workers, especially in the early years.

Leninists.[8] Although the group was involved in various external actions almost from the beginning — study groups, local strike support, interventions at leftist affairs, various workplace activities — members were extremely secretive about their Party affiliation. Typically, militants presented themselves in public as belonging to one or another of the many front groups (see fig. 12).

From 1978 through 1981, much of the DWP's practice centered on electoral work. Most of this was done through various front organizations, with most of the activity coordinated through the Grass Roots Alliance (GRA) while the Party was kept in the background. Militants pretended to be GRA organizers or volunteers and did not reveal their Party membership to other volunteers and supporters. The passage of Proposition 13 the previous year had changed California's tax base to favor the rich. This and related issues became fertile ground for Party activism. The GRA — and later the DWP and the GRA — were significant in raising public awareness about the effects of Prop. 13.

The Party's public emergence occurred at a celebration of a related electoral effort. On November 6, 1979, Party members and their supporters were gathered at a local club to await the voting results on Proposition P, a citywide ballot initiative sponsored by the GRA (and secretly the

Party) as a response to the recently passed Prop. 13. General Secretary Dixon appeared and spoke at the event, and a public document announcing the Party was issued. Afterward, militants were ordered to distribute the bright blue booklet around the city and elsewhere to important political contacts and supporters.[9] The unveiling of the Party met with a mixed reaction.

The Party grew to have 125 to 175 full-time militants, with other levels of general members who were recruited through or worked with the various front groups. As a leftist organization led by women with a unique line on proletarian feminism and a staunch critique of social democracy (also called petit bourgeois leftism), the DWP attracted intelligent, hardworking, dedicated women and men who were looking to make a commitment to the cause of social change.

From the beginning, new members were instilled with an utter and absolute respect for Dixon, a process that began in the recruitment phase. Dixon was talked about as the ultimate working-class heroine. She was lauded for knowing more about Marxism, world politics, revolution, and life than anyone else. She was praised as a genius and a revolutionary leader, in the tradition of Lenin and Mao. She was recognized as both the organizational and the theoretical leader. Central to the DWP's daily operations was a strict leadership principle that stated "the Party is always right." It also quickly came to mean that Comrade Marlene and the Party were synonymous.

The Development of Bounded Choice (Part 2)

During these early years of the formation of the DWP (1974–78), the four characteristic dimensions of cultic organization were reinforced strongly by Marlene Dixon and those who served in upper- and middle-level leadership positions in the Party. Each of these developments is key to the type of organization that took shape.

ESTABLISHING CHARISMATIC AUTHORITY

The charismatic relationship that Dixon established with members was most crucial to those who were in the initial grouping and to those who were drawn rather rapidly into the inner circle and top leadership positions. These members had a special bond with Dixon and believed in her ability to be a true revolutionary leader. They understood her unique qualities and cherished her as their leader — even while being intimidated by her. These militants, then, were instrumental in conveying this feeling to recruits and incoming members. A large part of the sense of community felt by this group of people revolved around Dixon as their leader, in spite of her excesses and abusive personality. They felt that if outsiders did not understand it, that was further proof of her uniqueness.

In those early months, whether or not it was outwardly acknowledged, Dixon quickly became the leader of the group. She brought structure and discipline; she formulated the group's basic belief system and led the study of it. Having floundered for some time on their own, for the most part, the women accepted Dixon as a hero figure and welcomed her knowledge and decisiveness. When it soon became clear that she was taking the lead, most of the women experienced a kind of elated relief, albeit with some trepidation because of her domineering personality. Some of those who were present at the founding meetings described Dixon's leadership presence.

Zola, for example, said, "Marlene was the leadership. There was no question about it. She was the motivating force. She was the organizer. She was the teacher to us all — and at that time she was a very good teacher."

Virginia commented: "Her role as the leader evolved. There was a need — she filled it. She wanted to do it. And so it happened. She was a very strong and domineering person."

And Michelle put it in context by saying, "We all wanted to be political. And Marlene presented 'together' politics. We latched onto that. The general feeling was that we wanted a sense of organizational stability; we were all frustrated with New Left or anarchistic models. Her ideas held together because it was an attempt to articulate a new transformation of politics — and the discipline part caught on. We were serious about ourselves."

Because of her lengthy absences when she went back to Canada, Dixon insisted on constant communication to be kept informed about what the others were up to. The others became accustomed to getting her input on everything. It became standard practice to always check with her before proceeding with any activity.

Rhonda explained: "We would go to several different phone booths and make these convoluted long-distance calls to her because of all the security we felt was needed. We would talk with her for an hour or so and get direction on what we were doing or should do next. I don't think a single independent decision was made without consulting her and getting her approval from the very beginning. We learned to do that very early on — so she wouldn't blow up about something."

When Dixon returned to the Bay Area on each of her university breaks, she made her presence known, "reclaimed the crown, as it were," as Virginia described it. Typically, Dixon would be highly critical of what the others had been doing, proving time and again their need for her leadership and guidance. Invariably, she found something or someone to "blow up about." These were not pleasant episodes. Dixon was good at slamming down her things and making a scene and expert at making others look stupid. Commonly she used ridicule combined with stern criticism to attack any independent decisions, that is, decisions she did not have the final say in. Before long Dixon became the sole arbiter of the functioning of the group. Her summation and analysis of a problem or a person's behavior was always at a much more sophisticated political level than any of the others could have come up with. Her views came to be accepted, with a mixture of awe, shame, and guilt.

In pondering those times, Virginia remarked: "A phenomenon occurred that was external to all of us, yet totally internal to who we were. Here we were with only one person with the faintest inkling of what a party was — so it was created totally in her image."

When Dixon was in town the group had to meet more often and for longer periods than when she was away. Eighteen-hour meetings were not uncommon; one founder recalled meeting all day on Christmas 1974. At these meetings they engaged in serious, lengthy discussions and much criticism, led by Dixon, who expressed superiority, frustration, and dismay at how "politically backward" the others were and how it fell to her to set the group back on the right path again. Over and over, mercilessly, Dixon pointed out the others' political naïveté and lack of seriousness. Though Dixon's returns always brought major upheaval, the other women, eager not to lose what they had begun, were willing to go along with this. They accepted it as a necessary part of the process. Meanwhile, recruits who were brought in at this time were either younger or about the same age as the other founders (but always, with one or two exceptions, younger than Dixon).

Many of them had much less political experience, or were made to think they did — in relation to Dixon's purported extensive activist background. Consequently, recruits and new members were just as likely to not make waves by questioning what was going on in the group. In a retrospective comment about those times, Trish said, "Dixon was able to bully the founders and early members. Compared to her, we were nobodies — or so we thought. She took advantage of the politically innocent and vamped on them. She chose a group in which she had no equals. It was ludicrous to think any one of us was her equal. She could totally control."

Another former member, Karen, who joined during the early period and who usually held a leadership position, remarked, "Marlene was no genius. But she did have an incredible ability to manipulate, and also she was more theoretically developed than those whom she first 'led' — and she talked circles around them."

Crucial to the legitimation of Dixon's charismatic authority during this period was the establishment of the Party leadership principle, following the issuance in early 1977 and discussion of a series of directives written by Dixon: "On the Development of Leninist Democracy," "The Nature of Leninist Democracy and Leadership," and "On Leadership." These directives were discussed intensively, illuminated with real-life examples, and constructed around specific criticisms of militants. This served to personalize the political lessons — some people were on the spot, while others were relieved not to be the center of attention.

The point of the first document, "On the Development of Leninist Democracy," was to expound on the organization's understanding of the word *democracy*. According to Dixon, "[D]emocracy *is* a method for the selection of leadership and a method of assuring that the most developed and tested comrades, the cadre, the bones of a Leninist party, govern the party."[10] Leadership was not about being popular, pleasant, or non-threatening. Because her claim to be the most experienced, developed, and tested was accepted by the members, her place as general secretary was assured.

The second document, "The Nature of Leninist Democracy and Leadership," was meant to instill the concept of instructed and uninstructed members. This lesson emerged out of a criticism of a new member who innocently recommended several book titles for the Party's study program. That a new member should presume to make such a suggestion indicated a lack of confidence in Dixon's leadership. The directive stated that "theoretical ability or leadership is developed only *within* the Party, it is tested by the Party and validated by the Party; it is earned and established *only within* the Party."[11]

Dixon boldly declared in a document studied throughout the organization: "I am the Party's principal theoretician at this time and laid the basis for our theoretical worldview. . . . A party is *not* a debating club, people do *not* come to leadership because they are the best debaters, and new members are *in no way competent* to debate the leadership of the Party because a debate by new members *must* occur *outside* the unity of the Party (since they are uninstructed)."[12]

For militants who wanted to stay in the organization, this study reinforced the idea that theirs was not to question, or even to suggest, but to learn and obey. Like all DWP directives, this ruling principle was set in the context of political necessity. To a serious revolutionary, contradicting this norm was out of the question, for it was clear that Dixon and the Party knew better.

The third directive, "On Leadership," was intended to affirm and secure Dixon's leadership after she had decided that an unprecedented, dangerous situation had emerged in the organization. The situation was described in the following serious manner: "The right of the central leadership to make authoritative judgments and determinations on the Party's line has been called into question by the leveling, presumptuous, arrogant and competitive worldview of new petty [sic] bourgeois militants."[13]

The directive stated: "The central leadership wishes to instruct new members, and to remind older militants, that the very existence of the Party — its growth, its sophistication and its power — is the validation of its leadership, and most especially the leadership of Comrade Marlene."[14] The document went on to say that "revolutionary leaders don't grow on trees" and listed Dixon's contribution to the Party — "in short, comrades, *all of it!*"[15]

By now, Dixon's role was clear and not to be obstructed: "Comrade Marlene and the Party are inseparable; [and] her contribution *is the Party itself,* is the unity all of us join together to build upon. The Party is now the material expression of that unity, of that theoretical world view. That world view is the world view of the Party, its central leadership and all of its members. And there will be no other world view. . . . This was the unity that founded the Party, this was the unity that safeguarded the Party through purge and two-line struggle, and this is the unity we will protect and defend at all costs. There will be no other unity."[16]

These two final documents, then, ensured no further challenges to Dixon's leadership, for any challenger would be regarded as either an incompetent, "uninstructed" new member or a hopeless "PB," or petit bourgeois. The former was regarded not as a serious challenger but as someone to be scorned. The PB was a reckless, selfish antirevolutionary who was attempting to create factions and take over the organization. The term was always uttered with venom and contempt. It was one of the worst criticisms a Party comrade endured.

All of this rested on the fact that the members had the utmost respect for Dixon as their leader. The interplay of two beliefs supported this adulation and caused militants to respond in the way they did. First, they believed that Dixon brought special abilities to the revolutionary political scene. Second, they believed that they were privileged to be members of Dixon's organization. With such an understanding, militants must earn the right to have a relationship with the great leader, and at the same time, they reflected back on her a worshipful stance that led her to feel justified in her actions.

In day-to-day practice, Dixon's leadership was heavy-handed and autocratic, leading one former cadre to describe the Party as "an organization run by one person." For those who chose to stay, it meant playing by the rules and norms as laid out in the founding documents. The cadre core, believing that the DWP was their best — indeed, only — political option, became increasingly bound to follow Dixon's direction. This bond grew stronger the longer someone stayed in the group. Part of the bond was feeling that one was part of a community and feeling responsible to others in that community.

In comparison to Heaven's Gate, we can see parallels with the ways in which Applewhite and Nettles were adored by their followers. In a similar manner, the students of Heaven's Gate felt honored to be part of the Class and willing to follow the lead of their Older Members.

DEVELOPING TRANSCENDENT BELIEF

Dixon and her followers were classic Marxist-Leninists in that they were "inspired by the self-sacrifice and discipline of the parties that defeated fascism."[17] They believed that volatile conditions existed and that the U.S. working class was in motion, evidenced by the political and social movements of the sixties and then other current events, such as labor strikes and urban riots. Dixon predicted that the conditions of austerity capitalism, begun in the 1970s, would deepen the polarization of the classes, giving rise to civil war in the United States. As a political entity, Dixon's party recognized the historical significance of being ready to "seize the time in an insurrectionary period."[18]

Believing in the effectiveness of the Marxist-Leninist model and trusting in their claim to uniqueness, Dixon and her cadres felt certain that they were the only hope for the emancipation of the U.S. working class. Their vision was built on two foundational ideas: the premise that a democratic-centralist party was necessary to lead the working class in its innate revolutionary desires; and the belief that the DWP, as led by Dixon, was the only group sophisticated enough in theory and serious enough in discipline to execute such a feat.

Viewing the rest of the Left as unserious and useless, Dixon directed her criticisms toward both what she identified as the petit bourgeois Left and the pseudo-Maoists of the New Communist Movement; neither offered a serious political option. One Party document after another described other leftist groups as being riddled with sexism, racism, cowardice, hypocrisy, anticommunism, and class arrogance. The only hope, then, was to build a new revolutionary party, as difficult as that would be in the "belly of the monster" and on the heels of a repressive era bolstered by a Cold War mentality. This meant being determined, serious, committed, and more than that even: it meant being *unfailing* in one's devotion. Not unlike Lenin's struggle with the social democrats of his time, Dixon convinced the other founders and early members to unite behind her vision — "a model of organizing that was unsurpassed for its ability to survive under adverse conditions."[19]

The DWP's guiding principles were established in the first year. They were

- Absolute respect for leadership
- The need to build and defend the Party
- Proletarian class standpoint as the measuring stick of all thoughts and activity
- The use of criticism/self-criticism as the mechanism for change
- The cadre ideal, exemplified by strict discipline and full-time commitment.

Typically, these principles were presented in documents written by Dixon and produced and distributed by the administrative staff. They were discussed in the various small group meetings, initially called Development Groups and later called Branch meetings. For the recalcitrant, there were special units called Remoulding Groups.[20]

As the organization evolved, the process of cadre development was also carried out in New Members Class and Party School sessions. Political education was one of the Party's priorities in training its members. "General study reflects the Party as a Communist 'school,' while particular study reflects Party ideology as a weapon. General study requires the militant to be a good student; specific study requires the militant to prepare to be a good Communist, active in political combat," wrote Dixon.[21]

Meetings were led by middle-level leaders who were trained at special leadership councils chaired by Dixon. These "middle levels," as they were called, had such titles as Political Officer, Executive Officer, and Party School Teacher. With some exceptions, because of expulsions or demotions (sometimes temporary), this was a fairly constant group of individuals who joined during the organization's formative years (1974–76), consisting of from ten to twenty cadres and usually including several men who had attained leadership positions. Some of these militants, joined by Dixon's personal staff, comprised the inner circle, which again remained a fairly constant body throughout the Party's existence. As time went on and Dixon receded from the daily life of the organization, leadership meetings were chaired by Dixon's second-in-command, Eleanor, or other high-level leadership personnel.

The moral imperative was intricately woven into the basic belief in the need for organization and for individual change. The two-line struggle between Dixon and Esther that took place in the first year established the principle of organization over party line. Over and above all else, the organization, based on the cadre party model, was to be built and defended.

A foundational document expounding on this idea was called "The Necessity for a Fighting Party."[22] Based on notes from a presentation by Dixon, it was first issued and studied Party-wide in December 1975. Inside the Party this document was referred to simply as "Freedom and Necessity." It was included in the first edition of *The Militant's Guide* and was studied line by line, over and over, almost to the point of memorization (see fig. 13).

In "Freedom and Necessity," Dixon made her case for a proletarian party based on Lenin's model of Bolshevism. She acknowledged Marxism as the lens for understanding "the system of monopoly capitalism as the necessity against which we struggle,"[23] but also she recognized the significance of Leninism for translating Marx's ideas into a "human instrumentality." Here Dixon introduced the concept of *unity of will* — the means by which a collection of individuals could change the course of history. The proletarian party was held forth as the actual manifestation of the collective conscious willing of those dedicated individuals who form a cadre forged by the discipline of democratic centralism. Dixon explained:

> It is the proletarian party that creates the capacity for human freedom to defeat necessity; that signals the beginning of the era when human beings consciously struggle towards the transformation of the realm of necessity to the realm of freedom. The proletarian party is the human effort to hurl mankind into the realm of freedom by recognizing the necessity (the conditions of capitalism) and seeking to transform it (socialist construction). In this way, the concepts of freedom (conscious willing) and necessity (history which we do not control) describe the essence of the proletarian party.[24]

Figure 13. The DWP was prolific and produced many books and other publications. These are some of the earliest ones, including *The Militant's Guide,* the Party's main indoctrination manual.

"Freedom and Necessity," then, was the internal battle cry of the DWP militant. It was the crutch that supported many a militant through various personal struggles over their commitment to the cause and to the organization. That was especially true during the formative years, when study of and indoctrination in the belief system and in the professed methodology for change was most intense. During this period of limited mass practice, most of the members' time was taken up with collective study and criticism. The rest of the time was used to produce documents and study materials. Almost nonstop meetings of small groups or units were held for the study and discussion of the group's founding documents and other carefully selected readings.

It was a conscious strategy on the part of Dixon and her top leaders to pursue the deliberate indoctrination of members in the early years, as evidenced by this statement in the DWP's written history: "In the early years of the Party's formation, cadre standards were extremely demanding. Many more members were recruited than were allowed to remain. It was the belief of the organization's leadership that the quality of the cadre would be decisive in the overall ability of the organization to carry out its goals and aims. Hence we pursued a highly selective cadre policy until we were ready to build the mass aspect of the Party."[25]

The type of study conducted during that period was almost nonexistent in the DWP's later years. Once the organization became involved in local electoral work and other forms of political practice (e.g., workplace activity, union work, and neighborhood causes) and especially after its public emergence in November 1979 and its growing outreach into intellectual circles via its research institute and publishing arm, internal study focused more on political lines and less on cadre development. Over time, even political study was given short shrift, as most militants suffered from a lack of time to comprehend, much less study or debate, the Party's theoretical positions or public stances.

Freedom and necessity, as a human ideal, was the linchpin of Dixon's ideological system. Members were taught that each militant must assume individual responsibility in the revolutionary process and that discipline was the material expression of will, neither blind nor conditional but guided by conscious obedience. According to Dixon, "The Party organizes itself into a series of particular necessities, welding its members together in thought and action, demanding the surrender of individualism into the greater social whole; the transformation into collective interdependence; and the subordination of our individual will to the collective will of the organization."[26]

If discipline was the necessity, what was the freedom? Freedom was explained as consciousness, transformation, creativity, and initiative. Freedom was found in the capacity to express oneself through the collective effort. Freedom was the choice to be a part of history: "Participation in a dialectical proletarian party unlocks the potentialities stifled within the bourgeois human being, giving birth to the Communist human being."[27] In other words, freedom was being a born-again Communist.

In a letter written approximately one year after the DWP's dissolution, I attempted to explain to former friends how this process happened in my case. I hoped to convey how I had been drawn to the group and to explain the appeal:

> Having been a loner for so many years, and suddenly finding myself with exciting political realizations coupled with a strong feminist leaning, I was immediately attracted to an organization founded by women, supposedly nondogmatic and serious. I was 30 years old and now willing to make a commitment. I had tried a lot of things and had come to realize that there really is strength in numbers.
>
> I was naturally wary upon joining (especially with all the secretiveness I

didn't really know exactly what I was joining), and accepting the discipline was the hardest for me. But overall I wanted to believe and to belong. I didn't want to be alone anymore and I wanted to do something meaningful with my life. For me, becoming part of a serious political organization seemed like a way to unselfishly make my mark on history.

I liked the idea of being part of an elite. I liked the claim that we were to be strong and without emotion. I liked the idea that personal choices and desires were to be subordinate to our political mission. I felt respected, cared for, recognized. What I didn't know was that playing by the rules meant losing myself, that total submission creates total dominance as a counterpart, and that the loss of self-respect, self-caring, and self-recognition brings on a slow and painful death.

But in the beginning I believed in it. I believed because politically and personally I wanted to find an answer, because this seemed to be a genuine attempt at building something different within the Left. From the onset, I yielded, painfully and sacrificingly, to every criticism. I gave up my style of dress, I changed my identity, I took on a Party attitude toward everything. And I was spotted as a leader and soon became one. I was trained by the top to despise my former self and remake myself in a Party-identified image. My pre-Party self-image as a strong, intelligent, independent woman was turned into a devotion to the Party. I really wanted this to work. Joining the Party, then, was the logical outcome of my political beliefs as they had developed and my personal beliefs in wanting to help create a better world. Although from the first I resisted the discipline, I had no reason to doubt the ideology; rather, I believed in it fiercely. I gave myself up to it — and in the fervor of those beliefs I wanted to help build the Party, to make it something strong and viable. And so I became a leader, a teacher, a recruiter.[28]

The exploration and transformation of one's class standpoint began as a new member entered the group. In the formative years a class history took up most if not all of the agenda of an eight- or ten-hour meeting. This initial examination was based on the person's written class history, which included a detailed description of family background and personal experience. The new member then made an oral presentation that was evaluated from the point of view of what had or had not been in the interest of the working class. The purpose of these class history discussions was to root out bad attitudes and "bourgeois thinking." Militants were taught that political backwardness would not only hinder that person's political development but also jeopardize a political activity in which he or she might be engaged.

Class history sessions became a relentless and often torturous political autopsy that did not end until the new member adopted the "correct class analysis" of his or her life up to the point of joining the organization. Class histories were an important part of reframing a militant's self-image

FIGURE 14. The author at a rummage sale in 1979 raising funds for the Tax the Corporation Initiative sponsored by the Grass Roots Alliance, one of the Party's mass organizations, used for recruitment and political clout. (Janja Lalich)

and sense of self, and also taught the norm of self-doubt, a crucial aspect of the worldview shift members experienced during the first weeks or months in the Party.

As the Party grew, class histories were done in New Members Class. The newly recruited members in the class were expected to participate in the dissection of the class history just presented by one of them. It was presumed that a class history would not be correct at first. The prevailing attitude was, how could an "uninformed" and "uninstructed" new member possibly have a correct analysis without the benefit of the Party's training? In that way each new member was initiated into the ritual of public exposure, denunciation and self-denunciation, and collective critiques. Invariably, new members were instructed to rewrite their class histories, sometimes more than once. The goal of this reframing process was to get new members to view and accept their personal histories from the correct political standpoint — that is, from the Party's point of view.

Much of this was adapted from the Chinese Communist thought-reform processes, for which Chairman Mao became so well known.[29] One of Mao's absolutist slogans — "Every kind of thinking, without exception, is stamped with the brand of a class" — became the cornerstone for the process of class-standpoint struggle in the DWP.

Its complement was another of Mao's ideas — that every criticism contains a kernel of truth and accepting that truth is vital to reforming class standpoint. Those Maoist ideas were basic tenets of the DWP's re-education process. The dialectic unfolded as follows: the ideal of exemplary practice was manifested through correct class standpoint, and correct class standpoint was possible only through the process of criticism/self-criticism. Dixon wrote: "Criticism serves praxis and political development; it is NOT a form of psycho-therapy. We do not indulge faults, we rectify them; we do not justify errors, we overcome them. Ours is a hard calling and a stern discipline; it is also liberation."[30]

Class-standpoint analysis plus criticism/self-criticism, the central features of cadre development, became the hallmark of the DWP's internal operation and a vital part of the transformative process that brought about the worldview shift necessary for acceptance as a cadre in the organization. Along with Dixon's (and then her second-in-command, Eleanor's) specific direction on how criticism sessions and class histories were to be carried out, the study of *The Training of the Cadre* sealed the mortar in the group's ideological foundation.[31] This manual was studied in Party School. The entire process of cadre development was presented as an effort to reach the cadre ideal. That ideal formed the basis by which militants were judged, regulated, disciplined, promoted, demoted, and/or expelled. The distinguishing characteristics of a cadre were described as follows: "Cadre is that individual in whom all emotional and unconscious elements have been reduced to a minimum and subjected to the control of an iron will. The cadre is obsessed with a purpose, which is the center of his/her existence. Party and cadre are indistinguishable."[32]

A two-page directive issued under the Central Committee logo, "The Cadre Ideal," summarized Dixon's vision of the cadre and made clear the extent of the demand. It was the ideal adhered to by members throughout the DWP's existence. Striving for the cadre ideal became the ultimate goal of each member, above all else. Through intense, directed study, a good militant came to understand that revolution was necessary but was not attainable without a cadre — and forming a cadre was possible *only* in the context of Dixon's Party, for no other organization on the Left had such a heightened degree of serious intent. The combativeness displayed by Dixon and the DWP against the Party's enemies — the petit bourgeois academics, the sellout union professionals, the corrupt media, the wimpy leftists — was evidence to recruits and members that Dixon and her Party were willing to go all the way. They believed Dixon when she said, "We have had a hard struggle indeed, for ours is in fact, as well as intent, a proletarian party."[33] If one was inclined to make a revolutionary commitment, the DWP was surely a serious option.

The goal for a militant, then, was to merge oneself with the totality of the Party, to become a "deployable agent," the very term idealized in Party literature as well as in meetings and criticism sessions. Militants were imbued with the idea that "only by identification with the Party can you have discipline and initiative within the same personality. The Party is the only means to reconcile this."[34] This complex understanding of initiative within discipline was used to reinforce the idea that members were in fact self-actualizing in their striving to meld with the organization:

> It is not enough to simply obey discipline (employee mentality). Cadres make the Party's orders their own; this is what it means to be unconditional in their discipline. Without this, how can you exercise initiative and have independence? Therefore, the criterion of your ability to see the unity you must have is not the correctness or incorrectness of one order — it is the totality, your ability to grasp the Party as a whole. You see the Party as the only instrument for realizing your goals. This is why the Party is right, even when it is wrong.[35]

The process of cadre development was to reach maturity in each militant when the demands of a proletarian class standpoint became self-imposed and were no longer dependent on criticism/self-criticism. At that point, internal pressures had become internalized. Militants felt that pressure quite directly for they were told repeatedly that "when the process is complete, an individual becomes a Communist such that if the entire Party was destroyed, he or she could rebuild it. That is the highest level. The highest ideal."[36] Thinking oneself capable of rebuilding the entire party seemed beyond the reach of most militants, yet the image emerged time and again in criticism sessions in which militants held forth that ideal as the moral yardstick by which they measured — and judged — their own and each other's practice. Free riders or role players were quickly flushed out in this intense and rigorous milieu.

The progression from a general desire for social change via proletarian revolution to the need for a fighting party via cadre development was the logical basis of the DWP's belief system. Its inculcation relied on the use of highly effective, probing techniques to generate the necessary personal transformation. In fact, such methods came to dominate the group's existence — an existence characterized by almost continual denunciation of militants and constant self-confession. Making a commitment to join and submit to the process of cadre transformation was not done lightly — on either side. The DWP led a carefully targeted recruitment program, choosing primarily from among networks of friends, which lent the necessary peer support. Meanwhile, internal organizational structures carefully monitored each militant's development.

Commitment crises, as they were called, happened at all levels of membership, and trained leaders guided militants through them. Some chose to leave the DWP at such times, but those who chose for the Party experienced relief, relished their acceptance, or reacceptance, into an elite force, and reaffirmed their deepening commitment to the cause. The demand for personal transformation was further justified by the urgency embedded in the group's message. Political exhortation, coupled with daily discussions of the increasing polarization manifest in a capitalist society in recession, helped to push struggling militants to choose for the working class — in the form of the DWP. The moral imperative linked readily with the sense of urgency embedded in the Party's rhetoric.

INSTITUTING SYSTEMS OF CONTROL

During these formative years, Dixon was very clear about creating an organization built around totally confining and all-encompassing systems of control: hierarchy and command, internal organization, rules, and regulations, discipline and punishment. It is to these systems that we now turn.

Hierarchy and Command. Although a variety of internal structures existed at different times in the DWP's history, all were based on a strict pyramid model: Dixon always at the top; Eleanor as second-in-command; various "trusted" militants who served staff, leadership, or intellectual functions; and the cadres at the bottom. Staff militants worked as Dixon's personal servants and aides; leadership militants ran the various work units; and the "Party intellectuals" provided the research and often the writing for Dixon's theoretical work. Some of these militants were also part of

Dixon's inner circle, spending long hours, many weekends, and most holidays with her.

Formally, most years, there was a two- or three-person Political Committee, with Dixon as general secretary; at times there was also a small Executive Committee, perhaps five or six top leaders. In addition, there was a Central Committee, which most years never met as a body and never served any purpose except to rubber-stamp various proposals or directives.

As for the day-to-day operation, there were various leadership councils, departments (e.g., the print shop and the administrative staff), and practice units (e.g., workplace and community groupings). Most of the power was centered in the administrative section, also called Staff. Here resided functions related to security, recruitment, finances, and militant development. The leadership of the subunits and all departments reported directly to Eleanor, sometimes to Eleanor and Dixon. Most leadership militants had several assignments, for example, serving a staff function and leading a work unit.

Vital to the smooth operation of this complex structure were Eleanor, as chief implementer of Dixon's wishes, and the middle-level leaders. Eleanor and the "middle levels" were relied on to transmit all guidance from Dixon and to see that the guidance was translated into actual work projects. Although the middle levels were crucial, being in leadership was a revolving-door experience. "[M]embers of leadership bodies and the inner circle around Dixon were periodically denounced or temporarily removed as a means of checking the power of anyone but Dixon," several former members wrote later in a published summation of the DWP.[37] In the final analysis, Dixon, as general secretary, was the powerhouse behind the DWP, and she instilled in her followers strict adherence to a leadership principle that allowed no challenges to her seat.

Decision Making. As a democratic-centralist organization, the DWP followed a military-style chain of command, which required that decisions and orders be carried out unconditionally and that, in principle, as Party documents declared, "the minority shall submit to the majority."[38]

Traditionally, democratic centralism entailed intense discussion and debate within an organization about a strategy or project, but once a decision was made, members were to stop pushing their own agendas and toe the line in accordance with the majority decision. It did not work that way in the DWP, for debate was nonexistent after the two-line struggle described earlier. Discussions were rote and followed the Party line advanced by the leaders in charge of a particular discussion. In actual practice, then, the DWP was always more centralist than democratic.

Eight former leaders explained their understanding of this fact: "The lack of democracy escaped few of us; we simply thought 'that's the way a Leninist party is *supposed* to be.'"[39] Similarly, a paper written after the DWP's dissolution and signed by thirty-three former members stated: "We have no past experience with debate or disagreement in the party."[40]

Essentially, militants were trained to accept orders with unquestioning obedience. They lived by the motto "The Party is right even when it is wrong."[41] The group had a written constitution, although other than when the document was passed by a Party Assembly vote, it was rarely used, except as a showpiece. The real decisions were made at the top of the pyramid. Ultimately, substantive decision making in the DWP did not rest with the members in general, or even with the middle-level leadership.

Levels of Membership. DWP membership categories included Trial, Candidate, and General Members; some years there were also Associate Members.[42] There were two categories of General Members: on-line (meaning rank and file) and cadre (divided into leadership and nonleadership militants). All General Members had full voting rights and were considered full-time, which meant they were to be on call, at the Party's disposal, twenty-four hours a day. Trial Members had no rights; they were to learn. If the Trial Membership stage was passed (based on study, level of participation, and good behavior), then appropriate leadership personnel recommended that the young militant be moved up to status of Candidate Member, with partial voting rights. Dixon had final say in these advancements.

Promotions occurred at the regular weekly meeting and involved a formal ceremony and a letter of confirmation to the militant on Central Committee letterhead. A pledge was read by the Branch Executive Officer, followed by affirmative responses from the eager candidate. The thrust of the pledge was vowing to make an even greater commitment to the class struggle and willingness to work hard. The new candidate pledged aloud before other comrades in the room that he or she would forever be a Communist and a loyal member of the Party. The ceremony ended with the present middle-level leaders pinning a red enamel star above the heart of the new Candidate Member, who then was hugged by both the Executive and Political Officers at the meeting. This was followed by congratulations and everyone standing to sing "The International," the anthem of Communists worldwide. In general, membership involved being a full-time cadre with the understanding that one was making a lifelong commitment to the Party and to the working-class struggle for emancipation.

Assignments. In addition to the weekly training meetings, militants had many duties and responsibilities, which varied over the years depending on the prevailing internal or external focus. Basic duties included writing reports, carrying out a work assignment, and meeting various quotas. Also, militants were expected to study the Party's political and theoretical lines as issued in either internal documents or external publications.

Other routine responsibilities were meeting or exceeding assigned quotas for fund-raising, selling the organization's paper, recruitment, obtaining signatures on petitions, and volunteer activation. Beginning with the group's involvement in electoral work in about 1978, fund-raising became and remained a major priority. Militants were required to sell a vast array of things: buttons with political slogans or the Party's name, posters, Party literature (books, journals, and pamphlets), raffle tickets, the political program, tickets to Party-sponsored political film screenings, even candy bars (see fig. 15).

Work assignments were almost always collective endeavors. At first, work was carried out at selected members' houses, those that the Party considered "secure" — for example, in a neighborhood that would not draw attention to all the comings and goings. Later, houses and commercial spaces were rented specifically as Party "facilities." Everyone worked at one or another of these locations, depending on their assignment. One house served as the staff headquarters for all internal administrative work. The production headquarters and the printing press were located in a warehouse space. Another rented house was the location of the data bank and research institute. Yet another served as a labor organizing center and public office for the Party's electoral efforts.

Dixon's city home and Eleanor's apartment were considered Party facilities, with certain militants assigned there to perform infrastructure duties (maid and clerical work). Facilities were run by a specific collective leadership, usually two or three people. As in the Branches, in the facilities a great deal of time was spent in meetings making collective criticisms of a militant for some error. So much time was spent in these sessions that on most days everyone had to stay later than the scheduled hours to accomplish their actual work assignments.

Controlling the daily environment was a major method of enforce-

FIGURE 15. Some of the many buttons produced by the DWP to publicize its various political campaigns.

ment. Members were expected to be at their assigned facility at all times, except when at an outside job or some other preapproved assignment or meeting. Each facility had a logbook for signing in and out, ensuring that militants were accountable for all their time.

Most often, work assignments had little to do with militants' skills or training, or with their preferences — especially when they were being "tested" as new members. For example, doctors were given production work, and academics and intellectuals might be assigned to the typing pool. Such an assignment was supposed to teach humility.

Rules and Regulations. The DWP operated by a strict code of conduct and some basic rules, among them

- Obey discipline and keep Party secrets.
- Put the Party first.
- Do what you say you're going to do.
- Remember, the Party is right even when it is wrong.
- No dope, especially no hard drugs, and no drinking while doing Party work.
- No gossip.

- Follow security guidelines and a strict need-to-know policy (that is, you know only what you need to know).

- Have only one sexual partner at a time.

Those rules and behavioral guidelines were conveyed in various ways: in print in the Party's constitution, *The Militant's Guide,* and specific directives; and orally through Branch and New Members study, political campaigns, and criticism sessions. Other rules and standards were transmitted as a new recruit entered the life of the Party and soon became aware that "nothing remains outside the eyes of the Party," a foundational principle of the cadre ideal.[43]

A great deal of attention was paid to the new member, who was rapidly involved in meetings and work and surrounded by other members. One of the first manifestations of their new life was when incoming members chose a new name. (My Party name was Emma. I chose it in memory of a sweet, shy, four-year-old whom I had known when I was living in Spain a few years before joining the Party. I did not select it because of Emma Goldman, the usual connection people made.) Once a Party name was chosen, only that name was to be used; and immediately new members learned others' Party names. Militants were never to reveal their real name to other members, not even to roommates. Party names were used in all meetings or gatherings, in all DWP facilities, and in all houses where members lived. For the new member, taking on a name was the first stage in losing his or her pre-Party identity and assuming a Party-molded one. Militants who violated the rule by mistakenly using their own or another member's real name were severely reprimanded for committing a security breach.

Members were instructed in other activities aimed at hiding their identities and locations. This included acquiring a post office or rental box for receiving all mail; establishing an alias for use on household utility bills; establishing an alias for use when subscribing to publications, particularly leftist publications; and changing the address on one's car registration and driver's license to either a "safe" address (e.g., the home of an apolitical friend) or a postal box. Although the entire membership did not live communally, soon after joining, militants were encouraged to live in a house with other members (a "Party house," all of which also had code names like Bus Stop, Pincushion, Shoebox). Given that militants lived on incomes equivalent to or less than the poverty level, once someone passed Trial Membership, communal housing quickly became a necessity. Typically, three to eight militants shared a house or an apartment. Sometimes roommates were assigned by the Party, but for the most part militants could choose their own roommates. In essence, the DWP was a communal group in that members were either in a Party facility, on an assignment with other militants, or at home with Party roommates. They were totally immersed in and surrounded by the Party and became increasingly dependent on the Party in all matters.

Finances and Security. All members were expected to pay weekly dues, based on their salaries. Dues were increased once the initial stage of membership was passed. Typically, this came as a great surprise to advancing Trial Members and was invariably cause for class-standpoint struggle. It was considered one of the "tests" of advancing cadres. The dues structure was set up so that each militant gave over all monies received above a group-determined living amount, set at approximately poverty-level standards. All monetary or substantial gifts (such as a car), job bonuses, legal settlements, and inheritances were turned over to the Party.

Security was a big part of daily life. In addition to code names, houses and facilities had security captains (chosen by Staff/Security) whose job was to ensure that security regulations were being followed and to communicate certain orders (e.g., earthquake procedures, guidelines for keeping documents, parking and telephone rules). All Party locations — even those with public faces, such as the DWP-operated businesses — were supposed to be secret locations.

Most years, militants were to park their cars at least two and a half blocks and around the corner from any DWP house or location. While at a facility, phone calls were not to be made or received, so that "the State" would not be able to trace calls to those locations. For many years, security rules forbade calls from one Party location to another, including the members' houses. Public telephones, at least two blocks away, were to be used for any call involving Party matters.

Members were instructed to be extremely cautious about not revealing personal information to each other, such as names, family information, where they worked, and so on. On one occasion, in early 1976, members were ordered to destroy anything that might reveal "hard" personal information (i.e., background, likes or dislikes, political leanings, sexual preference, family origin, etc.). The group did not yet own its paper shredders, so all militants were sent to an assigned location, where one by one they arrived, armed with great bundles and suitcases jammed with personal items. These were turned over for disposal. Three of us — all relatively new militants at the time — were assigned to burn everything. For three days and three nights, we threw documents, mementos, and hard data from the lives of our comrades into the fireplace: passports, photographs, diaries, poetry, artwork, treasured writings, packets of correspondence, health records, marriage certificates, and on and on. The reason given for this cleansing procedure was a security breach by one of the members that threatened the safety of the Party. The effect was the destruction of identities and memories — another step in the remolding process.

Sanctions. Given the emphasis on obedience and discipline, members understood that they could be sanctioned for not following rules or for in any way breaking the discipline. Militants were "punished" in a variety of ways besides submitting to collective criticism sessions and writing self-criticisms.

More practical sanctions, for example, were increased quotas, extra work duty, demotion from a particular position or function, removal from a practice, and instructions to leave a workplace or cease contact with a particular person. In more serious cases, there were periods of probation, suspension, or even house arrest (which could mean being confined and guarded by security forces).

Expulsion was the ultimate sanction. Most expulsions were handled privately between the member and the leaders. Other members learned about them by means of Branch announcements. Some expulsions came at the conclusion of trials, formal meetings at which a militant came before the rest of the members to be charged and publicly criticized. Sometimes in trials the accused was allowed to respond; sometimes, after a typically lengthy and harsh public denunciation, the accused militant was given the verdict and sent away without a chance to speak.

There were two types of expulsion — without prejudice and with prejudice. To be expelled *without prejudice* meant that the ex-member could be spoken to if seen, sometimes was allowed to work with one of the DWP front groups, often was expected to give a regular monthly "donation," and, in some cases, after a certain amount of time determined by leadership, was able to apply to rejoin. To be expelled *with prejudice* meant the person was declared an enemy and for all intents and purposes was considered to no longer exist. The expelled person was to be completely shunned; if members saw someone who had been expelled with prejudice — for example, in a store or on the street — they were to act as though the person was not there.

It was always the decision of top leaders as to who merited the extreme

punishment of expulsion with prejudice. Dixon gave the final approval on
all expulsions, with or without prejudice, even when recommendations
came from Eleanor or the Discipline and Control Board, a cadre committee that handled such matters. Most often, to be handed such a severe
sentence had nothing to do with the actual thoughts or actions of the
individual who was about to be shunned and become nonexistent. Generally, by means of criticism, staged trials, threats, and, at times, acts of
violence, expelled members were intimidated into years of silence and
would not think of speaking about their Party experiences, much less take
any action against the group.

Examples of the kinds of actions against expelled members are as follows: a founder being expelled was whisked from her house, everything
taken from her, and put on a plane to her parents' home across the country; an expelled militant was thrown out of his house, all of his clothes and
belongings discarded onto the street; a foreign-born, inner-circle militant
was put on a plane to Europe without a penny in her pocket. Many of
these actions were carried out by the Eagles, a special security force of
select militants who received physical fitness training from a Party cadre
who had been a Marine.[44] Other expelled militants were threatened and
extorted, given a schedule to repay the DWP for the "training" they had
received — often an amount in the thousands of dollars.

That type of violence and isolationist technique contributed to an us-
versus-them mentality, a feature found in many cults and certainly characteristic of this one. Declaring enemies drew battle lines and created a
feeling of superiority and righteousness among members, as well as a
sense of paranoia and hostility, as though these "enemies" truly posed a
threat to the organization.

The Party's First Purge.   Because the first mass expulsion of members was
central to the way in which the disciplinary structure took hold, it merits discussion here. Just after Christmas 1976, Dixon ordered the Party's
first real purge. Formally, it was called the Campaign Against Lesbian
Chauvinism and Bourgeois Feminism; in later years it was referred to
simply as "the lesbian purge." Though the membership was always mixed
(in both gender and sexual preference), in the early years there were quite
a number of lesbian members because much of the recruiting had been
done among friendship networks of the founders, eleven of whom were
lesbians. The purge was carried out under the political pretext that a
clique of lesbians in the Party were "bourgeois feminists"; Dixon provided
a new theoretical line on homosexuality to support her actions.[45] Over-

night, a number of female members were gone, with no explanation, and an investigative panel was questioning the rest of the members about their activities and testing their loyalty; a strict seal of silence was imposed to control information. After about a week, a pamphlet was produced and all the members were called to meetings to learn about an internal campaign to root out enemies "in our midst" — a clique charged with being exploitative, oppressive, and preventing the Party's growth.[46] The pamphlet explained that some female members had been expelled by the judgment of the leadership. Others, who had not yet been expelled (their fates were uncertain), were brought to stand before their comrades as they were formally charged with "crimes" and denounced collectively. This first purge served many purposes.

First, it established the Party's right to intervene in any aspect of members' personal lives and asserted its unmitigated power over their lives. The investigation that took place left nothing sacred; it included probing interviews (more like interrogations) and search-and-seizure tactics. In addition, because the purge happened so unexpectedly, it generated unspoken fear and uncertainty: someone could be in the group one day and gone the next — including a mate or a spouse. That uneasy feeling contributed to an ongoing atmosphere of watchfulness, terror, and condemnation.

Second, the purge helped to institute one of the DWP's main control mechanisms — the method of pitting people against each other so as to breed mistrust and foster loyalty only to Dixon. Actually, that precedent was begun in the first year when Virginia, Esther's best friend, was chosen to lead the investigation that culminated in the charges against Esther before her expulsion. Dixon reaffirmed the use of that tactic during the lesbian purge; eventually, over the years, every possible grouping or type within the DWP was subjected to such divisive treatment. There were campaigns against and purges of men, parents (i.e., militants with children), intellectuals, middle-level leaders, friendship networks, militants with political pasts, those from a middle-class (PB) background, and those with PB skills. In other words, not only were there no boundaries, but there were to be no bonds other than to the DWP. Such divisive tactics were implemented strategically throughout the years, ensuring that no one would trust anyone else.

Third, the Campaign Against Lesbian Chauvinism set the tone and style for future purges and mass trials. A booklet was produced almost overnight and distributed Party-wide for study and discussion. Accused militants were named, their "crimes" described, their punishments highlighted. Some were expelled without trial, never to be heard from again; others were ordered to come before their peers to face criticism and denunciation. After the trials, many women were suspended, unable to participate in any activity and cut off from contact with other members, for a period ranging from three weeks to six weeks.

And fourth, the purge served to break up a key friendship network. Among those named in the campaign were some of the founders and many who had been in the first ring of people to join soon after the founding. They were among the hardest workers, the most politically dedicated militants, and the most fervently loyal followers. Many were already in middle-level leadership positions. Perhaps Dixon thought they posed a threat to her, or perhaps she was testing the loyalty of her followers.

FORMING SYSTEMS OF INFLUENCE

Underlying the powerful systems of control in the DWP was what Dixon called unity of will. "Unity of will is the substance that harnesses us together," she wrote, "that creates our strength, endurance and flexibility. Unity of will is forged by discipline. *Discipline is the operation of the necessity of the party* . . . demanding the surrender of individualism into the greater social whole; the transformation of our bourgeois independence into a collective interdependence; and the subordination of our individual will to the collective will of the organization."[47]

In addition to this notion of collective will, another concept was taught in Party School, namely, that each individual's will was to merge with the Party. It was referred to as "bone of his bone and blood of his blood."[48] That image was used to convey the idea that eventually cadres would reach a point at which their will was so united with the Party that the two would be inseparable: at that point, the organization was no longer external to each person but an integral part of each militant's being.

Cadre Tension.   Cadre life was not easy, nor was it meant to be. Indeed, the very tension of "the constant pressure of Party authority" butting up against the member's independent spirit was recognized as the center of crisis and, therefore, growth for each militant.[49] Militants were taught that cadre development did not even really occur until the ideal was internalized — that is how long and hard the road was. At that point the hardship of daily life would become an accepted reality "because that is the way things must be if we are to achieve our purpose."[50] Living with — and confronting — the tension between self and the Party was the heart of the struggle.

In practical terms, this meant that inner turmoil was standard fare; militants accepted that feeling stressed, feeling conflicted, feeling confused were indications not that something was wrong but that something was right. Such internal struggle indicated that the militant was engaged in the process of self-transformation. In the end, the militant was rewarded by understanding that "this is a cadre party": "The demands we make on ourselves come from us. It's not the Party doing it to you. . . . We are agents of our own change." This idea was critical to each militant's sense of ownership and personal responsibility for the organization. At the same time, it meant that anxiety, fear, and guilt were everyday, seemingly self-generated emotions.

Integral to the DWP belief system, then, was crisis and struggle, testing, and a heightened awareness of the Party. Leadership militants responsible for training worked hard to implement such guidelines as "Don't break their spirit, but their individualism." At the same time, the militants did their part by living by the exhortations of an internal voice that repeated the lessons from their cadre training: "Submit but never break. Submission is not mindless, not blind; but submit without reservation. Submit with energy and commitment." Those challenging and somewhat contradictory mottos kept militants confused and on edge. Anxiety was embedded in the life of each cadre member. Like all other aspects, it was wrapped in a political aura and given a political justification. In cadre training, militants learned that to be a good Communist meant to be self-conscious, to be in constant tension with the Party. The idea was to be in continual struggle to shed old habits and attitudes so that the new cadre man or woman could emerge. The more that tension was felt, the more the person was engaged in the struggle. In that sense, anxiety became an accepted state of mind.

Peer Pressure. Meetings were one obvious place where peer pressure came into play. For example, the leaders would give a presentation on a change in the direction of some work or would open up a denunciation of a militant for some error. Each militant present was expected to say how much he or she agreed with what was just said. Ideally, each person said something different from what had already been said; but more to the point, each person was expected to agree with ("unite with") the thrust of what was happening and support the leadership position. Questions, should there be any, had to be couched within overall agreement. After years of this kind of participation, militants became quite incapable of creative or critical thinking, could only parrot each other, and had shrunken vocabularies riddled with arcane internal phraseology. For example, "bourgeois careerism," "PB self-indulgence," "need-to-know," "commandism," and "me-firstism" became everyday expressions. Afterward many members spoke of feeling "deadened" by this undemocratic experience and as though they lost a sense of themselves as thinking persons.

Reporting was another mechanism of peer pressure. The "one-help" system was a means by which members learned about, and were desensitized to, the practice of reporting on each other. This was a type of buddy system by which new members were assigned a helper (the one-help) to assist them in their integration into Party life. In weekly meetings, new members were to reveal to their one-help all thoughts, questions, or feelings about the organization. One-helps were supposed to help new members become "objective" about things, assist them in seeing things from "a Party point of view," and coach them in how to schedule their time so that they could figure out how to do even more for the organization.

Each one-help wrote detailed weekly reports about everything the new member said and did. Those reports were sent to Branch leadership, New Members teachers, Party School teachers, and Staff/New Members (the administrative team, who under Eleanor's direct guidance oversaw the training and development of all new members). To facilitate "breaking" the new member, these reports were used to monitor development and to identify an action or attitude that could serve as the basis of a group criticism in a future meeting. The more meat for criticism in the one-help report, the better the one-help. Just about every militant, at one time or another, was assigned to be a one-help to a new member. To be given that assignment was considered a sign of development and of the Party's trust. The one-help system helped to institutionalize incessant reporting on one another; it also helped to create an atmosphere of widespread fear of fellow comrades.

For example, I recruited a longtime friend, Stephanie, and we became housemates when she was still a relatively new member. (I needed a roommate because my two previous roommates had just been expelled during a campaign against middle-level leadership.) Although it was highly unusual to have a nonmember stay in a Party house, that summer Stephanie's mother was allowed to visit and stay with us for a week or two. This occurred while the Party was still completely clandestine.

Shortly after her mother left, Stephanie was harshly denounced in her Branch meeting for having addressed me by my real name, instead of my Party name, during the time her mother was visiting. The short-sightedness exemplified here is twofold. First, Stephanie's mother already knew me (or at least knew of me) before she came to stay with us, as Stephanie and I had been friends for some time before we each joined the Party. Before moving in, she had told her mother that she was going to be my housemate (although she had not revealed our Party affiliation). Certainly, it would have seemed bizarre to her mother if suddenly I had a different name. Second, and perhaps even more startling, I was the one who reported Stephanie for the security violation of having used my real name in front of her mother. In retrospect, I view this as a classic example of what is sometimes called black-and-white thinking commonplace among cult members.[51] And not only black-and-white, for its simplicity and lack of subtlety; but black-*is*-white, in what may be recognized by outsiders as ready acceptance of blatant contradictions.

Modeling. The top leaders were expected to be exemplary in terms of commitment, exhibited dedication, and willingness to struggle and be criticized. The motto was: "Don't ask of anyone what you yourself have not done." Certain members of the leadership circle underwent intense levels of criticism on a regular basis. Also, they were expected to make greater sacrifices and be willing to discuss them in meetings in order to be a model to lower-ranking militants.

The following is an example of the model/enforcer role. Frieda was the first parent in the Party. After some struggle, Frieda submitted to and united with the idea that she could raise her child on her time off, and she assured the Party that being a mother would not affect her commitment. In actuality, Frieda rarely had time off, and the child was raised primarily in a Party-run child care facility, where children received "superficial care but no real sustenance." Eventually, the Party adopted the attitude that it was "a selfish choice to have a child." Setting an example for others, Frieda, a true believer, modeled an exemplary attitude about the policy and helped to enforce the prevailing norms on parenting. At times, Frieda admitted later, she "was harder on others than necessary" to compensate for what she recognized as her own weak point.[52]

Another major aspect of modeling behavior was reflected in the relationship between leadership and nonleadership militants and the growing patterns of corrupt behavior. Essentially, nothing was to be questioned and there was no criticism of leadership, except on occasions when

Dixon called for a campaign against specific individuals. Total unity was expected, even while, concomitantly, militants were told to think for themselves and take initiative in their work. Yet anyone who disagreed or offered a criticism — member or nonmember — was labeled an enemy of the Party and hence an enemy of the working class. Disagreements were a rarity in the DWP. Typically, ones that were aired were handled swiftly, by the militant's capitulation or expulsion.

Commitment. There was an overriding sense that one's commitment to the Party was supposed to outweigh everything else. "A militant's first desire must be to serve, and not to lead," taught *The Militant's Guide.* Such intense dedication was routinely studied, often by using the example of Rubashov in *The Training of the Cadre.* Although the text names Rubashov as the protagonist, this was actually the story of the Soviet Communist leader and theoretician Nikolai Bukharin. In 1938, during the Stalin era, Bukharin signed a false confession knowing he would be found guilty of treason and shot. Militants learned that after much struggle and while imprisoned, Rubashov saw the light and united with his party. Ultimately, he said he was happy to be executed by the party. This was held up as exemplary devotion on the part of the cadre. Another historical example of the requisite depth of devotion was that of Chairman Mao allowing his closest friend and most beloved comrade, Lin Piao, to be shot.

The lesson was, Defend Communism and defend the Party to the end. In that vein, teachers asked militants in Party School, "Could you shoot someone?" Although a rhetorical question of sorts, the level of tension in the room during such a discussion was high. To give one's life for the Party was regarded as the highest honor.

COMPARING INTERNAL STRUCTURES

Rigid work routines and assignments were the mainstay of daily life in both the DWP and Heaven's Gate. Members worked on many projects over the years, projects that started and stopped at a moment's notice. When active, though, a project was top priority and required many hours of dedicated work. Related to this was the demand in both groups for flexibility: DWP militants were expected to "turn on a dime," and Heaven's Gate students learned that flexibility was one of their most important lessons, as it kept them "in tune" with the Next Level. That aspect further subjugated members to the leaders' decisions, and to some degree to their particular whims, desires, or paranoid tendencies that tended to motivate much of both groups' activities.

The DWP was ultimately a much larger group and had a far more complex structure. It was founded as a more formal organization; in some ways it attempted to structure itself after a political party or a labor union. The DWP developed an ongoing practice in areas where it had certain objectives: to effect change, make an impact, gain credibility. That feature led to structures and assignments that were oriented toward "external" work.

Attention to security matters was another central feature in these two groups, both of which were clandestine and secretive about their whereabouts. Likewise, members of both groups were secretive about their affiliation, the location of their homes and other facilities, their names, and so on. There were differences in the degree of clandestinity adopted by each group: Heaven's Gate remained clandestine for most of its twenty-three years, but it, like the DWP, worked through front groups and on occasion conducted public activities. The DWP was clandestine in the literal sense for only its first few years. After that, the group had a public presence in various forms, using front groups for this purpose while always keeping the core organizational functioning a secret. Much of the activity in both groups appeared to be a result of the leaders' seemingly paranoid behavior, as well as specific fears of outsiders, families of members, and the media. Moves were frequent, as were name changes; and a strict need-to-know policy kept members on edge and watchful.

In addition, both groups had a cache of arms. In the DWP, guns were used by Dixon as a display of power. This was an occasional occurrence, both in certain internal settings (mostly with members of her inner circle) and in meetings with outsiders, for example, when Dixon wanted to impress a visiting dignitary, such as a local labor leader or a respected leftist or intellectual. Heaven's Gate seemed less certain about the weapons it owned and ended up keeping them locked in a storage facility. This occurred rather late in the group's life, probably spurred on by the 1994 Waco incident, after which Applewhite's fears of outside intervention heightened.

Some organizational differences are apparent in the way new members entered each group. On joining Heaven's Gate, the person was expected to make an abrupt break with his or her prior life. In the DWP, the break was more gradual. Typically, it took a month or two — sometimes longer — before a militant became thoroughly integrated into the life of the Party and no longer had time for his or her prior commitments or interests. That difference extended to family life as well. Visits to friends or family members were controlled in both groups, although they were even rarer in Heaven's Gate. While members were with the group, typically, their parents did not know how to find them. The DWP was not quite as secretive, although visits home were rare and had to be approved by one's leadership, and militants' families were not encouraged to visit them. Such encounters were quite unlikely to happen.

In Heaven's Gate, there were no children at all; because celibacy was the rule, no children were born into the group, and recruits who had children were forced to leave them behind when they joined. In the DWP, on the other hand, children were tolerated, although militants were discouraged from having children. In general, abortions or some form of sterilization became the norm, which was a source of distress for some members who were not aware of the attitude toward having children when they joined. The DWP slogan "The children are our future" offers a glimpse of the kind of contradictory messages militants received. Mixed messages are a typical means of control: they cause the individual to question his or her ability to judge, and the confusion leads to the ongoing corrosion of self-confidence and the capacity to trust one's own judgment or perceptions. This is part of the illusion of choice found so often in cults.

Another difference was in relation to sexuality and intimacy. In Heaven's Gate, the object was to try to overtly eliminate gender differences; members did this in the way they dressed and behaved. There were no intimate relationships, no sex, no affection, or anything that could be considered such. This high degree of control did not occur in the DWP. Militants were allowed to have relationships, although there was little time for meaningful ones. In addition, personal relationships or the intimate aspects of members' lives were commented on and/or controlled by the Party. For example, couples were broken up during the lesbian purge; and later there were other cases of one spouse in a partnership being expelled while the one who "chose for the Party" was not allowed to see his or her former spouse — except for necessary interactions in cases where the couple had children. Sometimes a personal relationship was the subject of collective criticism when it somehow infringed on the Party or when, for some reason, Dixon took an interest in it. In some cases militants were forbidden to have relationships with each other or were instructed to end a relationship. In other cases militants were encouraged to begin a particular relationship because it served a political purpose or fantasy of the leader. And last but not least, especially given the group's origins in the gay community, gay members were discriminated against in the DWP: homosexual members were not allowed to be "out" in public, nor were they allowed to go to gay establishments.

In the DWP, there were numerous overt expressions of violent outbursts toward members, former members, and the outside world, including physical altercations, breaking and entering, threats, lies and slander campaigns, extortion, and a great deal of psychological violence. Such outwardly violent behavior was not seen in Heaven's Gate, although members experienced a fair amount of anxiety and fear.

The recruitment style of the groups also was different. Heaven's Gate recruited during the first year, and then, in April 1976, all recruitment was brought to a halt by Nettles. By contrast, DWP recruitment was ongoing and a required effort for members. Certain people were targeted as possible recruits. Recruitment officers were trained to oversee and guide recruitment in their Branches, and militants were encouraged continuously to submit names and profiles of potential recruits. Those lists were reviewed by an administrative section and specific guidance given on each person. In especially important cases, special recruiters were selected to be part of the team who met with targeted individuals.

On one level, Heaven's Gate was far stricter in terms of daily life. The leaders, by means of the procedures, dictated to the members where to live and how to live, eat, sleep, dress, and so on. The DWP was much less controlling in that way, although there were explicit instructions regarding household norms, roommates, personal relationships, and some clothing norms. But for the most part, militants were allowed to live where they could afford and with whom they wanted. In almost all cases, they lived with other members (or at least friendly Associate Members). Cadres were expected to live in a house with other Party members.

Yet, in spite of having a more relaxed code regarding the details of personal life, the DWP was a much harsher group in terms of both lifestyle and the ways in which members were treated by the leadership and each other. Members lived shabbily, did not eat well, did not have adequate health care, had no real family life, and were sleep-deprived and overworked most of the time. In addition, they lived under the intense pressure of harsh collective criticism and self-criticism.

THE POWER OF THE GROUP SETTING

As in Heaven's Gate, the group setting in the DWP offered each member a sense of belonging and a spirit of camaraderie. Many militants felt a renewed sense of self as a result of their commitment to a grand cause. They felt part of something very special.

On the other hand, the extent of self-renunciation required to meet the group's demands and strive for the ideal meant that the member also experienced personal losses, sometimes severe losses. First, there was the loss of individuality, independent decision making, and personal boundaries. And then, by following the demand for conformity, there was a loss of self and also, over time, of meaningful contact with the outside world. The flip side of comradeship was the incessant internal monitoring.

In both groups there was intense pressure to change, which creates a great deal of tension in a participant's life. Constant confession and self-exposure take their toll after a time. Ultimately, once a member internalized the belief system and the control and influence systems, he or she became a true believer, a deployable agent for the group, and perhaps a leader. In such a situation, there is always the potential for exploitation and abuse because the imbalance of power is so great.

Within a few years of the founding, Dixon had created an organization that exercised unquestionable charismatic authority under a powerful system of transcendent belief, reinforced by effective systems of control and influence. At this point, it seemed as though the members of the DWP were as trapped by bounded choice as those devoted individuals in the Heaven's Gate cult who took their own lives. But as we shall see as the story continues, there were significant differences between Heaven's Gate and the DWP, in both structure and membership, which ultimately led the latter to an entirely different and surprising conclusion.

CHAPTER 9

Decline and Fall

In the beginning, Dixon and her adherents were convinced that revolution was possible within their lifetimes. When that seemed less likely, the belief in Dixon's leadership and their own organization as the only viable alternative for social change kept militants going. All along they realized that Marx's utopian vision of a communist society was not within their sights; nonetheless, they believed that it was in their power to work toward socialism, the substructure of communist society.

In 1979 Dixon predicted that socialism was possible within the next two generations: "Socialism, or at least socialist construction, is both feasible and possible within nations and as an emergent world-economy by the year 2000."[1] That vision made the DWP's task ever more pressing. "The world we face is one of increasing crisis and danger," declared Dixon.[2] She predicted the fall of the American empire, rampant inflation, and increased hardship and suffering for the working class. She called on the militants to understand that their mission was to work to control and mitigate the increasing attacks on the working class.

Images of class war, brutality, and violence were ever present in Party literature, both in the internal documents militants studied and in the newspapers and leaflets they distributed on the streets. Getting their apocalyptic message out to the people was an urgent mission. And it was each militant's personal burden to carry the weight of that enormous struggle and live under the threat of the possibility of defeat if together they did not work hard enough to succeed. Militants heartily believed that the fate of the U.S. working class — indeed, the fate of humanity — rested in the daily expression of their commitment to the cause. Linking her vision to the history of the world Communist movement, Dixon wrote:

> Such periods, as preceded World War I and World War II, are supremely dangerous periods, both for the capitalists *and* the working classes. Why? Because the class struggle escalates inevitably into class war, and class war into violent and brutal reaction by the capitalist ruling class. Will we be equal to the danger? Or shall we be destroyed as were the workers' movements in Germany and Italy? Shall we be able to mobilize the masses of the people in their own self-defense, or shall we be butchered as were our comrades in generations past, in the fascist attacks executed in Italy and Germany? Will we stand and fight? Or will we run and be destroyed? Will our class be driven helplessly into imperial war and industrial slavery as were the working classes of Germany? Or will we defeat our class enemies as they were defeated in Russia, China, Cuba, Vietnam, Angola and so many other nations? What will be our fate? As men make history, ultimately, *we* shall decide. We shall decide our own fate. Then let us decide! Let us decide for humanity; let us decide for the future. The real choice that confronts us is simply this: Will we fight for socialism or will we be destroyed by a triumphant barbarism?[3]

Since her departure from academia and entry into the life of a professional revolutionary, Dixon emphasized time and again that besides the obvious enemy — the capitalist class, or bourgeoisie — there was another, the petite bourgeoisie, who more than once had sold out the working class: for example, in Germany, Spain, and Italy in the early 1900s and in Chile as recently as the early 1970s. An alliance with the PBs spelled certain death for proletarian revolution, an idea about which Dixon wrote profusely.[4] In early polemics against various leftist groups, Dixon expressed rage at her competitors, labeling them "the PB enemy."

A well-studied document issued in fall 1976, "The Directive on the Defense of the Party and the Party Line," exemplified Dixon's noncompromising and antagonistic attitude toward these sellouts.[5] The directive was intended for Party militants who were feeling queasy about the overt hostility in words and deeds toward other groups on the Left. Party insiders referred to the directive as "Listen, PB!" In it Dixon addressed individuals in the Party (and out), making clear there was no halfway point in regard to the Party's stance on this matter:

> If, like some little spoilt rats, you cannot even take losing some bullshit PB friends in the struggle, what the hell are you going to do when you might lose your life or your freedom? . . . And don't think that this Party is going to

make you a hot shot in the PB left or win any friends in the PB left for you: we aren't Christians, we don't turn the other cheek and we don't eat with our enemies. One-sided? You bet we're one-sided! We are on the side of the working class and that is the ONLY side we are on — and we are against all other sides! You don't live on both sides of the fence in this world or in this Party. . . . Every single militant in our organization must, absolutely must know, accept and be ready for the fact that we, as a Party, are a Party of heretics! . . . *YET THIS IS WHY THIS PARTY IS WORTH FIGHTING TO THE DEATH FOR.*[6]

With such fierceness burning in their minds and hearts, militants lived by another compelling idea that was hammered into them in Party School: "Without the Party there is no struggle, and without the struggle there is no future."[7] The task would not be easy, but the ultimate price was glory. Theirs was a struggle for all humankind. They considered themselves martyrs for the cause and believed that eventually they would earn the respect of the world's working classes.

Those who joined gave all. A core group of militants was wedded to that worldview; but over the years, despite their hard work and boundless devotion, their efforts at recruitment were less and less successful. Few new members stayed for any length of time after the formative years — although hundreds of people passed through for brief periods, either as Trial Members or as associates working with one of the front organizations. Two purges of non-full-time militants (one in late 1980, the other in mid-1982) solidified the DWP around Dixon and the remaining cadre. Those organizational contractions came during a time of increasing isolation, erratic political involvements and changing strategies, and the onset of intensified class-standpoint struggle inside the DWP.[8]

The Glory Days

During its twelve-year existence, the DWP was active and prolific. One structure after another was put into place — and then either abandoned or reformulated. As early as 1976 the group had its own print shop (first called Greenleaf Press, then Synthex Press), which grew into a full-service printing and publishing operation that serviced mainstream clients such as banks, catalog companies, and publishers throughout the San Francisco Bay Area. The press was a main source of income for the Party. Militants who worked there were not paid and were required to work long hours so that the press could underbid competitors. It was well run and accommodated every customer's needs.

FIGURE 16. The cover of an issue of *Our Socialism*, a political magazine published by the Party in its later years.

In addition, the press produced numerous materials for the Party: books, journals, newspapers, pamphlets, flyers, bulletins, direct mail solicitations, buttons, an endless array of products. Militants wrote and produced a weekly newspaper, the *Rebel Worker* (later *Plain Speaking*), which was sold on the streets. Everyone, except those at the very top, such

FIGURE 17. The author representing the Party's publishing house, Synthesis Publications, at the 1984 Frankfurt Book Fair in Germany. (Janja Lalich)

as Marlene and Eleanor and a few others, participated in paper sales. The average quota that militants had to meet was about seventy-five or eighty issues sold every other week. The Party also produced a theoretical news journal, *Our Socialism* (see fig. 16). At times, the newspaper and the journal were put out in bilingual English/Spanish editions. Also, the DWP produced two respectable academic journals, *Contemporary Marxism* and *Crime and Social Justice,* which solicited and published articles by well-known intellectuals on the Left.[9]

The Party's full-scale publishing house, Synthesis Publications, was bankrolled by one of the wealthy members, and from three to nine militants were assigned to work there (without pay). The publishing house exhibited at major book trade shows, such as the American Library Association, the American Booksellers Association, and the Frankfurt International Book Fair, and engaged in fairly large direct-mail campaigns, sending out catalogs and flyers to solicit orders and garner publicity. Books were also sold through regular trade channels and distributors. From 1981 until the Party's dissolution, one of my assignments was being in charge of the publishing operation. Dixon knew of my love for books and ideas.

One day in a meeting, she said to me, "Hah!" — she often started a pronouncement with a loud "Hah!" — "you always wanted to own a bookstore, right? Well, Comrade Emma, I'm going to give you better than that. I'm going to give you your own publishing house. Now you build me the best goddamned publishing house you can. Now get on with it!"

The publishing department worked long and hard. Over time, Synthesis gained a good reputation as a progressive publishing house, especially after it expanded beyond publishing only Dixon's work.[10] (See fig. 17.)

FORMING POLITICAL FRONTS

Several popular grassroots organizations (the Worker-Patient Organization, the Grass Roots Alliance, the Peace and Justice Organization, U.S. Out of Central America [USOCA]) were organized by the DWP. They were essentially front organizations in that they were totally controlled by the Party — a fact often kept in the background.

Those groups were involved in numerous activities. They sponsored local candidates and ballot measures in the San Francisco Bay Area, including the quite popular Tax the Corporations initiatives, Propositions P, V, and M, the latter of which succeeded in 1980 but was never implemented. Proposition P, on the November 1979 San Francisco ballot, received 48 percent of the vote. Proposition V, in June 1980, brought in 41 percent, even after much negative publicity about the DWP in the local press. And Proposition M, in November 1980, passed with 55 percent of the vote but was later declared illegal.[11] These initiatives were an attempt to have the city's largest corporations pay more local taxes and to have a certain percentage of the city budget designated for essential public services.

In about 1981 the DWP became active in the Peace and Freedom Party, a third-party alternative that had qualified for the ballot in California. The Party saw it as a way to make statewide inroads. As part of that effort, the DWP ran a candidate for governor on the Peace and Freedom Party ticket in 1982, which caused enough of an upset to get the conservative Republican George Deukmejian elected instead of the black Democratic candidate, Tom Bradley. It was the conclusion of many that if the votes cast for the DWP candidate had been cast for Bradley, he would have won.[12]

There were other front groups, which were meant to either intervene in or recruit from different sectors. These included the League for Proletarian Socialism and later the Institute for the Study of Labor and Economic Crisis, both of which targeted academics and intellectuals. Naturally, working-class causes and recruits were targeted also. Workplace efforts and labor-movement and union activity were the focus of Party-run entities such as the Rebel Worker Organization and the Worker-Patient Organization (active, in particular, at San Francisco General Hospital). DWP activists were placed in specific workplaces and unions, such as the International Longshoremen's and Warehousemen's Union (ILWU) and the Service Employees International Union (SEIU). U.S. Out of Central America organized and conducted delegations to Nicaragua, and lobbied Congress on various issues related to U.S. intervention policies (see fig. 18).

Not all of those "achievements" went without criticism. Over the years, the DWP was accused by the Left of splitting and wrecking a number of progressive groups and causes. A popular leftist newspaper, the New York-based *Guardian,* published an article on the DWP and its practices. The article listed a string of disputes with others on the Left that began in 1975 and ended in 1984.[13] These conflicts were with the West Coast Socialist Social Sciences conferences (1975, 1976); Health/PAC West, a medical research group (1976); the Mission Neighborhood Health Center, a low-income clinic in a Latino area of San Francisco (1979); NACLA-West, a group that researched and published on Latin American issues (1979); two local service workers' unions (1981 and 1983); the Communist Party and a local peace coalition (1983); the Peace and Freedom Party (1983); and CISPES and most of the other groups involved in Central America support work (1984).

In addition to being disruptive, the DWP was accused of creating confusion and dissension, causing splits, attempting takeovers and wanting all the credit, selling out rank-and-file causes, engaging in fraudulent prac-

FIGURE 18. The author speaking to Nicaraguan political activists while a member of a Party-sponsored delegation to Nicaragua in August 1984. (Janja Lalich)

tices, and generally working in an isolationist and sectarian manner.[14] For example, during one coalition effort surrounding a peace march, the DWP offered to print the posters and flyers — and then put the number of its own office as the contact number instead of the coalition number. When confronted, the DWP leadership feigned ignorance. This kind of activity was not highly thought of among other progressives.

As Elbaum noted, within the Left, the DWP was known to be "not above trying to psychologically and at times physically intimidate other activists on the left, ex-DWP members in particular."[15] There were several more widely known incidents, others known about only within the Party, and still others, of course, that only the Party's inner circle was aware of. Beginning in the Party's first year, "goon squads" would be sent out to harass and intimidate some "enemy" or other. These forays included acts of physical violence against people and property — assaults, spray-painting cars, trashing offices and homes, and the like. Special teams were assigned to carry out these actions, and Dixon would decide if, when, and how the details of these adventures would be conveyed to the rest of the members. Always, the DWP portrayed itself as the beleaguered champion of the working class, fending off spies, enemies, class traitors, and Red-baiters. That these actions merited violence was justified by the Party's rhetoric of working-class revolution and the cadre ideal.

THE APPEARANCE OF SUCCESS

Eventually militants were assigned to "stations" in Los Angeles, Nashville, Milwaukee, New York, and Washington, D.C. The impressive array of activities in the Bay Area and elsewhere was closely monitored and directed by Dixon, with the help of her inner circle of trusted lieutenants and the middle-level command structure. An equally astonishing array of internal structures existed to oversee and control the administrative functions, such as dues collection and finances, security, promotions and demotions, work assignments, and the dissemination of edicts and study guidelines.

The peak years of membership were 1980 and 1981. For several years, local organizing efforts had centered on issues related to the changing tax base brought about by California's passage of Proposition 13 in 1978. The DWP's analysis was this: the two "fat cat hustlers" who sponsored Prop. 13 took advantage of home owners' dislike of increasing property taxes to push through a bill that served only the interests of Big Business and would result in massive cutbacks to services and jobs throughout the state.[16] After Prop. 13 passed, the average home owner was supposed to feel some relief; but the gain was felt primarily by landlords and large corporations because Prop. 13 allowed for a 40 percent reduction in city businesses' share of local taxes. California's passage of this proposition set off similar tax-cutting movements across the country.

In one massive effort, Party militants gathered twenty-one thousand signatures of San Francisco residents who were opposed to Prop. 13 and its threat of cutbacks in city services. Through the GRA, militants worked on various electoral campaigns sponsored by the Party and also served as foot soldiers for other candidates and ballot measures approved by Dixon for strategic reasons. They put on events and fund-raisers and spoke at rallies, at City Hall, and in numerous public places. Militants made quite a name for themselves by getting up and speaking on the city buses, which always caused a stir. They gathered petition signatures and were generally a very visible (and noisy) presence in Bay Area politics. A high point during that period was a large demonstration in June 1978: an entire city block on which sat San Francisco's City Hall was wrapped in a lengthy, plastic-enclosed petition bearing thousands of signatures in support of the GRA's effort to save city services. Dixon and the militants were delighted to see that *Time* magazine captured the moment in full color. That kind of positive public work increased the Party's membership rolls by the hundreds.

But just as membership was at its peak, Dixon decided to draw the line on membership requirements. She concluded that having members at different levels with different degrees of commitment was detrimental to the full-time cadres. Most part-time members were expelled, and the mass organizations were dissolved. The cadres closed ranks, and the organization contracted in size. For many, this Menshevik purge, as it came to be called, was a significant turning point in organizational life.[17]

The Unraveling

The DWP's founding belief system, as explained to recruits and members, was to build a revolutionary, feminist organization that would fight for real change in the daily lives of the U.S. working class, eventually leading to the advent of socialism. In the early years, there was a great deal of emphasis on labor committees, workplace organizing, community efforts, and so forth. At one point, as described above, the DWP led a grassroots organization of nearly a thousand members who worked on local political issues; many of the peripheral members and supporters of that work were residents of the city's nonwhite communities. That was a genuine boon for the organization, as well as a morale booster for the militants.

Over time, because of Dixon's disenchantment with local issues and working-class causes, which she felt were not making enough of an impact and were reformist rather than revolutionary in nature, the focus changed from local work to international causes, from a biweekly newspaper distributed locally by the members to dense academic books and theoretical journals put out by the publishing arm and distributed through trade and academic outlets. Although militants still did some local organizing (usually in the form of support work for revolutionary struggles elsewhere, for example, in Central America), most members became increasingly distanced from what the DWP was espousing and from Dixon's aspirations.

DISILLUSIONMENT

At this time Dixon launched a new polemic in an attempt to establish herself once again as the sole upholder, this time, of the world working class.

She began to profess new theories on East-West polarization and the future of socialism.[18] Dixon had long been an adherent of the ideas of Immanuel Wallerstein and Andre Gunder Frank. She had gotten to know Wallerstein, an eminent sociologist and the originator of world-systems analysis, when they were both at McGill in the early 1970s. Wallerstein's theory rests on two basic premises: "the world-system as a unit of analysis, and the insistence that all social science must be simultaneously historic and systemic."[19] World-systems theory posits that the fundamental unit of analysis should be the world economy, not the nation-state.

For years, Dixon had regarded Wallerstein and Frank as her intellectual mentors; but as her sense of self expanded, she began to think of the two scholars as intellectual equals rather than mentors. Then in 1984 she attacked these two colleagues as being essentially antisocialist and anticommunist. She labeled them apologists for capitalism and called them cynical, pessimistic, and doomsayers. Her critical stance was based on their idea that modern-day socialist nations were doomed to failure because on entering the world economy, they in effect become capitalist.

At that juncture, Dixon was rejecting the possibility of there being a progressive, much less revolutionary, U.S. working class; also, she was recognizing the limitations of the Chinese revolution, long a beacon of hope to the DWP. As an alternative, Dixon adopted a position more favorable to the USSR. She began educating the Party in this major theoretical shift. Given this, it was not in Dixon's interest to regard the Soviets as capitalists; she had to rebel against Wallerstein and Frank. Debates on this issue, long held in private, were brought forward now to the DWP rank and file, as Dixon began to discuss publicly her disagreements with world-systems theorists.[20]

"There must be those who will guard the hope that the future will hold the dawn of a new age," she wrote.[21] Clearly, she saw herself as that guardian.

Concomitantly, Dixon began taking a greater interest in eastern Europe. Quite regularly she traveled to international conferences and meetings in western Europe, Yugoslavia, and Bulgaria. Her goal was to get an invitation to visit the Soviet Union. Much of the Party's work revolved around these international activities, which was rather alienating for the average militant. It was hard to make the leap from talking to people on the street about local ballot propositions to getting excited about what was going on in Bulgaria. No one dared speak it, but many a militant wondered what any of this had to do with the U.S. working class. Demoralization was widespread by 1984.

REVOLUTION WITHIN

Repeated criticisms of sectarianism, the high cost of Dixon's international travel, and various internal crackdowns in which a number of longtime cadres were expelled fueled a kind of despair among the remaining DWP members, as well as growing anger and frustration in Dixon herself. For more than a year, the Party had been discussing the failure of the Marxist-Leninist model. Dixon had concluded quite resolutely that the U.S. working class was not going to rise up. She declared that progressive, petit bourgeois political activists would be better allies. That stunning about-face was hard for militants to take after years of being inculcated with the idea that the PBs were the enemy and that they would hopelessly undermine the working-class struggle.

Dixon suggested not only a change in strategy but a new form of organization as well. She recommended getting rid of Marxism (without getting rid of Marx) and getting rid of the Party's Communist image (without getting rid of democratic centralism or the cadre). One proposed name for the new organization was Alliance Against American Militarism. Militants grappled as best they could with these issues, but they were exhausted, confused, and scared. Dixon's communiqués to her followers were harsher and less intelligible than ever before; she, too, seemed fed up.

In fall 1985 Dixon began talking about leaving with a small number of Party intellectuals and the few members with access to money. She said they would go to the East Coast to set up a think tank. She talked openly about getting rid of the "riffraff," meaning the rank-and-file militants who knew nothing of these discussions within the inner circle. Over the years, Dixon had become more and more dysfunctional, with clear signs of alcoholism and paranoia. Those of us in top leadership — Dixon's inner circle — kept the other Party members sheltered from the subjective and arbitrary nature of their leader's behavior and erratic decision-making style. Few, however, were spared the grueling eighteen-hour workdays and the endless sessions of unrelenting criticism/self-criticism.

In late October, feeling harassed and distraught, members of the inner circle staged a revolution of sorts. They broke the bonds of silence: first with each other; then revealing to the rest of the members what had really been going on behind the scenes. Dixon happened to be out of the country on one of her international adventures. Taking advantage of her absence, the inner circle called together the members and haltingly but honestly spoke out about the real nature of the Party. Hesitantly, militant after militant joined the chorus of the angry, disillusioned, frustrated, tired, and confused. Emotional and wrenching speak-bitterness sessions went on for a couple of weeks.

The night before Dixon's return, Party members convened and solemnly voted to expel their leader and dissolve the organization. Both votes were unanimous. A special committee was chosen to inform Dixon the next day, on her return from a trip to eastern Europe. Her city house was cleaned of weapons and guard dogs while an assigned team picked her up at the San Francisco airport. Once home, seated in her favorite plush leather recliner, Dixon looked out at the small group gathered around her and inquired about what had been going on in her absence.

"Well," she barked. "What's been going on? What do you have to report?"

Prepared ahead of time, one of the female leading cadres said, "We've come to tell you — well, we've come to tell you, the Party's over. The membership has met and taken a vote. The Party is dissolved and you have been expelled."

Dixon sat back in her chair, silent, not moving. After a moment, she slowly opened the rectangular marble box on the end table next to her. She took out a cigarette and held it up to her mouth. She waited. And waited. What seemed like a lifetime passed by in probably less than a minute. No one moved. No one came forward, as had been the practice, to light her cigarette.

"Hah!" she blurted. "Now I get it." And the cursing began.

DISSOLUTION

Marlene Dixon lost her organization after more than ten years as its supreme head. She had lived a life complete with all the perks and privileges of an unchallenged charismatic leader. Now she was sent on her way, as so many expelled militants had been over the years.

Meanwhile, DWP members tried to put their lives together and make sense of what had happened. Some moved away from San Francisco; others who had been called back for the dissolution meetings returned to the cities where they had been living. The Party's final demise came after another vote by mail in April 1986, which followed a series of heated discussions and a flurry of documents and position papers. During those months, sides were taken in intense debates among the now ex-membership regarding the continuation of political work, the possible formation of a new organization, and the fate of group assets. That vote was won by the majority, who favored the liquidation of assets to be shared among former cadres, most of whom had spent more than ten years of their lives "building the Party." Eventually, in August of the following year, an equal disbursement of group monies was parceled out to the approximately one hundred members who had been present at the earlier vote in November 1985. Each former member was eligible to receive $542.

Members' reactions to the breakup of their organization were varied. For those who had spent the good part of a decade or more totally devoted to the ideals and goals of the group, it was an extremely emotional event. A deep psychological impact was felt also, given the many years of hard work combined with the intense, very direct criticism experienced by almost everyone on an almost daily basis. The coup of sorts that dissolved the group was not capable of eradicating the individual aftereffects felt so deeply by these dedicated activists.

The Failure of Bounded Choice

In retrospect, we can see that the members of Heaven's Gate who ultimately sacrificed their lives were operating under a powerful cultic system that allowed them to perceive their actions as completely logical and inevitable. They had succumbed entirely to the emergence of a state of bounded choice within a self-sealing system of charismatic authority, transcendent belief, systems of control, and systems of influence.

DWP members, on the other hand, ultimately escaped an internally logical but self-destructive bounded choice and instead were able to dissolve their group. The DWP was undoubtedly a cult, and the core adherents' lives were constrained, controlled, and limited; nevertheless, DWP members were able to liberate themselves and, unlike the Heaven's Gate students, survive the experience. This very great difference in the DWP's termination can be attributed to certain combustible aspects of its structure.

THE DISSOLUTION OF CHARISMATIC AUTHORITY

We saw in Heaven's Gate and again in the DWP how the participant's engagement with the group was rooted in an extraordinary degree of commitment that evolved over time. It began with some sort of initial meeting or encounter with the leader or members of the group, or with being introduced to the group's ideology by other means. Once one joined, one's daily life was taken up with group activities and the social world became the world of the group. Through various processes, most members experienced a worldview shift, or conversion, out of which evolved a state of complete identification with the leader and the group and complete internalization of the group's worldview.

The role of the leader was central to each member's involvement in and commitment to the group. In many ways, especially in these two groups, this charismatic relationship was not only top-down but also essentially parental in nature. How the leaders behaved, in particular in relation to and in the presence of their members, had a great impact on the members' commitment and on the group's outcome.

Dixon behaved like a harsh, authoritarian parent. She was significantly less caring or nurturing toward Party militants than were Applewhite and Nettles toward their followers. Dixon's modus operandi was more akin to blatant one-way power than to a flexible style of relational authority. The latter, with its ongoing dynamic between leaders and followers, allows authority to have a more legitimate basis — and, consequently, engenders less rebellion within the ranks. The overt and harsh manner in which militants were criticized and blamed was impossible to ignore; after the Party's dissolution, numerous militants described the daily environment in the DWP as brutal and destructive. Although the DWP was known for its extremely subservient members who fawned on their leader, it is not hard to imagine that militants harbored also a seething resentment and profound distaste for the harshness of their lives.

In addition, eventually Dixon's way of handling organizational crises began to chip away at the stability of the organization itself. Over time, this allowed a tiny crack to occur in the armature of the self-sealed structure of the group. Within a year and a half, that crack grew until it could no longer hold the force of questioning and resistance from the inner circle and then the rank-and-file militants themselves. The Party was undergoing a sort of identity crisis, which Dixon named "the crisis of M-L," or Marxism-Leninism. She regarded it as a great turning point in the political career of the Party; little did she know how pivotal it would be.

During this period, Dixon expressed not only frustration but also disillusionment with the Marxist-Leninist model and was openly in despair at the end. Unfortunately for her, she seemed to have forgotten her role as charismatic leader to a devoted group of followers. Her self-centeredness and open derision of DWP militants went too far, especially when fueled by alcohol and coupled with a rejection of the very organizational model both cadres and rank-and-file militants had worked so hard to build over the years. Once the inner circle came forward and admitted to the corruption and deliberate manipulation at the highest levels of the organization, DWP members chose to give up the dream and dissolve the organization, traumatic as that act was.

THE WEAKNESS OF TRANSCENDENT BELIEF

Marlene Dixon expressed frustration numerous times over the fact that the Party was not accomplishing what she would have liked it to. She had always seen herself as a great revolutionary leader, but when things did not work out, she consistently laid the blame on the militants in general or on specific upper- or middle-level leaders. As the years passed, Dixon withdrew into her private world and was rarely present at meetings or gatherings. In the early years she had spent considerably more time at the Party facilities, conducting meetings and leading criticism sessions, sometimes even getting quite involved in the oversight of day-to-day work. But by the mid-1980s Dixon's appearances were few and far between; she stayed primarily at her comfortable and private country home, about one and a half hours north of San Francisco in a relaxed coastal town. Also, she began to travel internationally, removing herself even more from the daily life of the Party while at the same time requiring great expenditures of militant labor and organizational finances to support her travels.

In early 1984 Dixon introduced her major line change. Not only had she decided that it was *not* possible to advance to a "genuine workers' democracy in the foreseeable future," but also, and even more significant, she lost faith in the U.S. working class: "We have no illusions that the organized working classes of the core are revolutionary or that they will become a revolutionary force."[22] She was clearly in turmoil about the possibilities of working-class revolution; yet, having traveled for several years to eastern Europe, she became quite enamored with Bulgaria and the hope of being invited to the Soviet Union. That dilemma generated an internal intellectual struggle to reshape a vision that would be acceptable to her followers. Meanwhile, this fundamental shift in belief had a serious ripple effect throughout the Party.

Until that time, other line shifts or organizational shifts — even while they might have been traumatic or caused upheaval — always served the members in some way. For example, when most of the part-time members were expelled in the Menshevik purge, the cadres realized they were going to have to continue carrying the burden alone, but they were also mollified, because the new policy reinforced how special the cadres were. In that way, the purge bolstered each militant's internalized sense of elitism, as they rededicated themselves to the cause. They were the best, they were told; and certainly not everyone could be expected to be so dedicated and so strong.

Another line shift occurred in relation to children. Initially, the Party more or less supported the fact that a number of members had or were planning to have children. But suddenly it was no longer even remotely fashionable for militants to have children. Dixon and her top leaders decided to liquidate the Party's child care assistance, an around-the-clock service staffed by militants. Despite this reversal, militants still hung onto the Party slogan "The children are our future." They simply rationalized that their role was to create a revolutionary society that would benefit all people rather than attend to their own present-day needs.

In still other campaigns and purges, Party leaders were masterful at creating an us-versus-them atmosphere so that militants who chose for the Party felt staunchly righteous and honored to be in the DWP. But the line change introduced by Dixon in 1984 drove too much into the heart of each militant's dream. The logic and implications of that change were as follows:

- The U.S. working class is not revolutionary; therefore, the DWP must support struggles in the underdeveloped world where the revolutionary classes are found.

- The world socialist movement cannot hope to survive without the USSR as a socialist power; therefore, the DWP must support the USSR and other socialist states.

- The petit bourgeois progressives are the most active in solidarity work; therefore, the DWP should work in alliance with them.

- Having reaped the benefits of being situated in the "imperialist heartland," the U.S. working class is profoundly disinterested in change and is not going to get involved in leftist activity, certainly not Marxist-Leninist parties. Therefore, the DWP must change from being a Marxist-Leninist party and transform into something new while retaining the cadre, the discipline, and the democratic-centralist core.[23]

Dixon decided to impart these new ideas to her followers. A series of discussion documents were distributed and some actual discussions took place. They were more democratic in nature than in previous Party experience, although the tone was one of impatience and growing frustration.

"Let's get on with it," Dixon would say. In a communiqué to the cadres in early January 1984, called "Facing Reality," Dixon wrote:

LOOK AT DWP! DAMN IT, JUST LOOK! 110 people in one city, unable to win a single struggle; unable to force recognition of itself in the mass media; UNABLE TO RECRUIT!! Look at it. Face what it means. Face your responsibility for the crisis. But don't blame the Party, it's all we've got. I will, however, let you in on a secret: we are good, we can be great — but not if we don't grow up. I decided to talk straight and see who could take it; if you can't take the heat, I think it's time you got out of the kitchen.[24]

In the end, the line change was pushed through in "debates" described by some cadres as "tightly controlled 'lively discussions' to fully understand and come to unity with these positions. Dixon did not even personally attend the assembly, but sent papers that were discussed immediately after they were distributed."[25] By the time Dixon presented the line change, militants were experiencing a high level of demoralization and exhaustion. After years of working at a frenzied pace, many militants were far more attuned to the task at hand or an impending deadline than they were to grand political ideologies — and lacked the capacity to articulate them.

In reflecting on that period, longtime cadre Marguerite said of the line change, "Oh, that. That passed me right by. By then I was too tired."

Such a deep sense of depoliticization and demoralization was felt by others as well. For example, in her resignation letter sent around that time to the Party leadership, Doris wrote: "I am also disturbed that almost non-stop since Christmas there have been discussions and re-discussion about re-organization. We are internally weak, talking to ourselves while world-shaking events are taking place. People are in motion. People are in motion for example about South Africa. . . . And where are we? Why aren't we a leading part in this upsurge? Why aren't we at least an active part of this upsurge? Where is our base?"[26]

In another document written after the DWP's demise, three former leaders referred also to the growing sense of alienation within the ranks during the final years: "We witnessed our own depoliticization and that of many militants. . . . It became more and more obvious that we had no direction and the Eastern European focus didn't really make sense for an American party at this time."[27]

Unlike the more finessed handling of belief-system shifts in the Heaven's Gate cult (see chap. 5), this final crisis in the DWP was handled in such a way as to destabilize the members. Not only were these changes in direct violation of basic DWP beliefs, but they no longer served the militants' interests in any way.

The ramifications of this fundamental line shift were multifaceted.

First, militants had joined an organization that they thought was unique in its line on proletarian socialism and American Marxism, and now they were being asked to turn their backs on the U.S. working class. Second, believing their vitriolic, disruptive, and sometimes violent behavior had been justified in countless battles with the petit bourgeois Left, militants were now being asked to make alliances with the very class they had always understood as the biggest sellouts, as putting the working class at most risk for slaughter. Third, for years the DWP had been critical of the Soviet Union — its excesses, the Stalin purge trials, the bloodshed, the bureaucratic nature of the Soviet party — and now militants were being asked to tie their future to Soviet power. Fourth, and perhaps most startling, militants had spent years transforming themselves, submitting to harsh discipline and relentless criticism, in the belief that this was how to build a true fighting party, a Marxist-Leninist party, and now they were learning that the model was all wrong.

The damage done by Dixon's push was not just a crack in the belief system. These were fundamental shifts that amounted to a massive rupture that contributed mightily to the ultimate demise of the DWP.

THE BREAKDOWN IN SYSTEMS OF CONTROL

The DWP norm was work, work, and more work. Give everything, put the organization first, forget about the self and petty needs — these were maxims militants lived by. The rationale for any extreme action was that the end justifies the means. Because of the claims of its charismatic leader and its transcendent belief system, the Party considered itself an elite force with its own brand of morality — which meant militants could lie, cheat, be violent, manipulate, if these would serve the cause. In other words, do whatever it took to meet the goal.

After the Party's dissolution, in a letter to others, former cadre Toby commented on his own conflict in trying to sort through ethical issues related to the Party's corrupt practices, its front groups, and the resultant distortion of the DWP experience. He wrote: "We constantly exaggerated what we had accomplished. I know that we put out figures far in excess of what we were actually printing [referring to USOCA's Central America support political bulletins]. I know that the vast majority of distributors weren't real as they didn't pay for what we sent them. I don't know how many got distributed but I do remember boxes upon boxes of them piling up in New York. I always justified this in my mind because it was the Party doing it and the rest of the left was so corrupt and PB and we were the only serious organization that could be counted on to defend Nicaragua. Now that I know this is not the case, what seemed like justifiable explanations now look like inexcusable lies designed to build our organization at the expense of others. It was dishonest and the height of sectarianism."

Because they functioned as a collective and lived a communal lifestyle, militants thought of themselves as a tightly knit community. They regarded each other as comrades — at home, at work, at meetings, at the facility — and believed they would die for each other if need be. Within a brief period after joining, a cadre member had no other life but the Party. Anything else was an intrusion on a very special existence, the life of a dedicated cadre. They lived by Rubashov/Bukharin's words, which were reproduced in their training manual. As Bukharin capitulated during the Stalinist purge trials, he said to the world press:

> As the moment of death approaches and one goes out into the great loneliness, the thought of going out alone, unforgiven, apart from the party in which I have lived and which to me has been life itself, was a prospect I could not face; and, if by some miracle I should not die, life outside the party would to me be worse than death itself.[28]

Such a deep belief was shared by DWP cadres. This made it easier to monitor, scrutinize, report on, and control all parts of their lives.

The rationale or justification for all of it was sacrifice for the greater good. When the DWP ended, militants spoke of feeling "intellectually barren," "dead inside," and "depoliticized." They spoke of the "brutality and irrationality" of the DWP's internal operation; yet while they were involved in it, they believed they were doing what was necessary to meet the ideal. Toby, for example, said, "It is not about motives and sincerity! I went through the DWP with the best of motives, convinced I was fighting sectarianism, convinced I was doing what was absolutely best and needed for the movement. But I was wrong! I was sectarian, and only now that the veil of the DWP has been lifted can I see that."

As time went on in the organization, for most members, there was less and less contact with the outside world. Because militants could never explain to anyone outside the Party what they were involved in, why they were never home, why they were never available for socializing, how they earned a living, and so forth, it became easier simply not to see one's family or former friends. Militants' lives became dominated by the daily task, the daily criticism, and whatever political campaign (internal or external) was in focus at the time. Their harsh and unusual lifestyle was accepted as the sacrifice necessary for the political cause, for the achievements the DWP supposedly was making. Over and over, militants were taught that the kind of sacrifice they were making was difficult but doable — and necessary.

To seal the system even more tightly, militants were taught that cadre life was not meant for everyone; they were to feel honored to be part of the revolutionary cadre tradition. And finally, militants believed that they had an even weightier responsibility — because their leader, Marlene Dixon, was special and because the DWP alone was the only principled, truly Communist group remaining in the North American Left. Militants truly believed that there would be no leftist movement if it were not for them and their efforts, but especially if it were not for their leader.

Dixon lost her charismatic powers not only in relation to the rank-and-file cadre members but also, and most important, in relation to her inner circle. It was the rebellion at the top that allowed the systems of control to disintegrate and the mass revolt to occur. Most likely, it would not have happened otherwise, for the rank-and-file cadre members did not know about, did not witness, and did not experience the same things the higher ranking cadres did. The latter, having spent more — or most — of their time with Dixon, knew that she was often unreasonable or often went too far. For years they covered it up, until finally they reached their ethical (and emotional) limit.

Once Dixon lost her hold on her lieutenants and once the bond of silence was broken among them, the DWP crumbled. Perhaps this can be best understood in light of a social-psychological theory called doubling.[29] This concept has been used, for example, to explain how physicians in Nazi Germany could go every day to the camps to perform cruel experiments and have people murdered only to come home each evening to their wives and children and be caring fathers and family men. In the case of the Nazi doctors, doubling provided one vehicle for evil and one for survival. This is a type of dissociation in which a fully functioning autonomous self develops as the person adapts to an environment that might be producing tension between it and the preexisting "self." It is different from our normal understanding of psychological dissociation, however, because the individual continues to adapt to and is involved in his surroundings, whereas dissociation per se implies a disconnection from reality.

Similarly, someone living under a cultic regime may feel tension and anxiety over some of the precepts of the new worldview, but in staying with the group and complying with the demand for change, over time the individual begins also to express the cult's ideology in words and deeds, becoming, in that regard, a new person. This new persona may exist side by side, or in the shadows of, the old self. In this instance, where stalwart members of Dixon's inner circle revolted against their leader, the cult persona lost out to the preferences and value structure of the noncult persona.

THE DISSOLUTION OF SYSTEMS OF INFLUENCE

Coercive persuasion was used quite blatantly to change and retain members in the DWP. Early on, the leaders guided members through an intense and deeply probing indoctrination process. The effect was to change not only their political outlook but also their perception of themselves. Old views and attitudes were disconfirmed, with the aid of class-standpoint struggle and criticism/self-criticism, bolstered with such slogans as "Every kind of thinking is stamped with the brand of a class." A proletarian-socialist worldview was promoted and reinforced. That desired outlook was defined by Dixon but also constrained by her personal, psychological, and political weaknesses.

Nevertheless, under the impression that Dixon was a great revolutionary leader and that extreme internal practices were necessary and foolproof, members came to believe that only in the DWP could they find a viable political solution — one worth fighting for, and giving up habits, friends, and family for. But as the years passed, less and less of their Party work revolved around working-class causes; and, as an activist organization, the DWP became more and more isolated and subject to charges of sectarianism and cultism. Yet Dixon was able to retain a solid core of followers by assuring them that they were the *most revolutionary* and by overwhelming them with her intellectual output and their daily assignments and deadlines.

Over the years, the group's interest in and focus on transient causes waxed and waned; front groups were set up and dissolved; new members came and went. The DWP expanded and contracted, and contracted again and again, as a result of various crises and orchestrated purges, until eleven years after its founding, even Dixon complained aloud at having a mere 110 members. Like Heaven's Gate, the DWP was a defeated and moribund organization, and Dixon, the leader, was faced with a personal and organizational crisis.

To survive, organizations need an "open and evolving approach to the future. Cultures that embody closed visions and self-sealing values tend to die."[30] Certainly these words are prophetic in relation to both the DWP and Heaven's Gate, though their specific ways of dissolution differed radically.

Over time, the Heaven's Gate membership had dwindled and the hoped-for response to full-page ads and Internet appeals had not materialized. Applewhite's response was to make a "final call," this time assuring his followers that the time had come to leave this world. He used the appearance of the Hale-Bopp comet as his signal. That signal became the confirming evidence in a no-exit system. This is an example of what the organizational psychologist Edgar Schein calls change through coercive persuasion.[31] Applewhite and his thirty-eight followers took their own lives to follow that marker and transcend to the Next Level. In the case of Heaven's Gate, only negative change was possible because of the institutionalization and hardening of its self-sealing belief system and its overarching culture of conformity and compliance. The symbolic images of "other levels" and supreme beings and of students being prepared to "take off" — so useful and intriguing during recruitment and indoctrination — evolved from handy rhetoric to a hard-core ideological reality. The myths and images they lived by became the ones they died by.

In the DWP, the outcome was similar, yet strikingly different. Instead of mass suicide, the members engaged in mass revolt. Ironic in a Marxist sense, the outcome was dialectical: a final, negative change for the organization, and, ultimately, positive change for the participants.

Two events converged in the DWP that led to its demise. First, realizing that her organization was failing, Dixon called for a Party-wide discussion and debate about the ways in which the organization should evolve and conquer the crisis. In a sense, like Applewhite, Dixon, too, made a final call: we must change, she insisted, *but not completely*. She urged her followers to throw off the shackles of Marxist-Leninist stereotyping without loosening the yoke of constant criticism and democratic centralism. This was as much a no-exit system as Applewhite's. On some level, Dixon's vision of a non-Marxist party of loyal followers who would still heed her every word was as much an illusion as Applewhite's claim that the UFO they had been waiting for was trailing the Hale-Bopp comet. Yet Dixon led the DWP discussions with the idea that the prevailing M-L crisis was the confirming evidence her followers needed to heed her call that what was "out there" was still no good and that they, as DWP cadres, could make this transition. However, the same type of institutionalization and reification as found in Heaven's Gate was evidenced in the DWP, with its self-sealing belief system and its culture of compliance and conformity.

This situation left DWP militants awash in a sea of confusion and frustration, with but a slight glimmer of hope for the future. They wanted to act on these grand ideas presented by their leader but knew they could not. Their ingrained discipline permitted only careful treading on this new ground, and those who ventured forward with too much hubris were cut down and put in their place. After years of training as sycophants, how could they now muster the strength to voice their own opinions? Having witnessed comrades being criticized, demoted, put on trial, charged with crimes of me-firstism or factionalizing or independent thought, dare one contribute creative ideas to these discussions? And after one or two brave souls who voiced the opinion that some of the Party's features were "overkill" were soundly denounced by the general secretary for trying to undermine the process, what other militant would come forward with ideas of his or her own? Despite Dixon's effort at change, the usual trappings became clear, and militants were once more faced with the kind of double bind that characterized their lives in the Party.

Now, let us look at the second factor that brought the explosive mix to a head and led to the downfall of Dixon and her party. Dixon's call for change was complicated and eventually undermined by the behind-the-scenes discussions she was having with her inner circle and top-level leaders. While publicly, to the group as a whole, she was leading the cry of revolution and change, secretly she was plotting to defect from her very own organization. At a series of leadership meetings at her house, Dixon complained that the burden of carrying the Party was "driving [her] crazy": she was sick and tired of the militants with all their questions and what she perceived as their problems and incompetence; she felt overworked and as though she had no quality of life. She even admitted that she was going to a psychotherapist—something militants were forbidden to consider. She talked crassly with her trusted leadership circle about leaving behind the rank-and-file militants and going with a handful of cadres (the ones with money and the ones she considered intellectuals) to start anew in Washington, D.C. She envisioned setting up a leftist think tank, near the country's policy makers. At the same time, her reasoning known only to her, she advised her lieutenants to launch a Quality of Life campaign throughout the Party, so militants could assess their own lives.

With that act, Dixon inadvertently led even her most loyal inner circle to realize they could not reconcile Dixon's divergent ideas and contradictory requests. How could they go into meetings and encourage militants to talk openly about their feelings but at the same time hold them at bay? What Dixon was saying and doing went too much against the grain—and now this! It was too much for them.

Thus, while Dixon may have thought her usual coercive ploys would work, in fact, it all backfired on her. There were too many messages and too many examples of betrayal. How could she talk of dumping the rank-and-file members? How could she continually blame everything on the militants when her own life so completely violated Party norms? How could individual inner circle members know they would be safe, would be chosen, when the final plans were made? Behavior that had always been accepted as legitimate revolutionary authority now was looking more and more like blatant power-tripping and self-indulgence.

As a result, some of the high-ranking members who were in on those pivotal discussions bolted — psychologically — from Dixon's control. Dixon's idea that members should look at their own quality of life was taken at face value. Finally — and tragically — these militants came to see that their revolutionary fervor had been derailed and that their lives had been spent on an abusive treadmill that had served not the working class but only a megalomaniacal leader. With that realization, while Dixon was out of the country, Party members came together and for the first time ever discussed openly their life circumstances. By unanimous vote, DWP members chose to expel their leader and dissolve their organization.

• • •

All in all, it is difficult if not impossible to predict any group's outcome. The two cases examined here reveal a complex mixture of hard and soft, or extreme and mild, features. For example, one might consider that Heaven's Gate was a more pleasant group than the DWP, with its spartan lifestyle and harsh, incessant criticism of members. It appears that the students of Heaven's Gate lived better and had less stressful lives than did DWP cadres. Yet, ultimately, DWP members found the capacity to resist the tyranny of their leader and the organization they created. They finally had their revolution. And the four pillars of bounded choice — charismatic authority, transcendent belief, systems of control, and systems of influence — dissolved in a dramatic and remarkably quick denouement.

So, though at first glance it might appear that Heaven's Gate was a "nicer" group, the depth of the internalized commitment associated with it came as a result of intense indoctrination and sophisticated and daily means of influence and control that made an indelible impression on the members, whether or not they were in close contact with their leaders and other members. And, especially, we must not forget that those who followed Applewhite and Nettles did so in the belief that they had found a path to eternal life, to overcoming death. Instead, their leaders led them to a final, self-destructive bounded choice for an act that led them to their death, to precisely what they had hoped to avoid.

Although members of the DWP gained their freedom from the constraints of their organization, the toxic aftereffects of membership were long in dissipating. The euphoria some may have felt as they stepped freely out into the world in late 1985 and early 1986 often was overshadowed by the psychological, physical, and material impact of having spent so many years as devoted cadres in the confines of the DWP. They were physically worn down by the years of living under a grueling work schedule, and most members felt emotionally and psychologically battered by the years of criticism/self-criticism. Many had little or no family outside the group to which to turn, no means to start life over again, and few resources with which to reenter society. Recouping such losses became a priority for most former DWP members.

PART THREE

Theoretical Perspective

The True Believer

The Fusion of Personal Freedom and Self-Renunciation

As hard as it might be to fathom belonging to a cult, we know that thousands upon thousands do. Through arriving at an understanding of the pushes and pulls of such a commitment, we can see how it happens to so many of us. It is for that reason that I undertook to deconstruct the Democratic Workers Party and Heaven's Gate. It is my hope that this comparison will illuminate the parallels in these two groups and the extent to which cultic influences operated to transform at least some of the members from devotees to true believers.

The Significance of the Social Context

The DWP and Heaven's Gate evolved out of two quite different social phenomena — the New Communist Movement and the New Age movement. Yet parallel themes, or governing principles, emerged in both of these broad social movements that had a significant and lasting impact on the types of groups that were formed in the mid-1970s, including the DWP and Heaven's Gate. Events and decisions, on both an individual and an organizational level, illustrate that leaders and members alike were powerfully influenced by ideas and concepts held dear in their respective social milieus.

During the early 1970s, political activists and spiritual seekers were drawn to ideas, personalities, and activities present in their unique social environment. Through personal factors and circumstance, some of these individuals banded together under the guidance of Marshall Applewhite and Bonnie Nettles, in one case, and Marlene Dixon, in the other. Rather swiftly, two very circumscribed organizations emerged. Looking at this from the macro (sociohistorical) as well as micro (personal) perspectives allows us to grasp the interactive nature of the emergence of true believers in the two organizations. The individual responded to the situational context, from which the group itself emerged and developed.

To recap from chapters 2 and 6, three foundational themes in the New Communist and New Age movements were attractive to adherents. These were recognition of the importance of attaching oneself to a higher cause, recognition of the need for strong and wise leadership, and recognition of the need for personal transformation in order to attain one's desired goal. Thus a moral imperative, leadership, and personal transformation were represented structurally in both the DWP and Heaven's Gate.

Movement ideals were manifested through four organizational dimensions, charismatic authority, the transcendent belief system, systems of control, and systems of influence. These dimensions formed the framework within which each group was dissected and analyzed in this study. Each of these dimensions also played a key role in the development of bounded choice in each group's band of true believers.

Structures of Freedom and Constraint

Giddens's theory of structuration highlights the dual nature of social structures, that is, the interaction between the social system and the participants, or agents, in it.[1] This is relevant to any meaningful discussion of cults because so often this interaction is not considered. Frequently, the group is studied on an abstract level, without attention to the individual's role in the group or the impact of the social system on the participant. Structuration theory provides a mechanism for doing this.

According to Giddens, the defining dimensions of a social system are signification, domination, and legitimation.[2] Signification concerns the constitution of meaning; domination has to do with expressions of power via resource authorization and allocation; and legitimation is based in a code of conduct and upheld by normative sanctions. These three dimensions not only make up the social system but also inform the knowledge base of the agents, or actors, within the system, who, when they act, reproduce the system. Charismatic authority, transcendent belief system, and systems of influence and control — the structural dimensions of my bounded choice framework — have everything to do with meaning making, expressions of power, and codes of conduct. These dimensions are interlocking and interdependent, together forming the cult structure, or totalistic system. The meaning-making structures and processes are intertwined with the dimensions of domination and power, which are "inherent in social association."[3] For example, the belief in the revolutionary party and the cadre ideal was central to the acceptance of Dixon as the authority figure and to DWP members' acquiescence to the group's normative system of conduct and sanctions. Similarly, in Heaven's Gate the belief in the Next Level and the genderless creature was key to the acceptance of Applewhite and Nettles as authorities and to the students' acquiescence to the group's norms and sanctions. The following summary of this structural framework and the ways in which these fundamental dimensions came to life focuses primarily on the similarities rather than the differences in the two groups. When significant, differences are discussed.[4]

CHARISMATIC AUTHORITY: THE LEADER–FOLLOWER DYNAMIC

Charismatic authority involves the interactive relationship between the leaders and their followers. Significant features of this dimension were evident in both groups, such as claiming a lineage of authority, prophesying, evading proof, and claiming perfection for the leaders while demanding utter obedience from the followers. Although each group had its own language, symbols, or specific manifestations of these features, the effect of charismatic authority was strikingly similar in both groups. (See table 5, Appendix, for a list of the most salient features of charismatic authority and how they were manifested in each group.)

First, we have seen that charismatic leaders are considered "charismatic" because of the regard of others. This supports the view that charisma is a relationship.[5] In the case of the DWP and Heaven's Gate, the charismatic relationship between leader and followers, especially between the leader and his or her foundational followers, was crucial to the establishment and growth of the group. These early devotees bolstered the leader's sense of self as special and destined to lead. Also, they were responsible for the hard work of recruiting to increase the fold; this task rarely falls to the charismatic leader.

Claiming a lineage of authority afforded these leaders a level of authority to which loyal followers and new recruits responded — Marxism-Leninism in the case of Dixon, biblical and cosmic connections in the case of Nettles and Applewhite. An all-powerful leadership principle as a guiding precept was emphasized in both groups. The point was to defend the leaders at all costs for they were "the source," the connection to higher authority.

Over time, adherents came to believe that their very existence depended on their leaders. Heaven's Gate students said in their exit statements some version of "I am nothing without Ti and Do." As for DWP cadres, who were equally bound to their leader, that sense of attachment and dependency translated to "I am nothing without Comrade Marlene." Such was written in Party documents, raised in criticism sessions, and written again in militants' own self-criticisms. In both groups this immovable and strict leadership principle played out in daily life in the shape of authoritarian and autocratic rule with no democratic mechanism for the followers. Alike in another way, the leaders of both groups relied on an inner circle and various trusted devotees for a variety of reasons: for consultation, for implementing and maintaining the status quo, for personal attendance, for moral support, and for sharing good and bad times.

In both groups, the leaders were originators of a new belief system purported to be *the* formula for salvation. They began with guiding elements popular in their respective milieus: Dixon co-opted Marxism-Leninism and the concept of the disciplined, vanguard party; Nettles and Applewhite picked up New Age ideas of channeling, spirit entities, and other levels of existence, along with some concepts from Christian thought, such as the Heavenly Father. These adept leaders then added their own ideas, lending an original cast to their worldviews. In Dixon's case, the result was a combination of working-class and feminist theories, which she called proletarian feminism, as well as her version of world-systems analysis. For their part, Applewhite and Nettles combined spiritualist and religious ideas with beliefs in UFOs, interplanetary travel, and the ability to overcome death.

Dixon, Applewhite, and Nettles served as role models for their followers: they set the style and tone, and, in return, they were lauded as exemplary and perfect. All three demanded total devotion and veneration, creating a situation that bred in devotees increasing dependency on the group and the leaders. At the same time, all three kept their distance from their followers, limiting access and keeping some well-guarded secrets. Most members were not privy to where and how the leaders lived or where they were at any given time. The vast majority of members did not know such things as where the money went or how overall strategic decisions were made. Strict policies controlled and contained information. This extended to details about the leaders' backgrounds, which stifled within the group the possibility of honest discussion or evaluation of the leaders' performance as leaders. In both groups there was a double standard: leaders were not held to the strict standards they set for their followers.

All three leaders expressed feelings of paranoia, which were bolstered by both real and imagined enemies. These feelings were shared by the group members, which kept them unsettled and fearful. In some cases, the leaders instigated actions that heightened this tension between the group and "evil outsiders." In Dixon's group, it was assumed that every militant held bourgeois and petit bourgeois attitudes, if for no other reason than having grown up in "the belly of the monster." But tensions were exacerbated by the specific "external" enemies: other leftist activists, progressive academics, former members or supporters of the group, and the monolithic State and its surveillance forces (which in fact had shown no interest in the DWP's activities). Similarly, in Heaven's Gate every student was to hate and renounce "human" attachments. But the group also feared specific "external" enemies, which included mainstream churches and New Age competitors, families of members who were trying to communicate with or locate the group, former members who criticized the group, and the Luciferian forces in the form of evil discarnates whose goal, they supposed, was to distract the students from their mission.

As the two groups matured and instituted strict behavioral guidelines, norms, and ways of being, the charismatic authority shifted from the more classic, pure type to a more routinized form, as is often the case.[6] Such a process occurred in both groups but to a greater extent in the DWP because of its size and complex structure. Toward the end, Dixon was seen rarely and was more or less sequestered from the majority of Party members. Her aides and inner circle had regular contact with her, but sightings by others were few and far between. By contrast, in Heaven's Gate most members had a direct, almost daily relationship with their leaders, especially when they lived communally or in close proximity. Although Applewhite and Nettles always lived apart from their followers — in another tent, a trailer, a separate floor of a house, a closed-off room, or a separate house — once the Class was formed, they remained in regular contact and for long periods had daily meetings with their followers. This availability allowed the charismatic relationship to take on a personal cast in Heaven's Gate, whereas in the DWP charisma by proxy was the order of the day, as upper- and middle-level leaders were given authority to direct the daily work and criticism sessions.

The structural dimension of charismatic authority is extremely significant. In a sense, it is the root cause of everything that follows. Without the leader, there would be no draw, no call, no promise of an ideal. And without devotees responding to that call, there would be no group, no set of coordinated activities, and no followers granting the leader the authority to rule.

TRANSCENDENT BELIEF SYSTEM: IDEOLOGICAL UNDERPINNINGS

The transcendent belief system comprises the ideological underpinnings of the group. Specific features characterize this type of belief system, such as being motivated by a moral imperative, being deterministic, having a sense of urgency, being both all-inclusive (having all the answers) and exclusive (elitist), and dictating the true path, "the only way," along with specific methods of transformation. (See table 6, Appendix, for a list of the salient features of this dimension and how they were manifested in each group.)

A transcendent belief system has two major components, having to do with the promise and the path. Both were present in both the DWP and Heaven's Gate. First, the belief system in each group was transcendent in that it offered a path to salvation — political in the case of the DWP, (meta)physically eternal in the case of Heaven's Gate. Second, on a personal level, it was transformational. A unique aspect of each group's specific transcendent belief system is that it outlined and provided specific means by which believers were to conduct this personal transformation. In fact, personal transformation was a requirement for remaining on the path and reaching the promised goal. In that regard, the belief system offered both the context and the tools for change.

The belief systems of the DWP and Heaven's Gate were all-inclusive; that is, each group regarded its belief system as "the Truth," the only way to salvation. This made the group special and engendered the sense of privilege and specialness in its members. The reverse condition of being all-inclusive is exclusivity. Both groups were separatist, sectarian, and elitist. They ridiculed other groups and belief systems and thereby were able to justify the requirement that adherents separate from people and activities that were not part of the group's elitist system.

Each group operated under a moral imperative. The message was urgent and deterministic. DWP militants were instructed through directed study to come to a particular understanding of the universe that was delineated in the speeches and writings of General Secretary Dixon. A pivotal component of this understanding was the dictum that once a person acquired "class consciousness," he or she could not do anything else but follow the path Dixon laid out. How could someone turn away from the working class once the machinations of class forces under capitalism were understood? How could someone shirk the enormity of the task?

Meanwhile, Heaven's Gate students learned that they had a deposit of knowledge if they responded to Applewhite and Nettles's message. This deposit meant the students were part of a special Class of Next Level creatures who were training to go back home. The dictum in this case was, once they understood they were from outer space, they could not do anything else but follow the path laid out by their leaders. How could they turn away from this opportunity to overcome death, return home, and escape the destruction of planet Earth? Thus such moral imperatives were central to the magnetic appeal of each belief system.

The DWP and Heaven's Gate presented themselves as serious and different from other contemporary groups. The transformational process promoted and required by both groups was founded on impossible ideals. To achieve the ideal required strict adherence to rigid norms, a reclusive lifestyle, and a complete break with the thinking and attitudes of one's previous life. Through intensive and deliberate training and indoctrination programs, members were pushed to internalize the group's beliefs. They were reprimanded in a variety of ways if they failed to exhibit the appropriate behaviors or voice the appropriate opinions. The substance of the indoctrination programs in both groups was not unlike thought reform and coercive persuasion.[7] In the DWP and Heaven's Gate, change processes were based on highly emotional and psychologically intrusive stages that involved the rejection of the past and one's previous identity, a shift in values and the recoding of preferences, and the rebirth of a new self. In the DWP the goal was to become the new cadre man or woman, steeled and emotionless; in Heaven's Gate the ideal was to become a new creature from the Next Level, genderless and free of all human traits and emotions.

In sum, the transcendent belief system was integral to the formation and evolution of these two groups. And significantly, it was the source of the demand that each member change quite literally to fit the group's ideal. Such change was necessary in order to be eligible to be part of the group. Together, the two dimensions of charismatic authority and transcendent belief system made up the primary structural core of each group.

SYSTEMS OF CONTROL: ORGANIZATIONAL STRUCTURE

Systems of control are those elements concerned with the organizational structure and daily operations. I found specific characteristic features of organizational form, hierarchy, discipline, codes of conduct, and behavioral norms in both the DWP and Heaven's Gate. (See table 7, Appendix, for a list of the salient features of this dimension and their manifestations in each group.)

Each group had a pyramidal structure with rigid boundaries between it and the outside world and between internal divisions. Also, both were hierarchical, with top-down command structures that demanded unconditional obedience. Decision making was centralized; the leaders made all substantive organizational decisions, as well as many decisions affecting individuals, such as where they worked, whether or when they could visit families, what kinds of intimate relationships they could or could not have, and what they were to do with their time.

Rules and regulations were plentiful, some might say excessive. Members in both groups lived tightly controlled daily lives. Heaven's Gate certainly excelled in that realm in that every action was orchestrated by the "procedures" delineated in excruciating detail by Nettles and Applewhite. But the DWP was also a very restrictive group: members needed to get permission to conduct most aspects of their everyday lives, and most of their time was consumed by DWP assignments and activities, with little left for personal matters.

Both groups were collectively run and communal; money and other resources were pooled; and members lived with other members. Here again, Heaven's Gate was more strictly communal in the sense of sharing clothes and other belongings, eating all meals together, and living in a total group situation. The DWP was slightly more lax in this area. Almost every Party member lived in a house or apartment with other members, and all cadres were expected to be in a DWP facility at all times unless they were working outside the group. DWP members had their own money; but given that the amount they could keep from wages or otherwise was determined by the Party, expenditures on nonessential items were rare.

Therefore, like the Heaven's Gate students, DWP militants spent most of their waking hours in the presence of other cadres, and their lives were highly regulated.

Because of the leaders' fear and anxiety and because of the us-versus-them nature of their belief systems, both groups stressed security. This was rationalized by a need-to-know policy, meaning that a member needed to know only the bare minimum of information necessary to be a good member, and it was in one's interest not to know more. Guidelines restricted movement, phone calls, names, mail, and so on. Certain areas and buildings were off-limits, as were some topics of discussion. Security alerts and warnings had a stultifying effect on daily activities and daily life. In both groups members took on new names and were not to talk about personal backgrounds or emotional matters. Again, this restriction was more severely monitored in Heaven's Gate, but in the DWP it was considered "self-indulgent" and "PB" to talk about one's feelings, especially in terms of family, relationships, intimacy, lack of free time, and specific assignments. Also in both groups, the locations of work and living quarters were kept secret from outsiders and sometimes from new or lower-ranking members.

Both groups required total or near-total submission to the leader and the rules governing group life. A system of sanctions for violations of norms or rules existed in each group, relying to a large degree on self-reporting and peer reporting. Members were expected to be obedient, guided by the duties and obligations of having made a total commitment.

Several important studies shed light on the type of obedience found in the DWP and Heaven's Gate. One is Stanley Milgram's classic *Obedience to Authority*. Milgram led an experiment in the 1950s in which participants continued to administer what they thought were electric shocks to another person who could not be seen but could be heard. The reason most of the subjects (approximately 60 percent) persisted in giving "shocks" at increasing intensity, resulting in what they believed was increasing pain to the other person, was because they were given the order to do so by an authority figure (a doctor in a white lab coat) whom they did not oppose. Herbert C. Kelman and V. Lee Hamilton's *Crimes of Obedience* describes such incidents as the My Lai massacre during the Vietnam War, when American soldiers killed innocent civilians on their commander's orders.[8] The type of obedience that existed in the DWP and Heaven's Gate, wherein cadres and students followed orders without question, is similar to that described in these classic studies. As humans, we tend to follow through on our commitments, and we tend to respect and obey authority figures, even to our own detriment or the detriment of others. In this regard, the DWP and Heaven's Gate stalwarts who stood by their leaders and went along with certain actions or decisions were not so unusual.

Over time, in both groups, life became rigid, rule-bound, narrowly focused. The effect on members themselves was similar: rigid, dogmatic, single-minded. This state of being made it practically impossible for members to see any way through the boundaries of the system.[9] Rules and regulations hardened into a numbing and oppressive reality. These institutionalized systems of control were justified in each group by its overarching transcendent belief system. Members understood them to be the right of charismatic leadership and accepted them as such.

SYSTEMS OF INFLUENCE: SOCIAL CONTROLS

The final dimension of the structural framework is systems of influence, or the social controls that are part and parcel of the system. Once again, I found the same specific features in both the DWP and Heaven's Gate. (See table 8, Appendix.) Most important, a strict normative system and behavioral model based on an internalized attitude of constant striving toward the ideal was pivotal to the smooth functioning of both groups.

The crucial characteristics of social influence were self-monitoring, peer monitoring, and modeling oneself after approved behavior, exemplified by the leader, the ideal of the belief system, and other members. Adherents were expected to reject their former lives and interests, shed their pregroup identities, and take on a new group-molded identity. They were to have no loyalty other than to the leader and the group, and no interests other than working toward group-approved goals. The mechanisms used here were the same as those that tied the followers to their leaders, as discussed earlier. The object is the molding of identities in the image of the leaders. In the DWP the development of the changing self was monitored and furthered through a multitude of written and verbal reports and in individual and group criticism sessions. In Heaven's Gate there were similar mechanisms for reporting and daily sessions called slippage meetings to review "lessons." In both groups, then, ongoing criticism of errors in thought or deed was the norm.

Members' personal lives were governed by a strict moral code and rigid daily discipline, which propelled adherents to unite with the spirit of the collectivity and the leaders' demands. Enforced conformity was accepted by the members as necessary to accomplish their goals. The transcendent belief system held that this transformation was a personal choice. It was described in both groups as a "willing and willful transformation." This was an important aspect of securing members to their mission, for they clearly believed that they were the agents of their own transformation. They had made the commitment to change. No one was doing this *to* them; they were doing it to themselves — sometimes contentedly, sometimes begrudgingly — and they understood that it would not be easy.

A related ideal was that of the cog in the wheel. In Heaven's Gate no individual thinking was allowed whatsoever; students strove to be crew-minded, and any expression of individuality, considered human and therefore bad, was admonished by self and others. A student's mind was to merge with the Next Level Mind. In the DWP, on the other hand, this process of reduction and loss of individual thinking was more complex and more subtle. Militants were taught to "take initiative within the bounds of discipline." In actuality, taking initiative, or doing something without explicit guidance and instructions, was never allowed to happen. This extended to external activities such as union and workplace organizing, political rallies, grassroots work, and distribution of propaganda materials, as well as to "internal" activities such as meeting agendas, administrative work, and any number of tasks. More than once militants were publicly criticized or put on trial for "acting out" selfishly as a PB individualist. Yet the continual promotion and perpetuation of the concept kept members thinking that they were *supposed* to use their minds. This double-bind scenario proved one source of dissonance, and perhaps a crucial feature in the final outcome of the DWP.

The primary objective of the systems of influence was to get the individual member to identify completely with the leader and the group. In this way each member became what is known as a corporate actor. In such situations "the interests of all the members have a certain coherence."[10] When all the participants in a social system have identical interests, the result is a situation of optimal control for those in charge. In the DWP and Heaven's Gate, insofar as core members underwent a personal transformation that rendered them true believers and deployable agents, they were indeed corporate actors. In fact, they thrived on this very concept. It was the desired culmination of all their training. It was their longed-for ideal.

To achieve such a state of identification, the individual had to undergo certain psychic changes. Behaviors that elicit such a shift include acting to benefit others, identifying with successful persons, shared experiencing of consequential events, being dependent on another, and resting control in another.[11] DWP and Heaven's Gate members exhibited all five traits. They acted to benefit others, that is, the leader and the group. They identified with successful persons, that is, the leader and other high-ranking members. They shared consequential events, that is, events in the group context or events reframed by the leaders. They were dependent on another, that is, the leader and the group. And they rested control in another, that is, the leader. This powerful combination of group-oriented behaviors resulted in a level of trust, a willingness to obey, and a state of deployability that made it increasingly difficult for members to imagine life outside the group.[12]

· · ·

In the DWP and Heaven's Gate, the structural dimensions of charismatic authority, transcendent belief system, systems of control, and systems of influence were configured in such a way as to create a self-sealing system. (The crucial characteristics of each dimension of the organizational construct are shown in table 9, Appendix.) This is a type of closed system that reinforces itself and is not open to disconfirming evidence or other points of view. It is my general conclusion that the features discussed here (and illustrated fully in the preceding sections) are critical to a cultic system and were exemplified in the DWP and Heaven's Gate. In such systems, the person and the group become merged, creating, for the individual, an impermeable situation.[13] Boundaries between self, others, and the outside world are closed off and sealed.

AGENCY WITHIN BOUNDED SYSTEMS

Social structures are both constraining and enabling.[14] In these two cults, it is apparent that what constrained the followers enabled the leaders. On the other hand, the responsibility of authority constrained the leaders and enabled the followers.

This dialectic is found also on a structural level. In both groups, the overwhelmingly constraining structures also became enabling resources. The DWP's strict work requirements provide one illustration of this. For instance, militants were given quotas for fund-raising and selling newspapers and other items. This forced them to be creative. They needed to sell hundreds of papers or books of raffle tickets, gather scores of petition signatures or distribute political flyers, all on their "own" time, yet they were expected to be working at their assigned departmental facility and perform myriad other Party tasks. But getting out to sell things to the public provided militants with opportunities to experience themselves in other contexts, as well as to witness, experience, and confront other points of view. These situations and encounters gave militants slices of information — some of it for themselves, some for the group as a whole. For example, some information might encourage them to reevaluate (silently) their commitment to the group, while other information, when fed back to the group, such as the reactions of the people on the street to a headline in the Party's newspaper, might help the organization to reevaluate a particular strategy.

Likewise, in Heaven's Gate members encountered opportunities for change. Some, for example, held jobs in computer technology to help support the group. Those who worked in these out-of-craft tasks had more contact with the outside world and also learned new skills, which could be used if they left the group. At the same time, these skills enabled the group to have an elaborate presence on the World Wide Web, which allowed for other types of interaction and feedback on an organizational level.

In both groups, the leadership structure provided certain perquisites for the upper- and middle-level leaders: being privy to certain information, having a special relationship with the top leaders, being able to feel superior to others, and other privileges not shared by lower-ranking members. At the same time, some of the upper- and middle-level leaders found it difficult to reconcile their internal dissonance because they saw more and knew more conflicting information. That personal quandary might have led to inappropriate (from the organization's point of view) handling of their leadership responsibilities, especially vis-à-vis lower-ranking members.

The Bounded Reality of the True Believer

From this analytic comparison of the DWP and Heaven's Gate, I have extrapolated some general conclusions regarding charismatic commitment, membership selection processes, the nature of the charismatic relationship, varied group outcomes, and the self-sealing nature of ideological groups of this type. All five conclusions revolve around the compelling true believer reality that is bound up with the competing desire for personal freedom and demand for self-renunciation.

CHARISMATIC COMMITMENT

Participants' involvement in each group was rooted in a commitment that evolved from an initial attraction to the ideas of the leader, was consoli-

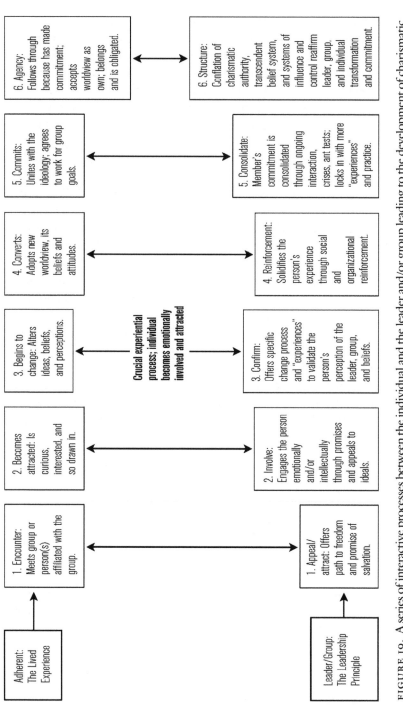

FIGURE 19. A series of interactive processes between the individual and the leader and/or group leading to the development of charismatic commitment.

dated through ongoing experiences in the group context, and, at least for some, resulted in a worldview shift, or conversion, that led to complete identification with the leader and the group as well as a life-altering internalization of the group's worldview.

Charismatic commitment is an interactive process, predicated on a charismatic relationship between leaders and their followers and between members and the group as a whole. It is a commitment bound up in intense devotion and personal sacrifice. In the cases here, members experienced the personal joy of having found an expression for their innermost desires — to have a life filled with purpose and meaning and to be part of a group. Both the DWP and Heaven's Gate promised their members a kind of personal freedom in their ultimate salvation, the everlasting reward for a life dedicated to the "correct" path and for being a faithful and hardworking member of the collectivity. Also, members experienced a sense of belonging, although at times they struggled intensely with their commitment because of the disparities between what they believed and what they were experiencing on a daily basis. That was especially true for DWP members, many of whom had extended contact with the outside world and therefore had more reality checks than did Heaven's Gate members.

Yet, offsetting this feeling of freedom, members engaged in continual self-renunciation. Denial of the personal in favor of the group was demanded by the leader, based on the precepts of the belief system, upheld by the disciplinary guidelines, and reinforced by the normative system. Commitment was expressed through ongoing participation in group practices, rituals, and work assignments that were time-consuming and sometimes grueling. But commitment was manifested also in changed thinking, attitudes, and behaviors as devotees strove to abide by the discipline and achieve the ideal. Ultimately, both groups produced true believers, a core group of dedicated, deployable agents who identified completely with the leader, the group, and its goals. (See fig. 19 for the interactive processes leading to charismatic commitment.) Each group's success in producing true believers was enhanced by the transformative process members engaged in to demonstrate their willingness to make a commitment.

Membership in these groups was grounded in the understanding that members were to undergo a personal transformation, the ideal of which was held forth in the group's belief system. In their respective groups, DWP cadres and Heaven's Gate students took part in calculated and ongoing programs of directed change. The goal of these programs was individual transformation: to alter beliefs, attitudes, thinking, and values.

Both groups employed psychological and social processes similar to those described in training and reeducation programs in Communist China, the former Soviet Union, North Korea, and elsewhere.[15] These processes, sometimes called thought-reform or brainwashing, include identity stripping, forced confessions, alternating periods of severity and leniency, and a symbolic death and rebirth ordeal[16] — all of which were evident in the DWP and Heaven's Gate.

A charismatic, cultic relationship requires cultivation and maintenance,[17] and these commitment processes constitute a primary method for meeting that need. Thus in both groups, not only was this transformative change process central to a person's involvement and individual enmeshment with the group, but it ensured that at least some of the members would make a total commitment and evolve into deployable agents.[18]

MEMBERSHIP SELECTION PROCESSES

Selection, self-selection, and deselection of members affected individuals, as well as the size and morale of the group. Selections were the outcome of an interactive process between leaders and followers and in some cases were one response to the dissonance experienced by members as a consequence of their group participation.

It is apparent that potential members were targeted by recruiters and occasionally by the leaders themselves. This tactic reveals a purposeful selection process whereby each group hand-picked those individuals who were already in some way primed for involvement in the group. Both groups used classic recruitment techniques such as flattery, positive reinforcement, peer pressure, involvement in group activities, emotional destabilization, persuasive arguments, and separation from usual routines and social supports.[19]

Especially in the early growth stages of the DWP, recruitment focused on leftist and feminist activists. Recruitment as a Party activity was prioritized through required reports and guided discussions in group meetings. Further refinement and eventual success was guaranteed by the transmission to militants of detailed instructions from Recruitment Officers and direction from the upper-level leadership. Similarly, in Heaven's Gate, potential recruits were targeted through introductory meetings held in and near progressive campuses and communities. Although these meetings were made known to the public through the distribution of posters, the information on the posters was designed to lure a certain type of person: that is, someone interested in exploring the unknown and the possibility of overcoming death. Posters and ads tapped into the prevailing interest in UFOs and other otherworldly phenomena of interest to New Agers. Thus, at this first level, each group respectively sought progressive-minded political activists or open-minded spiritual seekers, in particular, those who were dissatisfied with their political, religious, or self-awareness experiences. The two groups refined their efforts by flushing out idealistic individuals who were ready to join a greater cause and then engaging them in ever more intensified activities that fostered commitment and change.

That this selection process is interactive is a point sometimes overlooked in the study of cults. At the same time that the group spotted potential members, individuals self-selected by taking the first step toward involvement. Potential DWP joiners went to private discussions, study groups, or DWP-sponsored events. In most cases, they responded to the invitations and encouragement of friends, relatives, coworkers, or associates who were already in the group. Likewise, usually, potential Heaven's Gate joiners responded to a poster, an ad, or a media report. Some heard about The Two or their message from a friend, relative, or associate. Typically, these curious folks then went to a meeting or sought out the group.

In both cases, individuals whose curiosity was piqued decided to check it out. Although we do not know the internal motivation of all the members, the data indicate that at least some were frustrated with previous efforts in their lives (either political or spiritual), were trying to make sense of the world, and were looking for purpose and a sense of belonging. Their ages at time of recruitment ranged from early twenties to early fifties, with the average between twenty-seven and thirty-two. The degree of stability or involvement in their lives at the time varied: some were not attached or affiliated; others were quite entrenched in their personal and professional lives. From this one might conclude that the presence or lack of social stability is a less important factor in the decision to join than an intellectual or emotional pull toward the group, its leader, ideas, goals, and promise.

Deselection, too, is an interactive process between leader, members, and the group as a whole. First, in both examples, the leadership instigated purges and orchestrated tests to weed out less committed members and those who could not withstand the pressure. Second, some members left the group on their own, deciding that it just was not for them. Sometimes leaving came as a result of the demands of membership; sometimes it occurred because the person realized, consciously or not, that the reality of group life contradicted the professed ideal. In the DWP such a realization became more frequent as Dixon's interests and decisions took the group's daily work farther away from working-class projects and aims, which would have been more in line with the purported goal of the group. In Heaven's Gate contradictions were evident in the repeated failures of the prophecies: the Demonstration did not happen, the spaceships did not arrive to pick them up, Nettles died a "human" death, and what was supposed to take months (being "saved" by being lifted up to the Next Level) evolved into a project of years and decades.

In the end, doubters, rebels, the weak-willed, persistent nonconformists, the exhausted and confused, the physically frail — all these were among those who either left on their own accord or were expelled from the group.[20] Ultimately, in both groups, the deselection process helped to solidify the commitment of those who stayed. Greater was both the burden and the glory of remaining among the chosen few.

Because of these processes of selection, self-selection, and deselection, over time, both the DWP and Heaven's Gate were whittled down to a core of the most dedicated true believers. With each consolidation of that core, the leader's job of retaining followers (an urgent need for all charismatic leaders) was made a little bit easier.

THE CHARISMATIC RELATIONSHIP

The charismatic relationship in both the DWP and Heaven's Gate was essentially a parental one, characterized by rigid control. My data revealed a strong sense of attachment and, in some followers, induced regressive behavior; and on the part of the leaders, a high degree of desire to control.

In both groups, the leaders served as parent figures for their followers. I say this for several reasons. First, the groups provided everything for their followers, just as parents (ideally) do. Housing, finances, major life decisions — all were provided for or carried out within the norms and guidelines of each group's self-sealing system. Essentially, every aspect of life, or at least every meaningful aspect, was accounted for and directed by the leader or the leader's lieutenants. A member's every need was met, or was supposed to be met, by virtue of participation in the group. Of course, this was contingent on submission to the rules, regulations, and code of behavior. Both the DWP and Heaven's Gate can be identified as totalistic in part because of this all-encompassing feature of meeting members' basic needs.

Second, the authoritarian character of the relationship did not encompass simply the leader's dictates with regard to meeting the group's goals, as might be the case in a business, a nonprofit organization, or even other normative groups such as a commune or intentional community; rather, in the DWP and Heaven's Gate, the leader and the structure of the group intervened in all areas of a member's life. Members' recognition and acceptance of the charismatic authority brought them to believe that it was their leaders' legitimate right. Members submitted to that authority as one does to a parent—sometimes with guilt or shame, sometimes with anxiety, sometimes with relief, and almost always with a mixture of love and fear.

The personality regression apparent in at least some of the members, as well as the lack of independent thought and action on the part of members of both groups, indicated a type of developmental regression. I do not mean to suggest that followers were developmentally immature when they encountered the group; rather, I believe that this regression was induced, at least in part, by the group processes and interactions. The tendency to submit to authority is a basic human trait.[21] However, as one's submission becomes more "primal"—that is, as it comes to revolve around basic human needs and motives for human behavior—one tends to revert to a childlike state and become more and more dependent on the authority figure. This is even more the case when the means of survival and personal security are removed from the individual and placed in the hands of the group. In such situations the individual tends to lose a sense of self apart from the institution and may opt for a "kind of security [that will] destroy his freedom and the integrity of his individual self."[22]

One explanation proffered to account for this type of enmeshment is that cult members had not developed adequately as independent adults functioning in a self-satisfying way before they joined the group. I tend not to agree with that theory, at least in most cases. Why? Because the leader's part in this system cannot be ignored; his or her contribution to the regressive dynamic must considered in any assessment of members' behavior. If DWP or Heaven's Gate members regressed, more likely it was a result of the requirements of the system—not only the rigidity and invasiveness of the daily discipline, along with the prohibition against thinking or functioning as an individual, but also, and perhaps most significant, the demand to belittle oneself constantly in the face of greatness in the form of Dixon, Applewhite, and Nettles.

The parental nature of the charismatic relationship was reflected also in each leader's operating style—although, once again, this was manifested somewhat differently in the two groups. Comrade Marlene, general secretary of the DWP, behaved like a harsh, authoritarian parent; Ti and Do presented themselves as caring, nurturing parents. But this difference in style is overshadowed by each leader's desire to play the role of charismatic leader and be the controlling force in their followers' lives. The need to control led all three to create myths about themselves, assume the mantle of power, and set up rigid, ultra-authoritarian organizational structures that emanated directly from their specific guidance. All three thought of themselves as supreme beings and pushed their followers to the heights of adulation and emulation.

Also, in their respective groups, Dixon and Nettles and Applewhite instituted rules, normative guidelines, and procedures that infantilized their followers. Although the DWP touted the organizational principle of democratic centralism, according to which members were to function and think as creative adults, its structure was such that independent thinking was neither modeled by upper-level leaders nor condoned at any level. In Heaven's Gate independent thinking was literally banished, rendering the students all the more incapable of thinking for themselves and conducting their lives without their leaders and the group.

These sophisticated interactive processes are significant in their very mundaneness. The DWP cadre formed a tight-knit family, as did Heaven's Gate students. On some level, this was familiar territory, for there is nothing more ordinary — at least in U.S. society — than responding and succumbing to authority, especially parental authority.

VARYING GROUP OUTCOMES

The most striking difference between the DWP and Heaven's Gate is the way in which each group came to an end. The DWP was purposely dissolved by the members: they rejected their leader by expelling her, and Party members voted unanimously to disband the organization. At the other extreme, Heaven's Gate members responded "positively" to their leader's call to "exit": as a result, forty of them committed suicide.[23]

Four organizational features had a significant impact on these two very different outcomes: leadership style, which contributes to members' being more or less obedient; the response to and handling of crises, which either increases or decreases group cohesion; the leader's relations with followers, which either strengthen or weaken the charismatic bond; and worldview orientation in relation to the outside world, which either increases or decreases members' separation from people and activities outside the group. A positive or negative manifestation of each feature can contribute to forms of resistance to autocratic authority versus total acquiescence, to the point of self-destruction or other types of internal or external violence. In this case, "positive" means enhancing the self-sealed, or cultic, nature of the system, and "negative" means serving to unhinge the seal (see table 10, Appendix).

Leadership Style. Leadership style in the DWP was significantly harsher than that in Heaven's Gate. Social psychologists recognize that overt means of control are less effective than subtle ones.[24] It is widely believed that using coercion will tend to decrease rather than enhance the ability to elicit obedience.[25] Encouraging people simply to comply is not as effective as drawing on an internalized sense of obligation.[26] Although much of the rule following became implicit in both groups, nonetheless, a very controlling environment existed in both as well. Members expressed the type of internalized sense of commitment and identification that exemplifies the true believer who does not require constant supervision, yet performs his or her duties and remains loyal to the group.

Still, Dixon's harsher and more direct leadership style led her to be feared more than revered. Consequently, perhaps it was easier for militants eventually to break the charismatic bond. A more flexible form of relational authority, with its ongoing dialectic between leaders and followers, grants a more legitimate basis for authority — and, consequently, tends to engender less rebellion within the ranks. Though Heaven's Gate students were more overtly controlled on a daily basis, Nettles and Applewhite's style of leadership was softer, subtler, and more indirect than Dixon's.

The two Heaven's Gate leaders were also more fallible. At times they confessed that they did not know everything, and occasionally they appeared to be just as confused as their students, for example, if the Next Level did not come through with the expected event. This was especially true of Applewhite after Nettles died. This more sensitive leadership style allowed the students to feel a greater sense of loyalty toward and love for their leaders than was ever evident in the DWP. These disparate attitudes were clearly evident in written documents and in interviews and discussions with former members of both groups. Most of the deceased Heaven's Gate students spoke in their parting testimonials (and many other members and former members in interviews and elsewhere) of pleasant memories of Ti and/or Do and also referred to them with fondness, whereas no former DWP members expressed positive sentiments about their leader, Marlene Dixon.[27]

One conclusion from this is rather obvious: a soft-sell approach tends to have a more firmly binding effect. Yet another conclusion is that it might be more difficult for members in groups with a softer style of

242 THEORETICAL PERSPECTIVE

authority to see through the veil of power and begin to question the motivation of their leaders, or to reevaluate their own commitment to the group. This is, indeed, a double-edged sword.

Response to Crises. Typically, organizational crises resulted in a modification of goals or a change in certain elements of the belief system. In the DWP, however, changes in strategy and underlying beliefs, especially toward the end, cut too deeply into the basic foundation of the group, causing profound destabilization: the solution took a greater toll on the group than the crisis it was meant to resolve. Thus when the corrupt and arbitrary nature of their leader, and the collusion of the inner circle, was made known, DWP militants could no longer discern that crucial element of personal freedom in their required acts of self-renunciation.

By contrast, crises in Heaven's Gate were handled in a more orderly and more cohesive fashion. For example, in some instances, when their prophecies failed to materialize, Applewhite and Nettles, true to their subtle and indirect style of leadership, took some of the blame on themselves, which bound their followers even more closely to them. After a long night of waiting, when the spaceships did not arrive, the leaders and followers together recommitted to their cause. And when Nettles died, Applewhite carried out a commitment-inducing ceremony, giving each member a gold wedding band and making clear both his determination to carry on and his need for his followers. Over time, Applewhite introduced the idea of "shedding their bodies," a major shift from the initial explanation of individual metamorphosis from a human into a transformed creature who would be physically lifted up to the Next Level. The buildup toward the idea of dying in a human manner extended over several years, so that by the time Applewhite made the final call, his true believers were ready to follow.[28] In a way, by then, death had become just another fantastical image in a complex system of aliens, space wars, Luciferian forces, spaceships, spirit entities, and communication with departed souls. The mix of fantasy and reality in this group was so complete that death for Heaven's Gate members became just another "procedure."

Leader's Relations with Followers. In both the DWP and Heaven's Gate, there were primary and secondary layers of leadership. Trusted members were selected to serve as an inner circle around the leader(s) and as a body of upper-level leaders who helped to spread the message, train other members, and maintain the organizational systems of control.

In the DWP, however, the leadership structure was more sophisticated

THE TRUE BELIEVER 243

and far-reaching than that found in Heaven's Gate. In part, this had to do with the size of each group: the DWP was consistently a much larger group than Heaven's Gate ever was. In addition, this had to do with the type of group: the DWP's focus on "external practice" required more tiers of leaders who could operate and control various front groups and activities. The long-term impact of this tiered leadership structure took its toll on Dixon's charismatic hold on her followers, though. In that respect, the charismatic bond, at least for those members at the outer rings of the organization, was weaker in the DWP. Many rank-and-file members saw Dixon only rarely if at all. These members knew about their leader only from reports by their direct leadership cadres and from study and discussions in group meetings. This layered system of control had two significant ramifications: there were many more leadership secrets and far fewer contacts with the leader than in Heaven's Gate. Ultimately, it meant that Dixon's hold on her cadres was not as complete as that of Nettles and Applewhite on their students.

Heaven's Gate students always felt an intense, direct connection to their leaders, whom they revered as their Older Members. The goal of utter dependence on the leader was integral to the Heaven's Gate belief system and could not be compromised. Thus, while Heaven's Gate also had secondary levels of leadership in the form of Elders, Helpers, and Overseers, the extent of their control and influence on the other followers was not as encompassing as that exercised by the DWP's inner circle and upper- and middle-level leaders.

Certainly in larger groups it becomes necessary to mediate the charismatic authority of the top leader through other levels of leadership. This leadership by proxy might even be desirable to leaders who prefer not to get involved in the details of organizational life. Yet this very disconnection tends to weaken the leader-follower bond. And it can have catastrophic consequences for the leader and for the group as an entity, as was the case in the DWP.

Worldview Orientation. The DWP's worldview was oriented toward a real-world goal.[29] In its professed aim of fighting for social change and a better world, love was expressed for the working class specifically and for all humanity generally. Quite the opposite was true in Heaven's Gate, which professed a hatred for the world and for human life. This view must have made it easier for the students to take their own lives, for over the years they had been yearning to "leave this world."

And though both groups were apocalyptic, again, this was expressed in radically different ways. In the DWP the "apocalypse" was envisioned as the downfall of capitalism, the rising of the working class, and the emergence of worldwide socialism. The result was to be a better life, here on Earth, for all humankind. Meanwhile, the apocalyptic view in Heaven's Gate was eco-fatalistic. They awaited the "spading under," or total destruction, of planet Earth. Thus the Heaven's Gate vision of the world was a negative one in which only those accepted by and already ascended to the Next Level would be saved from total destruction.

In addition, the socially constructed reality of Heaven's Gate kept adherents more sequestered from the everyday life and routines of main-stream society. The DWP, too, had its own reality. However, because of its fundamental belief in proletarian principles and revolution, as well as its linkages to local and national political issues and the world socialist movement, its members, at least theoretically, were more closely con-nected to the "external" world. As withdrawn as militants were from the norms and aspirations of the dominant culture, they were not nearly as alienated from "this world" as Heaven's Gate students were.

. . .

All in all, leadership style, response to crises, the leader's relations with fol-lowers, and worldview orientation can have significant general and specific impacts on the life course of a group. These features help bring to fruition particular developments, tending in one or another direc-tion — either further sealing the group's atmosphere and strengthening the members' internalization of the belief system or loosening it and allowing movement and the potential for change.

THE SELF-SEALING SYSTEM

Systems of control and systems of influence served to bind the members to the group, manipulating some into compliance (sympathizers and gen-eral members) and others into obedience and deployability (true believ-ers). The processes inhering in these structural dimensions were thought-ful and deliberate, and interlocked in sophisticated ways with the other structural dimensions. That is, the systems of influence and the systems of control acted as reinforcers of but were also reinforced by charismatic authority and the transcendent belief system. The organizational outcome was a self-sealing, or closed, system. The outcome for at least some of the members was one of internalization and identification — or the fusion of personal freedom and self-renunciation.

Each of the four defining structural dimensions of the system served an important function in generating the vision of freedom (salvation), along with its demand for self-renunciation. Each dimension had a general purpose, a specific goal, a process or method for achieving that goal, and a desired effect or outcome (see table 11, Appendix).

The general purpose of the first dimension, charismatic authority, is to provide leadership. The specific goal is to be accepted as the legitimate authority and to offer direction. This is accomplished through privilege and command, and the hoped-for effect is that members will identify with the leader.

The purpose of the belief system is to provide a worldview, whose specific goal is to offer meaning and purpose through a moral imperative. This is accomplished by requiring that each member subject herself or himself to a process of personal transformation. The desired effect is the internalization of the belief system, which is to represent personal freedom in the sense of being connected to a greater goal and aspiring to salvation.

The purpose of the third dimension, systems of control, is to provide organizational structure. The specific goal is to establish a behavioral system and disciplinary code by means of rules, regulations, and sanctions. The hoped-for effect is compliance and, better still, obedience.

The purpose of the final dimension, systems of influence, is to provide a social system, or group culture. Institutionalized group norms and an established code of conduct by which members are expected to live is the specific goal. This is accomplished by various methods of peer and leadership influence and modeling. The desired effect is conformity, or the self-renunciation required for participation in the group and achieving the professed goal of the group.

Everything in these two groups fit together like a three-dimensional puzzle. Inside each group very little happened by chance. Even outside events were interpreted to coincide with the group's worldview, including the reframing, or reinterpretation, of leaders' and members' personal lives to fit the ideology. Daily life was highly controlled, with certain aspects literally orchestrated by the group. In some instances, there was blatant manipulation if not outright coercion. That was especially the case with respect to the methodology for and implementation of the required transformational process each member was expected to undergo. Members were given explicit guidance on how that process was to proceed. Once again, interpretive framing and reframing by the leader and other group members was crucial to achieving the desired goal. For the member, the goal was to perfect oneself against an impossible ideal and to criticize oneself for failing to do so all along the way. For the leader, the goal was to perfect a body of followers who would continually struggle for the impossible ideal, lauding the leader all along the way.

When this process works, leaders and members alike are locked into a self-sealing system in which every aspect and every activity reconfirms the validity of the system. Disconfirming information has no place. This closed system creates a bounded reality. In this context, organizational choices are made by the leader, for no one else is considered qualified or has the authority to do so. Personal choices, if and when they arise, are made in the context of bounded choice. First, choices are formulated within and constrained by the self-sealing framework and style of consideration, which always puts the organization first. Second, those choices are bounded by the constriction of each member's thought patterns, which, once more, always put the organization first.

·   ·   ·

The bounded choice framework and theory offer new ways to look at what happens to individuals who are caught up in cultic thinking. It helps us to understand the personal dilemma of true believers. These are individuals who are caught in the fusion of that sense of personal freedom to be gained from making a charismatic commitment and the demand for self-renunciation necessary to uphold the ideal. Also, this new perspective allows us to strip away our own moralistic and judgmental attitudes toward those who are living this sort of life of devotion and sacrifice. We may not agree with their actions or decisions, but perhaps we can now better understand what has motivated them.

Bounded Choice

*Cult Formation and the Development
of the True Believer*

The bounded choice framework and theory offers a new perspective on the identity shift and resultant behavior of at least some cult participants — that is, the most dedicated adherents, the true believers. Here I challenge prevailing theories at both ends of the spectrum. Both rational-choice and popular mind-control theories fall short in explaining cult behavior for they pay too little attention to the complexities and effects of knowledge and power in social systems, what is sometimes called the duality of structure. By contrast, the bounded choice model considers individual choice in the context of an authoritarian, transcendent, closed system.

Bounded Choice in Relation
to Other Conformity Theories

Bounded choice is connected to other theories on conformity and cognitive dissonance, yet is different from them. Some conformity theories address situations in which subjects know their actions are wrong but still go along with the crowd. Cognitive dissonance theories are concerned with internal conflict experienced by the person who continues to believe in or do something that does not fit with what the person recognizes as true. Bounded choice, on the other hand, incorporates the processes of conformity with the postdissonant state. It is perhaps the outcome of it. In bounded choice, the action fits the worldview.

CONFORMITY THEORIES

Some of the better known experiments on conformity were carried out by the social psychologist Solomon Asch.[1] The underlying thesis of his work had to do with being "caught in between the need to be right and the desire to be liked."[2] In these experiments several people in a room were asked to match the lengths of two lines. One by one, participants who were part of the setup of the experiment gave the wrong answer. Finally, when it was time for the subjects to answer, they chose the same wrong answer, even though they did not agree with it. The subjects in these experiments knew they were wrong, yet they went with the majority in order not to be different. Such behavior represents a kind of "public" conformity, a more superficial type of compliance whereby people pretend to agree.[3] In such cases, the subjects are not changed internally, as were at least the long-term members of the DWP and Heaven's Gate.

Undoubtedly, there were occasions in both groups when a member, because of normative influence, complied or conformed in full knowledge of being wrong about something. Typically, a person in such a situation is motivated by fear of negative social consequences, which in the cases of these two cults would have included criticism, ostracism, and possibly suspension or expulsion from the group. But there is a significant difference in the cult members' experiences from the experiences of the subjects in Asch's experiments: that difference is that over time the cult members shifted their personal worldview so as to be in alignment with the group's perception of things. This is a far more totalistic change or conversion process than the type of on-the-spot conformity evidenced by Asch's subjects. In that sense, the change among these cult members is more akin to other experiments on informational influence, in which the subjects conformed because they believed that the others were correct.[4]

Overall, once a person has adopted a cult's worldview, that person does not necessarily think a particular action is wrong, incorrect, or inappropriate because his or her perspective, value system, and preference structure have been reshaped by the group's transformational processes. The conformity in such instances is more "private" than public in the sense of being a true conversion or worldview shift.[5] The loyal cult member maintains the group's or leader's ideological perspective even when other members are not present, even when away from the group.

Certainly, conformity studies and theories are relevant to the interactional processes present in both the DWP and Heaven's Gate. Nonetheless, they fall slightly short; for we might surmise that if a person continued to go along with an activity or a behavior in the knowledge that what he was doing was wrong, presumably he would leave the group. Bounded choice theory addresses that person who has internalized the group worldview to such a degree that on those occasions when he is in full alignment with the cult mind-set, he no longer experiences a particular activity or pronouncement as wrong or questionable. The boundaries of his perceptions and his choices are tightly drawn and sealed by the interlocking nature of the cultic structure, its social system, and his role in it.

COGNITIVE DISSONANCE

Cognitive dissonance theory recognizes that a person experiences and is motivated by a type of psychological discomfort produced by two thoughts that do not follow, or by conflicting views of reality. When there is such inconsistency and/or conflict, a person tends to experience internal tension and is motivated to reduce the uncomfortable feeling. Yet people will continue to hold to their beliefs and behave accordingly even when a particular perception butts up against a different context or a different "reality." In that case, the person's behavior appears irrational or maladaptive. The classic example is the behavior of the adherents of a UFO cult studied by the social psychologist Leon Festinger and colleagues.[6] Instead of being disillusioned and disbanding their group at what was, at least from an observer's perspective, an obvious failed prophecy (the spaceships did not arrive as predicted), the cult members became even more fervent in their belief and continued to proselytize. The basis of this theory is that humans will tend to reduce the uncomfortable feeling caused by the dissonance by bringing their attitude in line with their behavior rather than changing the behavior.

At various times when DWP cadres or Heaven's Gate students were faced with baldly discrepant moments, surely they must have experienced cognitive dissonance. (I know that I did many times during my years of membership.) But cognitive dissonance is prebehavioral. It is about attitude and behavior, about the internal thought process of the individual faced with the dilemma of reconciling external and internal realities.

Bounded choice theory, on the other hand, is about decision making within the confines of the cult worldview. The goal of the training is to modify at least some of the members' thought processes (and preference structure) so that no recognized inconsistencies remain. Ultimately, the goal is to create the cult-formed persona. This is the context of bounded choice. Bounded choice is about decision making, not attitude change. The person has already been changed and her thought processes confined by the mental boundaries of the cult context.

GROUPTHINK

In groupthink the need for agreement takes priority over the motivation to obtain accurate knowledge and make appropriate decisions.[7] Groupthink is based on three factors: strong internal bonds, directive leadership, and the stress of perceived threat from outsiders. The classic example is that of U.S. President John F. Kennedy and his counselors fearing international conflict with Cuba over the Bay of Pigs.

Groupthink, while relevant to some degree, is the least applicable to my concerns here. Groupthink is about group, not individual, decisions. It is about "bad" decisions and defective decision making; it also implies a judgmental view. Bounded choice, on the other hand, is about individual decision making in a group context. It is meant not to be judgmental but to explain why someone makes the decision he makes under a given set of circumstances, holding to a particular worldview. If anything, its focus is on the claustrophobia of the internal and external structural boundaries rather than the threat of outside intervention or the concern for outside opinions.

• • •

The classic theories discussed above, although relevant to the processes explored in this book, are not as exact a fit as the bounded choice theory for explaining fully what happens to true believers in charismatic cults. To clarify how bounded choice comes about, I first highlight processes that are necessary at the structural level — in other words, how the cultic system develops and works to envelop the individual. I then describe what occurs at the individual level, that is, the social-psychological mechanisms at play that help to enclose the world of choices for the individual member. And last, I discuss the relationship of bounded choice to other theories on choice, as well as its relevance for us today as citizens in a world of increasing social and political polarization.

Cult Formation: The Self-Sealing Social System

In general, humans are knowledgeable about their situations and their inter-actions with others. According to Giddens, in most cases, if you ask a person why he or she did something, he or she can give you reasons.[8] Yet such a point of view does not preclude individuals from being limited in their knowledge or their power, both of which tend to have an effect on one's decision-making capabilities. All is not equal on most if not all playing fields.

Not only was power centralized in the DWP and Heaven's Gate, but knowledge was centralized, and access to it was limited or blocked in many ways. The degree and depth of knowledge available to group members were severely hampered in all four dimensions of the social structure:

- Charismatic authority: Leadership was secretive and inaccessible.

- Transcendent belief system: Group doctrine was inviolable and came down from on high.

- Systems of control: Rigid boundaries defined inaccessible space and topics closed to discussion or inquiry.

- Systems of influence: Internalized norms, all-pervasive modeling, and constant peer monitoring ruled out inappropriate questioning.

In both groups, then, the boundaries of knowledge were shut tight and reinforced in three specific ways — through the process of resocialization, through the use of ideology, and through social controls.[9]

RESOCIALIZATION INTO THE CULT IDENTITY

The works of Erik Erikson and Erving Goffman are critical to any under-standing of resocialization.[10] Giddens relied on these works in his description of the resocialization process as the systematic breaking down of the person in order to instill trust in the authority figure. He and others have pointed out that typical patterns of resocialization are found in specific situations, including the battlefield, prison camps, religious conversion, and forced interrogation. Known patterns of resocialization include launching a deliberate, sustained attack on ordinary routines; producing a high degree of anxiety in the person; stripping away socialized responses; and attacking the foundation of the basic security system grounded in the trust of others. In the target person, one can expect to see an upsurge in anxiety, regressive modes of behavior, succumbing to the pressures, and adopting a new attitude of trust in and identification with the authority figure(s). Giddens wrote: "The radical disruption of routine produces a sort of corrosive effect upon the customary behaviour of the actor, associated with the impact of anxiety or fear. This circumstance brings about heightened suggestibility, or vulnerability to the promptings of others; the correlate of such suggestibility is regressive behaviour. The outcome of these is a new process of identification — transitory in the mob case, more permanent in protracted critical situations — with an authority figure."[11]

The goal of resocialization, then, is the reconstructed personality. This reconstruction often revolves around one aim, "to get the individual to *identify* with the socializing agent."[12] The desired effect is a new self whose "actions will be dictated by the imagined will or purpose of the actor he has identified with. . . . It is then that will which generates the internal sanctions for future actions."[13] Such a process of resocialization was a central facet of membership in both the DWP and Heaven's Gate. It was the essence of the DWP's cadre transformation and of Heaven's Gate's transition to the genderless creature. The ultimate effect of such processes is not only a "violation of territories of the self"[14] but also, and perhaps more important, the generation of a state of personal closure, as the person closes himself off to outside knowledge or disconfirming evidence that might challenge this "new self."[15]

Resocialization is a great reinforcer of the status quo within the group. Equally significant, it serves as a hindrance to independent information gathering and a barrier to accessing sources of knowledge. In this context, the purpose of resocialization is to create a true believer — not a curiosity seeker or a critical thinker.

USING IDEOLOGY TO ENCLOSE THE SYSTEM

The second reinforcer of the boundaries of knowledge resides in the ideological realm. In the two cases examined here, the belief system became quite purposefully an ideological barricade. The constant striving for an impossible ideal that was the linchpin of membership caused members to feel consistently inadequate about themselves and their accomplishments. This kept them in a self-recriminating and self-critical behavioral and attitudinal mode.

This stultifying dynamic worked to stave off questioning the system or the "truths" of the system. Adherents were too busy criticizing themselves for their incessant failures and too consumed with working harder to achieve their goals — either the short-term ones set by the group or leader or the long-term goal of freedom and self-fulfillment as promised by the leader. The result was self-denial, exhaustion, and guilt. All of that was held neatly in place by the serious commitment each member made to the cause — and to the leader and other members of the group.

EXTERNAL AND INTERNALIZED
MECHANISMS OF CONTROL

The third reinforcer of closed boundaries was the use of specific social controls. Given the invasive and all-pervasive nature of the systems of influence and control found in Heaven's Gate and the DWP, the sociological concept of total institutions is useful here. These closed social systems are recognized for their "totalizing discipline," reshaped identity, and constraint.[16] The distinctive features of total institutions are interrogative procedures, removal of personal boundaries, forced and continual relations with others, and total control of time. Although many of the conditions of life in the DWP and Heaven's Gate are recognizably similar to those features, the differences must not be ignored. First, both groups were voluntaristic (except for children born or brought into the DWP), unlike the blatant confinement of the asylum, which was the locus of Goffman's class study on total institutions.[17] Second, membership in the two groups involved an attraction to, affinity for, and eventual adoption of a belief system that undergirded the adherent's acquiescence to the systems of control. Again, that is quite a different milieu from that experienced by an inmate in a locked ward in a mental hospital.

However, Goffman's analysis was meant to have broader applications. Thus abbeys, monasteries, convents, cloisters, and other retreats from the world were included in the category of total institutions. Now this might work for the Heaven's Gate group, whose members at times even referred to themselves as monks. But it would be difficult to squeeze the DWP into that category, especially with its stated mission of mass practice and social change. Although it was seclusive, the DWP was quite involved in worldly matters and in that sense could not be described as a retreat from the world. Nonetheless, the extent to which DWP cadres created and lived in a world unto themselves revealed that on some level they were just as cut off from the larger society as nuns in a cloister.

Despite these differences from the classic definition of a total institution, the constraining features of the systems of control and influence kept DWP and Heaven's Gate members from obtaining certain key information or having access to certain knowledge. The dimension of power is most prominent here. Above all, these true believers knew that the systems of control ensured the continuity of the group and the ongoing special (charismatic) relationship between leader and followers. In that sense every rule had a context, and every demand on members was justified by the ideology and the normative system that flowed from it. The overriding power of group authority figures was accepted as a given. The normative system was understood as a necessary mechanism of commitment and change, ultimately for the good of each participant who was striving to meet the ideal. Power in such a situation is both very real and quite subtle. Giddens said it precisely when he wrote, "Power relations are often most profoundly embedded in modes of conduct which are taken for granted by those who follow them, most especially in routinized behaviour, which is only diffusely motivated."[18] The success of these two groups was in their capacity to convince followers, who routinely convinced each other that they were acting of their own accord, for their own good.

Yet for all their efforts at good behavior, sanctions of all kinds existed in both groups. Members feared disapproval and punishment by means of a wide range of structural and social mechanisms — from slippage meetings and criticism sessions to ostracism and public trials and expulsion. DWP sanctions also included various forms of physical punishment, from double-duty work shifts to bodily harm. In effect, fully committed DWP cadres and Heaven's Gate students knew where the line was drawn. Their daily practice was the expression of their commitment. Any error was to be rooted out — with pleasure.

But the harshest sanction of all was internal — the devoted member's inner capacity to control urges, desires, actions, thoughts, and beliefs that were contrary to the group's teachings. Self-condemnation was everyday fare. These internalized sanctions were among the most powerful mechanisms of control. Ultimately, the individual cult member's ability to enact freedom of action was not restricted by lurking external forces or even by the confines of the system. Rather, at this point of the fusion of personal freedom and self-renunciation, at this point of personal closure, the individual may well become his own source of constraint.

The Social Psychology
of the Individual Change Process

Heaven's Gate and the DWP had widely divergent ruling ideologies. But the overall character of these groups was not belief-specific. Rather, what is relevant to our understanding here is the manifestation of broader principles of charismatic influence and control within the confines of each group's totalistic system. The demands in this milieu led to an individual worldview shift. The foundation for this was a social structure in which personal freedom (e.g., salvation), as aspired to by each participant, could be gained only through self-renunciation (transformation) of the highest order.[19] The charismatic commitment of each individual was stretched to mold the adherent into a deployable agent, or true believer. This was not achieved for every member of the group, however. For some, commitment was not that strong; they doubted major aspects of the belief system; they failed tests and either left or were ejected from the group; they did not have enough faith or lost faith in the leader — for one reason or another, they were not ready to take that leap. But for those who were, the parts were in place.

The interaction between the individual and the social structure is crucial at this stage. The four structural dimensions (charismatic authority, transcendent belief system, systems of control, and systems of influence) are interlocked and interdependent. They support and reinforce one another, creating the self-sealing system. For the person living within such a system, the conflation of these four dimensions generates an internal dualism, which, I believe, is the linchpin of a binding commitment and the genesis of the true believer. This internalized way of being becomes as much a part of the system as the mechanisms that engender it.

Let me explain what I mean by "internal dualism." Each of the structural dimensions creates a boundary inside and around the individual, and each dimension has a double-sided effect. These personal boundaries are grouped into four dualistic categories: purpose and commitment, love and fear, duty and guilt, and internalization and identification. (See table 12, Appendix, for the characteristic features of each dualistic category.)

PURPOSE/COMMITMENT

The cult member responds to the power of the group's beliefs and enjoys the strength of collective commitment. She believes she has found meaning and purpose. Yet this requires a commitment that demands single-mindedness, a way of thinking characterized by dogmatism and rigidity, and no identity outside the context of the group.

LOVE/FEAR

As much as members love their leaders, so do they fear them because of the power they hold over the members' lives, the threat of disapproval, and the expressions of paranoia that raise the specter of the "evil" outside world. Members also enjoy group solidarity and feel a sense of personal power and elitism; yet, at the same time, they fear peer shunning or withdrawal of support. It is a tightrope walk, with little room for error.

DUTY/GUILT

The member's sense of duty shares space with guilt, always a forceful human motivator. Feeling duty-bound and obligated, members find themselves participating in activities that in other circumstances may have violated a personal ethical code. Now the leader is the only moral arbiter. In some cases, through repetition, ritual, and other group activities, the member becomes desensitized to behavior previously considered unthinkable or objectionable. The longer a person remains with a group, the more invested he is, and potentially all the more complicit with group-dictated actions and behaviors. Life outside the group seems less and less an option.

IDENTIFICATION/INTERNALIZATION

Finally, by means of the processes of identification and internalization, the member feels in complete unity with the group and the leader. Although on occasion she may still experience dissonance or confusion over discrepancies, at the same time she has access to fewer and fewer outside sources of information and therefore little capacity for reality checks outside the bounds of the system. She feels completely separated from her own pregroup identities and cannot imagine life outside the group. Here the process has come full circle.

THE STATE OF PERSONAL CLOSURE

As these dualistic personal boundaries develop and strengthen, a state of personal closure begins to develop. We might think of personal closure as the individualized version of the self-sealing system on an organizational level. Closure is meant in the sense not of completion, which is one use of the term, but rather of a closing in of the self in a self-sealed world. Lifton described it as a "disruption of balance between self and the outside world."[20] He wrote:

> Pressured toward a merger of internal and external milieus, the individual encounters a profound threat to his personal autonomy. He is deprived of the

combination of external information and inner reflection which anyone requires to test the realities of his environment and to maintain a measure of identity separate from it. Instead, he is called upon to make an absolute polarization of the real (the prevailing ideology) and the unreal (everything else). To the extent that he does this, he undergoes a *personal closure* which frees him from man's incessant struggle with the elusive subtleties of truth.[21]

The personal closure that is the culmination of cultic life is profoundly confining because one is closed to both the outside world and one's inner life. This phenomenon is quite different from cognitive dissonance because it involves all aspects of one's life. It is also much more all-encompassing than our understanding of the normal processes of conformity because of the depth and extent of the internalization and identification. The quality of the belief change actually shifts members' value structure — either temporarily or permanently.[22] When such a shift occurs, individual choice is not an individual matter.

The Limited Choices of the True Believer

If we humans lived in an ideal world, we would be able to consider various options from among personal preferences and then choose a course of action.[23] But in the real world, we find ourselves in situations described by the economist, psychologist, and Nobel Laureate Herbert Simon as "bounded rationality." Through a process he dubbed *satisficing*, we tend to choose "good enough" solutions and courses of action. When people are faced with complexity and uncertainty, and "lacking the wits to optimize," they must settle for satisficing.[24] In a complex world such as ours, alternatives are not given but must be sought out. Importantly, the concept of bounded rationality rests on the idea that we cannot act with complete rationality due to limited resources that prevent us from having access to all the information or knowledge relevant to a particular problem.

By contrast, according to rational-choice approaches, a person is faced with all the options and chooses the best one. But a perfect situation is never possible. Instead, alternatives are presented sequentially, and typically we choose the first one that will allow us to meet our goal.[25] In general, we prefer to avoid uncertainty and therefore rely on tested decision-making rules and procedures in order to hasten out of the uncomfortable state of indecision. Not only are human cognitive abilities limited by power, speed, and capacity, but there are only so many alternatives and consequences a person can recognize at any given moment. For Simon, bounded rationality is a constant state of being for any human.

Now let us add the element of power to this mix. That old maxim "knowledge is power" is popular and so well known for the very reason that it is true, yet it is often forgotten. In social systems of all kinds, access to knowledge and information is systematically controlled by those in power. The conceptualizations of bounded rationality and rational choice are flawed in that they both "assume that information is a neutral commodity" that people can acquire.[26] But information is not neutral. In fact, it is vitally necessary in order for us to make an educated appraisal of our environment or an informed choice.[27]

Individual choice, then, becomes a matter of choosing from among a set of "givens" in any particular environment, and we see that a person's options are constrained by these givens.[28] In economic enterprises, givens are set forth by the company to aid employees in making decisions that will be congruent with corporate goals. However, normative groups also have goals, as well as integrated systems of influence and control that help to shape participants' choices and their perspectives on options. Members of cults, as one type of normative group, are constrained even more by the interlocking nature of the structural configuration of the charismatic authority, the transcendent belief system, and the systems of control and influence. This is depicted in figure 20, where charismatic authority and transcendent belief system are placed at the top of the pyramidal structure because they are primary. The systems of control and influence rely on and emanate from the top two dimensions but also uphold them and, in that sense, are regarded as foundational. The individual in a state of personal closure is illustrated graphically by the circle enclosed within the pyramid. This confluence of factors brings the cult member to a point where he or she will consider alternative possibilities *only* within the group framework.

In a group such as this, individual decisions are not a matter of satisficing, of choosing the "good enough" alternative. Rather, options are limited even further by the combination of the self-sealing nature of the system and the participant's rigid adherence to the norms and near-total identification with the leader and the stated goals. Above I categorized broadly the effects of the cultic social system on the individual as dualisms: love and fear, purpose and commitment, duty and guilt, and identification and internalization. Each dualistic set corresponds to a major dimension of the system and enables the further enmeshment of the individual (see fig. 20). For example, issues of love and fear come up most often in relation to charismatic authority. Purpose and commitment are most relevant to a person's adoption of the belief system. Duty and

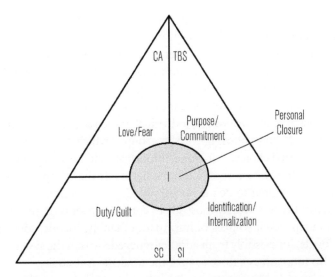

FIGURE 20. The interlocking and interactional dimensions of the social structure create a bounded reality and contribute to a state of personal closure for the individual participant. Charismatic authority (CA) and a transcendent belief system (TBS) are crucial to the creation of such a reality, while the systems of control (SC) and the systems of influence (SI) uphold the other two structural dimensions and reinforce the confines of the bounded reality. Enmeshed in such a social system, the individual (I) is apt to become closed off to ideas and experiences outside this system.

guilt intersect most often with the systems of behavioral control. And identification and internalization are primarily the product of the systems of attitudinal influence.

Yet those effects do not stand alone. They interrelate and intersect with all the other aspects of the system, creating personal boundaries that are claustrophobic in nature. The individual becomes enmeshed in the four organizational dimensions. Through charismatic authority, the member has come to identify with the leader. Through the transcendent belief system, the member has adopted and internalized the utopian worldview. Through the systems of control, the member has accepted daily behavioral controls. And through the systems of influence, the member has internalized the group norms and attitudes.

Thus in closed, self-sealing groups, not only is rationality bounded, as it is in all environments; but further, choices are bounded. According to Simon's theory of bounded rationality, choices are limited because of the uncertainty and complexity of the social context. But in a context of bounded choice, a person's perceptions and, hence, decision-making processes are constrained even further. The social context of cultic totalism is one of hyper-certainty and ultra-rationalization, resulting in both external and internalized sanctions. (See fig. 21.) Almost everything is set up, figured out, taken care of: there is only one way to be, to think about things, to perceive the world. The individual in such a setting is faced with being "rational" and choosing for the group — which can be described only as a bounded choice — or being "irrational" and breaking out of the mold, in which case he would find himself outside the group, in another context (or struggling to define himself in another context). Reinforcers of this latter process would most likely come from outside the system (such as independent sources of information, family, friends, concerned professionals), or possibly from another renegade within the system who would also function as a force against the totalistic collectivity.

Under bounded choice, free will has not been taken away, but it has been restricted and distorted. The individual cult member acts and is responsible for his or her actions — but these actions must be recognized as occurring in a specific context. It becomes difficult to conclude that such an individual is operating out of rational choice. First, such cases do not exist. Second, in groups such as the DWP and Heaven's Gate, choices are severely limited for the person who stays in the system. Not only are choices limited, but the actual decision-making process is hampered by the true believer's internal voices, which are in complete alignment with the self-sealing system. In this way, behaviors or actions that might look crazy or irrational to the outsider look completely rational from the perspective of the person inside the bounded reality of the cult.

This, of course, bring us to the thorny issue of leaving cults and cultic situations. What are the barriers, real and imagined? How does a person make that move? What aids and what hinders that process? What is the thinking process? The decision-making process? Those are questions and issues that continue to intrigue us. Innovative research is needed for an understanding of how individuals who so desire can break free from a situation of bounded choice, no matter its context.

Generally, we need to better understand present-day manifestations of cultic thinking and totalistic systems and their effects on our society. Although the two groups discussed in this book may be regarded as extreme and unusual, in fact, the people in them were in many ways no different from everyday citizens. They were by no means crazy or suffering from psychological maladies — at least not when they joined.

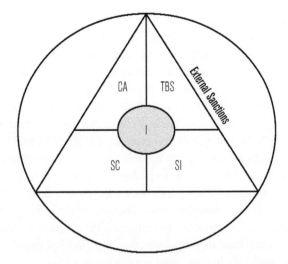

FIGURE 21. The interactional and structural elements leading to the state of bounded choice include the four interlocking dimensions of charismatic authority (CA), transcendent belief system (TBS), systems of control (SC), and systems of influence (SI). The true believer is constrained by "external" sanctions coming from the group and, perhaps more important, internalized sanctions coming from within.

Nor were they evil, ill-intentioned, or stupid. For the most part, they were just people who had a deep desire for a better life and found a way to act on it that they thought was right for them. Unfortunately, their idealism was betrayed by the very systems in which they participated, the very structures they worked so hard to uphold.

Bounded Choice as a Larger Social Phenomenon

Whenever the subject of cults comes up, confusion, distortions, and misunderstandings prevail, along with fear, skepticism, and ridicule. It is my hope that the ideas presented here and the bounded choice perspective will prove useful as a new model for looking at these groups and understanding the lives of the dedicated individuals in them. For the most part, cult members are giving and idealistic, hardworking and loyal, trustworthy and loving. They are people who yearn for a better world — here or in the hereafter. Is that so bad? Do they deserve ridicule, hatred, and lack of support whether they are in the group or have left it? I don't think so. People who try something new, something different, are pioneers. Perhaps they frighten us because they threaten what we imagine is the status quo. Perhaps they hurt us when they choose not to remain in our lives. Perhaps they even harm us with their occasional acts of violence. But we should not forget or deny the courage, endurance, and strength of will it takes to step into the unknown. Sometimes these pioneers find happiness and good times, peace and personal resolution. And sometimes they find that their loyalty and willingness to please, to work hard, to give all have been taken advantage of. Sometimes the leader, group, or belief turns out to be something other than the person thought when joining. Yet we, as a society, have so much to learn from these individuals and their experiences. For on some level they represent the desire in all of us to better ourselves or the world we live in, or to reach a better place.

Bounded choice is a general process that may occur in cults, but also it may be present in many other contexts. I can think of any number of situations in which people confine themselves to a rigid worldview, closed and sealed off from others, rather than become exposed to a variety of perspectives. Obvious examples are radical religious fundamentalists, political terrorists, and other types of extremists, such as those in extreme right-wing organizations, the Christian Identity movement, and various ultraright groups and survivalist or separatist compounds. We need only look at some recent examples: Timothy McVeigh, convicted and executed for bombing the federal building in Oklahoma City; William L. Pierce, author of *The Turner Diaries*, the bible of many white supremacists, which includes a blueprint for a bombing almost exactly like the one McVeigh carried out; members of The Order, who killed Alan Berg, a Jewish radio talk show host in Denver; and members of the Army of God and other extreme anti-abortionists. All of these individuals exhibit the kind of single-mindedness and adherence to a self-sealing ideology typical of the true believer mind-set. Even closer to home, a next-door neighbor might be stockpiling for what he believes to be an impending apocalyptic event; another might be pinning all her hopes (and funds) on an elaborate pyramid scheme or the divinations of a New Age guru; and yet another might be throwing all caution to the wind by ingesting unproven but highly touted potions for health and wellness. Or nearby youngsters might be as trapped in their own pained, seclusive world as were the two teenagers who ignited the rampage at Columbine High School in Littleton, Colorado, several years ago. With the increasing political polarization in our country and the widening social gap between rich and poor, I can foresee idealistic activists swelling the ranks of many small left- and right-wing political cults.

Closed thinking and self-sealing systems take hold in myriad everyday contexts. Respect for authority, duty and self-sacrifice, dedication to an ideal, and service to others are widespread mores of our culture. Not surprisingly, they were also central to the formation and evolution of both the DWP and Heaven's Gate. Those same principles are found in many settings — both beneficial and harmful. Given the current interest in alternatives to mainstream ways of knowing and being, it is important that more and more people have access to information and perspectives that will help them come to a balanced view of the benefits *and* risks of involvement in groups or situations that proffer new and radical solutions. By using the four-part framework and model presented here, it may be possible to assess situations in which extremism, harm, and violence may flourish.

Likewise, with the current threats of extreme fundamentalism and ongoing acts of domestic and international terror, it cannot but help us to have a greater understanding of the mind-set of the true believer. When the Heaven's Gate true believers committed suicide, most people turned the other way, saying, "Well, it was their choice. That's what they believed in, and anyway, they didn't hurt anyone else." But when true believers of another kind flew airplanes into the Twin Towers and the Pentagon, we were horrified at the loss of innocent lives. And rightly so. Condemnation for the terrorist perpetrators was plentiful. But what about those hijackers who were not aware of being on a suicide mission? Do we judge them the same way?

The more we can learn about the social and individual forces that can bring someone to that place of ultimate self-sacrifice for a cause, the better off we all are. Certainly no one in their right mind would question the immorality of the World Trade Center bombers. But what brought them to that place? What choices did they have? And as for the Heaven's Gate students, the many who died at Jonestown, the DWP cadres, and the countless other cult members confined and constrained by bounded choice, doesn't it harm all of us when groups of individuals among us are deprived of freedom of choice? In that regard, I hope this book will open up new ground for exploring these issues and take us one step closer to comprehending why we, as humans in search of meaning and purpose, so often thrust aside our sense of self, personal integrity, and clear thinking for the sake of some lofty, often elusive offering.

Appendix

TABLE 1. Charismatic Authority: Positive and Negative Characteristics

Positive	Negative
Enjoys special relationship, either directly or by proxy	Must defend leader and group at all costs
Expectation of salvation	Double standard: leader considers self above the law, exempt from norms
Feels needed, among the chosen few	Increasingly dependent relationship with group and leader; loss of personal autonomy
Security of having leadership	Unequal power relations: leader remains unchallenged, tends to be autocratic; leader is always right
Shares in sense of community	Potential for uncritical obedience; no real input from base
Has a sense of purpose	Access to knowledge is limited; leadership has secrets
Intrigued by charismatic and mysterious leader	Unrealistic obligations; must deny any leadership weaknesses
Feels special because leader is special	Unrealistic expectations; denies possibility of leadership burnout

TABLE 2. Transcendent Belief System: Positive and Negative Characteristics

Positive	Negative
Higher calling	Overly righteous
Sense of purpose	Becomes dogmatic
Special	Exclusive
Provides answers, meaning	All-or-nothing, totalistic
Offers path to salvation	Push to become a true believer
Lure of freedom	Self-renunciation outweighs freedom
Hope for future	Closed worldview; dead end

TABLE 3. Systems of Control: Positive and Negative Characteristics

Positive	Negative
Sense of purpose	Reified and dogmatized
Orderliness to life	Little or no independent action; no democracy
Sense of accomplishment	Overworked, burned out
Security of strength in numbers	Elitist attitudes; weak elements purged
Most if not all personal needs met	Little or no personal time (or money)
Group system of justice	Fear of rejection; ejection
Hierarchical structure; clear lines of authority	Reinforces class relations; leadership secrets and privilege
Increased sense of responsibility	Anxiety; guilt; fear of making mistakes

TABLE 4. Systems of Influence: Positive and Negative Characteristics

Positive	Negative
Sense of belonging	Loss of sense of self, individuality
Enjoys sense of comradeship	Peer monitoring and reporting to leadership
Strives to be better	Pressure to change; tension
Role models for each other	Overly conformist; cut off from outside
Sense of commitment	Becomes overly obedient; deployable agent
Born again; renewed self	Self-exposure; constant confession
Part of something greater, so submit to authority	Potential for exploitation, abuse

TABLE 5. Salient Features of Charismatic Authority as Manifested
in Heaven's Gate and the DWP

Feature	Heaven's Gate	Democratic Workers Party
Claims a lineage	Biblical and cosmic connections	Marxism-Leninism and Maoism
Leadership principle	Defend at all costs: "I am nothing without Ti and Do"	Defend at all costs: "I am nothing without Comrade Marlene"
Leader is perfect	Ti and Do lauded as exemplary	Dixon lauded as exemplary
Unique	Unlike other New Age groups	Unlike other Left or radical groups
Experiences awakening	At Gold Beach: Ti and Do are the "two witnesses" from the Bible	In academia: Dixon "figured it all out," develops her vision
Specialness of leader	"Ti and Do are the Next Level Representatives"	"Revolutionary leadership doesn't grow on trees"
Privilege for followers	Chosen, select: "Next Level doesn't need anyone"	Chosen, select: "The DWP is not for everyone"
Privilege for leader	Enjoys double standard	Enjoys double standard
Prophetic	The end of civilization as we know it — soon!	The overthrow of capitalism; socialism by the year 2000
Issue of proof	Don't question: "knowing through faith"	Don't question: "uninformed," "uninstructed"
Leader imparts formula for salvation	The overcoming process; willful transformation	Cadre development; collective conscious willing
Leader is source	Do is Jesus; Ti is God	Comrade Marlene is the Party
Leader as innovator	Creative blend of New Age, UFO, and Christian beliefs	Creative blend of proletarian feminism, Marxism, and fighting party
Level of authority	"Chain of Mind": abject obedience, total compliance	Chain of command: abject obedience, total compliance
Evidence	"Deposit of knowledge"	"Class consciousness"
Oratory style	Hypnotic, intense	Evocative, intense
Leadership style	Subtle authoritarian; soft	Overtly authoritarian; hard
Followership style	Obsequious, subservient	Obsequious, subservient

TABLE 6. Salient Features of the Transcendent Belief System as Manifested in Heaven's Gate and the DWP

Feature	Heaven's Gate	Democratic Workers Party
Transcendent	Resurrection is life; "ticket to heaven"	Revolution is life; salvation for humanity
Requires personal transformation	Metamorphosis: transition to genderless creature, Next Level being; must rid self of human traits and programming	Class-standpoint struggle: become cadre, the new Communist man or woman; must rid self of bourgeois traits and programming
Moral imperative	"The Two speak the truth; I had to follow them"	"Dixon's class analysis puts it all into place; how could I do anything else?"
Rests on internalized belief	Deposit of knowledge, recognition	Class consciousness; proletarian class stand
Deterministic	Everything by Next Level "design"	Life unfolds per Marxist economic determinism
Urgent	"The end of the Age is here"	"The world we face is one of increasing crisis and danger"
Includes both the context and the tools for change	The Class: tests, lessons, slippage meetings	The Party: cadre tests, crises, criticism sessions
Path to freedom	To choose for the Next Level	To choose for the working class
Heretical	Persecuted; cult-baited	Persecuted; cult-baited and Red-baited
Separatist	Sectarian and seclusive	Sectarian and seclusive
External enemies: "us versus them"	Corporate Lucifer, "discarnate beings," organized religion, critics, families	Capitalist class, petite bourgeoisie, other leftists, critics, former members
Internalized enemy	"Influences," spirit entities controlled by Lucifer	Bourgeois and petit bourgeois (PB) class standpoint
All-encompassing	Explains everything	Explains everything
Exclusive	The only way; elitist	The only way; elitist

TABLE 7. Salient Features of the Systems of Control as Manifested in Heaven's Gate and the DWP

Feature	Heaven's Gate	Democratic Workers Party
Organizational form	Pyramid structure	Pyramid structure
Hierarchy	Top leader: Older Members, co-leaders, Ti and Do Inner circle Elders, Helpers, overseers	Top leader: General Secretary Second-in-command Inner circle Middle-level leaders
Command structure	Military-like "Chain of Mind"	Military-like chain of command
Discipline	Unconditional obedience	Unconditional obedience
Decision making	Centralized in Ti and Do	Centralized in Dixon
Indoctrination setting	Daily, recurring meetings; work units	Weekly, sometimes daily meetings; work units
Duties as a member	Full-time "tasks" and meetings	Full-time "assignments" and meetings
Group environment	Communal	Communal but in small units
Recruitment style	Subtle, seductive	Aggressive, pressured
Expected personal transformation	Shed previous (human) identity; reject past; break contact with former life	Submerge previous (pre-Party) identity; reject past; break contact with former life
Financial obligation	Members asked to turn over or give up all resources; collective finances	Members required to turn over all income above base amount set by DWP; select other resources collectivized
Code of conduct	Strict, via procedures, "17 Steps," "Major Offenses"	Strict, via Central Committee directives, *Militant's Guide*
Behavioral norm	Acquiescent, exemplified in Next Level genderless creature	Acquiescent, exemplified in Communist cadre ideal
Security measures	Clandestine; guarded, paranoid atmosphere	Clandestine; guarded, paranoid atmosphere
Sanctions	More indirect; mild; slippage sessions for public "lessons"	Direct; severe; public criticism sessions and trials
Commitment goal	Become a deployable agent: instrument of the Next Level	Become a deployable agent: instrument of the Party

TABLE 8. Salient Features of the Systems of Influence as Manifested in Heaven's Gate and the DWP

Feature	Heaven's Gate	Democratic Workers Party
Proof	"Soul deposit"; "deposit of knowledge"	Marxist analysis; class consciousness
Behavioral model	"What would my Older Member have me do?"	"What would a good Bolshevik do?"
Change process	Willful overcoming	Willing cadre transformation
Choice	"Free will"	"Freedom and necessity"
Overall attitude	Conformity, martyrdom: "be of like mind with Next Level Mind"; prepare to leave this world	Conformity, martyrdom: be one with the collective; "we are all dead men on leave"
Reward expectation	Reborn as new creature; go to Next Level	Reborn as cadre Communist; be part of making history
Self-renunciation	No "human" attachments	No "PB" self-indulgence
Training mechanism	Tests, "lessons"	Cadre tests, cadre crises
Evidence of striving	Constant tension	Cadre tension; "nervous toughness"
Peer pressure	"Check partner"; task team	"One-help"; work unit and Branch
Collective spirit	Detest individual thinking; "be crew-minded"	Criticize "me-firstism"; comradeship over all
Self-monitoring	Expose errors; slippage notes	Discipline reports; self-criticism
Attitude toward criticism	No defensiveness; take the blame	No defensiveness; look for the kernel of truth
Attitude toward former life	Forget the past, literally; no talk	Reject and reframe the past through class histories; no talk
Privacy; boundaries	Next Level knows all; reads all thoughts	"Nothing remains outside the eyes of the Party"
Relations with outside world	Silence critics via slander, nonviolent; controlled visits with family	Silence critics via slander, sometimes violent; controlled visits with family
Emotions	Anticipation; anxiety; guilt	Generalized anxiety; guilt; fear
Internalized fears	"Luciferian programming" will distract from training	"Bourgeois programming" will sabotage cadre development
Sense of threat	Fear of being "sent out"	Fear of expulsion

TABLE 9. Critical Features of Cultic Structure as Evidenced in Heaven's Gate and the Democratic Workers Party

Charismatic Authority (Leader-Follower Dynamic)	Transcendent Belief System (Ideological Underpinnings)	Systems of Control (Organizational Structure)	Systems of Influence (Social Controls)
Stress on leadership principle: autocratic, no feedback	All-inclusive: the Truth; the only way; elitist, special	Hierarchical top-down command structure	Strict behavioral model: constant striving for ideal
Personal myth: awakening, prophetic	Urgent and deterministic	Pyramid formation and rigid boundaries	Personal choice; willing transformation
Leader as role model: sets style and tone, lauded as perfect	Personal transmission from leader	Administered by excessive rules and regulations	Assume new identity; reject former interests
Leader as originator of belief system; has formula for salvation	Transcendent: offers ultimate solution and path to freedom	Discipline: tight controls on daily life, communal	Monitoring by leadership and peers; reporting
Leader dependent on followers	Moral imperative: it must be done	Collective units for indoctrination, work	Internalized self-monitoring
Limited access to leader; mysterious; secretive; don't question	Separatist and heretical: excludes and ridicules other belief systems	Total or near-total submission: unconditional obedience	Unite with collective spirit: conformity; no individual thinking
Double standard: leadership privileges	Founded on impossible ideal	Decision making centralized in leader	No loyalty other than to leader
Leader paranoid; has real and/or imagined enemies	Based on need for members' personal transformation; shed previous identity	Heightened sense of security: guidelines; secrets; off-limits areas and topics	Constant exposure of errors in attitude and deed; no privacy
Followers in awe of leader; privilege to be with	Members must internalize	System of sanctions	Life governed by strict code; norms internalized
Charismatic relationship between leader and followers	Offers context and tools for change	Duties, obligations; full-time commitment	Identification with leader and group

TABLE 10. Organizational Outcomes of Heaven's Gate and the Democratic Workers Party

Organization	Leadership Style	Response to Crises	Leader's Relations with Followers	Worldview Orientation	Outcome
Heaven's Gate	Soft, indirect, subtle veil of power	Tightly controlled; resolved in members' interests	Direct and personal; members feel connected to leader	Want to reject the world and leave it; no reason to go to outside world	Organizational implosion, personal collective obedience, self-destruction
DWP	Hard, direct; obvious face of power	Tightly controlled but not always resolved in members' interests	Mediated, impersonal; members don't feel as connected to leader; eventually easier to disconnect	Want to change the world and save it; retain attachment to outside world	Organizational explosion, personal and collective resistance and self-preservation

TABLE 11. Matrix of Purpose and Effects of the Four Structural Dimensions of the Self-Sealing System

Dimension	General Purpose	Specific Goal	Process/Method	Effect
Charismatic authority	Offer and establish leadership	Legitimate authority (direction)	Leadership privilege and command	Personal identification with leader
Transcendent belief system	Provide worldview and goals	Moral imperative (meaning and purpose)	Requires personal transformation	Internalization of utopian ideology (personal freedom)
Systems of control	Establish organizational structure	Behavioral system (discipline)	Abide by rules, regulations, and sanctions	Compliance and obedience in words and deeds
Systems of influence	Institute social system (organizational culture)	Group norms (code of conduct)	Respond to peer influence and modeling	Conformity of thought (self-renunciation)

TABLE 12. Characteristics of Personal Closure

Purpose and Commitment	Love and Fear	Duty and Guilt	Identification and Internalization
Characterized by decency, loyalty	Feels love for leader and group	Feels obligated to participate	Feels complete unity with leader
Finds meaning	Enjoys group solidarity	Feels duty-bound to the belief system	Identifies with other members
Finds purpose	Feels personal power; sense of elitism	Is invested in group's goals and successes	Strives at all times to accomplish goals
Is single-minded	Fears loss of meaning	Won't renege on commitment	Lacks energy; is passive
Lacks information	Fears loss of purpose	Blames self for group failures	Feels confused at disparities
Has dualistic worldview; rigid, black-and-white thinking	Experiences and/or fears authority figure's disapproval, withdrawal of support	Feels complicit: cannot imagine leaving behind others who he or she recruited, chastised, held to group norms	Experiences cognitive inefficiencies because of mental and/or physical exhaustion
Responds to power of belief	Experiences and fears peer disapproval or shunning	Feels shame over separating from past: cut ties, expressed hatred for past and others	Is cut off from other sources of information; lacks reality checks
Enjoys strength of collective commitment	Feels paranoia about evil outside world; fears disapproval of outside world	Feels obligated to leader; cannot imagine leaving	Feels complete loss of pregroup identities; would not know where to go
No identity outside group context	Feels unable to function outside group context	Feels obligated to others: leaving would mean more work for them	Cannot imagine life outside the group

Notes

Preface

1. Robert Jay Lifton, *Destroying the World to Save It: Aum Shinrikyo, Apocalyptic Violence, and the New Global Terrorism* (New York: Metropolitan Books, 1999).

2. Walter Laqueur, *The New Terrorism: Fanaticism and the Arms of Mass Destruction* (New York: Oxford University Press, 1999).

3. Eric Hoffer, *The True Believer: Thoughts on the Nature of Mass Movements* (New York: Perennial, 1951), 10.

4. Benedict Carey, "Method without Madness?" *Los Angeles Times,* July 30, 2002; Reuel Marc Gerecht, "The Gospel According to Osama Bin Laden," *Atlantic Monthly,* January 2002, 46–48; Rohan Gunaratna, *Inside Al Qaeda* (New York: Columbia University Press, 2002); Paulo Pontoniere, "Lessons from the Al Qaeda Cult Handbook" (AlterNet.org, 2001 [accessed February 27, 2003]); available from www.alternet.org/print.html?StoryID = 11895.

5. Pontoniere, "Lessons from the Al Qaeda Cult Handbook."

6. I thank Hal Mansfield for our discussions on the similarities and differences of cults and terrorist groups.

7. In keeping with DWP tradition and style, I capitalize "Party" when referring to the DWP.

8. See, for example, Janja Lalich, "The Cadre Ideal: Origins and Development of a Political Cult," *Cultic Studies Journal* 9.1 (1992): 1–77; "How I See It Today" (Pelham, N.Y., 1987); and "A Little Carrot and a Lot of Stick: A Case Example," in Michael D. Langone, ed., *Recovery from Cults: Help for Victims of Psychological and Spiritual Abuse* (New York: Norton, 1993), 51–84.

9. See, for example, Janja Lalich, "Dominance and Submission: The Psychosexual Exploitation of Women in Cults," *Women & Therapy* 19.4 (1996): 37–

52; "Introduction: 'We Own Her Now,'" *Cultic Studies Journal* 14.1 (1997): 1–3; "Repairing the Soul after a Cult Experience," *Creation Spirituality Network Magazine,* spring 1996, 30–33; and Madeleine Landau Tobias and Janja Lalich, *Captive Hearts, Captive Minds: Freedom and Recovery from Cults and Abusive Relationships* (Alameda, Calif.: Hunter House, 1994).

10. One result of this work was the special edition of the *Cultic Studies Journal* focusing on women in cults. See Janja Lalich, ed., "Women under the Influence: A Study of Women's Lives in Totalist Groups" [Special Issue], *Cultic Studies Journal* 14.1 (1997).

1. Introduction

1. At the time of the suicides there were some former members and sympathizers who were not actively part of the group but continued to believe in Heaven's Gate leaders Marshall Applewhite and Bonnie Nettles and their worldview.

2. For the negative position on apostates, see, for example, David G. Bromley, ed., *The Politics of Apostasy: The Role of Apostates in the Transformation of Religious Movements* (Westport, Conn.: Praeger, 1998). For my position, see Janja Lalich, "Pitfalls in the Sociological Study of Cults," in Thomas Robbins and Benjamin Zablocki, eds., *Misunderstanding Cults: Searching for Objectivity in a Controversial Field* (Toronto: University of Toronto Press, 2001), 123–55.

3. For an interesting and thorough view of this controversy, with perspectives from various sides of the debate, see Benjamin Zablocki and Thomas Robbins, eds., *Misunderstanding Cults: Searching for Objectivity in a Controversial Field* (Toronto: University of Toronto Press, 2001).

4. This definition and subsequent explanation was presented in my Ph.D. dissertation, "Bounded Choice: The Fusion of Personal Freedom and Self-Renunciation in Two Transcendent Groups" (Fielding Graduate Institute, 2000), and later published in "Pitfalls in the Sociological Study of Cults."

5. See the following by Robert Jay Lifton: "The Appeal of the Death Trip," *New York Times Magazine,* January 7, 1979, 26–27, 29–31; "Cult Violence, Death, and Immortality" (paper presented at the American Psychiatric Association, San Diego, Calif., 1997); *Destroying the World to Save It: Aum Shinrikyo, Apocalyptic Violence, and the New Global Terrorism* (New York: Metropolitan Books, 1999); *The Future of Immortality and Other Essays for a Nuclear Age* (New York: Basic Books, 1987); *Revolutionary Immortality: Mao Tse-tung and the Chinese Cultural Revolution* (New York: Random House, 1968); *Thought Reform and the Psychology of Totalism* (New York: Norton, 1961); "'Totalism' Ideology of Cults Helps Explain Violent Acts," *Psychiatric News,* July 4, 1997.

6. Benjamin D. Zablocki, "Exit Cost Analysis: A New Approach to the Scientific Study of Brainwashing," *Nova Religio* 1.2 (1998): 217.

7. Benjamin D. Zablocki, "The Blacklisting of a Concept: The Strange History of the Brainwashing Conjecture in the Sociology of Religion," *Nova Religio* 1.1 (1997): 96–121; "Exit Cost Analysis," 216–49.

8. Zablocki, "Exit Cost Analysis."

9. Lifton, *Thought Reform and the Psychology of Totalism*.

10. Edgar H. Schein, *Coercive Persuasion* (New York: Norton, 1961); "Groups and Intergroup Relationships," in Walter E. Natemeyer and Jay S. Gilberg, eds., *Classics of Organizational Behavior* (Danville, Ill.: Interstate Printers and Publishers, [1970] 1989), 172–78; *Organizational Culture and Leadership*, 2d ed. (San Francisco: Jossey-Bass, 1992).

11. Max Weber, *From Max Weber: Essays in Sociology*, ed. and trans. H. H. Gerth and C. Wright Mills (New York: Oxford University Press, 1946); *The Sociology of Religion* (Boston: Beacon Press, [1922] 1964).

12. John Lofland, *Doomsday Cult: A Study of Conversion, Proselytization, and Maintenance of Faith* (New York: Irvington, [1966] 1981); John Lofland and N. Skonovd, "Patterns of Conversion," in Eileen Barker, ed., *Of Gods and Men: New Religious Movements in the West* (Macon, Ga.: Mercer University Press, 1983), 1–24.

13. John Lofland and Rodney Stark, "Becoming a World-Saver: A Theory of Conversion to a Deviant Perspective," *American Sociological Review* 30 (1965): 862–75.

14. Rosabeth Moss Kanter, *Commitment and Community: Communes and Utopias in Sociological Perspective* (Cambridge, Mass.: Harvard University Press, 1972).

15. Anthony Giddens, *Central Problems in Social Theory: Action, Structure and Contradiction in Social Analysis* (Berkeley: University of California Press, 1979); *The Constitution of Society: Outline of the Theory of Structuration* (Berkeley: University of California Press, 1984).

16. Herbert A. Simon, "A Behavioral Model of Rational Choice," *Quarterly Journal of Economics* 69 (1955): 99–118; *Models of Thought*, vol. 1 (New Haven, Conn.: Yale University Press, 1979); "Rational Choice and the Structure of the Environment," *Psychological Review* 63 (1956): 129–38.

17. Robert Jay Lifton, *The Nazi Doctors* (New York: Basic Books, 1986); *Revolutionary Immortality; Thought Reform and the Psychology of Totalism; The Future of Immortality and Other Essays for a Nuclear Age*.

18. It is difficult to estimate membership in cult groups for a number of reasons. Some groups are so secretive we know very little if anything about them. Other groups tend to boast and exaggerate their numbers. Many people pass through such groups rather quickly. Some groups have varying levels of membership, again making it difficult to ascertain exact numbers, depending on whether the count includes full-time, part-time, sympathizers, and so on. Michael Langone, editor of the *Cultic Studies Review*, addresses some of these very issues in "Prevalence" (American Family Foundation, n.d. [accessed January 4, 2003]), available from www.csj.org/infoserve_freeinfo/cso/Prevalence.htm.

19. Few survived this debacle. Survivors included several members of Jones's security guards who enforced the administering of the poisonous potion. Other survivors were several followers who hid and Jonestown attorneys Mark Lane

and Charles Garry, who managed to flee into the jungle and escape death. See John R. Hall, *Gone from the Promised Land: Jonestown in American Cultural History* (New Brunswick, N.J.: Transaction Books, 1987); Deborah Layton, *Seductive Poison: A Jonestown Survivor's Story of Life and Death in the Peoples Temple* (New York: Anchor Books, 1998); Martin Merzer, "Cultists Commit Mass Suicide in Guyana," November 28, 1978 (accessed January 2, 2003), available from wire.ap.org/APPackages/20thcentury/78jimjones.html.

20. Layton, *Seductive Poison.*

21. Anthony Storr, *Feet of Clay—Saints, Sinners, and Madmen: A Study of Gurus* (New York: Free Press, 1997).

22. Amy Waldman, "Little Trace of Late Bhagwan at His Commune," *San Francisco Chronicle,* December 13, 2002, K6.

23. Judith Miller, Steven Engelberg, and William Broad, *Germs: Biological Weapons and America's Secret War* (New York: Simon & Schuster, 2001).

24. Marion S. Goldman, *Passionate Journeys: Why Successful Women Joined a Cult* (Ann Arbor: University of Michigan Press, 1999).

25. Stuart A. Wright, ed., *Armageddon in Waco: Critical Perspectives on the Branch Davidian Conflict* (Chicago: University of Chicago Press, 1995).

26. Jean-François Mayer, "'Our Terrestrial Journey Is Coming to an End': The Last Voyage of the Solar Temple," *Nova Religio* 2.2 (1999): 172–96.

27. Ibid.

28. This is not unlike the activities of some domestic groups that preach Armageddon, beginning with the Manson family in 1969. Such ideas were integral to Charles Manson's belief system. After the seven Tate-LaBianca murders, Manson's followers used their victims' blood to scrawl such words as "Political Piggy," "Rise," and "Helter Skelter" on the refrigerator and walls, hoping to deflect blame as well as incite a race war, which Manson preached was inevitable and the white man's just due. See, for example, Karlene Faith, *The Long Prison Journey of Leslie Van Houten: Life Beyond the Cult* (Boston: Northeastern University Press, 2001). Timothy McVeigh, inspired by the racist book *The Turner Diaries,* apparently had similar motivations when on April 19, 1995, he bombed the Alfred P. Murrah Federal Building in Oklahoma City, which took the lives of 168 people and injured 500 more. See, for example, Richard Serrano, *One of Ours: Timothy McVeigh and the Oklahoma City Bombing* (New York: Norton, 1998). In both these cases, the perpetrators thought they were starting "the revolution."

29. See also Mark Juergensmeyer, *Terror in the Mind of God: The Global Rise of Religious Violence* (Berkeley: University of California Press, 2000); Lifton, *Destroying the World to Save It;* Miller, Engelberg, and Broad, *Germs;* Kyle B. Olson, "Aum Shinrikyo: Once and Future Threat?" *Emerging Infectious Diseases* 5.4 (2000) [serial on-line] [accessed December 29, 2001]; available from www.cdc.gov/ncidod/EID/vol5o4/olson.htm.

30. This information was verified by Jean-François Mayer of the University of Fribourg in Switzerland, a leading authority on this group. Personal communication via e-mail.

31. Nori J. Muster, *Betrayal of the Spirit: My Life behind the Headlines of the Hare Krishna Movement* (Urbana: University of Illinois Press, 1997).

32. E. Burke Rochford Jr., "Child Abuse in the Hare Krishna Movement: 1971–1986," *ISKCON Communications Journal* 6.1 (1998): 43–69; "Family Formation, Culture, and Change in the Hare Krishna Movement," *ISKCON Communications Journal* 5.2 (1997): 61–82; Storr, *Feet of Clay.*

33. Nirshan Perera, "$400 Mn Lawsuit against ISKCON Dismissed," *rediff.com,* October 2, 2001.

34. Carl T. Hall, "Clone Experts Fear the Worst for 'Eve,'" *San Francisco Chronicle,* December 29, 2002, A1, A6; Gina Kolata, "Experts Are Suspicious of Claim of Cloned Human's Birth," *New York Times,* December 28, 2002, A16.

35. Dana Canedy, "Sect Claims First Cloned Baby," *New York Times,* December 28, 2002, A16; Michael Friscolanti, "Aliens, Free Love at Core of Sect," *National Post,* December 28, 2002; Ingrid Peritz, "Raelians Seek Path to Human Immortality," *Globe and Mail,* December 28, 2002, A5.

36. Malcolm Ritter, "Journalist Overseeing Test of 'Clone' Throws in Towel," *San Francisco Chronicle,* January 7, 2003, A2.

37. Editorial, "Raelians Owe Us Proof or Explanation," *The Gazette* (Montreal), January 7, 2003.

38. Michael Taylor, "SLA's Legacy a Violent Void," *San Francisco Chronicle,* November 11, 2002, A1, A12.

39. Associated Press, "Radical Group Claims It Set SUVs on Fire," *San Francisco Chronicle,* January 5, 2003, A7.

40. Lofland and Skonovd, "Patterns of Conversion."

41. Lewis R. Rambo, *Understanding Religious Conversion* (New Haven, Conn.: Yale University Press, 1993).

42. Although *worldview shift* is preferable to me as a term for identifying this life-altering process, at times I use *conversion* and intend for the two terms to carry the same meaning.

43. Kurt Lewin, *Resolving Social Conflicts: Selected Papers on Group Dynamics* (Washington, D.C.: American Psychological Association, [1948] 1997), 49.

44. Leon Festinger, *A Theory of Cognitive Dissonance* (New York: Row, Peterson, 1957).

45. Lofland and Skonovd, "Patterns of Conversion."

46. Karen Breslau and Colin Soloway, "'He's a Really Good Boy,'" *Newsweek.MSNBC.com,* December 3, 2001, available at www.msnbc.com/news/666792.asp; Kevin Fagan and Pamela J. Podger, "American's Road to Taliban Fighter," *San Francisco Chronicle,* December 5, 2001, A1, A14; Don Lattin and Kevin Fagan, "John Walker's Curious Quest," *San Francisco Chronicle,* December 14, 2001, A24; Evan Thomas, "A Long, Strange Trip to the Taliban," *Newsweek,* December 17, 2001, 30–36.

47. Lifton, *Thought Reform and the Psychology of Totalism.*

48. I thank Barnett Pearce for introducing me to this concept in his book *Communication and the Human Condition* (Carbondale: Southern Illinois University Press, 1989).

49. Jerry MacDonald presents the concept of a bicameral normative system—two sets of rules, one benign when everything is going as the leader wants it, and one coercive, when the leader's control is threatened. See "'Reject the Wicked Man'—Coercive Persuasion and Deviance Production: A Study of Conflict Management," *Cultic Studies Journal* 5.1 (1988): 59–121.

50. Giddens, *The Constitution of Society*.

51. Lifton, *Revolutionary Immortality*.

52. Jane Braaten, *Habermas's Critical Theory of Society* (Albany: State University of New York Press, 1991); Lukes, *Power: A Radical View;* Richard Sennett, *Authority* (Boston: Faber & Faber, 1980).

53. Janja Lalich, "Mimesis and Metaphors in the Discourse of Heaven's Gate Students" (paper presented at the Society for the Scientific Study of Religion, San Diego, Calif., November 7, 1997).

54. Giddens, *The Constitution of Society*.

55. DWP data were drawn largely from archival material, including a vast collection of documents, position papers, and correspondence (more than one hundred pieces) written by members, individually and collectively, during and immediately after the group's demise and dissolution. The majority were written by DWP members of all levels and length of membership but also included documents by nonmember supporters and associates, as well as published accounts by former members after the group's dissolution. Articles about the DWP published in the mainstream and leftist media were also used as secondary source material to corroborate other data and also as partial evidence of the group's societal impact and efforts at impression management. Additional DWP data were drawn from transcripts and notes from formal interviews, in-depth discussions, and informal conversations with former members, relatives and friends of members, and organizational and professional associates. The majority of these took place between 1986 and 1991. Requests for updates or clarification took place between 1998 and 2002. In some instances I was seeking out specific information, especially about the group's history before I was a member or about specific incidents. I spoke with ten of the thirteen founders of the group, plus more than fifty members who had functioned at various levels while in the DWP and who had varying points of view during and after its demise. One founding member refused my request for an interview. (This initial research on the DWP culminated in my work "The Cadre Ideal: Origins and Development of a Political Cult," *Cultic Studies Journal* 9.1 [1992]: 1–77; and "A Little Carrot and a Lot of Stick: A Case Example," in Michael Langone, ed., *Recovery from Cults: Help for Victims of Psychological and Spiritual Abuse* [New York: Norton, 1994], 51–84). Included in the data were personal observations based on my own long-term participation in the group. I was among the first rung of recruits to join in mid-1975, immediately after the group's founding year, and remained a member until the demise of the group in late 1985 and its final dissolution in 1986. I was a high-ranking member, consistently part of leadership bodies and the inner circle around the leader. At various times, I was on the Central Committee; served as head of Party-wide recruitment training and was

responsible for the content and conduct of New Members Classes; and served as Branch Executive Officer, Branch Political Officer, and Party School Teacher. Working with one of the top leaders, I was also responsible for the centralized training of Party School Teachers and various Branch officers. I was assigned leadership of the Party's publishing house, was part of various executive councils and the Discipline and Control Board, and served as an aide to the leader, especially on international travel. Most of those years I was privy to much information not revealed to the general membership and participated in countless leadership meetings, discussions, and decisions. Thus some of the data used in this study were drawn from my own experiences, observations, and perceptions as a member; my later writings about the organization and my experiences in it; and my recollections of events and discussions with other members, before, during, and after my involvement. Included are recollections of personal encounters, travels, and discussions with the leader.

Heaven's Gate data were drawn from archival material, including personal testimonials by members and former members, both in print and in audiovisual format, media interviews with former members after the 1997 suicides, and a former member's personal diary written during his first several months with the group. Data sources also included articles and book chapters published about the group — both academic and popular — and correspondence by family members of group participants. I relied in particular on the work of Robert Balch and David Taylor, who have done extensive sociological research since the 1970s, when they began monitoring developments in the group. This includes my conversations and personal communications with Balch. Media reports date from the 1970s to the present. These data were supplemented by interviews with several long-term members of the group, one of whom was among the original group of adherents, and who was at times part of the inner circle around the leaders. These tape-recorded, open-ended interviews were five to ten hours in length. Two others interviewed had been inconsistent members in that they were in and out of the group from the first year until quite near the end. These open-ended interviews were about two hours in length and were also tape-recorded. Also included were interviews and discussions with three short-term members and fifteen relatives, friends, and professional associates of the leaders or members dating to 1994. These interviews were from one to three hours long. Tape-recorded interviews were transcribed by a professional transcriber, and the transcriptions were checked against the recording to ensure accuracy.

56. This is akin to Herbert Simon's concept of bounded rationality. See Simon, *Models of Thought.*

57. Lifton, *Thought Reform and the Psychology of Totalism.*

2. Gurus, Seers, and New Agers

1. Information on the Hale-Bopp comet is from the NASA Web site, http://encke.jpl.nasa.gov/hale_bopp_info.html [accessed October 31, 2000].

2. Written instructions indicate that the cult members died in shifts, with members of one segment of the group helping another, cleaning up, then proceeding with their own suicides. The two final helpers were found with plastic bags over their heads. Other similar bags with elastic bands around them were found in trash receptacles behind the house, indicating they had been used on others, then removed once death was confirmed. See Pamela Kramer, Brandon Bailey, Tracy Seipel, Rodney Foo, and Renee Koury, "Cult's Recipe for Death," *San Jose Mercury News,* March 28, 1997, 1A, 26A.

3. Seth Hettena, "Rancho Santa Fe — The Good Life," *San Francisco Chronicle,* June 5, 2002, 2.

4. Robert W. Balch and David Taylor, "Making Sense of the Heaven's Gate Suicides," in David G. Bromley and J. Gordon Melton, eds., *Cults, Religion and Violence* (New York: Cambridge University Press, 2002), 209–28.

5. This section is not intended to present a thorough review of the New Age movement, its history or overall societal implications. For such a review, see, for example, W. J. Hanegraaff, *New Age Religion and Western Culture: Esotericism in the Mirror of Secular Thought* (Albany: State University of New York Press, 1998); Paul Heelas, *The New Age Movement* (Cambridge, Mass.: Blackwell, 1996).

6. Wade Clark Roof, *Spiritual Marketplace: Baby Boomers and the Remaking of American Religion* (Princeton, N.J.: Princeton University Press, 1999).

7. Arthur A. Dole and Michael D. Langone, "Strongly Held Views about the New Age: Critics versus Experts," *Cultic Studies Journal* 11.1 (1994): 1–28.

8. Russell Chandler, *Understanding the New Age* (Grand Rapids, Mich.: Zondervan, 1993), 27.

9. Marilyn Ferguson, *The Aquarian Conspiracy* (Los Angeles: Tarcher, 1987), 380.

10. Ibid., 23.

11. Aldous Huxley, *The Doors of Perception and Heaven and Hell* (Harmondsworth: Penguin, 1959).

12. Baba Ram Dass, *Be Here Now* (San Cristóbal, New Mex.: Lama Foundation, 1971); Timothy Leary, *The Politics of Ecstasy* (London: Paladin, 1970).

13. Charles Y. Glock and Robert N. Bellah, "Introduction to Part I: New Religious Movements in the Asian Tradition," in Charles Y. Glock and Robert N. Bellah, eds., *The New Religious Consciousness* (Berkeley: University of California Press, 1976), 1–4.

14. Rodney Stark and Roger Finke, "A Rational Approach to the History of American Cults and Sects," in David G. Bromley and Jeffrey K. Hadden, eds., *The Handbook on Cults and Sects in America, Part A* (Greenwich, Conn.: JAI Press, 1993), 109–26.

15. Mia Farrow, *What Falls Away: A Memoir* (New York: Bantam Books, 1998).

16. The 1990s version of that philosophy can be seen in the postmodern rejection of Western science and "left-brain thinking" and the vast popular interest in mystical healing arts and personal transformation through "feeling states."

17. Ferguson, *The Aquarian Conspiracy.*

18. Again, these summaries are not meant to be definitive but are included to convey core concepts relevant to this study. There are many good books that provide in-depth expositions of each of these religious and spiritual movements.

19. Hanegraaff, *New Age Religion and Western Culture,* 382.

20. Kay Alexander, "Roots of the New Age," in James R. Lewis and J. Gordon Melton, eds., *Perspectives on the New Age* (Albany: State University of New York Press, 1992), 30–47.

21. Jacques Lacarriere, *The Gnostics* (San Francisco: City Lights Books, 1989).

22. Ruth Brandon, *The Spiritualists: The Passion for the Occult in the Nineteenth and Twentieth Centuries* (Buffalo, N.Y.: Prometheus Books, 1984); Ann Braude, *Radical Spirits: Spiritualism and Women's Rights in Nineteenth-Century America* (Boston: Beacon Press, 1989); Barbara Goldsmith, *Other Powers: The Age of Suffrage, Spiritualism, and the Scandalous Victoria Woodhull* (New York: Knopf, 1998).

23. Alison Winter, *Mesmerized: Powers of Mind in Victorian Britain* (Chicago: University of Chicago Press, 1998).

24. Michael F. Brown, *The Channeling Zone: American Spirituality in an Anxious Age* (Cambridge, Mass.: Harvard University Press, 1997); Jon Klimo, *Channeling: Investigations on Receiving Information from Paranormal Sources* (Los Angeles: Tarcher, 1987).

25. Eileen Campbell and J. H. Brennan, *Body Mind & Spirit: A Dictionary of New Age Ideas, People, Places, and Terms* (Rutland, Vt.: Tuttle, 1994), 212.

26. Ibid., 39. Also see Peter Washington, *Madame Blavatsky's Baboon: A History of the Mystics, Mediums, and Misfits Who Brought Spiritualism to America* (New York: Schocken, 1995).

27. C. G. Jung, *Memories, Dreams, Reflections* (New York: Vintage, 1965).

28. Donald Stone, "The Human Potential Movement," in Glock and Bellah, eds., *The New Religious Consciousness,* 95.

29. Abraham H. Maslow, *Toward a Psychology of Being,* 2d ed. (Princeton, N.J.: Van Nostrand, 1968).

30. Leonard George, *Alternative Realities: The Paranormal, the Mystic and the Transcendent in Human Experience* (New York: Facts on File, 1995), 215.

31. This raises the question of whether the peak experience is in fact "spiritual," or the attainment of self-actualization, or whether it is only *felt* to be so — and often quite temporarily — by the experiencer.

32. Ferguson, *The Aquarian Conspiracy,* 31.

33. Gregory Bateson, *Mind and Nature: A Necessary Unity* (New York: Bantam Books, 1980); *Steps to an Ecology of Mind* (New York: Ballantine Books, 1978).

34. Bateson, *Steps to an Ecology of Mind,* 305.

35. Ibid., 306.

36. Ferguson, *The Aquarian Conspiracy,* 34.

37. Ibid., 31.

38. Philip Cushman, "Iron Fists/Velvet Gloves: A Study of a Mass Marathon Psychology Training," *Psychotherapy* 26.1 (spring 1989): 23–39; Leonard L. Glass, Michael A. Kirsch, and Frederick A. Parris, "Psychiatric Disturbances Associated with Erhard Seminars Training, I: A Report of Cases," *American Journal of Psychiatry* 134 (1977): 245–47; Janice Haaken and Richard Adams, "Pathology as 'Personal Growth': A Participant Observation Study of Lifespring Training," *Psychiatry* 46 (1983): 270–80; Michael A. Kirsch and Leonard L. Glass, "Psychiatric Disturbances Associated with Erhard Seminars Training, II: Additional Cases and Theoretical Considerations," *American Journal of Psychiatry* 134 (1977): 1254–58; Morton A. Lieberman, "Effects of Large Group Awareness Training on Participants' Psychiatric Status," *American Journal of Psychiatry* 144 (1987): 460–64; Peter Marin, "The New Narcissism," *Harper's*, October 1975, 45–50, 55–56; Michael Persinger, N. J. Carrey, and L. A. Suess, *TM and Cult Mania* (North Quincy, Mass.: Christopher, 1980); Steven Pressman, *Outrageous Betrayal: The Dark Journey of Werner Erhard from est to Exile* (New York: St. Martin's Press, 1993); Margaret T. Singer and Richard Ofshe, "Thought Reform Programs and the Production of Psychiatric Casualties," *Psychiatric Annals* 20.4 (1990): 188–93; Margaret Thaler Singer, *Cults in Our Midst: The Hidden Menace in Our Everyday Lives* (San Francisco: Jossey-Bass, 1995); Margaret Thaler Singer and Janja Lalich, *"Crazy" Therapies: What Are They? Do They Work?* (San Francisco: Jossey-Bass, 1996); Irvin D. Yalom and Morton Lieberman, "A Study of Encounter Group Casualties," *Archives of General Psychiatry* 25 (1971): 16–30.

39. Marin, "The New Narcissism."

3. The Beginning

1. I use pseudonyms for former members who did not take part in the suicide and use members' assumed cult names (ending in -*ody*) for those who died. For the leaders, who were public figures, I use both real names and their assumed group names. Unless otherwise cited, all quotations by former members are from author interviews. Brent's diary is cited with permission. Unless otherwise cited, all quotations by members who died in the collective suicide are from their own videotape, *Students' Exit Statement*, dated March 21, 1997; from individual exit statements in the group's published book, available at www.heavensgate.com (accessed March 30, 1997); and, in the cases of Jstody and Rkkody, from recorded interviews before their deaths. (The latter two individuals were not in the group at the time of the collective suicide and committed suicide individually in the months following.) Unless otherwise cited, quotations attributed to Applewhite (aka Do) are from his videotaped statement, *Do's Final Exit*, dated March 19, 1997, and from his talks on the twelve-part *Beyond Human* video series, dated 1992 and 1993, produced and used by the group for recruitment and training purposes. See chapter 1, note 55, for further details on Heaven's Gate data.

2. Rex Dalton, "Tragedy Painful, Familiar to Man Who Lost Mom to Applewhite Cult," *San Diego Union-Tribune*, March 29, 1997, A11.

3. Lynn Simross, "Like Lambs, Cultists Who Follow Bo, Peep Are Being Fleeced," *Sunday Plain Dealer,* November 16, 1975, 8.

4. Rosemary Barnes, "He Had So Much Potential": Sister Calls Applewhite Born Leader (Caller-Times Interactive [Corpus Christi, Tex.], March 29, 1997 [on-line], available at www.caller.com/newsarch/news3673.html.

5. Mary Lee Grant, "College Roommate Remembers Herff as Social Butterfly" (Caller-Times Interactive [Corpus Christi, Tex.], March 30, 1997 [on-line], available at www.caller.com/newsarch/news3679.html.

6. Robert W. Balch and David Taylor, "Heaven's Gate: Implications for the Study of Commitment to New Religions" (unpublished ms., 1998).

7. Robert W. Balch, "Bo and Peep: A Case Study of the Origins of Messianic Leadership," in Roy Wallis, ed., *Millennialism and Charisma* (Belfast: Queen's University, 1982), 13–72.

8. See James S. Phelan, "Looking For: The Next World," *New York Times Magazine,* February 29, 1976, 12, 58–59, 62–64. In later writings Applewhite indicates that for the most part he felt that this article was a decent, accurate, and "generally quite objective" representation of The Two, their beliefs, and their movement. See Do, "'88 Update — the UFO Two and Their Crew: A Brief Synopsis," in Representatives from the Kingdom of Heaven, eds., *How and When "Heaven's Gate" (The Door to the Physical Kingdom Level above Human) May Be Entered* (Santa Fe, New Mex.: Heaven's Representatives, 1996) (hereafter referred to as *Heaven's Gate Book*).

9. Do, "'88 Update," III-3.

10. *Beyond Human,* session 1.

11. Balch, "Bo and Peep."

12. Robert W. Balch, "Waiting for the Ships: Disillusionment and the Revitalization of Faith in Bo and Peep's UFO Cult," in James R. Lewis, ed., *The Gods Have Landed* (Albany: State University of New York Press, 1995), 142.

13. Todd Berger, "Lost in Space," *San Francisco Focus,* May 1997, 36.

14. Phelan, "Looking For: The Next World."

15. Berger, "Lost in Space," 36.

16. Ibid.

17. Robert B. Cialdini, *Influence: The New Psychology of Modern Persuasion* (New York: Quill, 1984).

18. Although it is typical in academic research to disguise informants, I have done little to change Brent's identity, although I have given him a pseudonym to be consistent with my treatment of other former members. Brent specifically asked me during his interviews to *not* disguise his information.

19. Phelan, "Looking For: The Next World."

20. "Flying Saucery in the Wilderness," *Time,* August 27, 1979, 58.

21. Tables 1 through 4 in the Appendix detail relevant characteristics of these structural polar opposites, illustrating the complex, sometimes contradictory nature of this type of social system.

22. Most references to charisma in the literature, and possibly also in the public mind, are connected to male charismatic persons. Yet there are numerous

examples of female charismatic personalities. Such a list would include spiritualist leaders Madame Blavatsky and Victoria Woodhull; leaders of new religious movements such as Aimee Semple McPherson, Elizabeth Clare Prophet, and Mother Ammachi; political leaders Cleopatra, Joan of Arc, Sojourner Truth, Emma Goldman, Rosa Luxemburg, Eva Peron, and Gloria Steinem. When discussing charismatic figures in general in this book, as much as possible without being cumbersome, I alternate the gender to facilitate a broadening recognition of female charismatic leaders and also because two of the leaders discussed in this book are women.

23. Do, "Aids in Approaching This Material," in *Heaven's Gate Book*, iii.

24. All from Phelan, "Looking For: The Next World."

25. Rachel Coughlan, ed., *Heaven's Gate: Inside Story* (British Broadcasting Company, London, 1997).

26. Anthony Giddens, *Central Problems in Social Theory: Action, Structure and Contradiction in Social Analysis* (Berkeley: University of California Press, 1979), 197.

27. This is what Smelser called a "value-oriented belief": "Adherents see a new world, not merely an improvement of individuals or a reform of institutions — even though the latter are aspects of regeneration. The potential for regeneration may rest in a personal savior, in impersonal values such as liberty or communism, in national destiny, or in a combination of these. In any case the value-oriented belief involves a preoccupation with the highest moral bases of social life." See Neil J. Smelser, *Theory of Collective Behavior* (New York: Free Press, 1962), 122.

28. Robert W. Balch and David Taylor, "Salvation in a UFO," *Psychology Today*, October 1976, 58, 60–62, 66, 106.

29. Jacques Vallee, *Messengers of Deception: UFO Contacts and Cults* (Berkeley, Calif.: And/Or Press, 1979), 74.

30. See, for example, Andrew Ortony, ed., *Metaphor and Thought*, 2d ed. (New York: Cambridge University Press, 1993).

31. Dvora Yanov, "Ecologies of Technological Metaphors and the Theme of Control," *Technē: Journal of the Society for Philosophy and Technology* 1.3–4 (1996): 11.

32. George A. Miller, "Images and Models, Similes and Metaphors," in Andrew Ortony, ed., *Metaphor and Thought*, 2d ed. (New York: Cambridge University Press, 1993), 397.

33. Ludwig Fleck used the term "thought collective" to describe scientific communities in which people held the same beliefs and thought alike. See Ludwik Fleck, *Genesis and Development of a Scientific Fact* (Chicago: University of Chicago Press, 1977). My modification here to "thought community" is meant to distinguish it from solely scientific milieus and to suggest an even greater degree of conformity in thought and deed.

34. Herbert C. Kelman and V. Lee Hamilton, *Crimes of Obedience: Toward a Social Psychology of Authority and Responsibility* (New Haven, Conn.: Yale University Press, 1989).

35. Ibid., 55.

36. Ibid., 75.

37. *Beyond Human*, session 11.

4. Evolution of the Charismatic Community

1. I refer readers to Balch's and Balch and Taylor's research and writings, which extend from 1976 to 2002 (see bibliography). These two scholars have done meticulous historical research on this group, providing the most precise time line possible.

2. Robert W. Balch and David Taylor, "Seekers and Saucers: The Role of the Cultic Milieu in Joining a UFO Cult," *American Behavioral Scientist* 20.6 (1977): 839–60.

3. Robert W. Balch, "Bo and Peep: A Case Study of the Origins of Messianic Leadership," in Roy Wallis, ed., *Millennialism and Charisma* (Belfast: Queen's University, 1982), 13–72; Robert W. Balch and David Taylor, "Making Sense of the Heaven's Gate Suicides," in David G. Bromley and J. Gordon Melton, eds., *Cults, Religion and Violence* (New York: Cambridge University Press, 2002), 209–28; Balch and Taylor, "Salvation in a UFO," *Psychology Today*, October 1976, 58, 60–62, 66, 106; Balch and Taylor, "Seekers and Saucers"; and my own research.

4. Benjamin D. Zablocki, *Alienation and Charisma: A Study of Contemporary American Communes* (New York: Free Press, 1980).

5. Phelan, "Looking For: The Next World."

6. It is during this period that Balch infiltrated the group and wrote an article based on the experience, in which he stated that there was not much indoctrination in the group. See Balch and Taylor, "Salvation in a UFO." Unfortunately, his conclusion about the group at that time became a source of proof that such groups were not really brainwashing their members. It is in part that misconception that I am addressing in this book by elucidating the subtleties of indoctrination efforts that are more indirect than direct but nonetheless are quite influential. Bracketing for the time being the larger debate over definitions and usage of the term "brainwashing," the fact that during a particular moment in a group's history blatant indoctrination is not evident to researchers by no means justifies concluding that there is no such thing as brainwashing in this or any other group.

7. Balch, "Bo and Peep."

8. Do, "'88 Update — the UFO Two and Their Crew: A Brief Synopsis," in *Heaven's Gate Book*, III-9.

9. Do, "Undercover 'Jesus' Surfaces before Departure," in *Heaven's Gate Book*, 1–3.

10. Max Weber, "The Nature of Charismatic Authority and Its Routinization," in S. N. Eisenstadt, ed., *Max Weber: On Charisma and Institution Building* (Chicago: University of Chicago Press, [1947] 1968), 48–65; "The Pure

Types of Legitimate Authority," in Eisenstadt, ed., *Max Weber: On Charisma and Institution Building;* "The Social Psychology of World Religions," in H. H. Gerth and C. Wright Mills, eds., *From Max Weber: Essays in Sociology* (New York: Oxford University Press, 1946), 46–47; "The Sociology of Charismatic Authority," in Gerth and Mills, eds., *From Max Weber; The Sociology of Religion,* trans. E. Fischoff (Boston: Beacon Press, [1922] 1964).

11. Weber, "The Nature of Charismatic Authority and Its Routinization," 48.

12. Weber, "The Sociology of Charismatic Authority," 245.

13. Ibid., 247.

14. Max Weber, "Bureaucracy," in Gerth and Mills, eds., *From Max Weber,* 242.

15. Max Weber, "Religious Rejections of the World and Their Directions," in Gerth and Mills, eds., *From Max Weber;* Weber, "The Social Psychology of World Religions."

16. Both context and the idea of psychological preconditioning are important to consider here. For example, if John Doe is told or thinks that a "magical" being is about to enter the room and speak, then John may very well attribute some degree of magic, or specialness, to the speaker, to the event, and to what he, John, experienced, or thinks he experienced, during the event because of the "demand characteristics" and expectations of the setting. Another person may be told the same thing and yet see nothing magical. And finally John Doe may not be told anything and still have a "magical" moment. These varying experiences have to do with both context and personal traits. See, for example, Michael A. Kirsch and Leonard L. Glass, "Psychiatric Disturbances Associated with Erhard Seminars Training, II: Additional Cases and Theoretical Considerations," *American Journal of Psychiatry* 134 (1977): 1254–58; Martin Orne, "On the Social Psychology of the Psychological Experiment: With Particular Reference to Demand Characteristics and Their Implications," *American Psychologist* 17 (1962): 776–83.

17. Weber, "The Sociology of Charismatic Authority," 249.

18. Weber, "The Nature of Charismatic Authority and Its Routinization," 50.

19. Weber, "The Social Psychology of World Religions," 295.

20. This sentiment is reinforced by some of the early articles on the origins of the group. See, for example, Robert W. Balch, "The Evolution of a New Age Cult: From Total Overcomers Anonymous to Death at Heaven's Gate," in William W. Zellner and Marc Petrowsky, eds., *Sects, Cults, and Spiritual Communities: A Sociological Analysis* (Westport, Conn.: Praeger, 1998), 1–25.

21. Ti and Do, "Prospective Candidate Letter," 1975, 1.

22. Do, "Undercover 'Jesus' Surfaces before Departure," 1-3.

23. *Beyond Human,* session 7.

24. James R. Gaines, "Cults: Bo-Peep Flock," *Newsweek,* October 20, 1975, 32.

25. James Brooke, "Former Cultists Tell of Believers Now Adrift," *New York Times,* April 2, 1997, A1, A10.

26. Do, "'88 Update," 3-5.

27. "Flying Saucery in the Wilderness," *Time,* August 27, 1979, 58.

28. *Beyond Human,* session 6.

29. Ibid.
30. Ibid., session 7.
31. Ibid.

5. Denouement

1. *Heaven's Gate Book,* 1996, vii.
2. Cheryl Clark, "Cultist Applewhite Had a Severe Heart Disease," *San Diego Union Tribune,* April 12, 1997, available at www.uniontrib.com/reports/cult_suicide/news_1n12reports.html.
3. Benjamin Zablocki, "The Birth and Death of New Religious Movements" (paper presented at the Association for the Sociology of Religion, Washington, D.C., August 12, 2000).
4. Interview on "California Report," KQED Radio, San Francisco, March 30, 1997.
5. Irving Hexham and Karla Poewe, "UFO Religion: Making Sense of the Heaven's Gate Suicides," *Christian Century,* May 7, 1997, 439–40.
6. Interview on "California Report."
7. This couple joined in August 1996, after first making contact with the group via the Internet. They left behind four young children, including two-week-old twins, and drove across country with their nest egg of about $14,000. They met up with the group in Las Vegas. Three days later they met Applewhite, who praised them for being "advanced students." In response, they joined the group and turned over their life savings. After that the couple were separated and not allowed to be together. The husband said that about three weeks into it, his wife wanted to leave. He said that Applewhite took her alone into a room for about an hour. Speaking slowly and deliberately during a televised interview, he recounted what happened: "They came out and he told me, 'She's staying.' I looked at [my wife] and she was changed." Several months later he decided to leave the group because he was alarmed by Applewhite's continual talk of the violent ending of other groups, such as those at Jonestown and Waco. When his wife learned from him that he was planning to leave, she retrieved Applewhite to speak to her husband. That time Applewhite's efforts to convince someone to stay did not work. The man's wife stayed behind and died with the others six months later. Tom Keenan, "Sole Survivor," *Dateline,* National Broadcasting Company, 1997.
8. *Beyond Human,* session 8.

6. Revolutionaries, Rebels, and Activists

1. The New Communist Movement had a counterpart in Europe, which is not addressed here. See, for example, David Caute, *The Year of the Barricades: A Journey through 1968* (New York: Perennial, 1988); Dick Howard, *Defining the*

Political (Minneapolis: University of Minnesota Press, 1989). For an excellent in-depth study of the New Communist Movement in the United States, see Max Elbaum, *Revolution in the Air: Sixties Radicals Turn to Lenin, Mao and Che* (London: Verso, 2002). This section is not meant to be a definitive recounting of the NCM or of the leftist movements of the era. My intention is to convey the general atmosphere at the time, as well as specific principles inhering in the NCM that are relevant to this study.

2. Maurice Isserman, *If I Had a Hammer: The Death of the Old Left and the Birth of the New Left* (New York: Basic Books, 1987).

3. Max Elbaum, "Maoism in the United States," in Mari Jo Buhle, Paul Buhle, and Dan Georgakas, eds., *Encyclopedia of the American Left* (New York: Oxford University Press, 1998), 471–75.

4. Ibid.

5. Richard P. Appelbaum, *Karl Marx* (Newbury Park, Calif.: Sage, 1988), 9.

6. Karl Marx and Frederick Engels, *The Communist Manifesto* (New York: International Publishers, 1948), 9.

7. The Russian Social Democratic Workers' Party split into two factions in 1903. Lenin led the Bolshevik faction in favor of a small, disciplined party of professional revolutionaries. The Menshevik faction pushed for a large mass party, more loosely organized and without the discipline and full-time commitment of the Bolsheviks. In the October Revolution of 1917, the Bolsheviks overthrew the revolutionary provisional government, of which the Mensheviks were a part. In 1918 the Bolsheviks became the Russian Communist Party and over the next several years suppressed all other political groups. See J. S. Levey and A. Greenhall, eds., *The Concise Columbia Encyclopedia* (New York: Avon Books, 1983), 97.

8. I am indebted to the work of Max Elbaum for the formulation of this summary. See Max Elbaum, "Where's the Party?" 1997.

9. Ibid.

10. Elbaum, "Maoism in the United States."

11. Theodore H. E. Chen, *Thought Reform of the Chinese Intellectuals* (Hong Kong: Hong Kong University Press, 1960).

12. Several excellent books depicting this period have been written in recent years by Chinese who lived through it. See, for example, Anchee Min, *Red Azalea* (New York: Pantheon Books, 1994). Another excellent work is Lifton's on the concept of revolutionary immortality: Robert Jay Lifton, *Revolutionary Immortality: Mao Tse-tung and the Chinese Cultural Revolution* (New York: Random House, 1968).

13. Elbaum, "Where's the Party?"

14. I am deliberately not addressing here the Trotskyist organizations that existed at this time, as they are not pertinent to this discussion. For that history, see Dennis Tourish, "Ideological Intransigence, Democratic Centralism, and Cultism: A Case Study from the Political Left," *Cultic Studies Journal* 15.1 (1998): 33–67; Dennis Tourish and Tim Wohlforth, *On the Edge: Political Cults Right and Left* (Armonk, N.Y.: Sharpe, 2000); Tim Wohlforth, *The Prophet's Children: Travels on the American Left* (Atlantic Highlands, N.J.: Humanities Press, 1994).

15. William G. McLoughlin, *Revivals, Awakenings, and Reform: An Essay on Religion and Social Change in America, 1607–1977* (Chicago: University of Chicago Press, 1978), 205–6.

16. Ibid., 6.

17. Isserman, *If I Had a Hammer.*

18. James Miller, *"Democracy Is in the Streets": From Port Huron to the Siege of Chicago* (New York: Simon & Schuster, 1987), 317.

19. Rebecca E. Klatch, *A Generation Divided: The New Left, the New Right, and the 1960s* (Berkeley: University of California Press, 1999).

20. Caute, *The Year of the Barricades,* 59.

21. Robert N. Bellah, "New Religious Consciousness and the Crisis in Modernity," in Charles Y. Glock and Robert N. Bellah, eds., *The New Religious Consciousness* (Berkeley: University of California Press, 1976), 77–92; Wade Clark Roof, *A Generation of Seekers: The Spiritual Journeys of the Baby Boom Generation* (San Francisco: HarperSanFrancisco, 1993); Steven M. Tipton, *Getting Saved from the Sixties: Moral Meaning in Conversion and Cultural Change* (Berkeley: University of California Press, 1984).

22. Elaine Brown, *A Taste of Power: A Black Woman's Story* (New York: Pantheon Books, 1992); David Hilliard and Lewis Cole, *This Side of Glory: The Autobiography of David Hilliard and the Story of the Black Panther Party* (Boston: Little, Brown, 1993); Hugh Pearson, *The Shadow of the Panther: Huey Newton and the Price of Black Power in America* (Reading, Mass.: Addison-Wesley, 1994).

23. Elbaum, "Maoism in the United States."

24. For a more detailed understanding of the social and intellectual roots of the New Left and their implications, see Wini Breines, *Community and Organization in the New Left, 1962–1968: The Great Refusal* (New Brunswick, N.J.: Rutgers University Press, 1989); Todd Gitlin, *The Sixties* (New York: Bantam Books, 1987); Howard, *Defining the Political;* Klatch, *A Generation Divided.*

25. Elizabeth Wheaton, *Code Name Greenkil: The 1979 Greensboro Killings* (Athens: University of Georgia Press, 1987), 12.

26. Once again, I thank Max Elbaum for jogging my memory on the historical facts on these two schools.

27. Elbaum, "Maoism in the United States."

28. Ibid., 475.

7. The Founding of the Democratic Workers Party

1. Other than Dixon, who is a public figure, and those who published articles under their real names, all names of DWP members are pseudonyms.

2. Some of the material in this section is drawn from Janja Lalich, "The Cadre Ideal: Origins and Development of a Political Cult," *Cultic Studies Journal* 9.1 (1992): 1–77.

3. Marshall Kilduff, "The Unusual Group behind Proposition V," *San Francisco Chronicle,* May, 30 1980, 7.

4. Suman Chatterjee, "Interview with Marlene Dixon: On the U.S. Left Today" (unpublished document, 1985), 2.

5. Ibid.

6. Malcolm G. Scully, "New Demonstrations Hit U.S. and Canadian Campuses; Several States Weigh Measures to Control Disruptions," *Chronicle of Higher Education,* February 24, 1969, 1.

7. See, for example, Chatterjee, "Interview with Marlene Dixon," 2.

8. On-line at www.feminist.org/research/chronicles/fc 1969.html (accessed June 12, 1999).

9. Edward Shils, "Totalitarians and Antinomians," in John H. Bunzel, ed., *Political Passages: Journeys of Change through Two Decades, 1968–1988* (New York: Free Press, 1988), 22–24.

10. At Dixon's urging at least six of the students who were in this circle later moved to San Francisco to join the DWP; this number was confirmed by several of those who joined.

11. Information from www.dnai.com/~hi_there/people's_park.html, accessed January 1, 2002, as well as Robert N. Bellah, "The New Consciousness and the Berkeley New Left," in Charles Y. Glock and Robert N. Bellah, eds., *The New Religious Consciousness* (Berkeley: University of California Press, 1976), 77–92; Robert S. Ellwood, *The Sixties Spiritual Awakening: American Religion Moving from Modern to Postmodern* (New Brunswick, N.J.: Rutgers University Press, 1994).

12. See Marlene Dixon, "The Sisterhood Ripoff: The Destruction of the Left in Professional Women's Caucuses," *Bulletin of Women in Canadian Sociology* 11.2 (1975); "Why Women's Liberation," *Ramparts,* December 1969; "Women's Liberation: Opening Chapter Two," *Canadian Dimension,* June 1975, 56–68.

13. There was one woman, Letitia, who was about two years older than Dixon. Letitia was the partner of Eleanor, who became Dixon's second-in-command. Letitia was expelled in late 1975.

14. Workers Party, *The Founding of the Workers Party* (San Francisco: Synthesis Publications, 1979), vi.

15. These are all in *Synthesis,* 1977, II, 1–2.

16. See, for example, Robin Baker et al., *Splitting & Wrecking at Health/Pac West: The League for Proletarian Socialism in Action* (San Francisco: Author, 1976); Pat Morgan, "A Comment to 'Jacque' and the League for Proletarian Socialism," *UMSS Newsletter,* December 1976.

17. This episode is described in a book by Dixon, *Things Which Are Done in Secret* (Montreal: Black Rose Books, 1976).

18. Chatterjee, "Interview with Marlene Dixon," 2.

19. Democratic Workers Party, *The History of the Democratic Workers Party* (San Francisco: OS Publications, 1984), C25; hereafter referred to as *DWP History.*

20. See, for example, *DWP History,* B28, C2.

21. Members of the Weather Underground and other armed groups had been accused of bombing a police headquarters, a bank, a utility station, and an

ROTC facility, among others, as well as being instrumental in Timothy Leary's escape from a California maximum-security prison. These were identified at the time as acts of domestic terrorism. See, for example, on terrorist activity, Hearings before the Subcommittee to Investigate the Administration of the Internal Security Act and Other Internal Security Laws, of the Committee of the Judiciary, U.S. Senate, 93d Cong., 2d sess. (Washington, D.C.: Government Printing Office, 1974); and, on the Weather Underground, Report of the Subcommittee to Investigate the Administration of the Internal Security Act and Other Internal Security Laws, of the Committee on the Judiciary, U.S. Senate, 94th Cong., 1st sess. (Washington, D.C.: Government Printing Office, 1975).

22. Frank S. Meyer, *The Moulding of Communists: The Training of the Communist Cadre* (New York: Harcourt, Brace, 1961).

23. Democratic Workers Party, *The Training of the Cadre* (n.p., n.d.).

24. *The Militant's Guide* is a collection of founding documents. See Democratic Workers Party, *The Militant's Guide* (San Francisco: Synthesis Publications, 1979). The book was distributed to each militant for training and education. A statement on the copyright page cautioned: "*The Militant's Guide* is to be read with care and studied only under the guidance of Party teachers." For years, it was an "internal document," kept hidden from public view. In the 1980s, however, as the DWP emerged into new forms of work and more public approaches, the guide was edited and sold along with other DWP publications. Interestingly, much of the editing consisted of replacing the numerous appearances of the word *Communist* with *socialist*.

25. Alan Bryman, *Charisma and Leadership in Organizations* (London: Sage, 1992).

26. Sandi Dolbee and Susan Gembrowski, "Closing Heaven's Gate," *San Diego Union-Tribune*, March 23, 1998, B1, B4-5.

27. Marlene Dixon, *The Future of Women* (San Francisco: Synthesis, 1983), 188.

28. Ibid.

29. Ibid., 189.

30. Democratic Workers Party, *The Training of the Cadre*, 59.

31. Meredith Maguire [pseud.], "Returning to Humanity," in Madeleine Landau Tobias and Janja Lalich, *Captive Hearts, Captive Minds: Freedom and Recovery from Cults and Abusive Relationships* (Alameda, Calif.: Hunter House 1994), 217.

32. Democratic Workers Party, *The Militant's Guide*, 273.

33. Ibid., 254, 55.

34. Ibid., 254.

35. David Roche, "Learning to Love," in Tobias and Lalich, *Captive Hearts, Captive Minds*, 238.

36. Maguire, "Returning to Humanity," 216.

37. Eight former DWP leaders, untitled manuscript, December 15, 1987, 9.

38. Ibid., 8.

39. Maguire, "Returning to Humanity," 220.

8. The Cadre Formation

1. Over time, eight of the twelve founders, minus Dixon, were expelled (technically, one withdrew early on under pressure). Three of the four who were not expelled were relegated to low-level, nonleadership positions; they were seen as hardworking, loyal followers. Of those who were expelled, four were readmitted after some time had elapsed and after they furnished proof of their willingness to "submit" to the organization; one person stayed only a short time after being readmitted.

2. From Bertolt Brecht, "To Posterity," in H. R. Hays, trans., *Selected Poems of Bertolt Brecht* (New York: Grove Press, 1959), 177.

3. This is from a document entitled "Re: Middle Level Leadership," March 17, 1986, 1–2. It was written by three members of the leadership, including me, during debates among the members that followed the DWP's dissolution. We wrote it for the reason stated on page 1 of the document: "We believe that the militants in middle level leadership who enforced the norms and discipline of the Party and managed information internally as well as externally have a particular responsibility for the Party going on as long as it did in the way that it did. Each of us as signers of this document served at various times for varying lengths of time as middle level leadership, sat on leading bodies (formal and informal), and were at times on the Central Committee. Some of our experiences were similar; some were different — we hope that by sharing and opening up these experiences to ex-DWP members we will help bring clarity to what went on and what led to the eventual demise of the Party."

4. For a detailed description of how this took place and the power struggles that ensued, see Janja Lalich, "The Cadre Ideal: Origins and Development of a Political Cult," *Cultic Studies Journal* 9.1 (1992): 1–77.

5. Democratic Workers Party, *The Militant's Guide* (San Francisco: Synthesis Publications, 1979), 57.

6. Ibid.

7. Ibid., 77–88.

8. Democratic Workers Party, *The History of the Democratic Workers Party* (San Francisco: OS Publications, 1984), A4 (hereafter cited as *DWP History*); and personal observation.

9. Workers Party, *The Founding of the Workers Party* (San Francisco: Synthesis Publications, 1979).

10. Marlene Dixon, "On the Development of Leninist Democracy," in *DWP History*, C45.

11. Marlene Dixon, "The Nature of Leninist Democracy and Leadership," in *DWP History*, C48.

12. Ibid., C48, C50.

13. Marlene Dixon, "On Leadership," in *DWP History*, C53.

14. In the original version of this document, Dixon's Party name, Comrade Kim, was used. However, her name was changed to Comrade Marlene when

this document was reissued in a written history meant for distribution especially to eastern European countries, which at that time were still part of the Soviet bloc. See Dixon, "On Leadership," C54.

15. Ibid.

16. Ibid., C55.

17. *DWP History,* B32.

18. Ibid., B50.

19. Ibid., A1.

20. Dixon always used the British spelling *remoulding,* lifted from the title of Meyer's book, *The Moulding of Communists.* I would argue also that it was an example of her pretensions and attitude of self-importance.

21. Marlene Dixon, "On the Study of Official Party Positions, Part I," in *DWP History,* C58.

22. Marlene Dixon, "The Necessity for a Fighting Party," *Proletarian Socialism: Journal of the Workers Party for Proletarian Socialism* 1 (1977): 3–7.

23. Ibid., 3.

24. Ibid., 6.

25. *DWP History,* C16.

26. Dixon, "The Necessity for a Fighting Party," 6.

27. Ibid., 7.

28. Janja Lalich, "How I See It Today," (unpublished ms., Pelham, N.Y., 1987), 3–4.

29. Theodore H. E. Chen, *Thought Reform of the Chinese Intellectuals* (Hong Kong: Hong Kong University Press, 1960); Robert Jay Lifton, *Thought Reform and the Psychology of Totalism* (New York: Norton, 1961).

30. Marlene Dixon, "Principles of Dialectical Leadership," in *DWP History,* C41.

31. Democratic Workers Party, *The Training of the Cadre* (n.p., n.d.).

32. Ibid.

33. Ibid., iii.

34. From my Party School teacher's notes.

35. Dixon, "On the Development of Leninist Democracy," C24.

36. From my Party School teacher's notes.

37. Peter Siegel, Nancy Strohl, Laura Ingram, David Roche, and Jean Taylor, "Leninism as Cult: The Democratic Workers Party," *Socialist Review* 17.6 (1987): 65.

38. Democratic Workers Party, *The Militant's Guide,* 329.

39. Eight former DWP leaders, untitled manuscript, December 15, 1987, 14.

40. "Plain Speaking," March 12, 1986, 5.

41. Marlene Dixon, "The Cadre Ideal," in *DWP History,* C23–C24.

42. See "Constitution of the Democratic Workers Party," adopted August 1981.

43. This principle was taught repeatedly in Party School and other meetings. Taken here from my notes as a Party School teacher.

44. Eagles also served as Dixon's personal bodyguards, monitors during demonstrations, disrupters, goons, and rabble-rousers, as needed. Dixon rarely

went anywhere (including to DWP facilities) without her large Rottweiler, who was a trained guard dog, plus at least one attendant or Eagle bodyguard.

45. The new line was that the DWP had been wrong in saying that militants could be gay. Now the Party taught that "gay" implied petit bourgeois self-indulgence and ultimately support of the bourgeois system. The DWP support-ed the general right to sexual preference for all people, but militants were not to be openly homosexual during their political work (which meant on the job or at any DWP activity). Also, they were forbidden to go to gay establishments. For the DWP's public presentation of this episode, see "A Living Example," in Marlene Dixon, *The Future of Women* (San Francisco: Synthesis Publications, 1983), 181-217.

46. Ibid.

47. Dixon, "The Necessity for a Fighting Party," 6.

48. Democratic Workers Party, *The Training of the Cadre*, 51.

49. Ibid., 45.

50. This quote, along with much of the material in this section, is drawn from my Party School teacher's notes from sessions in the late 1970s and early 1980s.

51. Madeleine Landau Tobias and Janja Lalich, *Captive Hearts, Captive Minds: Freedom and Recovery from Cults and Abusive Relationships* (Alameda, Calif.: Hunter House, 1994).

52. "Re: Middle Level Leadership," 4.

9. Decline and Fall

1. Democratic Workers Party, *The Militant's Guide* (San Francisco: Synthesis Publications, 1979), 28, 29.

2. Ibid., 30.

3. Ibid., 30-31.

4. For example, pt. 3, "Against Social Democracy: In Defense of the Work-ing Class," 89-173; and pt. 4, "On Socialism: The Contradictions of Socialist Construction," 177-225, in *The Militant's Guide*.

5. Marlene Dixon, "Directive on the Defense of the Party and the Party Line," in *The Militant's Guide*, 95.

6. Ibid., 95-100.

7. From my Party School teacher's notes.

8. The article by Peter Siegel, Nancy Strohl, Laura Ingram, David Roche, and Jean Taylor, "Leninism as Cult: The Democratic Workers Party," *Socialist Review* 17.6 (1987): 60-85, provides an excellent summary of the DWP's politi-cal practices during those years and the effects on morale of the sudden shifts in direction.

9. For example, articles by Immanuel Wallerstein, Andre Gunder Frank, James Petras, Bernard Magubane, Samir Amin, Frank Bonilla, Pedro Vuskovic, Nzongola-Ntalaja, and Lourdes Arguelles. It is unlikely that these scholars knew

of the connection to the DWP or had knowledge of how it functioned. Many simply regarded it as another academic, albeit very progressive, journal.

10. Examples are *Karl Marx Remembered* and *Black Socialist Preacher* by the historian Philip Foner; chapters by Abdul Alkalimat (Gerald McWorter), Doug Gills, and James Jennings, and a foreword by Manning Marable in *The New Black Vote: Politics and Power in Four American Cities;* a preface by George Wald in *Guatemala: Tyranny on Trial* and a foreword by Harvey Cox in *On Trial: Reagan's War against Nicaragua,* both books based on testimony of the international Permanent Peoples' Tribunal sessions, focused respectively on Guatemala (held in 1983) and on Nicaragua's charges against the United States (held in 1984); and *The Contras: Interviews with Anti-Sandinistas* by Dieter Eich and Carlos Rincón (Synthesis bought the English-language rights to this book at the Frankfurt Book Fair, translated it, and published it for U.S. sale). Most likely, none of these scholars was aware that the DWP was behind these publications.

11. Siegel et al., "Leninism as Cult."

12. Ibid., 73.

13. John Trinkl, "USOCA: An Asset or a Liability?" *Guardian,* May 16, 1984, 2, 19.

14. Ibid.

15. Max Elbaum, "On the DWP's Demise: What Leninism Is and Is Not," *Frontline,* August 3, 1987, 2, 15.

16. See, for example, "You Can't Force Jarvis Down Our Throats!" by Dixon in the June–July 1978 issue of the *Rebel Worker* newspaper.

17. This is in reference to the split between the Mensheviks and Bolsheviks before the Russian Revolution. The Mensheviks were considered part-time revolutionaries and therefore not serious. See also chap. 6, note 7, for a fuller discussion of this event.

18. Marlene Dixon, "East-West, North-South: The Global Environment and the Future of Socialism" (paper presented at the Socialism in the World Roundtable, Cavtat, Yugoslavia, 1985); "Foreword: World-Systems Theory and Marxism," *Contemporary Marxism* 9 (1984).

19. Immanuel Wallerstein, *The Essential Wallerstein* (New York: New Press, 2000).

20. See, for example, Democratic Workers Party, "Global Marxism Versus Academic World-Systems Theory? A Select Annotated Bibliography" (1984), 1–13.

21. Ibid., 5.

22. Suman Chatterjee, "Interview with Marlene Dixon: On the U.S. Left Today," unpublished document, 1985, 4, 7.

23. This summary is based on DWP documents and communiqués distributed during the last two years of the Party, most of them written by Dixon and some by Party militants; my recollection of the Party discussions about the line change; subsequent interviews and discussions with former members; and Siegel et al., "Leninism as Cult."

24. Marlene Dixon, "Facing Reality," January 15, 1984, 1–2.

25. Siegel et al., "Leninism as Cult," 76.

26. Doris, resignation letter, May 17, 1985, 2. Only a few top leaders read Doris's resignation letter. Such communications, especially if they contained criticisms of the Party, were kept secret and withheld from the members. Doris distributed her letter for everyone to see during the discussions that occurred after the Party was disbanded.

27. "Re: Middle Level Leadership," March 13, 1986, 7.

28. Quoted in Democratic Workers Party, *The Training of the Cadre*, 32.

29. Robert Jay Lifton, *Destroying the World to Save It: Aum Shinrikyo, Apocalyptic Violence, and the New Global Terrorism* (New York: Metropolitan Books, 1999); *The Future of Immortality and Other Essays for a Nuclear Age* (New York: Basic Books, 1987); *The Nazi Doctors* (New York: Basic Books, 1986).

30. Gareth Morgan, *Images of Organization* (Thousand Oaks, Calif.: Sage, 1997), 102.

31. Edgar H. Schein, *Organizational Culture and Leadership*, 2d ed. (San Francisco: Jossey-Bass, 1997), 327-29.

10. The True Believer

1. Anthony Giddens, *The Constitution of Society: Outline of the Theory of Structuration* (Berkeley: University of California Press, 1984), 25.

2. Ibid.

3. Ibid., 32.

4. Georg Simmel wrote: "Similarity, as fact or as tendency, is no less important than difference. In most varied forms, both are the great principles of all external and internal development." Georg Simmel, *The Sociology of Georg Simmel* (New York: Free Press, 1950), 30.

5. Max Weber, *The Sociology of Religion,* trans. E. Fischoff (Boston: Beacon Press, [1922] 1964); Benjamin D. Zablocki, *Alienation and Charisma: A Study of Contemporary American Communes* (New York: Free Press, 1980).

6. Max Weber, "The Sociology of Charismatic Authority," in H. H. Gerth and C. Wright Mills, eds., *From Max Weber: Essays in Sociology* (New York: Oxford University Press, 1946), 196-244.

7. Robert Jay Lifton, "Cult Formation," *Harvard Mental Health Letter* 7.8 (1991), 5-6; *Thought Reform and the Psychology of Totalism* (New York: Norton, 1961); Edgar H. Schein, *Coercive Persuasion* (New York: Norton, 1961).

8. Herbert C. Kelman and V. Lee Hamilton, *Crimes of Obedience: Toward a Social Psychology of Authority and Responsibility* (New Haven, Conn.: Yale University Press, 1989); Stanley Milgram, *Obedience to Authority: An Experimental View* (New York: Harper & Row, 1974).

9. Peter L. Berger and Thomas Luckmann, *The Social Construction of Reality* (New York: Anchor Books, 1967); Lynne G. Zucker, "The Role of Institutionalization in Cultural Persistence," in Walter W. Powell and Paul J. DiMaggio, eds., *The New Institutionalism in Organizational Analysis* (Chicago: University of Chicago Press, 1991), 83-107.

10. James S. Coleman, *Foundations of Social Theory* (Cambridge, Mass.: Belknap Press, 1990), 398.

11. Ibid., 517–19.

12. This relates to Zablocki's work on the "exit costs" incurred by cult members who become deployable agents. Zablocki has argued that it is extremely difficult to leave groups in which there is a demand for a personal transformation that results in a member's preference structure being modified to conform with the group's goals. See Benjamin D. Zablocki, "Exit Cost Analysis: A New Approach to the Scientific Study of Brainwashing," *Nova Religio* 1.2 (1998): 216–49.

13. Giddens, *The Constitution of Society.*

14. Ibid.

15. Theodore H. E. Chen, *Thought Reform of the Chinese Intellectuals* (Hong Kong: Hong Kong University Press, 1960); Robert Chin and Ai-li S. Chin, *Psychological Research in Communist China: 1949–1966* (Cambridge, Mass.: MIT Press, 1969); William Hinton, *Fanshen: A Documentary of Revolution in a Chinese Village* (New York: Vintage Books, 1966); John Wilson Lewis, *Leadership in Communist China* (Ithaca, N.Y.: Cornell University Press, 1963); Robert Jay Lifton, "Methods of Forceful Indoctrination: Psychiatric Aspects of Chinese Communist Thought Reform," in Maurice Stein, Arthur J. Vidich, and David Manning White, eds., *Identity and Anxiety: Survival of the Person in Mass Society* (Glencoe, Ill.: Free Press, 1960), 480–92; *Revolutionary Immortality;* and *Thought Reform and the Psychology of Totalism;* Meyer, *The Moulding of Communists;* Anchee Min, *Red Azalea* (New York: Pantheon Books, 1994); Allyn Rickett and Adele Rickett, *Prisoners of Liberation: Four Years in a Chinese Communist Prison* (New York: Anchor Books, [1957] 1973); Schein, *Coercive Persuasion.*

16. Lifton, *Thought Reform and the Psychology of Totalism.*

17. Robert Jay Lifton, "The Appeal of the Death Trip," *New York Times Magazine,* January 7, 1979, 26–27, 29–31.

18. The conversion process from recruit to deployable agent in relation to cults or new religious movements has been described in various ways. One useful model is that of Lofland and Stark, based on their field research in the early 1960s of the first American branch of the Reverend Sun Myung Moon's Unification Church, located in Oakland, California. The most significant aspects of their model that link with my descriptions here relate to the intensive interactive process and the emotional relationship between recruit and recruiter and eventually between new member and group. Lofland and Stark discuss tension building, turning points, absence of "extra-cult attachments," and affective bonds and positive feelings toward the group. See John Lofland and Rodney Stark, "Becoming a World-Saver: A Theory of Conversion to a Deviant Perspective," *American Sociological Review* 30 (1965): 862–75.

19. Philip G. Zimbardo and Michael R. Leippe, *The Psychology of Attitude Change and Social Influence* (New York: McGraw-Hill, 1991).

20. A question not addressed here is the relationship between leaving and professional ability. For example, are "leavers" more likely to have skills and abil-

ities that will afford them greater opportunities for survival once outside the group? Or the reverse: are certain ones "stuck" because they have a more difficult time trying to imagine survival on the outside? This raises important issues for future study. I thank my colleague Cynthia Siemsen for bringing this to my attention.

21. Erich Fromm, *Escape from Freedom* (New York: Avon Books, [1941] 1965).

22. Ibid., 38.

23. This number does not include Applewhite but does include the two followers, Rkkody and Jstody, who committed suicide in the months after the group's collective suicide in March 1997 in which thirty-eight followers died. There may have been other suicides of former followers who remained believers, although I am not aware of any.

24. Robert C. Cialdini, *Influence: The New Psychology of Modern Persuasion* (New York: Quill, 1984); Kelman and Hamilton, *Crimes of Obedience;* Zimbardo and Leippe, *The Psychology of Attitude Change and Social Influence.*

25. Kelman and Hamilton, *Crimes of Obedience,* 93.

26. Cialdini, *Influence.*

27. It is interesting to ponder the gender shifts that come into play here. Dixon, a woman, was a much harsher and more insensitive leader than Applewhite, a man. How much did Applewhite's homosexuality influence his style of leadership? Or was he more influenced by being "second" to Nettles? Again, I thank Cynthia Siemsen for pointing out these intriguing issues.

28. This is not unlike Jim Jones's "White Night" suicide drills in which his followers were given a drink and told they would die within minutes. Such sessions started in 1975 and prepared Jones's followers for the final White Night three years later, when his 912 followers (including 276 children) were served a potion of Fla-Vor-Aid poisoned with potassium cyanide. See Deborah Layton, *Seductive Poison: A Jonestown Survivor's Story of Life and Death in the Peoples Temple* (New York: Anchor Books, 1998).

29. Max Weber's work in this area is relevant here. He discussed this-world and otherworldly orientations of various cultures and religions. See Weber, "Religious Rejections of the World and Their Directions," in Gerth and Mills, eds., *From Max Weber,* 323–59. Roy Wallis presented a typology of three distinct types of new religious movements: world-accommodating, world-affirming, and world-rejecting. According to his typology, both the DWP and Heaven's Gate would fall into the third category, which comprises movements seeking to establish a new world order. See Roy Wallis, *The Elementary Forms of the New Religious Life* (London: Routledge & Kegan Paul, 1983).

11. Bounded Choice

1. Solomon Asch, "Effects of Group Pressure upon the Modification and Distortion of Judgment," in M. H. Guetzkow, ed., *Groups, Leadership, and Men*

(Pittsburgh: Carnegie, 1951), 177–90; "Studies of Independence and Conformity: A Minority of One against a Unanimous Majority," *Psychological Monographs* 70.9 (1951).

2. Sharon S. Brehm and Saul M. Kassin, *Social Psychology,* 3d ed. (Boston: Houghton Mifflin, 1996), 335.

3. Ibid.

4. M. Sherif, *The Psychology of Social Norms* (New York: Harper, 1936).

5. Brehm and Kassin, *Social Psychology,* 336.

6. Leon Festinger, *A Theory of Cognitive Dissonance* (New York: Row, Peterson, 1957); Leon Festinger, Henry W. Riecken, and Stanley Schachter, *When Prophecy Fails: A Social and Psychological Study of a Modern Group That Predicted the Destruction of the World* (New York: Harper & Row, 1956).

7. Irving Janis, "Groupthink," in Walter E. Natemeyer and Jay S. Gilberg, eds., *Classics of Organizational Behavior* (Danville, Ill.: Interstate Printers & Publishers, 1989), 179–87.

8. Anthony Giddens, *The Constitution of Society: Outline of the Theory of Structuration* (Berkeley: University of California Press, 1984).

9. Ibid.

10. Erik H. Erikson, *Identity and the Life Cycle* (New York: Norton, [1959] 1980); and *Identity: Youth and Crisis* (New York: Norton, 1968); Erving Goffman, *Asylums* (Garden City, N.Y.: Anchor Books, 1961); and *The Presentation of Self in Everyday Life* (Garden City, N.Y.: Doubleday Anchor, 1959).

11. Anthony Giddens, *Central Problems in Social Theory: Action, Structure and Contradiction in Social Analysis* (Berkeley: University of California Press, 1979), 126.

12. James S. Coleman, *Foundations of Social Theory* (Cambridge, Mass.: Belknap Press, 1990), 295.

13. Ibid.

14. Goffman, *Asylums.*

15. Lifton described personal closure in this way: "Rather than stimulating greater receptivity and 'openness to the world,' they encourage a step backward into some form of 'embeddedness' — a retreat into doctrinal and organizational exclusiveness, and into all-or-nothing emotional patterns more characteristic (at least at this stage of human history) of the child than of the individuated adult." Lifton, *Thought Reform and the Psychology of Totalism,* 436.

16. Giddens, *The Constitution of Society,* 155.

17. Goffman, *Asylums.*

18. Giddens, *The Constitution of Society,* 176.

19. This is akin not only to the social environments but also to the thought-reform processes described by Lifton in his studies of and commentaries on Communist China, Jonestown, Aum Shinrikyō, the Manson Family, and others. See Lifton, *Destroying the World to Save It* and *Thought Reform and the Psychology of Totalism.* It is consistent also with Zablocki's work on charismatic communities, cultic movements, and hypercompliance in charismatic groups. See Zablocki, *Alienation and Charisma;* "Exit Cost Analysis"; "Hyper Compliance

in Charismatic Groups," in David D. Franks and Thomas S. Smith, eds., *Mind, Brain and Society: Toward a Neurosociology of Emotion, Social Perspectives on Emotion* (Stamford, Conn.: JAI Press, 1999), 287–310; *The Joyful Community* (Baltimore, Md.: Penguin Books, 1971).

20. Lifton, *Thought Reform and the Psychology of Totalism,* 421.

21. Ibid.

22. Kelman and Hamilton, *Crimes of Obedience;* Zablocki, "Exit Cost Analysis."

23. Herbert A. Simon, *Models of Thought,* vol. 1 (New Haven, Conn.: Yale University Press, 1979).

24. Ibid., 3.

25. Ibid.

26. Neil Fligstein, "The Structural Transformation of American Industry," in Walter W. Powell and Paul J. DiMaggio, eds., *The New Institutionalism in Organizational Analysis* (Chicago: University of Chicago Press, 1991), 315.

27. Giddens, *The Constitution of Society.*

28. Herbert A. Simon, *Administrative Behavior,* 3d ed. (New York: Macmillan, 1976), 79.

Bibliography

Alexander, Kay. "Roots of the New Age." In James R. Lewis and J. Gordon Melton, eds., *Perspectives on the New Age*. Albany: State University of New York Press, 1992, 30–47.

Appelbaum, Richard P. *Karl Marx*. Newbury Park, Calif.: Sage, 1988.

Asch, Solomon. "Effects of Group Pressure upon the Modification and Distortion of Judgment." In M. H. Guetzkow, ed., *Groups, Leadership, and Men*. Pittsburgh: Carnegie, 1951, 177–90.

——. "Studies of Independence and Conformity: A Minority of One against a Unanimous Majority." *Psychological Monographs* 70.9 (1951).

Associated Press. "Radical Group Claims It Set SUVs on Fire." *San Francisco Chronicle*, January 5, 2003, A7.

Baker, Robin, Elinor Blake, Dan Feshbach, and Ellen Shaffer. *Splitting & Wrecking at Health/Pac West: The League for Proletarian Socialism in Action*. San Francisco: Author, 1976.

Balch, Robert W. "Bo and Peep: A Case Study of the Origins of Messianic Leadership." In Roy Wallis, ed., *Millennialism and Charisma*. Belfast: Queen's University, 1982, 13–72.

——. "The Evolution of a New Age Cult: From Total Overcomers Anonymous to Death at Heaven's Gate." In William W. Zellner and Marc Petrowsky, eds., *Sects, Cults, and Spiritual Communities: A Sociological Analysis*. Westport, Conn.: Praeger, 1998, 1–25.

——. "Waiting for the Ships: Disillusionment and the Revitalization of Faith in Bo and Peep's UFO Cult." In James R. Lewis, ed., *The Gods Have Landed*. Albany: State University of New York Press, 1995, 137–66.

Balch, Robert W., and David Taylor. "Heaven's Gate: Implications for the Study of Commitment to New Religions." Unpublished manuscript, 1998.

——. "Making Sense of the Heaven's Gate Suicides." In David G. Bromley and J. Gordon Melton, eds., *Cults, Religion and Violence.* New York: Cambridge University Press, 2002, 209–28.

——. "Salvation in a UFO." *Psychology Today,* October 1976, 58, 60–62, 66, 106.

——. "Seekers and Saucers: The Role of the Cultic Milieu in Joining a UFO Cult." *American Behavioral Scientist* 20.6 (1977): 839–60.

Barnes, Rosemary. "'He Had So Much Potential': Sister Calls Applewhite Born Leader" [on-line] *Caller-Times Interactive* (Corpus Christi, Tex.), March 29, 1997. Available at www.caller.com/newsarch/news3673.html.

Bateson, Gregory. *Mind and Nature: A Necessary Unity.* New York: Bantam Books, 1980.

——. *Steps to an Ecology of Mind.* New York: Ballantine Books, 1978.

Bellah, Robert N. "The New Consciousness and the Berkeley New Left." In Charles Y. Glock and Robert N. Bellah, eds., *The New Religious Consciousness.* Berkeley: University of California Press, 1976, 77–92.

——. "New Religious Consciousness and the Crisis in Modernity." In Charles Y. Glock and Robert N. Bellah, eds., *The New Religious Consciousness.* Berkeley: University of California Press, 1976, 333–52.

Berger, Peter L., and Thomas Luckmann. *The Social Construction of Reality.* New York: Anchor Books, 1967.

Berger, Todd. "Lost in Space." *San Francisco Focus,* May 1997, 34, 36–39, 143.

Braaten, Jane. *Habermas's Critical Theory of Society.* Albany: State University of New York Press, 1991.

Brandon, Ruth. *The Spiritualists: The Passion for the Occult in the Nineteenth and Twentieth Centuries.* Buffalo, N.Y.: Prometheus Books, 1984.

Braude, Ann. *Radical Spirits: Spiritualism and Women's Rights in Nineteenth-Century America.* Boston: Beacon Press, 1989.

Brehm, Sharon S., and Saul M. Kassin. *Social Psychology.* 3d ed. Boston: Houghton Mifflin, 1996.

Breines, Wini. *Community and Organization in the New Left, 1962–1968: The Great Refusal.* New Brunswick, N.J.: Rutgers University Press, 1989.

Breslau, Karen, and Colin Soloway. "'He's a Really Good Boy.'" *Newsweek*.MSNBC.com, December 3, 2001.

Bromley, David G., ed. *The Politics of Apostasy: The Role of Apostates in the Transformation of Religious Movements.* Westport, Conn.: Praeger, 1998.

Brooke, James. "Former Cultists Tell of Believers Now Adrift." *New York Times,* April 2, 1997, A1, A10.

Brown, Elaine. *A Taste of Power: A Black Woman's Story.* New York: Pantheon Books, 1992.

Brown, Michael F. *The Channeling Zone: American Spirituality in an Anxious Age.* Cambridge, Mass.: Harvard University Press, 1997.

Bryman, Alan. *Charisma and Leadership in Organizations.* London: Sage, 1992.

Campbell, Eileen, and J. H. Brennan. *Body Mind & Spirit: A Dictionary of New Age Ideas, People, Places, and Terms.* Rutland, Vt.: Tuttle, 1994.

Canedy, Dana. "Sect Claims First Cloned Baby." *New York Times,* December 28, 2002, A16.

Carey, Benedict. "Method without Madness?" *Los Angeles Times,* July 30, 2002.

Caute, David. *The Year of the Barricades: A Journey through 1968.* New York: Perennial, 1988.

Chandler, Russell. *Understanding the New Age.* Grand Rapids, Mich.: Zondervan, 1993.

Chatterjee, Suman. "Interview with Marlene Dixon on the U.S. Left Today." Unpublished document, 1985.

Chen, Theodore H. E. *Thought Reform of the Chinese Intellectuals.* Hong Kong: Hong Kong University Press, 1960.

Chin, Robert, and Ai-li S. Chin. *Psychological Research in Communist China: 1949–1966.* Cambridge, Mass.: MIT Press, 1969.

Cialdini, Robert B. *Influence: The New Psychology of Modern Persuasion.* New York: Quill, 1984.

Clark, Cheryl. "Cultist Applewhite Had a Severe Heart Disease" [on-line]. *San Diego Union Tribune,* April 12 1997. Available from www.uniontrib.com/reports/cult_suicide/news_1n12reports.html.

Coleman, James S. *Foundations of Social Theory.* Cambridge, Mass.: Belknap Press, 1990.

Coughlan, Rachel, ed. *Heaven's Gate: Inside Story.* British Broadcasting Company, London, 1997.

Cushman, Philip. "Iron Fists/Velvet Gloves: A Study of a Mass Marathon Psychology Training." *Psychotherapy* 26.1 (spring 1989): 23–39.

Dalton, Rex. "Tragedy Painful, Familiar to Man Who Lost Mom to Applewhite Cult." *San Diego Union-Tribune,* March 29, 1997, A11.

Dass, Baba Ram. *Be Here Now.* San Cristobal, New Mex.: Lama Foundation, 1971.

Democratic Workers Party. "Global Marxism Versus Academic World-Systems Theory? A Select Annotated Bibliography." N.p., 1984.

———. *The History of the Democratic Workers Party.* San Francisco: OS Publications, 1984.

———. *The Militant's Guide.* San Francisco: Synthesis Publications, 1979.

———. *The Training of the Cadre.* N.p., n.d.

Dixon, Marlene. "The Cadre Ideal." In Democratic Workers Party, *History of the Democratic Workers Party.* San Francisco: OS Publications, [1976] 1984, C23–C24.

———. "Directive on the Defense of the Party and the Party Line." In Democratic Workers Party, *The Militant's Guide.* San Francisco: Synthesis Publications, 1979, 94–100.

———. "East-West, North-South: The Global Environment and the Future of Socialism." Paper presented at the Socialism in the World Roundtable, Cavtat, Yugoslavia, 1985.

———. "Foreword: World-Systems Theory and Marxism." *Contemporary Marxism* 9 (1984).

———. *The Future of Women.* San Francisco: Synthesis Publications, 1983.

———. "The Nature of Leninist Democracy and Leadership." In Democratic Workers Party, *The History of the Democratic Workers Party*. San Francisco: OS Publications, [1977] 1984, C48–C49.

———. "The Necessity for a Fighting Party." *Proletarian Socialism: Journal of the Workers Party for Proletarian Socialism* 1 ([1975] 1977): 3–7.

———. "On Leadership." In Democratic Workers Party, *The History of the Democratic Workers Party*. San Francisco: OS Publications, [1977] 1984, C53–C57.

———. "On the Development of Leninist Democracy." In Democratic Workers Party, *The History of the Democratic Workers Party*. San Francisco: OS Publications, [1977] 1984, C45–C46.

———. "On the Study of Official Party Positions, Part I." In Democratic Workers Party, *History of the Democratic Workers Party*. San Francisco: OS Publications, [1977] 1984, C58–C60.

———. "Principles of Dialectical Leadership." In Democratic Workers Party, *History of the Democratic Workers Party*. San Francisco: OS Publications, [1974] 1984, C26–C43.

———. "The Sisterhood Ripoff: The Destruction of the Left in Professional Women's Caucuses." *Bulletin of Women in Canadian Sociology* 11.2 (1975).

———. *Things Which Are Done in Secret*. Montreal: Black Rose Books, 1976.

———. "Why Women's Liberation." *Ramparts,* December 1969.

———. "Women's Liberation: Opening Chapter Two." *Canadian Dimension,* June 1975, 56–68.

Do. "Aids in Approaching This Material." In Representatives from the Kingdom of Heaven, eds., *How and When "Heaven's Gate" (The Door to the Physical Kingdom Level above Human) May Be Entered*. Santa Fe, New Mex.: Heaven's Representatives, 1996, iii–iv.

———. "'88 Update—The UFO Two and Their Crew: A Brief Synopsis." In Representatives from the Kingdom of Heaven, eds., *How and When "Heaven's Gate" (The Door to the Physical Kingdom Level above Human) May Be Entered*. Santa Fe, New Mex.: Heaven's Representatives, 1996, 3-1-19.

———. "Undercover 'Jesus' Surfaces before Departure." In Representatives from the Kingdom of Heaven, eds., *How and When "Heaven's Gate" (The Door to the Physical Kingdom Level above Human) May Be Entered*. Santa Fe, New Mex.: Heaven's Representatives, 1996, 1-3-4.

Dolbee, Sandi, and Susan Gembrowski. "Closing Heaven's Gate." *San Diego Union-Tribune,* March 23, 1998, B1, B4–5.

Dole, Arthur A., and Michael D. Langone. "Strongly Held Views about the New Age: Critics Versus Experts." *Cultic Studies Journal* 11.1 (1994): 1–28.

Editorial. "Raelians Owe Us Proof or Explanation." *The Gazette* (Montreal), January 7, 2003.

Elbaum, Max. "Maoism in the United States." In Mari Jo Buhle, Paul Buhle, and Dan Georgakas, eds., *Encyclopedia of the American Left*. New York: Oxford University Press, 1998, 471–75.

———. "On the DWP's Demise: What Leninism Is and Is Not." *Frontline,* August 3, 1987, 2, 15.

——. *Revolution in the Air: Sixties Radicals Turn to Lenin, Mao and Che.* London: Verso, 2002.

——. "Where's the Party?" Unpublished manuscript. Oakland, Calif., 1997.

Ellwood, Robert S. *The Sixties Spiritual Awakening: American Religion Moving from Modern to Postmodern.* New Brunswick, N.J.: Rutgers University Press, 1994.

Erikson, Erik H. *Identity: Youth and Crisis.* New York: Norton, 1968.

——. *Identity and the Life Cycle.* New York: Norton, [1959] 1980.

Fagan, Kevin, and Pamela J. Podger. "American's Road to Taliban Fighter." *San Francisco Chronicle,* December 5, 2001, A1, A14.

Faith, Karlene. *The Long Prison Journey of Leslie Van Houten: Life Beyond the Cult.* Boston: Northeastern University Press, 2001.

Farrow, Mia. *What Falls Away: A Memoir.* New York: Bantam Books, 1998.

Ferguson, Marilyn. *The Aquarian Conspiracy.* Los Angeles: Tarcher, 1987.

Festinger, Leon. *A Theory of Cognitive Dissonance.* New York: Row, Peterson, 1957.

Festinger, Leon, Henry W. Riecken, and Stanley Schachter. *When Prophecy Fails: A Social and Psychological Study of a Modern Group That Predicted the Destruction of the World.* New York: Harper & Row, 1956.

Fleck, Ludwik. *Genesis and Development of a Scientific Fact.* Chicago: University of Chicago Press, 1977.

Fligstein, Neil. "The Structural Transformation of American Industry." In Walter W. Powell and Paul J. DiMaggio, eds., *The New Institutionalism in Organizational Analysis.* Chicago: University of Chicago Press, 1991, 311–36.

"Flying Saucery in the Wilderness." *Time,* August 27, 1979, 58.

Friscolanti, Michael. "Aliens, Free Love at Core of Sect." *National Post,* December 28, 2002.

Fromm, Erich. *Escape from Freedom.* New York: Avon Books, [1941] 1965.

Gaines, James R. "Cults: Bo-Peep Flock." *Newsweek,* October 20, 1975, 32.

George, Leonard. *Alternative Realities: The Paranormal, the Mystic and the Transcendent in Human Experience.* New York: Facts on File, 1995.

Gerecht, Reuel Marc. "The Gospel According to Osama Bin Laden." *Atlantic Monthly,* January 2002, 46–48.

Giddens, Anthony. *Central Problems in Social Theory: Action, Structure and Contradiction in Social Analysis.* Berkeley: University of California Press, 1979.

——. *The Constitution of Society: Outline of the Theory of Structuration.* Berkeley: University of California Press, 1984.

Gitlin, Todd. *The Sixties: Years of Hope, Days of Rage.* New York: Bantam Books, 1987.

Glass, Leonard L., Michael A. Kirsch, and Frederick A. Parris. "Psychiatric Disturbances Associated with Erhard Seminars Training, I: A Report of Cases." *American Journal of Psychiatry* 134 (1977): 245–47.

Glock, Charles Y., and Robert N. Bellah. "Introduction to Part I: New Religious Movements in the Asian Tradition." In Charles Y. Glock and Robert N. Bellah, eds., *The New Religious Consciousness.* Berkeley: University of California Press, 1976, 1–4.

Goffman, Erving. *Asylums*. Garden City, N.Y.: Anchor Books, 1961.

——. *The Presentation of Self in Everyday Life*. Garden City, N.Y.: Doubleday Anchor, 1959.

Goldman, Marion S. *Passionate Journeys: Why Successful Women Joined a Cult*. Ann Arbor: University of Michigan Press, 1999.

Goldsmith, Barbara. *Other Powers: The Age of Suffrage, Spiritualism, and the Scandalous Victoria Woodhall*. New York: Knopf, 1998.

Grant, Mary Lee. "College Roommate Remembers Herff as Social Butterfly" [on-line]. *Caller-Times Interactive* (Corpus Christi, Tex.), March 30, 1997. Available at www.caller.com/newsarch/news3679.html.

Gunaratna, Rohan. *Inside Al Qaeda*. New York: Columbia University Press, 2002.

Haaken, Janice, and Richard Adams. "Pathology as 'Personal Growth': A Participant Observation Study of Lifespring Training." *Psychiatry* 46 (1983): 270–80.

Hall, Carl T. "Clone Experts Fear the Worst for 'Eve.'" *San Francisco Chronicle*, December 29, 2002, A1, A6.

Hanegraaff, W. J. *New Age Religion and Western Culture: Esotericism in the Mirror of Secular Thought*. Albany: State University of New York Press, 1998.

Hays, H. R., trans. *Selected Poems of Bertolt Brecht*. New York: Grove Press, 1959.

Heelas, Paul. *The New Age Movement*. Cambridge, Mass.: Blackwell, 1996.

Hettena, Seth. "Rancho Santa Fe – The Good Life." *San Francisco Chronicle*, June 5, 2002, 2.

Hexham, Irving, and Karla Poewe. "UFO Religion: Making Sense of the Heaven's Gate Suicides." *Christian Century*, May 7, 1997, 439–40.

Hilliard, David, and Lewis Cole. *This Side of Glory: The Autobiography of David Hilliard and the Story of the Black Panther Party*. Boston: Little, Brown, 1993.

Hinton, William. *Fanshen: A Documentary of Revolution in a Chinese Village*. New York: Vintage Books, 1966.

Hoffer, Eric. *The True Believer: Thoughts on the Nature of Mass Movements*. New York: Perennial, 1951.

Howard, Dick. *Defining the Political*. Minneapolis: University of Minnesota Press, 1989.

Huxley, Aldous. *The Doors of Perception and Heaven and Hell*. Harmondsworth: Penguin, 1959.

Isserman, Maurice. *If I Had a Hammer . . . The Death of the Old Left and the Birth of the New Left*. New York: Basic Books, 1987.

Janis, Irving. "Groupthink." In Walter E. Natemeyer and Jay S. Gilberg, eds., *Classics of Organizational Behavior*. Danville, Ill.: Interstate Printers & Publishers, 1989, 179–87.

Juergensmeyer, Mark. *Terror in the Mind of God: The Global Rise of Religious Violence*. Berkeley: University of California Press, 2000.

Jung, C. G. *Memories, Dreams, Reflections*. New York: Vintage, 1965.

Kanter, Rosabeth Moss. *Commitment and Community: Communes and Utopias in Sociological Perspective*. Cambridge, Mass.: Harvard University Press, 1972.

Keenan, Tom. "Sole Survivor." *Dateline.* National Broadcasting Company, New York, 1997.

Kelman, Herbert C., and V. Lee Hamilton. *Crimes of Obedience: Toward a Social Psychology of Authority and Responsibility.* New Haven, Conn.: Yale University Press, 1989.

Kilduff, Marshall. "The Unusual Group Behind Proposition V." *San Francisco Chronicle,* May 30, 1980, 1, 7.

Kirsch, Michael A., and Leonard L. Glass. "Psychiatric Disturbances Associated with Erhard Seminars Training, I: Additional Cases and Theoretical Considerations." *American Journal of Psychiatry* 134 (1977): 1254–58.

Klatch, Rebecca E. *A Generation Divided: The New Left, the New Right, and the 1960s.* Berkeley: University of California Press, 1999.

Klimo, Jon. *Channeling: Investigations on Receiving Information from Paranormal Sources.* Los Angeles: Tarcher, 1987.

Kolata, Gina. "Experts Are Suspicious of Claim of Cloned Human's Birth." *New York Times,* December 28, 2002, A16.

Kramer, Pamela, Brandon Bailey, Tracy Seipel, Rodney Foo, and Renee Koury. "Cult's Recipe for Death." *San Jose Mercury News,* March 28, 1997, 1A, 26A.

Lacarriere, Jacques. *The Gnostics.* San Francisco: City Lights Books, 1989.

Lalich, Janja. "Bounded Choice: The Fusion of Personal Freedom and Self-Renunciation in Two Transcendent Groups." Ph.D. dissertation, Fielding Graduate Institute, 2000.

———. "The Cadre Ideal: Origins and Development of a Political Cult." *Cultic Studies Journal* 9.1 (1992): 1–77.

———. "Dominance and Submission: The Psychosexual Exploitation of Women in Cults." *Women & Therapy* 19.4 (1996): 37–52.

———. "How I See It Today." Unpublished manuscript. Pelham, N.Y., 1987.

———. "Introduction: 'We Own Her Now.'" *Cultic Studies Journal* 14.1 (1997): 1–3.

———. "A Little Carrot and a Lot of Stick: A Case Example." In Michael D. Langone, ed., *Recovery from Cults: Help for Victims of Psychological and Spiritual Abuse.* New York: Norton, 1993, 51–84.

———. "Mimesis and Metaphors in the Discourse of Heaven's Gate Students." Paper presented at the Society for the Scientific Study of Religion, San Diego, Calif., November 7, 1997.

———. "Pitfalls in the Sociological Study of Cults." In Thomas Robbins and Benjamin Zablocki, eds., *Misunderstanding Cults: Searching for Objectivity in a Controversial Field.* Toronto: University of Toronto Press, 2001, 123–55.

———. "Repairing the Soul after a Cult Experience." *Creation Spirituality Network Magazine,* spring 1996, 30–33.

———, ed. "Women under the Influence: A Study of Women's Lives in Totalist Groups" [Special Issue]. *Cultic Studies Journal* 14.1 (1997).

Langone, Michael D. "Prevalence." American Family Foundation, n.d.. Available at www.csj.org/infoserve_freeinfo/cso_free/Prevalence.htm.

Laqueur, Walter. *The New Terrorism: Fanaticism and the Arms of Mass Destruction.* New York: Oxford University Press, 1999.

Lattin, Don, and Kevin Fagan. "John Walker's Curious Quest." *San Francisco Chronicle,* December 14, 2001, A24.

Layton, Deborah. *Seductive Poison: A Jonestown Survivor's Story of Life and Death in the Peoples Temple.* New York: Anchor Books, 1998.

Leary, Timothy. *The Politics of Ecstasy.* London: Paladin, 1970.

Levey, J. S., and A. Greenhall, eds. *The Concise Columbia Encyclopedia.* New York: Avon Books, 1983.

Lewin, Kurt. *Resolving Social Conflicts: Selected Papers on Group Dynamics.* Washington, D.C.: American Psychological Association, [1948] 1997.

Lewis, John Wilson. *Leadership in Communist China.* Ithaca, N.Y.: Cornell University Press, 1963.

Lieberman, Morton A. "Effects of Large Group Awareness Training on Participants' Psychiatric Status." *American Journal of Psychiatry* 144 (1987): 460–64.

Lifton, Robert Jay. "The Appeal of the Death Trip." *New York Times Magazine,* January 7, 1979, 26–27, 29–31.

———. "Cult Formation." *Harvard Mental Health Letter* 7.8 (1991): 5–6.

———. "Cult Violence, Death, and Immortality." Paper presented at the American Psychiatric Association, San Diego, Calif., 1997.

———. *Destroying the World to Save It: Aum Shinrikyo, Apocalyptic Violence, and the New Global Terrorism.* New York: Metropolitan Books, 1999.

———. *The Future of Immortality and Other Essays for a Nuclear Age.* New York: Basic Books, 1987.

———. "Methods of Forceful Indoctrination: Psychiatric Aspects of Chinese Communist Thought Reform." In Maurice Stein, Arthur J. Vidich, and David Manning White, eds., *Identity and Anxiety: Survival of the Person in Mass Society.* Glencoe, Ill.: Free Press, 1960, 480–92.

———. *The Nazi Doctors.* New York: Basic Books, 1986.

———. *Revolutionary Immortality: Mao Tse-tung and the Chinese Cultural Revolution.* New York: Random House, 1968.

———. *Thought Reform and the Psychology of Totalism.* New York: Norton, 1961.

———. "'Totalism' Ideology of Cults Helps Explain Violent Acts." *Psychiatric News,* July 4, 1997.

Lofland, John. *Doomsday Cult: A Study of Conversion, Proselytization, and Maintenance of Faith.* New York: Irvington, [1966] 1981.

Lofland, John, and N. Skonovd. "Patterns of Conversion." In Eileen Barker, ed., *Of Gods and Men: New Religious Movements in the West.* Macon, Ga.: Mercer University Press, 1983, 1–24.

Lofland, John, and Rodney Stark. "Becoming a World-Saver: A Theory of Conversion to a Deviant Perspective." *American Sociological Review* 30 (1965): 862–75.

Lukes, Steven. *Power: A Radical View.* Houndsmill: Macmillan Education, 1974.

MacDonald, Jerry Paul. "'Reject the Wicked Man' — Coercive Persuasion and Deviance Production: A Study of Conflict Management." *Cultic Studies Journal* 5.1 (1988): 59–121.

Marin, Peter. "The New Narcissism." *Harper's,* October 1975, 45–50, 55–56.

Marx, Karl, and Frederick Engels. *The Communist Manifesto*. New York: International Publishers, 1948.

Maslow, Abraham H. *Toward a Psychology of Being*. 2d ed. Princeton, N.J.: Van Nostrand, 1968.

Mayer, Jean-François. "'Our Terrestrial Journey Is Coming to an End': The Last Voyage of the Solar Temple." *Nova Religio* 2.2 (1999): 172–96.

McLoughlin, William G. *Revivals, Awakenings, and Reform: An Essay on Religion and Social Change in America, 1607–1977*. Chicago: University of Chicago Press, 1978.

Meyer, Frank S. *The Moulding of Communists: The Training of the Communist Cadre*. New York: Harcourt, Brace, 1961.

Milgram, Stanley. *Obedience to Authority: An Experimental View*. New York: Harper & Row, 1974.

Miller, George A. "Images and Models, Similes and Metaphors." In Andrew Ortony, ed., *Metaphor and Thought*. 2d ed. New York: Cambridge University Press, 1993, 357–400.

Miller, James. *"Democracy Is in the Streets": From Port Huron to the Siege of Chicago*. New York: Simon & Schuster, 1987.

Miller, Judith, Steven Engelberg, and William Broad. *Germs: Biological Weapons and America's Secret War*. New York: Simon & Schuster, 2001.

Min, Anchee. *Red Azalea*. New York: Pantheon Books, 1994.

Morgan, Gareth. *Images of Organization*. Thousand Oaks, Calif.: Sage, 1997.

Morgan, Pat. "A Comment to 'Jacque' and the League for Proletarian Socialism." *UMSS Newsletter*, December 1976, 1–4.

Muster, Nori J. *Betrayal of the Spirit: My Life Behind the Headlines of the Hare Krishna Movement*. Urbana: University of Illinois Press, 1997.

Olson, Kyle B. "Aum Shinrikyo: Once and Future Threat?" *Emerging Infectious Diseases* 5.4 (2000). Available at www.cdc.gov/ncidod/EID/vol5no4/olson.htm.

Orne, Martin. "On the Social Psychology of the Psychological Experiment: With Particular Reference to Demand Characteristics and Their Implications." *American Psychologist* 17 (1962): 776–83.

Ortony, Andrew, ed. *Metaphor and Thought*. 2d ed. New York: Cambridge University Press, 1993.

Palmer, Susan Jean. "Women in the Raelian Movement: New Religious Experiments in Gender and Authority." In James R. Lewis, ed., *The Gods Have Landed: New Religions from Other Worlds*. Albany: State University of New York Press, 1995, 105–35.

Pearce, W. Barnett. *Communication and the Human Condition*. Carbondale: Southern Illinois University Press, 1989.

Pearson, Hugh. *The Shadow of the Panther: Huey Newton and the Price of Black Power in America*. Reading, Mass.: Addison-Wesley, 1994.

Perera, Nirshan. "$400 Mn Lawsuit against ISKCON Dismissed." *rediff.com*, October 2, 2001.

Peritz, Ingrid. "Raelians Seek Path to Human Immortality." *Globe and Mail*, December 28, 2002, A5.

Persinger, Michael, N. J. Carrey, and L. A. Suess. *TM and Cult Mania.* North Quincy, Mass.: Christopher, 1980.

Phelan, James S. "Looking For: The Next World." *New York Times Magazine,* February 29, 1976, 12, 58–59, 62–64.

Pontoniere, Paulo. "Lessons from the Al Qaeda Cult Handbook." AlterNet.org, 2001. Available at www.alternet.org/print.html?StoryID = 11895.

Pressman, Steven. *Outrageous Betrayal: The Dark Journey of Werner Erhard from est to Exile.* New York: St. Martin's Press, 1993.

Rambo, Lewis R. *Understanding Religious Conversion.* New Haven, Conn.: Yale University Press, 1993.

Rickett, Allyn, and Adele Rickett. *Prisoners of Liberation: Four Years in a Chinese Communist Prison.* New York: Anchor Books, [1957] 1973.

Ritter, Malcolm. "Journalist Overseeing Test of 'Clone' Throws in Towel." *San Francisco Chronicle,* January 7, 2003, A2.

Rochford, E. Burke, Jr. "Child Abuse in the Hare Krishna Movement: 1971–1986." *ISKCON Communications Journal* 6.1 (1998): 43–69.

———. "Family Formation, Culture, and Change in the Hare Krishna Movement." *ISKCON Communications Journal* 5.2 (1997): 61–82.

Roof, Wade Clark. *A Generation of Seekers: The Spiritual Journeys of the Baby Boom Generation.* San Francisco: HarperSanFrancisco, 1993.

———. *Spiritual Marketplace: Baby Boomers and the Remaking of American Religion.* Princeton, N.J.: Princeton University Press, 1999.

Schein, Edgar H. *Coercive Persuasion.* New York: Norton, 1961.

———. "Groups and Intergroup Relationships." In Walter E. Natemeyer and Jay S. Gilberg, eds., *Classics of Organizational Behavior.* Danville, Ill.: Interstate Printers & Publishers, [1970] 1989, 172–78.

———. *Organizational Culture and Leadership.* 2d ed. San Francisco: Jossey-Bass, 1992.

Scully, Malcolm G. "New Demonstrations Hit U.S. and Canadian Campuses; Several States Weigh Measures to Control Disruptions." *Chronicle of Higher Education,* February 24, 1969, 1.

Sennett, Richard. *Authority.* Boston: Faber & Faber, 1980.

Serrano, Richard. *One of Ours: Timothy McVeigh and the Oklahoma City Bombing.* New York: Norton, 1998.

Sherif, M. *The Psychology of Social Norms.* New York: Harper, 1936.

Shils, Edward. "Totalitarians and Antinomians." In John H. Bunzel, ed., *Political Passages: Journeys of Change through Two Decades, 1968–1988.* New York: Free Press, 1988, 1–31.

Siegel, Peter, Nancy Strohl, Laura Ingram, David Roche, and Jean Taylor. "Leninism as Cult: The Democratic Workers Party." *Socialist Review* 17.6 (1987): 60–85.

Simmel, Georg. *The Sociology of Georg Simmel.* Ed. Kurt H. Wolff. New York: Free Press, 1950.

Simon, Herbert A. *Administrative Behavior.* 3d ed. New York: Macmillan, 1976.

———. "A Behavioral Model of Rational Choice." *Quarterly Journal of Economics* 69 (1955): 99–118.

———. *Models of Thought.* Vol. 1. New Haven, Conn.: Yale University Press, 1979.

———. "Rational Choice and the Structure of the Environment." *Psychological Review* 63 (1956): 129–38.

Simross, Lynn. "Like Lambs, Cultists Who Follow Bo, Peep Are Being Fleeced." *Sunday Plain Dealer,* November 16, 1975, 1, 8.

Singer, Margaret Thaler. *Cults in Our Midst: The Hidden Menace in Our Everyday Lives.* San Francisco: Jossey-Bass, 1995.

Singer, Margaret Thaler, and Janja Lalich. *"Crazy" Therapies: What Are They? Do They Work?* San Francisco: Jossey-Bass, 1996.

Singer, Margaret T., and Richard Ofshe. "Thought Reform Programs and the Production of Psychiatric Casualties." *Psychiatric Annals* 20.4 (1990): 188–93.

Smelser, Neil J. *Theory of Collective Behavior.* New York: Free Press, 1962.

Stark, Rodney, and Roger Finke. "A Rational Approach to the History of American Cults and Sects." In David G. Bromley and Jeffrey K. Hadden, eds., *The Handbook on Cults and Sects in America, Part A.* Greenwich, Conn.: JAI Press, 1993, 109–26.

Stone, Donald. "The Human Potential Movement." In Charles Y. Glock and Robert N. Bellah, eds., *The New Religious Consciousness.* Berkeley: University of California Press, 1976, 93–115.

Storr, Anthony. *Feet of Clay—Saints, Sinners, and Madmen: A Study of Gurus.* New York: Free Press, 1997.

Taylor, Michael. "SLA's Legacy a Violent Void." *San Francisco Chronicle,* November 11, 2002, A1, A12.

Thomas, Evan. "A Long, Strange Trip to the Taliban." *Newsweek,* December 17, 2001, 30–36.

Tipton, Steven M. *Getting Saved from the Sixties: Moral Meaning in Conversion and Cultural Change.* Berkeley: University of California Press, 1984.

Tobias, Madeleine Landau, and Janja Lalich. *Captive Hearts, Captive Minds: Freedom and Recovery from Cults and Abusive Relationships.* Alameda, Calif.: Hunter House, 1994.

Tourish, Dennis. "Ideological Intransigence, Democratic Centralism, and Cultism: A Case Study from the Political Left." *Cultic Studies Journal* 15.1 (1998): 33–67.

Tourish, Dennis, and Tim Wohlforth. *On the Edge: Political Cults Right and Left.* Armonk, N.Y.: Sharpe, 2000.

Trinkl, John. "USOCA: An Asset or a Liability?" *Guardian,* May 16, 1984, 2, 19.

United States Senate. Committee on the Judiciary. Hearings before the Subcommittee to Investigate the Administration of the Internal Security Act and Other Internal Security Laws. 93d Cong., 2d sess. Washington, D.C.: Government Printing Office, 1974.

———. Report of the Subcommittee to Investigate the Administration of the Internal Security Act and Other Internal Security Laws. 94th Cong., 1st sess. Washington, D.C.: Government Printing Office, 1975.

Vallee, Jacques. *Messengers of Deception: UFO Contacts and Cults.* Berkeley: And/Or Press, 1979.

Waldman, Amy. "Little Trace of Late Bhagwan at His Commune." *San Francisco Chronicle,* December 13, 2002, K6.

Wallerstein, Immanuel. *The Essential Wallerstein.* New York: New Press, 2000.

Wallis, Roy. *The Elementary Forms of the New Religious Life.* London: Routledge & Kegan Paul, 1983.

Washington, Peter. *Madame Blavatsky's Baboon: A History of the Mystics, Mediums, and Misfits Who Brought Spiritualism to America.* New York: Schocken, 1995.

Weber, Max. "Bureaucracy." In H. H. Gerth and C. Wright Mills, eds., *From Max Weber: Essays in Sociology.* New York: Oxford University Press, 1946, 196–244.

———. *From Max Weber: Essays in Sociology.* Eds. H. H. Gerth and C. Wright Mills. New York: Oxford University Press, 1946.

———. "The Nature of Charismatic Authority and Its Routinization." In S. N. Eisenstadt, ed., *Max Weber: On Charisma and Institution Building.* Chicago: University of Chicago Press, [1947] 1968, 48–65.

———. "The Pure Types of Legitimate Authority." In S. N. Eisenstadt, ed., *Max Weber: On Charisma and Institution Building.* Chicago: University of Chicago Press, [1947] 1968, 46–47.

———. "Religious Rejections of the World and Their Directions." In H. H. Gerth and C. Wright Mills, eds., *From Max Weber: Essays in Sociology.* New York: Oxford University Press, 1946, 323–59.

———. "The Social Psychology of World Religions." In H. H. Gerth and C. Wright Mills, eds., *From Max Weber: Essays in Sociology.* New York: Oxford University Press, 1946, 267–301.

———. "The Sociology of Charismatic Authority." In H. H. Gerth and C. Wright Mills, eds., *From Max Weber: Essays in Sociology.* New York: Oxford University Press, 1946, 245–52.

———. *The Sociology of Religion.* Trans. E. Fischoff. Boston: Beacon Press, [1922] 1964.

Wheaton, Elizabeth. *Code Name Greenkil: The 1979 Greensboro Killings.* Athens: University of Georgia Press, 1987.

Winter, Alison. *Mesmerized: Powers of Mind in Victorian Britain.* Chicago: University of Chicago Press, 1998.

Wohlforth, Tim. *The Prophet's Children: Travels on the American Left.* Atlantic Highlands, N.J.: Humanities Press, 1994.

Workers Party. *The Founding of the Workers Party.* San Francisco: Synthesis Publications, 1979.

Wright, Stuart A., ed. *Armageddon in Waco: Critical Perspectives on the Branch Davidian Conflict.* Chicago: University of Chicago Press, 1995.

Yalom, Irvin D., and Morton Lieberman. "A Study of Encounter Group Casualties." *Archives of General Psychiatry* 25 (1971): 16–30.

Yanov, Dvora. "Ecologies of Technological Metaphors and the Theme of Control." *Technē: Journal of the Society for Philosophy and Technology* 1.3–4 (1996). http://scholar.lib.vt.edu/journals/SPT/v1n3n4/Yanow.html.

Zablocki, Benjamin D. *Alienation and Charisma: A Study of Contemporary American Communes.* New York: Free Press, 1980.

———. "The Birth and Death of New Religious Movements." Paper presented at the Association for the Sociology of Religion, Washington, D.C., 2000.

———. "The Blacklisting of a Concept: The Strange History of the Brainwashing Conjecture in the Sociology of Religion." *Nova Religio* 1.1 (1997): 96–121.

———. "Exit Cost Analysis: A New Approach to the Scientific Study of Brainwashing." *Nova Religio* 1.2 (1998): 216–49.

———. "Hyper Compliance in Charismatic Groups." In David D. Franks and Thomas S. Smith, eds., *Mind, Brain and Society: Toward a Neurosociology of Emotion.* Stamford, Conn.: JAI Press, 1999, 287–310.

———. *The Joyful Community.* Baltimore, Md.: Penguin Books, 1971.

Zablocki, Benjamin, and Thomas Robbins, eds. *Misunderstanding Cults: Searching for Objectivity in a Controversial Field.* Toronto: University of Toronto Press, 2001.

Zimbardo, Philip G., and Michael R. Leippe. *The Psychology of Attitude Change and Social Influence.* New York: McGraw-Hill, 1991.

Zucker, Lynne G. "The Role of Institutionalization in Cultural Persistence." In Walter W. Powell and Paul J. DiMaggio, eds., *The New Institutionalism in Organizational Analysis.* Chicago: University of Chicago Press, 1991, 83–107.

Index

Following usage in the text, the Democratic Workers Party is referred to as DWP. Page numbers in italics refer to photographs.

activism: cult members and personal history of, 66; disillusionment and, 120–21, 129; era of, 118–21; liberation movements and, 121–22; secrecy and, 122–23

agency, 232–33

Alcoholics Anonymous, 127

Aleph, 11

Alpert, Richard (Ram Dass), 34

androgyny ideal. *See* gender

Animal Liberation Front, 14

anticult movement, 4–5

anxiety, 107–8, 185, 213–14, 229

apocalyptic beliefs, 11, 278n28; DWP and, 193, 243–44; Heaven's Gate and, 42, 48–49, 96, 243–44

Applewhite, Marshall: aging of, 93, 95; appearance of, *46, 49, 53, 55, 65, 72, 100*; arrest and jail time of, 47–48, 70, 84; background of, 43–45; charismatic authority and, 43, 53, 54–56, 79–80; death of Nettles and, 91–93, 104, 108; emotional style of, 89; gender and, 78, 83; guns and, 189; health of, and mass suicide, 97–98; on mental telepathy, 108; names of, 25, 42, 43, 49, 50, 52, 71, 72, 82; New Age movement and, 31,

102; sexuality of, 43–44, 103, 300n27; spiritualism and, 36. *See also* Heaven's Gate leadership; *other* Heaven's Gate *headings*

The Aquarian Conspiracy (Ferguson), 33, 34–35, 38, 39

Army of God, 262

Asahara, Shoko, 11

Ascended Masters, 36–37

Asch, Solomon, 248

Assagioli, Robert, 35

Atta, Mohammed, xvi

Aum Shinrikyō and, 11

authority: authoritarianism, 207; language and, 58; legal, 79; obedience to, 58, 79, 229–30, 240, 241; as relationship, 58, 207; resocialization and, 251–52; socialization for obedience to, 58, 240. *See also* charismatic authority; lineage of authority

Away Team, 27, *27*, 96. *See also* Heaven's Gate

Balch, Robert, xxi, 57, 287n6

Bateson, Gregory, 39

Beatles, 34

Beat poets, 33

beliefs. *See* DWP beliefs; Heaven's Gate beliefs; transcendent belief system

Berg, Alan, 262

Bible, 55, 102

bicameral normative system, 280n49

bioterrorism, 10

black-and-white thinking, 187

Black Panther Party, 121

Blavatsky, Helena Petrovna, 36–37, 45

Bo, 52. *See also* Applewhite, Marshall

Bolshevik cadre party, 115–16, 290n7, 297n17

bonding, conversion and, 7, 66–67

Bo Peep cult. *See* Heaven's Gate

bounded choice: about decision making vs. attitude change, 250; acting against one's own interest and, 19, 77, 98–101, 206, 229–30, 260; cognitive dissonance theory compared to, 247, 249–50; conformity theories compared to, 247–49; context of, 246; defined, 2, 14–15; DWP analysis, 137, 192, 206, 217–18; failure of, 206; free will and, 100–101, 260; groupthink compared to, 250; Heaven's Gate analysis, 53–54, 77, 98; illusion of choice and, 190; juncture of emergence (*see* charismatic commitment); knowledge boundary control and, 251–54; non-cult contexts for, 262–63; structural dimensions creating, 258–61; works cited, summary of, 7. *See also* personal closure; self-sealing systems

bounded rationality, 7, 257–58, 259

bounded reality, 20, 281n56

brainwashing: apparent vs. indirect, 287n6; defined, 6; denial/redefinition of, as characteristic, 143–44; as term, 4; use of, 61, 236

Branch Davidians (Waco, TX), 10

Brecht, Bertoldt, 150

Bukharin, Nikolai, 188

Castro, Fidel, 121

charismatic authentication, 78

charismatic authority: beleaguered leader, 99; characteristics required of, 137–40; commitment and relation of, 234, 236; defined, 17, 78; dependency (*see* dependency on leader); deselection of members as solidifying, 238; discipline and, 79; dualism of, 54, 254–57, 258–59, 265, 273, 285n21; DWP analysis, 137–40,

160–65, 206–8, 223–26, 267, 271; "failed" miracles and, 90; gender and, 285–86n22; gratitude to leaders, 98–99, 106; Heaven's Gate analysis, 54–56, 77–80, 98–101, 137–38, 223–26, 267, 271; knowledge as issue in, 19, 251; language and, 58, 138–39; lineage (*see* lineage of authority); manipulation and, 79–80, 162–63; obedience to, 58, 229–30, 240, 241; personal boundaries created by, 255–56, 258–60, 261, 273; psychological preconditioning and, 78–79, 288n16; purpose and effects of, 244–46, 272; resocialization and, 251–52; routinization of, 225–26; social relation as intrinsic to, 17, 54, 78–79, 138, 222–26, 238–40; specialness of followers and, 54, 56, 74, 135, 137, 191, 208–9, 213; as structural dimension, summarized, 223–26, 271, 272; style of leadership and, 56, 83, 240, 241–42, 300n27; submission to (*see* submission); tables summarizing characteristics of, 265, 267, 271, 272; Weber on, 7, 78, 79. *See also* self-sealing systems; systems of control; systems of influence; transcendent belief system

charismatic commitment: crisis management and maintenance of, 242; defined, 14, 18–19; dualism and, 255, 258–59, 273; as fusion of personal freedom and self-renunciation, 14–15, 17–19, 234, 244–46, 255, 301n19; as interactive process, 233–36; lapses of, 18; primary works on, 7; renewal of, 18; struggle with, 234; transformation and (*see* personal transformation requirement); variation in, 255. *See also* bounded choice; DWP commitment; Heaven's Gate commitment; self-sealing systems

chemical warfare, 11

children: DWP and, 187, 190, 209; Heaven's Gate and, 190, 289n7

Chinese Communist Party, 117–18, 135, 156, 172, 203, 236

choice: bounded rationality, 257–58, 259; rational choice, 257–58. *See also* bounded choice

Christianity, Heaven's Gate and, 53, 55, 77–78, 101–2

CISPES, 199

class history sessions, 132–33, 170–72

class-standpoint struggle: class history

sessions and, 132–33, 170–72; as coercive persuasion, 214; as daily atmosphere, 145; defined, 117–18; as first priority, 158; internalization of, 173; process and expectations of, 170–72. *See also* criticism/self-criticism; Democratic Workers Party

closure. *See* personal closure

coercive persuasion, 214, 215, 241

coercive persuasion conversion, 15

Coercive Persuasion (Schein), 6

cognitive dissonance theory, 247, 249–50, 257

COINTELPRO, 122–23

Cold War, 6, 118

collective contagion conversion, 15

collective unconscious, 37

Columbine High School, 262

commitment. *See* charismatic commitment; DWP commitment; Heaven's Gate commitment

The Communist Manifesto (Marx and Engels), 115

communal living: DWP and, 179–80, 186–87, 191, 212, 228–29; as foundational, 228–29; Heaven's Gate and, 67, 71, 75, 86, 104–6, 228, 289n7; interest in, generally, 67

communication: as charismatic requirement, 137–38; Marlene Dixon's style of, 137–38, 198, 204, 205, 209–10; DWP security and, 161–62, 180; Heaven's Gate style of, 68–69, 89, 157–58. *See also* language

Communism, 114–18, 203, 204, 290n7, 297n17. *See also* Democratic Workers Party (DWP); New Communist Movement

Communist Party–U.S.A., 117, 119

conformism: DWP and, 144–45; Heaven's Gate and, 89; as societal norm, 89; theories of, 247–49, 257. *See also* systems of influence

contradictions and mixed messages: agency and, 232–33; black-and-white thinking and, 187; on children, 187, 190, 209; cognitive dissonance theory and, 249–50; dissolution of DWP and, 214–17; leaving the group and, 237–38; as means of control, 190. *See also* dualism

control. *See* systems of control

conversion. *See* worldview shift

corporate actors, 231

Crimes of Obedience (Kelman and Hamilton), 229

criticism: DWP and (*see* criticism/self-criticism); Heaven's Gate error-review, 74, 84–85, 230, 254; as norm, 230, 254

criticism/self-criticism: background of Marlene Dixon and, 128; as coercive persuasion, 214, 215; defined, 117–18; dependency on Dixon reinforced in, 224; dissolution of group and, 206; emotional suppression as requirement of, 146–47; function of, 172; hierarchy of DWP and, 162–63, 204; internalization as requirement of, 145–46, 172, 173; language of, 185–86; New Communist Movement and, 123; peer pressure in, 185–87; process and expectations of, 144–47; reporting on others, 186–87. *See also* class-standpoint struggle; Democratic Workers Party

"cult apologists," 4

"cult bashers," 4–5

cultic social systems. *See* bounded choice; self-sealing systems; structural dimensions

cults: conventional wisdom regarding, 1–2; defined, 5; ideologies of, generally, 6–7; as label, xvii–xviii, 4–5; prior studies of, 3–5, 7; statistics regarding, 8, 277n18; types of, generally, 8–14. *See also* bounded choice

Cultural Revolution, 117

"cult wars," 6–7

Debray, Regis, 121

democratic centralism, 116, 163–64, 175–76, 204, 209, 215

Democratic National Convention, Chicago 1968, 120

Democratic Workers Party (DWP): assets liquidation of, 205–6; bounded choice analysis, 137, 192, 206, 217–18; charismatic authority analysis, 137–40, 160–65, 206–8, 223–26, 267, 271; children, policy on, 187, 190, 209; as cult, 125, 206; daily life, tenor of, 144, 191, 207, 212–13, 217; facilities of, 177, 179; feminism and, 113, 125, 126, 147, 224; front groups and study groups, 151–52, 158–60, *159*, 189, 198–99; gays and lesbians and, 125, 135, 147, 148, 182–84, 190–91;

Democratic Workers Party *(continued)*
guns and, 189, 205; methodology of
study, 20, 280–81n55, 291n11; names used
by, xvii, 158–59, 204, 275n7; political
activities of, 159–60, *171*, 198–201, *200*,
201–2, 211–12, 214; public emergence
of, 159–60, 169, 189; publishing house
of, *197*, 198, 297n10; submission to, as
required, 144, 170, 185, 207; systems of
control analysis, 141–43, 174–84, 211–
14, 228–30, 269, 271; systems of influence analysis, 143–48, 184–88, 214–17,
230–32, 270, 271; timetable for revolution, 149; as vanguard party, 134–37,
147–48, 185; violence and, 182, 191, 200–
201, 254. *See also entries beginning with*
DWP, *following*
DWP beliefs, 146; cadre ideal, 172–74,
184–85; class consciousness as concept,
141, 143; crisis of Marxism-Leninism,
204, 207, 208–11, 215; democratic
centralism, 116, 163–64, 175–76, 204,
209, 215; discipline of, 136, 141; ends
justifying means, 150, 211–12; guiding
principles, 166; international focus,
change to, 202–3, 208, 210; socialism
as goal, 193, 202; transcendent belief
analysis, 140–41, 165–74, 208–11, 226–
28, 268, 271. *See also* class-standpoint
analysis; criticism/self-criticism
DWP commitment: acceptance of Dixon's
direction, 165; crises of, 174, 242; differ-
ing degrees of, as problem, 195, 202,
208–9; freedom and necessity and, 168–
69; promotion of members and, 176; as
total, 174, 188, 195, 206–7
DWP dissolution: aftermath, 205–6,
218; bounded choice and, 206, 217, 218;
charismatic authority and, 206–8; crisis
of Marxism-Leninism and, 204, 207,
208–11, 215; defection from Party
planned by Dixon, 204, 216–17;
demoralization of members, 202, 203,
204, 210–12, 213, 215–17; impact on
members, 206, 212, 218; international
focus of DWP and, 202–3, 208, 210;
revolution of inner circle, 204–6, 213–
14, 216–17; systems of control and, 211–
14; systems of influence and, 214–17;
transcendent beliefs and, 208–11
DWP leadership, 174–75; Central

Committee, 135, 175; communication
among, 161–62; dependence on Dixon,
161–63; directives establishing, 163–64;
dissolution of DWP and, 204–6, 213–
14, 216–17; double standard for Marlene
Dixon and, 155–57, 204, 207–8, 213,
216–17, 294n3; dualism and, 233;
formation of party and establishment of
Dixon in, 130–31, 135, 136, 155, 158, 160–
65; inner circle, 167, 174–75, 201, 204–6,
213–14, 216–17, 242–43; internal
structures overseen by, 201; layered
structure of, 243–44; middle levels,
166–67, 175, 184, 201; modeling by, 187–
88, 224, 230; sanctions and expulsions,
157–58, 167, 175, 182, 184, 294n1; second-
in-command, 156, 174, 175. *See also*
Dixon, Marlene
DWP members: ages of, 131, 292n13;
androgyny/gender and, 142–43;
"cadres" or "militants" as terms for, 113;
categories of, 176–77; ceremony for
promotions of, 176–77; communal
living of, 179–80, 186–87, 191, 212, 228–
29; comradeship, 142, 212; criticism of
(*see* criticism/self-criticism); demoralization of, 202, 203, 204, 210–12, 213,
215–17; dependency on Dixon, 161–63,
224–25, 238–40, 243; dues required of,
179–80; fund-raising quotas, 144, 177,
232; instructed vs. uninstructed, 163–
64, 171–72; interactive process of
selection/self-selection, 236–38; living
conditions of, 179–81; loyalty to Dixon,
127, 142, 157, 160, 183–84, 188, 241; men
as, 135, 147, 154; motivations for joining,
147–48, 169–70; names taken by, 154–
55, 179, 186–87; "no gossip" rule for,
139, 142; numbers of, 113, 154, 160, 201,
202, 214; one-help system, 186–87;
personal effects of, destroyed, 180–81;
purges, 182–84, 190, 195, 202, 208–9;
relationships and, 190–91; rules and
regulations for, 142, 178–80, 191;
sexuality and, 143, 182, 190–91, 196n45,
296n45; silencing of, 139, 142; specialness felt by, 135, 137, 191, 208–9, 213;
work assignments for, 144, 155, 177–78,
188–89, 232–33
DWP recruitment and training, 165–74,
191; anxiety and, 185; cadre ideal, 172–

74, 184–85; Dixon's private meetings, 138; as interactive process, 236–37; loyalty to Dixon stressed in, 157, 160; loyalty to Party stressed in, 188; narrative of author's, 150–54, 169–70; New Members Class, 166, 171–72; one-help system, 186–87; Party School, 166–67, 172, 184, 188, 195, 295n43; seriousness of, 136–37, 173; study/front groups, 151–52, 158–60, *159*, 189, 198–99; waning, 195. *See also* class-standpoint struggle; criticism/self-criticism; DWP publications

DWP secrecy: atmosphere of, 135, 136, 153, 154–55, 229; double standard of leadership and, 155–57, 204, 207–8, 213, 216–17, 294n3; emotional matters, 229; front groups, 151–52, 158–60, *159*, 189, 198–99; Party affiliation, 158–59, 189; publishing ventures hiding DWP control, 296–97n9-10; Remoulding Groups, 166, 295n20; resignations and, 298n26; sanctions, 139, 156, 158, 179, 181–84, 186–87, 191, 204, 254

DWP security: communication and, 161–62, 180; destruction of personal items, 180–81; of Marlene Dixon, 205, 295–96n44; Eagles (security force), 182, 295–96n44; fear and, 189, 225, 229; living quarters and, 179, 180–81; names and, 179, 186–87; work sites for members and, 177

dependency on leader: DWP and, 161–63, 224–25, 238–40, 243; as foundational, 224–25; Heaven's Gate and, 68, 71, 72–73, 82, 89, 90, 99, 100, 106, 238–40, 243; layers of leadership mediating, 242–43; regressive dynamic and, 239–40

deployable agents, transformation to: DWP and, 173; exit costs and, 299n12; Lofland and Stark on, 299n18; processes of commitment and, 236; terrorism and, xvi–xvii. *See also* self-sealing systems; true believers

deterministic undercurrent, 141

developmental regression, 239–40

Di Mambro, Joseph, 11

discipline: charismatic authority requiring, 79; DWP and, 136, 141; Heaven's Gate and, 77, 87–88; terrorism and, xvi. *See also* systems of control

dissent disallowed. *See* independent thought or action as unacceptable

dissociation, 213

Dixon, Marlene: academia and, 127–29, 133–34, 150, 203; as authoritarian parent, 207, 238–40; communication style of, 137–38, 198, 204, 205, 209–10; devotion to, 126–27, 164–65, 207; double standard regarding, 155–57, 204, 207–8, 213, 216–17, 294n3; emotional style of, 158, 162, 204, 205; financial support of, 139, 155, 180, 208; leadership style of, 241–42, 272, 300n27; lineage of authority claimed by, 127–32, 133, 134–35, 138–39, 160; name in Party, 294–95n14; personal service given to, 155, 177, 205; personal style and appearance of, 126–27, 130, 154; seclusion and inaccessibility of, 157, 208, 225; theoretical orientation of, 125, 126, 139–40, 167, 202–3, 208–11, 215. *See also headings at* Democratic Workers Party

Do, 52, 71. *See also* Applewhite, Marshall

"The Doors of Perception" (Huxley), 34

double standards for leadership: DWP and, 155–57, 204, 207–8, 213, 216–17, 294n3; as foundational, 225; Heaven's Gate and, 142

doubling, 7, 213

drugs, 33, 34, 38, 40

dualism of social system, 54, 232–33, 254–57, 258–59, 265–66, 273, 285n21

duty and guilt, dualism of, 256, 259, 273

Earth Liberation Front (ELF), 14

Eastern beliefs and practices, 33, 34, 35, 37

eco-fatalistic apocalypticism, 42, 48–49, 96, 243–44

eco-terrorism, 14

Elbaum, Max, 116, 125, 200

emotions: Marlene Dixon and displays of, 158, 162, 204, 205; DWP and suppression of, 146–47, 229; Heaven's Gate and suppression of, 60–61, 67–68, 86–89, 229; of Heaven's Gate leaders, 89

encounter movement, 37–38

enemies: DWP and declaration of, 182, 183, 194–95, 200–201, 209, 225; Heaven's Gate and, 225. *See also* separatism

Engels, Friedrich, 115

Erikson, Erik, 251
Esalen, 38
exit costs, 299n12
extremists, bounded choice and, 262–63

family. *See* children; isolation from family
and friends
FBI infiltration and investigations, 122–23,
136, 153, 225
fear: as atmosphere in DWP, 138, 183, 185,
191, 241; as atmosphere in Heaven's
Gate, 70, 80, 83–84, 107–8, 138, 191;
and love, dualism of, 255–56, 258, 273;
submission to authority and, 239
feminism, DWP and, 113, 125, 126, 128, 131–
32, 147, 224
Ferguson, Marilyn, 33, 34–35, 38, 39
Festinger, Leon, 249
financial support of leaders: DWP, 139, 155,
180, 208; as expectation, 139; Heaven's
Gate, 67, 71, 75, 106, 139, 289n7
First International, 115
Fleck, Ludwig, 286n233
former members, as study informants, 3–4
Fourth Great Awakening, 119
Frank, Andre Gunder, 203
freedom and necessity, 167–69, 184
free will, 100–101, 160, 230–31
friends. *See* isolation from family and
friends
Full Moon Coffeehouse, 123–24

Garry, Charles, 277–78n19
gays and lesbians: DWP and, 125, 135, 147,
148, 182–84, 190–91; Heaven's Gate
members, 51, 67–68; political activism
and, 123–24. *See also* homosexuality
gender: charismatic authority and, 285–
86n22; DWP and, 142–43; Heaven's
Gate and, 78, 83, 108, 142–43, 190;
leadership style and, 300n27
Giddens, Anthony, 7, 222–23, 251–52, 254
Gnosticism, 35, 102
Goffman, Erving, 251, 253
Grass Roots Alliance (GRA), 159–60, 171,
198, 201–2
groupthink, 250
group tie conversion, 15
Guevara, Che, 121
guilt: duty and, dualism of, 256, 259, 273;
self-transformation and, 16, 253

Guinea and Pig, 49, 52. *See also* Heaven's
Gate leadership, names for
guns, 189, 205

Hale-Bopp comet, 25–26, 28, 30, 96, 215
Hamilton, V. Lee, 229
Hare Krishna movement, 12–13
Health/PAC West, 199
Hearst, Patricia, 13, 79, 122
"Heaven and Hell" (Huxley), 34
Heaven's Gate: bounded choice analysis,
53–54, 77, 98; charismatic authority
analysis, 54–56, 77–80, 98–101, 137–38,
223–26, 267, 271; continued believers of,
92–93, 99, 276n1, 300n23; daily life,
tenor of, 62, 144, 217; guns and, 189;
Internet and, 25, 29, 30, 77–78, 95–96,
233; methodology of study, 20, 280–
81n55, 284n1; names of group, 30, 82, 93,
96; systems of control analysis, 58–59,
83–89, 104–6, 142–43, 228–30, 269;
systems of influence analysis, 59–62,
89–90, 106–8, 143–44, 230–32, 270,
271; as thought community, 57–58,
286n33. *See also headings beginning with*
Heaven's Gate, *following*
Heaven's Gate beliefs: basic tenets of, 81;
body as "vehicle" in, 83, 85, 92, 95, 103;
Christianity and, 53, 55, 77–78, 101–2;
the Class, 71–77; coercive persuasion
and, 215; crew-mindedness, 73, 142; the
Demonstration, 48, 69–71, 101; deposit
of knowledge, 74, 82, 143, 227; discipline, 77, 87–88; eco-fatalistic apocalypticism, 42, 48–49, 96, 243–44;
failed miracles and, 90; gender and, 78,
83, 108, 142–43, 190; metamorphosis of
body, 57, 80–83, 95, 242; metaphors
and, 57–58; New Age and (*see* New Age
movement); obedience and, 58; overcoming death (Next Level immortality), 26, 48–49, 57, 60, 80–83; overcoming humanness, 59, 60–62, 67–68,
75–76, 80–83, 85–89, 103–4; procedures as part of, 88–89; reading list for
members, 102; sexuality, denial of, 67–
68, 77, 87, 88–89, 143, 190; shifts in, 26,
95, 101, 242; transcendent belief analysis, 57–58, 80–83, 101–4, 140–41, 226–
28, 268, 271
Heaven's Gate commitment: bounded

choice and, 217–18; crisis management and, 242; daily life as demonstration of, 62, 254; "final exam," 90; isolation from family and friends, 62; requested levels of, 89–90; as total, 49–50, 59, 62; wedding ritual, 92, 242; written notes declaring, 62, 90

Heaven's Gate leadership (Nettles and Applewhite): awakening of, 48–49; charismatic authority analysis and, 54–56, 77–80, 98–101, 137–38, 223–26, 267, 271; communication with members, 68–69, 157–58; criminal behavior of, 47–48; death of Nettles and, 91–93, 98, 104, 108; dependence on, by members, 68, 71, 72–73, 82, 89, 90, 99, 100, 106, 238–40, 243; double standard and, 142; early formation of, 42–47; fallibility and, 85, 241; financial support of, 67, 71, 75, 106, 139, 289n7; hierarchy of, 47, 53, 58–59, 98, 104, 300n27; homosexuality and, 43–44, 103, 300n27; language use of, 57–58, 65, 72, 138; lineage of authority claimed by, 55, 56, 77–78; loyalty to, 52, 90, 142, 241; modeling by, 60–62, 65, 89, 90, 104, 224, 230; names for, 26, 42, 47, 49, 50, 52, 55, 71, 72, 82; Older Members, 47, 72; paranoia of, 84, 225; parental relationship to members, 72–73, 82, 238–40; public relationship between, 47, 53; review of member actions by, 74, 84–85, 230, 254; seclusion and disappearances of, 47, 52, 70–71, 142, 225; secrecy and, 47, 189, 229; style of leadership of, 56, 83, 241–42, 272, 300n27; trust in, by members, 59, 106; upper- and middle-level (Elders, Helpers, and Overseers), 50, 233, 242–43. *See also* Applewhite, Marshall; Nettles, Bonnie

Heaven's Gate mass suicide, 26–31, *29*; bounded choice and, 98–109, 215, 217–18; as choice, 263; exit videos and documents, 30, 98–99, 100–101, 107, 284n1; health of Applewhite and, 97–98; as "life" not death, 99–101, *100*, 242; media coverage of, 12, 28, 29–31, 96; method of, 26, 30, 96–97, 282n2; procedures written for, 97, 242; suicides occurring afterward, 92–93, 99–100, 300n23

Heaven's Gate members: ages of, 30, 66; bonding between, 66–68, 92; castration of, 2, 30; check partners, 67–68, 87–88; clothing worn, 27, *27*, 86; communal living, 67, 71, 75, 86, 104–6, 228, 289n7; communication style of, 89; decision making process when away from group, 104–5; dependency on leaders, 68, 71, 72–73, 82, 89, 90, 99, 100, 106, 238–40, 243; diet and exercise regimen, 27, 73, 75–76, 77; error-review of, 74, 84–85, 230, 254; fear as atmosphere and, 70, 80, 83–84, 107–8, 138, 191; free will of, 100–101; gays and lesbians, 51, 67–68; interactive process of selection/self-selection, 236–38; language use by, 65; leaving group, 59, 79–80, 84, 90, 237–38, 289n7; mimicking leaders, 60–62, 65, 89, 90, 104, 224, 230; name change required for, 72; number of, 30, 63, 64, 71, 84, 95, 215; self-monitoring and -reporting, 88; socioeconomic status of, 66–67; specialness felt by, 56, 74; thoughts, lack of privacy in, 107–8; work and projects of, 75–77, 84, 90, 93, 104–6, 188–89, 233

Heaven's Gate recruitment, 191; check partners and, 67, 68; earliest, 47–49, 55; early 1990s, 93–95; early Hollywood, 49–52, 55–56; "final call," 93–96, 215, 242; initiation pattern, 45; as interactive process, 236–37; meeting format, 63–66, *65*

Heaven's Gate rules and procedures: the Class, 71–77; consulted for decision making, 105; establishment of, 71, 73, 87–89, 191; for suicide, 97, 242

hierarchy: as foundational, 228–30; Heaven's Gate and, 47, 53, 58–59, 98, 104, 300n27; as societal norm, 59; terrorism and, xvi. *See also* DWP leadership

hippie movement, 120

Ho Chi Minh, 121

Hoffer, Eric, xv

homosexuality: Applewhite and, 43–44, 103, 300n27; DWP's theoretical line on, 182, 296n45; New Communist Movement and, 125. *See also* gays and lesbians

Human Individual Metamorphosis (H.I.M.), 82

human potential movement, 37–40, 117–18
Huxley, Aldous, 34, 35

idealism. *See* personal freedom
identification: and internalization, dualism of, 256, 259, 273; resocialization and, 252. *See also* worldview shift
ideology. *See* transcendent belief system
independent thought or action as unacceptable, 231; DWP and, 142, 144, 161–62, 167, 184–85, 187–88, 231, 240; Heaven's Gate and, 60–62, 65, 104–5, 106, 231, 240
individualism. *See* independent thought or action as unacceptable
influence. *See* systems of influence
inner circle: comparison of, 242–43; defined, 79; of DWP, 167, 174–75, 201, 204–6, 213–14, 216–17, 242–43; as foundational, 224; of Heaven's Gate, 50, 79, 233, 242–43. *See also* DWP leadership
inner knowing, Gnosticism and, 35
Institute for the Study of Labor and Economic Crisis, 199
"The International," 176–77
International Society for Krishna Consciousness (ISKCON), 12–13
Isis Unveiled (Blavatsky), 36
isolation from family and friends: Applewhite and Nettles and, 43, 45, 142; double standard and, 142; DWP and, 146, 186–87, 189–90, 212, 218; as foundational, 227; Heaven's Gate and, 82, 107, 189, 190, 289n7

Jones, Jim, xvii, xviii, 8–9, 300n28
Jonestown, xvii, xviii, 8–9, 277–78n19, 300n28
Jouret, Luc, 11
Joyu, Fumihiro, 11
Jung, Carl G., 35, 37, 38

Kanter, Rosabeth Moss, 7
Kataribabo, Dominic, 12
Kelman, Herbert C., 229
Kennedy, John F., 120
Kennedy, Robert, 120
Kent State University, 120
Kibwetere, Joseph, 12
Kilgore, James, 13
King, Martin Luther, Jr., 120

Klug, Clarence, 49–50, 55
knowledge: choice and, 257–58; control of, 251–54; divine, lineage claims and, 55, 77–78; promise of, and charismatic authority, 19, 251
Koresh, David, 10
Krishnamurti, J., 35

bin Laden, Osama, xvi
Lalich, Janja: as DWP recruit, 150–54, *152*, 169–70; methodology of, 3–4, 19–21, 280–81n55; motivation for study, xviii–xx; name used in DWP, 179; as New Communist Movement recruit, 123–24, *171*; as participant observer, 20; Synthesis Publications and, *197*, 198
Lane, Mark, 277–78n19
Langone, Michael, 277n18
language: authority and, 58; DWP and, 134, 138, 295n20; Heaven's Gate and, 57–58, 65, 72, 83, 105; metaphors, 57–58. *See also* communication
leader as necessity, principle of: as foundational theme, 222, 224; New Age movement and, 32; New Communist Movement and, 124, 125. *See also* charismatic authority; DWP leadership; Heaven's Gate leadership
leadership: dualism of, 233; layers of, 242–43; style of, 56, 83, 241–42, 272, 300n27. *See also* DWP leadership; Heaven's Gate leadership
League for Proletarian Socialism, 199
Leary, Timothy, 34, 292–93n21
leaving the group: DWP, 174; exit costs, 232, 299n12; Heaven's Gate and, 59, 79–80, 84, 90, 237–38, 289n7; as interactive process, 237–38; as "irrational," 260; professional ability and, 299–300n20; questions on issue of, 260; worldview shift and, 18. *See also* DWP recruitment and training, sanctions
LeBaron, Ervil, 79
Lenin, Vladimir Ilyich, 115–16, 290n7
Leninism, Dixon and, 167, 204, 207, 208–11, 215, 224
lesbian purge, 182–84, 190
lesbians. *See* gays and lesbians; homosexuality
Lewin, Kurt, 15
liberation movements, 121–22
Liberation School, 124

Lifton, Robert Jay, xv, 5, 6, 7, 16, 20, 127, 256–57, 301nn15, 19
Lindh, John Walker, 16
lineage of authority: DWP and, 127–32, 133, 134–35, 138–39, 160; as foundational, 224; Heaven's Gate and, 55, 56, 77–78
Lin Piao, 188
Little Red Book, 121
Lofland, John, 7, 15, 299n18
love and fear, dualism of, 255–56, 258, 273
loyalty: to Marlene Dixon, 127, 142, 157, 160, 183–84, 188, 241; to Heaven's Gate leadership, 52, 90, 142, 241

MacDonald, Jerry, 280n49
Maharishi Mahesh Yogi, 34
Malcolm X, 120
manipulation: charismatic authority and, 79–80, 162–63; terrorism and, xvi
Manson family, 79, 278n28
Maoism. See New Communist Movement
Mao Zedong, 117–18, 121, 156, 172, 188
Marx, Karl, 114–15
Marxism, Dixon and, 167, 204, 224
Marxism-Leninism model, DWP crisis of, 204, 207, 208–11, 215
Marxist-Leninist-Mao Tse-tung Thought, 118
Maslow, Abraham, 35, 38
May 1968, 119, 124
May, Rollo, 38
McLoughlin, William, 119
McVeigh, Timothy, 10, 262, 278n28
media: cults as portrayed in, 12, 14; Heaven's Gate mass suicide coverage, 12, 28, 29–31, 96; personal myth and legend of Dixon and, 128
mediums, 36
membership: idealism of, 260–62; infantilization of, 72–73, 82, 238–40; interactive selection processes, 236–38; sanctions of, generally, 229, 254, 260. See also DWP members; Heaven's Gate members; leaving the group
Menshevik purge, 195, 202, 208–9
Mensheviks, 290n7, 297n17
Mesmer, Franz Anton, 36
Meyer, Frank, 136
Milgram, Stanley, 229
militants. See DWP members

Mission Neighborhood Health Center, 199
mixed messages. See contradictions and mixed messages
modeling: DWP and, 187–88, 224, 230; as foundational, 230; Heaven's Gate and, 60–62, 65, 89
Moon, Sun Myung, 299n18
moral imperative: of DWP, 141, 167, 174, 211–12, 227; as foundational theme, 222, 227; Heaven's Gate and, 108–9, 141, 227; lineage of authority to protect, 224; of New Age movement, 31–32, 39; of New Communist Movement, 124–25
The Moulding of Communists: The Training of the Communist Cadre (Meyer), 136
Movement for the Restoration of the Ten Commandments of God, 12
Mwerinde, Credonia, 12

NACLA-West, 199
names: of Marshall Applewhite, 25, 43, 49, 50, 52, 71, 72, 82; of Marlene Dixon, 294–95n14; of DWP, xvii, 158–59, 204, 275n7; of DWP members, 154–55, 179, 186–87; of Heaven's Gate, 30, 82, 93, 96; of Heaven's Gate members, 72; of Bonnie Nettles, 26, 49, 50, 52, 71, 72, 82
need-to-know policy, 189, 229
Nettles, Bonnie: appearance of, 46, 53, 65, 72; background of, 43, 44–45; charismatic authority of, 80; death of, 91–93, 98, 104, 108; double standard and, 142; gender-bending and, 78; as medium and psychic, 36, 43, 45, 54, 108; names of, 26, 42, 49, 50, 52, 71, 72, 82; as "never wrong," 85; New Age movement and, 31, 43, 53, 102; parental attitude of, 72–73, 239–40. See also Heaven's Gate leadership; other Heaven's Gate headings
New Age movement, 31–41, 224; change demanded by, 32; moral imperative of, 31–32, 39; overview, 32–34, 40–41, 53; parallel themes as social context, 221–22; reliance on leaders, 32; religious and spiritual influences, 34–37; self-actualization, 38–40, 73, 173, 283n31; technologies of change, 37–40
New Communist Movement (NCM), 113–25; as antihomosexual, 125; criticism/self-criticism and, 123; Dixon's criticisms of, 166; emergence of, 121–23;

New Communist Movement *(continued)*
feminism dismissed by, 125; groups, examples of, 118; leader needed, principle of, 125; Maoism and, 117–18; Marxist-Leninist model for, 115–17, 118; moral imperative of, 124–25; overview, 113–14, 124–25, 148; parallel themes as social context, 221–22; personal transformation, call for, 125; sociocultural influences on formation of, 118–21; typical recruits to, 123–24
New Left: criticisms of DWP by, 199–201; defined, 119; disillusionment with, 121–22, 136, 151; Dixon's criticisms of, 133–34, 166, 203
new religious movements, 4, 6–7
Nixon, Richard, 120
"no gossip" rule, 139, 142
norms. *See* systems of influence

obedience, 58, 79, 229–30, 240, 241
Obedience to Authority (Milgram), 229
Oklahoma City bombing, 10, 262, 278n28
Old Left, 114, 119
Olson, Sara Jane, 13
oratory skills, 137–38. *See also* communication; language
The Order, 262
Order of the Solar Temple (OTS), 10–11
organizational outcomes, summary of differences in, 240–44, 272
Osho Commune International, 10

paranoia, 84, 204; as foundational, 225
parental relationship of leaders, 72–73, 207, 238–40
Peace and Freedom Party, 199
peak experiences, 38–40, 73, 283n31
Peep, 52. *See also* Nettles, Bonnie
peer pressure. *See* systems of influence
People's Park incident, 129–30
Peoples Temple, xvii, xviii, 8–9, 277–78n19, 300n28
Perls, Fritz, 38
permanent helpers. *See* inner circle
personal closure: characteristics of, 255–56, 273; cognitive dissonance distinguished from, 257; conformity theory distinguished from, 257; defined, 20–21, 256–57, 301n15; primary works on, 7, 20; resocialization and, 252; structural dimensions creating, 255–56, 258–60,

261. *See also* bounded choice; personal transformation requirement; self-sealing systems
personal freedom: crisis management and loss of, 242; fusion with self-renunciation *(see* charismatic commitment); salvation path as, 226–27, 234. *See also* self-renunciation; true believers
personal mystical conversion, 15
personal transformation requirement, principle of, 16, 18–19; anxiety and guilt and, 16, 107–8, 185, 213–14; closure and *(see* personal closure); coercive persuasion and, 214–15, 245; doubling and, 213; DWP and, 140–41, 143–48, 173–74, 192, 213–17, 227–28; exit costs and, 299n12; as foundational theme, 222, 226–28, 231–32, 234–36, 245–46; free will and, 230–31; function of, 57; Heaven's Gate demand for, 57, 69–70, 80–83, 95, 140–41, 227–28, 242; New Age and, 37–40; New Communist Movement and, 124, 125; resocialization, 251–52. *See also* self-renunciation; transcendent belief systems
Phoenix 19, 84
Pierce, William L., 262
political social psychology, 16. *See also* bounded choice
Post, Jerrold, xvi
power: charisma as relationship of, 7, 19; imbalances of, 192; taken for granted, 254. *See also* authority; charismatic authority
Prabhupada, Srila, 12
Prairie Fire Organizing Committee, 122
pre-party formations, 118, 134–37
Progressive Labor Party, 121
proletarian feminism, 126, 224
Proposition 13, 159–60, 201
psychics, 36
psychological precondition, 78–79, 288n16
purpose and commitment, dualism of, 255, 258–59, 273

Al-Qaeda, xvi, 16

Raëlians, 13
Rajneesh, Bhagwan Shree, 9–10
Ram Dass, 34
rational choice, 257–58
Reagan, Ronald, 130

Rebel Worker Organization, *159*, 199
recruitment: age at, generally, 237; as inter-active process, 236–37. *See also* DWP recruitment and training; Heaven's Gate recruitment
Red Squads, 122, 123, 136
regressive dynamic, 238–40
reincarnation, 37
religious studies paradigm, 4, 6–7, 32, 253, 300n29
Representative incarnate ("the Rep"), 82. *See also* Heaven's Gate leadership
resocialization, 251–52
Rogers, Carl, 35, 38
Roof, Wade Clark, 32
rules, 18, 142, 228–30, 240, 280n49; of DWP, 142, 178–80, 191. *See also* Heaven's Gate rules and procedures
Russian Communist Party, 114–16, 290n7
Russian Social Democratic Workers' Party, 290n7
Ryan, Leo J., 8–9

San Francisco Liberation School, 124
satisficing, 257, 258
scarcity principle of influence, 50
Schein, Edgar, 6, 215
secrecy: Heaven's Gate and, 47, 189, 229; leftist activists and, 123; terrorism and, xvi; vanguard-party theory and, 115, 116. *See also* DWP secrecy; security
The Secret Doctrine (Blavatsky), 36
security: as foundational, 229; Heaven's gate and, 189. *See also* DWP security
self, doubling and the, 213
self-actualization, 38–40, 73, 173, 283n31
self-conversion, 15, 16
self-interest, acting against one's: bounded choice and, 19, 77, 98–101, 206, 229–30, 260; obedience to authority and, 229–30
self-renunciation: androgyny principle and, 143; DWP and, 143, 144–48, 170–72, 184–85, 192; as exhausting, 16; as foundational, 234; fusion with personal freedom (*see* charismatic commitment); Heaven's Gate and, 60–62, 82, 85–86, 89, 103, 144; as internalized control, 254. *See also* personal freedom; personal transformation; true believers
self-sacrifice. *See* self-renunciation
self-sealing systems, 244–46, 272; agency

within, 232–33; defined, 17, 232; dimensions of (*see* structural dimensions); dissolution of, 214–17; individualized version of (*see* personal closure); leaving the group (*see* leaving the group); non-cult contexts of, 262–63; self-renunciation and personal freedom fused in (*see* charismatic commitment). *See also* bounded choice
self-transformation. *See* personal transformation
sensitivity training, 37
separatism: defined, 5–6; differences in, 244; DWP and, 141, 146, 244; as foundational, 226–27; Heaven's Gate and, 85, 104, 141, 244
September 11, 2001, xv, xvi, 263
sexuality: DWP and, 143, 182, 190–91, 196n45, 296n45; Heaven's Gate and denial of, 67–68, 77, 87, 88–89, 143, 190
Sheela, Ma Anand, 9
Shils, Edward, 128
Simmel, Georg, 298n4
Simon, Herbert, 7, 257, 258, 259
situational conversion, 15
Smelser, Neil J., 286n27
social context, 221–22. *See also* New Age movement; New Communist Movement
socialism, 115, 117, 193, 202, 203, 209
social stability as factor, 237
Soliah, Kathleen, 13
spiritualism, 36, 45, 46, 54, 108
Stalinism, 116, 188
Stark, Rodney, 7, 299n18
structural dimensions: boundaries of knowledge reinforced by, 251–54; dualism of, 54, 232–33, 254–57, 258–59, 265–66, 273, 285n21; purpose and effects of, 244–46, 272; summary of, 222–33; tables summarizing, 265–72. *See also* charismatic authority; systems of control; systems of influence; transcendent belief system
structuration model, 7, 222–23
student movement, 119–21
Students for a Democratic Society (SDS), 119–20
submission, 229–30; DWP and, 144, 170, 185, 207; Heaven's Gate and, 58; regressive dynamic and, 238–40; social norm of, 58, 240

Symbionese Liberation Army (SLA), 13, 79, 122
Synanon, 127
Synthesis Publications, *197*, 198, 297n10
systems of control: boundaries closed by, 253–54; defined, 17, 58, 228; dualism of, 54, 232–33, 254–57, 258–59, 266, 273, 285n21; DWP analysis, 141–43, 174–84, 211–14, 228–30, 269, 271; Heaven's Gate analysis, 58–59, 83–89, 104–6, 142–43, 228–30, 269; layered, 242–43; obedience, 58, 229–30, 240, 241; personal boundaries created by, 255–56, 258–60, 261, 273; purpose and effects of, 244–46, 272; as structural dimension, summarized, 222–23, 228–30, 271, 272; tables summarizing characteristics of, 266, 269, 271, 272. *See also* charismatic authority; self-sealing systems; systems of influence; transcendent belief system
systems of influence: boundaries closed by, 253–54; defined, 17, 59–60, 228; dualism of, 54, 254–57, 258–59, 266, 273, 285n21; DWP analysis, 143–48, 184–88, 214–17, 230–32, 270, 271; Heaven's Gate analysis, 59–62, 89–90, 106–8, 143–44, 230–32, 270, 271; personal boundaries created by, 255–56, 258–60, 261, 273; purpose and effects of, 244–46, 272; as structural dimension, summarized, 222–23, 230–32, 271, 272; tables summarizing characteristics of, 266, 270, 271, 272. *See also* charismatic authority; self-sealing systems; systems of control; transcendent belief system

Taliban, 16
Tax the Corporations Initiatives, *171*, 198
Taylor, David, 57
Teilhard de Chardin, Pierre, 35
telepathy, 107–8
terrorism: Aum Shinrikyō and, 11; bounded choice and, 262–63; Earth Liberation Front and, 14; Rajneesh group and, 9, 10; Symbionese Liberation Army (SLA), 13, 79, 122; true believers and, xv, xvi–xvii, 262–63
Theosophy, 36–37, 43, 45, 53
Third International, 115
thought collective, 286n33
thought community, 57–58, 286n33. *See*

also brainwashing; independent thought or action as unacceptable
Thought Reform and the Psychology of Totalism (Lifton), 6
Ti, 52, 71. *See also* Nettles, Bonnie
total institutions, 253–54
totalism: defined, 5–6; Heaven's Gate and, 83; as key to self-sealing systems, 57; members' needs and, 238. *See also* self-sealing systems
Total Overcomers Anonymous (T.O.A.), 93. *See also* Heaven's Gate
transcendent belief system: alienation and, 102; as barricade, 252–53; defined, 17, 56–57; dualism of, 54, 254–57, 258–59, 266, 273, 285n21; DWP analysis, 140–41, 165–74, 208–11, 226–28, 268, 271; Heaven's Gate analysis, 57–58, 80–83, 101–4, 140–41, 226–28, 268, 271; origination of, as foundational, 224; personal boundaries created by, 255–56, 258–60, 261, 273; personal transformation as requirement of (*see* personal transformation); purpose and effects of, 244–46, 272; as salvation path, 226–27, 234; as structural dimension, summarized, 222–23, 226–28, 271, 272; tables summarizing characteristics of, 266, 268, 271, 272; totalizing nature of (*see* totalism). *See also* charismatic authority; DWP beliefs; Heaven's Gate beliefs; self-sealing systems; systems of control; systems of influence
true believers: commitment as producing, 234; as goal in worldview shift, 16; retention of, 238; terrorism and, xv, xvi–xvii, 262–63. *See also* bounded choice; charismatic commitment; deployable agents
The Turner Diaries, 262, 278n28
The Two, 50. *See also* Heaven's Gate leadership

ufology: defined, 42; Hale-Bopp comet and, 25; Heaven's Gate and, 48, 57, 82, 96, 102, 215
UFOs. *See* ufology
Unification Church, 299n18
unions, 199
unity of will, 167, 184
University of Chicago, 127–28
urgency, as characteristic, 140

U.S. Out of Central America (USOCA), 198, 199, *200*, 211–12
USSR, 115–17, 203, 208, 209, 211, 236, 290n7, 297n17

Vallee, Jacques, 57
value-oriented belief, 286n27
vanguard party: DWP as, 134–37, 147–48, 185; Russian, 115–16, 290n7
Vietnam War, 119, 121–22, 229
violence: bounded choice and assessment of, 262–63; DWP and, 182, 191, 200–201, 254
Vorilhon, Claude, 13

Wallerstein, Immanuel, 203
Wallis, Roy, 300n29
Weather Underground, 122, 292–93n21
Weber, Max, 7, 78, 79, 300n29
wedding ritual, 92, 242
West Coast Socialist Social Sciences conferences, 199

What Is to Be Done? (Lenin), 115
Women and the State study group, 151–52
women's movement (feminism), 113, 125, 126, 128, 131–32, 147, 224
Worker-Patient Organization, 198, 199
world-systems theory, 125, 203
worldview shift: cognitive dissonance theory compared to, 249–50; conformity theory compared to, 248–49; defined, 15; Lofland and Stark model, 299n18; methods used to achieve, 16; orientation of worldview, 243–44, 300n29; primary works examining, 7, 15; as transformational process, 15–16, 207, 231–32, 234; types of conversion experiences, 15, 16. *See also* moral imperative; self-sealing systems; true believers

Zablocki, Benjamin, 6, 299n12, 301n19

Compositor:	BookMatters
Text:	10/13 Galliard
Display:	Galliard
Printer and binder:	Edwards Brothers, Inc.